NEW DEAL PLANNING

NEW DEAL PLANNING
The National Resources Planning Board

Marion Clawson

Published for Resources for the Future
By The Johns Hopkins University Press
Baltimore and London

Copyright © 1981 by Resources for the Future, Inc.

All rights reserved
Manufactured in the United States of America

Published for Resources for the Future
By The Johns Hopkins University Press, Baltimore, Maryland 21218

Library of Congress Catalog Card Number 80-8777
ISBN 0-8018-2595-4

Library of Congress Cataloging in Publication Data

Clawson, Marion, 1905-
    New Deal planning.

    Bibliography: p.
    Includes index.
    1. United States.   National Resources Planning Board.
I. Resources for the Future.   II. Title.
HC106.3.C646   353.0082′3   80-8777
ISBN 0-8018-2595-4

RESOURCES FOR THE FUTURE, INC.
1755 Massachusetts Avenue, N.W., Washington, D.C. 20036

Resources for the Future is a nonprofit organization for research and education in the development, conservation, and use of natural resources and the improvement of the quality of the environment. It was established in 1952 with the cooperation of the Ford Foundation. Grants for research are accepted from government and private sources only if they meet the conditions of a policy established by the Board of Directors of Resources for the Future. The policy states that RFF shall be solely responsible for the conduct of the research and free to make the research results available to the public. Part of the work of Resources for the Future is carried out by its resident staff; part is supported by grants to universities and other nonprofit organizations. Unless otherwise stated, interpretations and conclusions in RFF publications are those of the authors; the organization takes responsibility for the selection of significant subjects for study, the competence of the researchers, and their freedom of inquiry.

This book is a product of RFF's Renewable Resources Division, Kenneth D. Frederick, director. It was edited by Joan Tron-Ruggles and indexed by Sydney Schultz. It was designed by Elsa Williams.

RFF editors: Ruth B. Haas, Jo Hinkel, Sally A. Skillings

Contents

Foreword   xiii

Preface and Acknowledgments   xv

1   An Overview   1
   Purpose of this Chapter   2
   The NRPB: Child of the Depression and the New Deal   2
   Tasks and Roles   3
   Organization and Structure   4
   Output of Reports   7
   The NRPB in the Federal Structure   9
   Why and How the NRPB Was Killed   10
   The NRPB's Legacy   13
   Does the United States Today Need a
      Reconstituted NRPB?   15

I.   ORIGIN AND SETTING

2   The Situation From Which the Board Arose   21
   Back to Normalcy—Post-World War I and the 1920s   22
   Crash and Depression   23
   The New Deal   25
   Recovery Versus Reform   27

3   Predecessors of the Board   30
   Study of Recent Social Trends   30

Studies of America's Capacity   33
Agricultural Planning   34
National Capital Park and Planning Commission   34
Governmental Measures During the
   Hoover Administration   35
Conclusion   36

II. HISTORY, ORGANIZATION, OPERATION

4   The Evolution of the Board and Its Predecessor
    Agencies   39
    Beginnings   41
    National Planning Board   42
    National Resources Board   44
    National Resources Committee   46
    National Resources Planning Board   47

5   Actors in the Board's Operations   52
    President Franklin Delano Roosevelt   52
    Harold L. Ickes   55
    Frederic A. Delano   58
    Charles E. Merriam   60
    Merriam–Eliot Differences   65
    Two Old-Boy Networks   68
    Supporting Actors   69

6   Organization, Structure, and Functioning   72
    Policy or Directing Boards   72
    Central Office Staff   75
    Committees   77
    Use of Consultants   79
    The NRPB's Field Organization   80
    Relationships to State and Local Planning Organizations   81
    Summary and Evaluation   84

7   The Roles Played by the Board   86
    Idea Development and Stimulation   87
    Planning as a Governmental Activity   89
    Planning as the NRPB and Its Officials Saw It   92
    Planning as the NRPB's Opponents Saw It   94
    NRPB Helps Develop Planning as a
       Governmental Activity   97

Published Reports of the NRPB as a Measure
  of Its Activities   99

III. SUBSTANTIVE FIELDS AND ACTIVITIES

8   NRPB Reports Concerning Natural Resources   107
    The 1934 Report   107
    Subsequent History and Work of the
      Water Committee   115
    Subsequent History and Work of the
      Land Committee   119
      Minerals and Energy   121
    Summary and Evaluation of the NRPB's Activities
      in Natural Resources   123

9   NRPB Reports Concerning People and Their Lives   125
    Population Studies   125
    Housing   131
    Research   133
    Welfare and Security   136
    Summary and Evaluation   142

10 NRPB Economic Inquiries and Reports   144
    Public Works   145
    Consumer Incomes and Expenditures   148
    Industrial Organization and Location   152
    General Economic Studies   155

11 NRPB Concerns With Transportation and Urban
    Structure   158
    Transportation Studies   158
    Urban Structure   162
    Conclusion   164

12 NRPB Reports on Planning   165
    The NRPB Promotes Regional Planning   166
    The NRPB Stimulates and Helps State Planning   171
    The NRPB Helps Make City Plans   172
    Summary   174

13 The NRPB as War and Postwar Planner   176
    In Defense and War Planning   177
    In Postwar Planning   181

IV. THE NRPB IN THE STRUCTURE OF AMERICAN GOVERNMENT

14 The NRPB in Relation to State and Regional
Planning Organizations   189
Washington, Regions, and States   189
How the NRPB Sought to Influence Regional and State
Planning   191
Where and How the Field Organization Fitted into the
Overall NRPB Structure   194
Role of State Planning Agencies in Their States   196
If the NRPB Had Become Permanent   197

15 The NRPB and Other Executive Branch Agencies   199

16 The NRPB and FDR   208
FDR and Conservation   208
The 1934–1939 Period   210
1940 to Near the End of the NRPB   213

17 The NRPB and Congress   214
Relations of the NPB, NRB, and NRC with Congress
Prior to 1939   215
Relations of the NRPB and Congress, 1939 to 1942   218
Some of NRPB's Chief Actors—Again   220
The NRPB's Field Organization in Relation
to the Congress   222

V. DEMISE AND LEGACY

18 Why and How Congress Killed the NRPB   225
Publications in 1942 and 1943   226
Appropriations for Fiscal 1944 in the House of
Representatives   228
Appropriations for Fiscal 1944 in the Senate   229
Immediate Consequences and Attitudes   233
Who Was Responsible for the NRPB's Demise   235

19 How Hard Did FDR Fight to Save the NRPB?   237

20 The Legacy   242
Published Reports   242

NRPB Functions Taken Over Elsewhere in the
   Federal Government   243
The NRPB and Regional, State, and Local Planning   248
The NRPB's Influence on U.S. Planning of the
   Late 1970s   249
The NRPB's Alumni   250
NRPB Functions Taken Over by Private Groups   250
Later Public Programs Proposed in NRPB Studies   252
Intellectual Attitude Toward Planning and
   Social Action   253

21   An Appraisal   255
How Important Was the NRPB?   255
How Well Did the NRPB Play Its Roles?   259
Could Some Other Federal Agency Have Filled These
   Roles Equally Well or Better?   260
Why Did the NRPB Not Do Better?   260
Might the NRPB Have Survived, Had It Been
   Different?   261

22   Does the United States Need a Reconstituted
      NRPB Today?   264
Major National Problems That Might Seem to Argue
   for a New NRPB   266
Overall National Planning Since 1943   269
The State of Planning in the United States Today   273
What Are the Lessons from the Past?   277
An Idea Stimulator/Financer?   279
As a Coordinator of Federal Programs?   281
As Part of a Major Federal Economic
   Operating Agency?   283
A Reconstituted NRPB—Yes or No?   284

APPENDIXES

Appendix A   Documentary History of Official Actions
             Related to the National Resources
             Planning Board   289

Appendix B   Chronological List of Major Reports   322

Index   349

Foreword

Resources for the Future has a long tradition of conducting studies of government agencies that administer natural resource programs and policies. Usually these studies have been of agencies that have responsibility for managing or developing a particular resource such as water, energy, or the forests—or that have a particular managerial or development function for a range of resources. The resulting books add richness, diversity, and realism to the other RFF offerings emphasizing economic performance and technology. While this book is in the RFF tradition of institutional studies, it is unusual both with respect to the agency chosen for study and the exhaustive nature of the coverage. It is unusual in another respect as well—it is about an agency that has not been in existence for many years and that has little or no prospect of being reconstituted in its original form.

Although RFF's primary mission is to study those natural resource issues that relate directly to current problems, I believe that publishing a book like this one about an expired agency is exceedingly relevant to current needs.

This is so because one of the most pressing current problems facing our federal establishment is the propensity of each agency and department to view problems from the standpoint of its own particular mission. The result is that a comprehensive viewpoint is often lacking and the interrelations among problems are neglected, with the resolution within a department or agency being on the basis of the political power or strength of a particular interest. The more politically difficult problems usually find their way to the president's office which must then deal with them on the basis of inadequate analysis and preparation. The National Resources Planning Board, whose experience is analyzed in this book, was created in 1933 to anticipate emerging problems and to provide a more comprehensive viewpoint than that supplied by the established agencies of government. The experience of this agency—its successes and failures—are most germane as we try to grapple with similar problems in the contemporary scene.

It was important that this analysis be completed now, not only because the lessons learned can be put to immediate use but also because any extensive delay would have resulted in a loss of much invaluable information from the people who were involved in the agency in one way or another. Human mortality is such that the number of living persons with such knowledge is becoming ever smaller. The author of this book, Marion Clawson, is admirably suited to the task. He brings to it not only his enormous scholarly and research talents but the fact that he was active professionally at the time the National Resources Planning Board was in existence and knew many of those active in its affairs. The pages that follow reflect both this capacity and experience.

It is appropriate that this foreword also note the contribution of Gilbert F. White, former chairman of the Board of Directors of Resources for the Future. Dr. White recognized the importance of the study, the need for it to be completed at this time, and also that Marion Clawson was uniquely qualified to do this difficult and important work. White's encouragement and support was most important to the initiation and completion of this effort just as it has been for so many developments at Resources for the Future.

Washington, D.C.   Emery N. Castle
January 1981   President, Resources for the Future

Preface and Acknowledgments

The purposes of this book are to analyze and describe the National Resources Planning Board (NRPB) and its direct predecessor agencies[1] in the setting of their times, and to draw from that description and analysis any lessons their experience offers us today.

I do not attempt to describe and analyze the New Deal as a whole. I do try to look at the NRPB as one part of the New Deal, but the focus is always on the NRPB.

I have approached the NRPB in this book from three different but interrelated angles:

1. In terms of its political and administrative history; how it was formed, how it operated, who were its chief actors, and how and why it was abolished. This is the kind of approach that a political scientist or a historian might take.

2. In terms of the content of the NRPB's work, especially its published reports. What did it contribute, in a substantive or professional

---

[1] Throughout this book, in the interest of simplification of exposition "National Resources Planning Board" (NRPB) will be used to stand for the Board and all its predecessors, unless the contrary is specifically noted. The organizations under this general heading are: National Planning Board (July 20, 1933 to June 30, 1934), National Resources Board (July 1, 1934 to June 7, 1935), National Resources Committee (June 8, 1935 to June 30, 1939), and National Resources Planning Board (July 1, 1939 to August 31, 1943). The last was abolished as of August 31, 1943, with its affairs all wound up by December 31, 1943.

way? My training and experience as a resource economist naturally lead me to look at the economic significance of this work, but I also try to look at the substantive contributions in other professional fields.

3. In terms of the relevance of the NRPB's experience for the problems of the United States in the 1980s. The NRPB was the most nearly comprehensive national planning organization this country has ever known. Many of the problems with which it struggled in the 1930s and early 1940s are with us today, and it might well be argued that the national situation is as serious today as in the 1930s. What, if anything, in the NRPB experience might be emulated, or avoided, or applied today?

I intend the audience for this book to be all persons who are interested in government, in natural resources, in economic and social studies, and in planning generally. My approach is not highly specialized nor, I hope, overly technical in any professional field.

It has often been said by the alumni of the NRPB and by those reasonably familiar with its operations that there has been no systematic study or evaluation of the NRPB. I believed this statement when I began work on this book, but I found that there was a great deal more research on it than I realized. A number of graduate students have made careful and detailed studies of it. I have drawn extensively on three of these. Each is an excellent piece of scholarship. The approach in each was primarily toward the first of my three angles of interest. I found their citations of congressional hearings, executive orders, board minutes and correspondence, and other government documents most helpful, particularly in directing me to the same documents. I found references to other dissertations and theses but I did not use any others than these three, listed chronologically as follows:

1. Landon G. Rockwell, "National Resources Planning: The Role of the National Resources Planning Board in the Process of Government," Princeton University, May 1942; I obtained a Xerox print directly from the university.

2. Philip L. White, "The Termination of the National Resources Planning Board," a master's thesis in political science, Columbia University, 1949. I obtained a microfilm of this thesis from the university. Partly as a result of my correspondence and discussions with him, Dr. White (now a professor of history at the University of Texas) is conducting further research on this subject, with the expec-

tation of publishing a book. I am particularly indebted to him for some materials in chapter 5, which I otherwise would not have known about, but I have found his thesis most helpful in total. I hope very much that his book is completed and published.

3. Philip K. Warken, "A History of the National Resources Planning Board, 1933–1943," Ohio State University, 1969. I obtained a print of this dissertation from University Microfilms International, Ann Arbor, Michigan. Dr. Warken, now a professor of history at the U.S. Naval Academy, informs me that his dissertation has been published by Garland Publishers (New York, 1979) and that the publication was by a photographic process, so that the page references to the dissertation are accurate for the book as well. Throughout this book, I have referred to his dissertation, not to his book, because I actually worked from the dissertation.

I also found that there is a good deal more information about and analyses of the NRPB, scattered through various books primarily devoted to other subjects, than I at first had realized. Naturally, I have used all such material that I could find.

A particularly rich source of material about the NRPB is its own reports. There is literally a five-foot shelf of printed reports and a vastly larger bulk of mimeographed reports. While some of the Board's activities did not result in published reports, most of its activities did, and the reports are a good index to its total activities. Through the kindess of Virginia Hartley, I obtained an almost complete set of the printed reports and some of the major mimeographed reports which had been the personal copies of the late Robert W. Hartley. These have been most helpful to me; they have formed the basis for my second major approach to the NRPB, namely, its substantive or professional accomplishment. The availability on my bookshelf of this set of reports, ready to my hand whenever I wanted one, has been timesaving in the extreme. I also inherited some of Hartley's personal files with copies of numerous documents useful to the first of my approaches to the NRPB, namely, its organizational history.

I have interviewed a number of surviving alumni of the NRPB, including (listed alphabetically) Jack Alterman, Thomas C. Blaisdell, Jr., Charles W. Eliot, 2nd, Joseph L. Fisher, Wilbert G. Fritz, Lincoln Gordon, Maynard Hufschmidt, Glenn E. McLaughlin, John Miller, Ralph J. Watkins, Gilbert F. White, and Abel Wolman. I also interviewed William

E. Warne, never an employee of the NRPB but one who worked closely with its water committee. Since it has been more than thirty-five years since the NRPB was abolished, many of the persons active in its operations have died in the intervening years, and the survivors are naturally no longer young. I have relied on these interviews more for the first of my three angles of approach than for the other two. I have quoted directly or referred specifically to these interviews only sparingly, but I have used the knowledge gained from the interviews very extensively and I want to express my thanks to the persons named. They are not, of course, to be held responsible for my interpretation.

The congressional act which terminated the NRPB directed that its files be placed in the National Archives, and this was done. The National Archives has prepared three mimeographed reports listing and describing NRPB records transferred to it: (1) *Record Group No. 187; Records of the National Resources Planning Board—Preliminary List of the Published and Unpublished Reports of the National Resources Planning Board, 1933–1943,* by Lester W. Smith, with the assistance of Estelle Rebec and Mary Frances Handley, The National Archives, SR 3 (46-3), March 1946; (2) *Preliminary Inventories: Number 50, Central Office Records of the National Resources Planning Board,* compiled by Virgil E. Baugh, 1953; and (3) *Preliminary Inventories: Number 64, Records of the Regional Offices of the National Resources Planning Board,* compiled by Virgil E. Baugh, 1954. In addition to a listing of the records, these reports include short but very useful accounts of the NRPB, including its history, changes in its organization, its functions, and the like. These reports are available to scholars, although they are not really publications for general distribution and have not been advertised by the National Archives nor widely distributed by it. Each is absolutely essential to anyone seeking to use National Archives material on the NRPB. The volume of this material is very great—1,600 individual documents of one kind or another, or 1,000 cubic feet of record material. While they are all indexed and all listed in these publications of the Archives, their volume makes any use of them a major time-consuming task. When I began my research for this book, I expected to make extensive use of the materials in the National Archives. In the end, my use of these materials was more limited than I had expected for two reasons, one indicated above, and the other, because I found that, to a substantial extent, others had done the necessary detailed searching of these records, or of those in the Roosevelt library at Hyde Park, so that I could to a large extent rely on their work. This was particularly true of the dissertations and theses. I have, however, found the National Archives material crucial on a few matters.

In this connection, I am pleased to give recognition to the substantial help I have had from Dr. Harold T. Pinkett, Chief, Natural Resources Branch, National Archives. In particular, he carefully checked the data in table B-1 in appendix B. Dr. Pinkett not only saved me from much time-consuming work but also gave me the assurance of accuracy in my references to NRPB publications.

After the NRPB was officially terminated as of August 31, 1943, Charles W. Eliot, 2nd, its director, and Harold A. Merrill, its executive officer, remained to close out its offices. They compiled a *Guide to the Files of the National Resources Planning Board and Predecessor Agencies—Ten Years of National Planning, 1933–1943;* and Eliot wrote a *Final Report—Status of Work, National Resources Planning Board.* In the latter, Eliot outlined his ideas at that time as to a desirable permanent national planning agency. Each report is dated December 31, 1943; each was mimeographed; Merrill has told me that only 100 copies were ever made of either, hence the distribution was limited. Since the nation was at war at the end of 1943, and preoccupied with that war, it is doubtful if these reports would have attracted much attention in any case. The second of these reports is labeled "confidential." Since the NRPB went out of existence at the date of these reports, the reports were actually mimeographed by the Bureau of the Budget. I obtained a copy of each from Merrill and I have used each extensively. These reports are in the files at the National Archives. They are absolutely indispensable to anyone seriously interested in NRPB history. Although written under what must have been difficult conditions, they contain a vast amount of highly valuable information.

Special mention must be made of the role of Professor Albert Lepawsky, University of California, Berkeley, now retired. In the early 1960s, Resources for the Future made a grant to the University of California to enable Professor Lepawsky to make a critical evaluation of the NRPB. He has published at least three articles on the subject, which have been used and noted in this book, and is currently working on a book about the Board. His interest in the subject and his diligent search for reference materials have stimulated my interest in the subject also, and thus I am particularly indebted to him for more than my specific references to his publications.

This book consists of twenty-two chapters grouped into five major parts. The first chapter is an overview, an interpretative summary of the whole book, written in the hope that it will entice readers to read the rest of the book rather than to consider that they have gained the essence of it from this summary. Part I is concerned with the origin and setting—from what did the NRPB arise and why? Part II is concerned with the evolution of the NRPB, its actors, its general organization and functioning, the various roles it played, and an overall view of its publication record. These first two parts are primarily concerned with the first of my three angles of approach to the NRPB—the legislative, organizational, administrative, and personnel history of the organization. Part III has six rather long chapters on the substantive work of the NRPB—natural resources, people, economics, transportation and urban structure, the NRPB as a stimulator of planning, and as a postwar planner. These are directly related to the second of my angles of approach—what the NRPB was concerned with, in a substantive way. Part IV deals with the NRPB in the structure of American government; four short chapters deal with its relation to state and local planning, its relations with the president and with other parts of the executive branch, and its relations with Congress. Part V is concerned with how and why Congress killed the NRPB, the president's role in trying to save it, its bequest to the future, my appraisal of its performance, and a consideration of the role that a reconstituted NRPB might play in the United States today and in the future. Chapter 22, the final chapter, examines the case for a new or reconstituted national planning board.

Perhaps I should try to inform the reader of my philosophical approach to a study of this kind. I believe that what individuals or groups have as an attitudinal base is important; that how they decide what are "facts" in any situation, how they analyze such facts as they consider, and how they draw conclusions from their analyses are important. But I think it is difficult always to be sure of the attitudes and philosophies of other persons and difficult to describe such attitudes in terms meaningful to every reader. Accordingly, I put much more emphasis on what persons or groups actually do, as the most significant expression of what they think and feel. The focus of this book is thus on events and actions, not on motives and thoughts of actors.

In the preparation of this book, I have been aided by a great many people. First of all, there are the numerous scholars, including the authors of the dissertations and theses listed, whose work I have used and acknowledged throughout the text. Then there are the persons whom I interviewed, listed above. Several of my colleagues at Resources for the Future, in addition to two included among the interviewees, have been most helpful; here I include Emery N. Castle, Herbert C. Morton, and Kenneth D. Frederick.

A review draft of this entire manuscript was circulated to a lengthy list of interested and informed persons in the fall of 1979. My special thanks go to Charles W. Eliot, 2nd, for his comments on this review draft. He had been, first, executive officer and then director of the NRPB and its predecessor organizations, having served throughout the entire history, including the liquidation of the Board. As a result, his knowledge of the agency is more detailed and more nearly complete than that of any other person. He has preserved a personal file of nearly all NRPB material, to which he referred frequently in commenting upon this manuscript. His detailed comments apply to nearly every page and most of them have been incorporated into this final book. He must not, of course, be held responsible for my interpretation or for my selection of ideas and facts to include or to leave out.

In addition to Eliot, comments were received from the following reviewers: Jack Alterman, the late Charles S. Ascher, Roy F. Bessey, Thomas C. Blaisdell, Jr., Eveline M. Burns, Joseph L. Fisher, Wilbert G. Fritz, Luther Gulick, Peter Hall, Maynard M. Hufschmidt, Herbert Kaufman, Albert Lepawsky, Glenn E. McLaughlin, John Miller, Robert H. Nelson, Harold T. Pinkett, Rutherford H. Platt, Wayne D. Rasmussen, James L. Sundquist, Conrad Taeuber, Philip W. Warken, William E. Warne, Gilbert F. White, Philip L. White, Aaron Wildavsky, Abel Wolman.

I am pleased here to acknowledge the great help I have had from these reviewers but, of course, they are not to be held responsible for what I finally chose to say here.

The manuscript has been edited by Joan Tron-Ruggles and I am glad to acknowledge my indebtedness to her for much of its clarity and felicity of expression. I am also deeply indebted to several present or former secretaries at RFF, for their diligence, skill, and cheerfulness in typing this long manuscript; included here are Harriet Belden, Lorraine Van Dine, Maybelle Frashure, John Mankin, Sylvia Steadham, and my most recent and very able secretary, Avery Gordon. To all of the many people who have helped me (including any others I may have inadvertently omitted) go my thanks; and, if this book meets a real need with its readers, they too will have benefited from the persons who have helped me.

Washington, D.C.   Marion   Clawson
January 1981

1

An Overview

Do the society and the economy of the whole United States or the efficiency of the federal government require some form of central planning of the national economy, or central coordination of federal government programs, or some common direction to the numerous public programs? The awkwardnesses, conflicts, overlappings, and missed opportunities of diverse, uncoordinated, often unrelated, and frequently opposed efforts of public agencies and private parties are all too evident to any alert observer. In 1980, national efforts to deal with inflation, unemployment, and energy problems of the nation each provide ample and serious examples of the lack of coordination at the federal level. But could any form of central coordination be developed that would do better? Might any attempt in this direction bring other and more serious ill consequences than do the present confusion and diversity?

Formation and effectuation of a national policy to create a central planning organization, or a reasoned decision not to create one, involve many difficult questions and many kinds of important considerations. The role of the United States in international affairs; the role of the federal government in domestic affairs; the relation between the executive branch, the Congress, and the judiciary; the operations within each of these branches; and many other factors should be considered in arriving at a national decision on this matter. This book has a much more modest intent than to provide an answer to these questions: my concern is a critical analysis of the one official comprehensive national planning agency this country has ever had, namely, the National Resources Planning Board, in order to ascertain what lessons that experience has for present day governmental and national planning efforts. What was the NRPB, how did it function, what did it do, and why was it abolished? How far did it succeed in doing what it tried to do? What is there in its experience that is useful for the nation today? These are the questions to which this book is addressed.

Purpose of this Chapter

The purpose of this chapter is to present an overview of the whole book. It is more an overview than a summary because, while it covers the same broad range of subject matter, it does not provide an exact summary nor one strictly in sequence with the later chapters. It is more interpretive than precise. The reader is asked to accept many statements on faith, with full exposition and support in later chapters.

The NRPB: Child of the Depression and the New Deal

Beginning in late 1929 the United States plunged into the deepest, longest, severest, and most devastating economic depression of its history. The depression was worldwide. Stock market and agricultural commodity prices in the United States each fell to a small fraction of their pre-depression levels; industrial output and gross national product alike fell by more than half; many millions of workers were unemployed; and real hardship ensnared millions of families. Worst of all was the indecision and uncertainty about what to do, the general mood of helplessness giving way to sullen resentment, and the threat of actual civil strife—although it was unclear who should attack whom. The best pundits of the day and the leading businessmen were equally divided and equally helpless. On March 4, 1933, when President Franklin Delano Roosevelt was inaugurated, most banks were closed. One of his first official acts was to declare a bank holiday, closing all banks for a few days.

In 1932, it was not so much Roosevelt who was elected as Hoover who was defeated.[1] The country knew not what to expect of Roosevelt

---

[1] Rexford G. Tugwell, *Roosevelt's Revolution: The First Year—A Personal Perspective* (New York, Macmillan Publishing Co., 1977).

for the very good reason that he did not know himself what he was going to try to do. During the campaign he had followed completely contradictory advice—on the one hand, proclaiming the need for a balanced budget and on the other hand, proposing programs for the assistance of the unemployed that would necessarily cost large sums.

In Roosevelt's famous first "Hundred Days" about a score of important pieces of legislation were enacted or new agencies created—the Tennessee Valley Authority, the Securities and Exchange Commission, the Emergency Banking Act, unemployment relief measures, the Public Works Administration, the Agricultural Adjustment Administration, home owners loan program, the National Industrial Recovery Act, and several others. These did not directly involve the NRPB, since the National Planning Board was not established until later that year, but the rapid enactment of this legislation is significant as a measure of the times. The Emergency Banking Act was passed by the Congress and on the president's desk for signature just eight hours after the draft bill had left that same desk, bound for Congress. The country and the Congress were in a mood for action—almost any action that extended hope of relief. A new mood swept the country. "The only thing we have to fear is fear itself," said Roosevelt, and fear substantially receded under the new president.

One of the major early new programs was a greatly expanded public works program, placed under Harold L. Ickes, as public works administrator. He was also secretary of the interior and a relative newcomer to Washington. Foreseeing the need to coordinate such public works with each other and with other governmental programs, Charles W. Eliot, 2nd, a young planner with the National Capital Park and Planning Commission, in early 1933 proposed to Ickes the establishment of a national planning organization. Such an agency, the National Planning Board, was established in the Public Works Administration in July 1933.

Tasks and Roles

At the first meeting of the new National Planning Board in the summer of 1933, it decided to group its work and activities under four headings

1. Planning and programming of public works
2. Stimulation of city, state, and regional planning
3. Coordination of federal planning activities
4. Research

With some modest redefinitions and extensions—some of its own choice, some placed upon it by the president—these remained the basic tasks of the NRPB (in its various names) for the ten years of its life.

I find it more useful, for my analysis of the NRPB, to group its activities and its objectives in a twofold breakdown: (1) idea development and stimulation, and (2) planning and coordination in general. For the first of these it conducted its own research, financed or helped to find funds and manpower for research by other agencies, served as a catalyst and synthesizer of existing information into comprehensive reports, and was a publisher and disseminator of reports. On the whole, the NRPB was quite successful in this general role. It produced a large number of reports, some quite outstanding for their time. These reports surely developed ideas and stimulated thinking—and opposition.

On its second main role, that of planning and program coordination, the NRPB's record is spottier and harder to measure. Some excellent work was done on water development planning but this stirred the opposition of the Rivers and Harbors Congress. Some of its attempts to formulate national policy, such as in welfare and social services, were highly controversial and not accepted during the life of the NRPB.

My judgment, based upon a careful study of the NRPB's problems and accomplishments, is that these two major roles were basically incompatible for any single organization. In order to be useful, research results had to be disseminated. This called for reports, publicity, and public discussion. The NRPB served the president in this role of idea stimulator because it also served the whole country. Its program coordination role, however, was strictly for the president. The NRPB always considered itself an adviser to the president, so much so that some Board members refused—unwisely, I think—to talk to the Congress themselves if they could avoid it, and instructed their staff to do likewise.

Organization and Structure

Although the NRPB had four names, corresponding to four different versions of its basic existence, it maintained a closely similar organization and (for the times) a remarkably continued group of personalities. There was always a board, though its membership and to some extent its role changed over its life. There was always an executive officer or director (basically the same job under different titles) and the same man filled the position from the beginning to the end. There was always a Washington staff; it grew larger as time went on, and it came to play a much larger role toward the end than at the beginning of the NRPB's life. Extensive use was made of committees for various subjects or problems—committees sometimes drawn exclusively from employees in other federal agencies, sometimes wholly of nonfederal employees, more often of mixed federal and nonfederal membership, and typically including a staff member of the NRPB.

Extensive use was also made of temporary or part-time employees—often university professors working during the summer or part-time during the rest of the year. Many of the employees were retained on the personnel rolls as unpaid consultants after their assignments were over, to be drawn upon (and paid) when new need for their expertise arose. There was a field organization, attached to the regional commissions, which the NRPB established or encouraged.

But the NRPB did change over the years, and in more ways than its name. At the end of the first year, the National Planning Board became the National Resources Board; the major changes were to make the organization an adviser to the president rather than to the administrator of public works and to add to the three-man citizen governing board six cabinet members (or administrators of cabinet rank). The second name change, another year later, to National Resources Committee was solely due to the fact that the National Industrial Recovery Act, which had been the legal basis for the two first boards, was declared unconstitutional by the Supreme Court, and the authority of the Emergency Relief Act was substituted for it. The third name change, to National Resources Planning Board, was accompanied by more basic changes: the cabinet members were dropped from the Board, the three citizen members being thereafter solely responsible; the Board now met directly with the president, rather than having Harold L. Ickes (its chairman in the two previous incarnations) as its formal contact; the Board now had to go to Congress for its appropriations (formerly the president had allotted it emergency funds); and its legal basis and the rationale for its existence were increasingly challenged in the Congress. The NRPB made more extensive though less easily defined changes in its methods of operation internally.

There were a number of major actors in or responsible for the NRPB. There was President Roosevelt. One of Roosevelt's characteristics, of direct relevance to the NRPB, was his willingness, even his desire, to talk with people of widely differing backgrounds and ideas. Another was his stimulating them to believe that he agreed with them when, in fact, he was only being pleasant and receptive, without real commitment.

Harold L. Ickes, secretary of the interior, administrator of the Public Works Administration, and chairman of the National Resources Board and National Resources Committee, was a man of great drive, overwhelming ego, serious emotional insecurity, great devotion to the president, and an indefatigable defender of his bureaucratic turf, including the NRPB when he headed it. Once he was no longer its head, he paid no more attention to it and never again mentioned it in his famous secret diaries.

The top citizen member of the Board throughout, and its chairman during its first and final forms, was Frederic A. Delano, uncle to the president. Nearing 70 years of age when the NRPB began, he was obviously nearing 80 when it was terminated; his energies gradually ran out. A very distinguished public servant and planner, he leaned over backward to avoid ever trying to capitalize on his relationship to the president—so much so that another chairman would undoubtedly have tried to play a more vigorous role with the president. His reputation, his position, his charm, and his ability to work with different persons undoubtedly were great assets. He was much liked and respected by the staff and generally accessible to it.

The vice chairman of the Board when Delano was chairman, and an influential member at all times, was Charles E. Merriam, professor of political science at the University of Chicago. Like Delano, he was part-time. Each served two days a month for the NRPB on a formal or paid basis, but each devoted many more hours to reading or writing reports or otherwise working on NRPB matters. Merriam was widely regarded at the time as a man of great intellectual powers. He had a conviction, amounting almost to a phobia, that the Board must deal only with the president, that it should avoid the Congress as far as it was possible to do so, and that its staff should likewise avoid Congress as far as possible.

The top staff man throughout the ten years was Charles W. Eliot, 2nd, descendant of a noted New England family. He was the top staff man of the National Capital Park and Planning Commission before the National Planning Board was established, and was a protege of Delano. With his background in city planning, which in large part Delano shared, he wanted to develop plans which could be put into action.

A serious problem throughout the NRPB's life was major and serious differences between Merriam and Eliot. Merriam wanted the NRPB to be a federal counterpart of the private Social Science Research Council, which he had headed or in which he had been a major figure in the several years before the New Deal. He was much less interested in the public works aspect of the NRPB's operations than was Eliot. The two never quarrelled openly and violently, as far as I can learn, though relations were often difficult, cool, or hostile. Continuity of staff is generally considered an asset for a government agency, but this assumes that the personalities fitted together well to begin with. If this condition is not met, continuity can be a liability.

Output of Reports

Although some of the NRPB's work, such as some of its coordinating activities, did not result in published reports available to the public, by far the greater part of its work did result in such reports and they give a good idea of the scope and thrust of its total activities. In appendix B I have included 370 printed and "major" mimeographed reports as a measure of the NRPB's total activity. The range of subject matter covered by these reports is very great: a number deal with specific natural resources, such as water, land, energy, or minerals; some deal with industry, research and transportation; others with population, housing, and welfare; still others with planning generally, public works, cities, state planning, regional planning, and war and postwar planning; and some with economic topics such as income and expenditures, and interest rates.

These reports as a whole included more than 43,000 pages. The printed reports typically began with an edition of 5,000, and were reprinted when demand exceeded the original supply. Pamphlets for popular use were prepared for many of the major printed reports. A good many reports, sometimes preliminary versions, were mimeographed, generally for limited distribution; but these may have been highly influential in quickly reaching persons directly and closely concerned with some problem or subject. Many of the reports included recommendations for legislation, for action, for expenditure of public funds, for organization, or for research. The printed reports were typically transmitted by the Board to the president, and generally by him to the Congress. Many of the reports were excellent examples of editing and drafting.

The first reports, under the National Resources Board and National Resources Committee particularly, were typically the output of committees. Later, reports were more often the output of staff. This shift in authorship quite probably simplified the problems of organizing, conducting, and writing of reports, but it also deprived the NRPB of the support from other agencies which their active participation nearly always secured. I cannot but wonder if this shift in operations was a mistake.

While there is naturally a good deal of variation among as large a body of reports as the NRPB published, on the whole I am today highly impressed with their caliber, particularly when one evaluates them in light of the standards of professional competence, of research technology—there were no computers then!—and of data availability.

It is difficult now to measure the impact of these reports at the time. Some received a lot of public attention—and much of it critical, especially when a report proposed new and different policies. My impression, partly resulting from my memories and of my own reactions to some of these reports at the time, partly based on my relatively recent reading of the reports and of the reactions to them, is that the NRPB reports were, in general, highly influential—more so in developing ideas, stimulating discussion, and encouraging thinking than they were in producing results along the lines recommended. Some of the latter came much later. One of the NRPB's truly major reports recommended "cradle-to-the-grave" social programs on a scale and a coverage which offended many people, including influential senators, at the time—but its recommendations have in substantial measure been enacted since then. The NRPB's work in the water planning field has been basic to everything that has happened in U.S. water planning since then.

And yet, the publications of the NRPB are little used, indeed nearly unknown today. One is likely to have a hard time finding the reports in a library; they will rarely be cited in recent professional studies, even when they would have been relevant. Though many NRPB publications are outdated, many others contain concepts, analyses, and even data which are still directly relevant. The professional researcher today would be well advised to see what the NRPB had to say on his subject.

The NRPB in the Federal Structure

The NRPB was only one of many federal agencies at the time, and its relationships with other parts of the federal government and with states was an important aspect of its existence.

During the nine years that the NRPB was advisory to the president, the Board as a whole, its executive officer or director, and sometimes other members of its staff, met with the president at intervals of about a month until the war broke out, after which they met with him only about twice a year. Their relationships with the president were friendly, even cordial. The meetings were typically loosely organized and generally inconclusive as to specific actions or decisions. The president would often reminisce or tell anecdotes. The Board would generally refrain from trying to get a positive decision from him, either drawing its own conclusions as to his position on some matter, or submitting a separate written communication asking for his blessing on some proposed activity. It is impossible for me now to judge how influential the NRPB was with the president; he certainly got some ideas and some stimulation from it, but equally certainly it was not his only source of ideas—he sought stimulation from many quarters and many kinds of people. While he gave it some coordination tasks, such as the preparation of a long-range program of public works from the materials submitted by the construction bureaus, in general he did not rely much on the Board as an action arm of his office or of his personality.

The NRPB from the beginning sought the cooperation and help of other federal agencies and in this it was generally successful. When committees were established on some subject, bureaus or other agencies that might reasonably be expected to be interested were asked to nominate someone to the committees. The NRPB always insisted that these committee members drawn from the bureaus should serve in an individual or personal capacity, not as formal representatives of their agencies; but it is clear that in this the NRPB was not wholly successful, for many an agency man actively defended what he thought were his agency's interests. Efforts were made to get truly top people from the agencies, with the result that the nominal committee member was often represented by a substitute. It seems fairly clear that other agencies generally felt that NRPB auspices were an excellent way to get their ideas before a larger public than they had managed to previously—as well as noting the fact that the NRPB was, after all, in the Office of the President, with all that this connotes for a federal agency. In later years, as the NRPB gradually shifted to doing more of its own research and report writing, the role of other federal agency personnel somewhat diminished.

One conspicuous exception to the NRPB's generally good relations with federal agencies was the Corps of Engineers; or more accurately, the Rivers and Harbors Congress, which was the mentor and supporter of the Corps. That congress included many senators and congressmen; they wanted the Corps to bring pork barrel projects to them directly, not through the president and the Bureau of the Budget. The Corps and the Rivers and Harbors Congress opposed giving basic legislative authority to the NRPB, opposed its specific public works coordination efforts, and was one—though perhaps only a minor one—of the forces involved in the NRPB's demise. Relationships between technical staff of the Corps and NRPB staff were generally good.

In contrast to its relationships with the president and with the executive branch generally, the NRPB's relationships with the Congress were very bad. During the first six years of its existence under various names, the NRPB operated wholly on funds allocated to it by the president from his emergency funds; it did not have to go to Congress for appropriations, and thus escaped the kind of scrutiny which appropriation requests invariably bring. Some attempts were made during these years to give the NRPB legislative authority, to replace its authority conferred by executive order; but these efforts were not successful—and, in my judgment, were not skillfully made. In its last four years, the NRPB was required to seek appropriations, and this opened it up to extensive and often highly critical review by the Congress. By this time, some of its reports were stirring increased opposition in the Congress.

The NRPB's very bad relations with the Congress were the direct outcome of some of the personalities on the Board or staff. Delano was respected by congressmen. But he was unwilling to politic with members of the Congress, individually or in committees. Merriam not only avoided contact with the Congress, individually and in committees, as much as he could, but he forbade Eliot and other staff people to make any more such contacts than were necessary. Eliot would have liked to have developed friendly relations with potential friends in Congress, but he was forbidden by Merriam and the Board from doing so, and some commentators have suggested that he would have been a poor emissary in any case.

When the war in Europe cast its shadow of ultimate war for the United States, the NRPB was gradually shoved aside in many ways.

After some initial activities in "defense" planning, the defense and war planning was taken over by other agencies. The president did assign responsibility for postwar planning to the NRPB, and considerable effort was directed to this end. With some modest exceptions, much of this postwar planning was not directly translated into action, perhaps because the NRPB was out of existence by the time the war ended, but largely because postwar economic conditions were greatly different than anticipated. But at least some of the ideas generated by such postwar planning did indirectly lead to actions after the war.

The NRPB had its own regional organizations. These varied from active and quite able in the Pacific Northwest, in New England, and in the Southeast to little more than token organizations in some other regions. Considerable time was required to arouse interest in regional planning and to get a regional organization formed and functioning; had the NRPB survived permanently, its regional organizations would surely have become much more effective, perhaps in a relatively few years. The NRPB greatly stimulated the formation of state planning agencies, in part by helping them get various federal emergency funds, but the state organizations were, strictly speaking, not part of the NRPB's organization. In general, its relationships with state planning agencies seem to have been cordial and constructive. The regional organizations folded up with the NRPB's demise; the state organizations were curtailed, in general, with some surviving, and with some of the survivors being transformed into economic development agencies. One of the most curious aspects of the NRPB's operations was its extremely limited use of the political and public relations resources which the regional and state agencies provided. Although the record is not entirely clear, apparently it was only when the NRPB was under fatal attack that any real effort was made to mobilize the political power which its field relationships provided.

Why and How the NRPB Was Killed

In 1943 Congress killed the NRPB by the simple device of refusing to make any further appropriations for it and by forbidding it to accept any funds not appropriated to it. Provision was made for its liquidation and for the transfer of all its records to the National Archives.

There is no single or simple explanation for the action by the Congress; on the contrary, a number of factors, each of which may have been serious but none of which alone would probably have been fatal, combined in 1943 to produce the death of the NRPB:

1. There had been a rising tide of criticism in the Congress and in the press about some NRPB studies. In particular, its lengthy report on *Security, Work, and Relief Policies,* with its advocacy of a cradle-to-the-grave program of welfare, had drawn much criticism. So had a pamphlet on monetary and fiscal policy, *After the War—Full Employment,* by Alvin H. Hansen of Harvard. One of the Board's last major reports, *National Resources Development Report for 1943,* was another which drew much criticism from critics who argued that Roosevelt sought dictatorial powers. There were others as well. The Board was increasingly pictured as left-wing, socialistic, visionary, impractical, opposed to free private enterprise, and so forth.

2. The 1942 congressional elections had seen a marked swing toward the political right. There had been a substantial net Republican gain in both Senate and House, and a number of liberals in each house had been defeated. The elections fairly well reflected the political mood of the country at the time.

3. There was a strong, and often emotional, concentration on winning the war, and anything not directly and obviously contributing to that end was often severely criticized in the Congress and elsewhere. One of the lines of argument was that the NRPB's work duplicated that of other agencies and did not contribute to the war effort.

4. For ten years congressional hostility and opposition to President Roosevelt had been rising. His repeated election victories had fanned rather than assuaged this hostility in many quarters. The Congress dared not deny him what he asked in the name of the war effort, but it took out much of its opposition on spite attacks on New Deal programs which were not, or seemed not, directly aiding the war effort.

5. The Corps of Engineers or the Rivers and Harbors Congress had a continuing opposition to the NRPB, as noted earlier. This seems not to have been as intense at the end as it had been earlier, but it was clearly one factor affecting the attitude of some members of Congress.

In early 1943, in considering the appropriations for fiscal 1944 (which began on July 1, 1943), the House Appropriations Committee voted against any appropriation for the NRPB. No real effort was made to reverse the committee when the appropriation bill came to the House for vote; such efforts as were made by the Board's would-be friends were too ill informed and too weak to be effective.

Following this House action, strenuous battles over the NRPB appropriation for fiscal 1944 were made in the Senate Appropriations Subcommittee and Committee, and on the Senate floor. The final Senate action was an appropriation of only $200,000—not enough to keep even a skeletal NRPB functioning, and barely enough to provide for its liquidation. The final appropriation act adopted this figure and also provided that it could not be augmented by transfers from other sources. There is reason to believe that President Roosevelt made a less than all-out drive for the continuance of the NRPB and that he had become reconciled to its demise. He was absorbed fully in the war and he was forced to jettison programs that were or seemed dispensable, partly to satisfy his critics and partly simply because he had not the time nor the energy to fight every battle.

Although the actual end of the NRPB came in 1943, I argue that its end should have been foreseen several years earlier. I specifically pick out 1939, when the National Resources Planning Board replaced the National Resources Committee, as the date when either drastic revisions in the Board's structure, functioning, and personnel should have been made or its demise had to be accepted as inevitable. Such changes would have included a willingness to meet potential congressional friends half way, to have modified the NRPB's activities by dropping some of the more controversial parts, and to make major personnel changes. Had these changes been made, the NRPB would have been changed but might have survived. The latter is, of course, speculative since no one can say positively today what the consequences would have been of some sharply different course.

The NRPB's Legacy

The NRPB left a substantial legacy in various forms. First, many men who have achieved outstanding careers in the years since 1943, and who are still active professionally, were connected with the NRPB in one capacity or another during early and formative years in their professional lives. These include Joseph L. Fisher, research organization president and congressman; Milton Friedman, professor, Nobel Prize winner, and outstanding economist; J. K. Galbraith, also professor, outstanding economist, and U.S. ambassador to India; Lincoln Gordon, university president and ambassador to Brazil; Wassily Leontief, university professor and Nobel Prize winner; Paul Samuelson, also professor and Nobel Prize winner; Malcolm Toon, U.S. ambassador to several countries; and Gilbert F. White, college president and university scholar, among others. In addition, a number of outstanding older persons, now largely retired from active professional work, were also connected with the NRPB in one capacity or another; and many outstanding scholars and professional workers of the day were on one or more NRPB committees. All of these people made contributions to the Board but it may reasonably be assumed that each of them gained something from his or her own NRPB experience.

A more tangible legacy was the number of reports compiled under NRPB auspices and published by it. I have noted that these reports are today largely forgotten and ignored, to an unfortunate and undeserved degree. They might well be uncovered again, as an archeological dig uncovers the remains of an earlier civilization, discovered to be interesting, often valuable, and sometimes jewels.

Some of the NRPB's policy recommendations which were most controversial at the time, such as its proposals for welfare programs, have been translated into government programs today. Whether one supports or whether one opposes those programs, the influence of the NRPB was probably considerable.

Some of the specific functions undertaken by the Board, or the logical modern derivatives of those functions, have been taken over by other agencies. The Council of Economic Advisers has taken over some of the NRPB's economic analysis and reporting function, the National Science Foundation has taken over some of its function of stimulating and financing research, and the executive departments generally have far stronger and more effective planning units today than they had in the 1930s. There have also been a number of special presidential or presidential–congressional commissions which have undertaken specific analytical and planning tasks. It would be impossible to measure exactly how far these developments owe their existence or their form to the NRPB experience, but I judge that the NRPB did exert a significant influence here.

There has been an enormous expansion of government planning at all levels—federal, state, and local—in the past two decades, as is discussed in more detail in the next section. I believe, much of this would have occurred irrespective of the NRPB, but I judge that the Board's promotion of and its technical contributions to the conduct of planning were important factors in the actual development of planning over the years since its demise.

The NRPB stimulated the formation of a number of private groups and influenced their programs. The Brookings Institution, the National Planning Association, the Committee for Economic Development, the Potomac Institute, the Rand Corporation, the Twentieth Century Fund, and the American Assembly of Columbia University have in some degree carried on work similar to that the NRPB did or were influenced by the NRPB or both. Special mention should be made of Resources for the Future (RFF), both because it fits into this general category and because Charles W. Eliot, 2nd, the executive officer or director of the NRPB throughout its entire life, played an influential role in the creation of RFF. As with the other legacies of the Board, it is impossible to measure exactly the degree of its influence.

Lastly, and overlapping a good deal with all the foregoing, I believe the NRPB left a legacy of ideas and concepts about economics, about natural resource planning, about social research, and about the role of government in national affairs. Again, it is impossible to measure its precise effect and to disentangle it from the effects of many other contemporaneous activities. But I think the NRPB did have a significant intellectual and conceptual impact.

Does the United States Today Need a Reconstituted NRPB?

What would a reconstituted NRPB do, how should it operate, what could it reasonably expect to accomplish, and, on balance, would such an organization be worthwhile? What lessons can be learned from the Board of the 1930s and 1940s? To what extent should a reconstituted NRPB, if one were to be established, operate only in a national office and to what extent should it also have regional offices?

There are at least three general or broad roles which a reconstituted NRPB might play in the United States today:

1. It might be an idea stimulator/financer, as the original NRPB was in part. That is, it might itself conduct research on contemporary problems, or it might stimulate others to conduct more or different research than they would do if left to themselves, or it might finance research, or any combination of these modes of action.

2. It might serve as a general coordinator of federal planning and of federal programs, operating out of the president's office and serving as his arm to a considerable degree.

3. It might serve as a major federal economic planner and operator, seeking to fill the role which the War Production Board filled in World War II or which the National Industrial Recovery Administration tried unsuccessfully to fill during the worst of the Great Depression.

A need for a new agency in any of these roles can easily be argued. New, innovative, imaginative ideas for a nation, for any institution, or for a private business are always in short supply, and it may be argued that any organization which might possibly fill this role is worth a try, even if it should turn out to be not very productive.

The need for better coordination of federal planning and of federal programs is painfully apparent in 1980 and has been recognized as such by every president since Roosevelt. It is not generally appreciated how very extensive is planning in the federal government today, and how much the federal government dominates the planning by states and local governments. The inconsistencies and conflicts among federal programs which are so often aired in the information media have their counterpart in the federal or federally dominated planning programs, which have not had the same degree of attention from the information media.

It is also obvious that the United States today faces extremely difficult economic problems and that its various federal economic programs are neither well-coordinated or very effective. In times of great emergency in the past, such as the two World Wars and the Great Depression, the United States set up comprehensive economic planning and operating organizations with great powers. How serious does an emergency have to be for such an effort to find strong public as well as majority legislative support?

Just as it is possible to marshal arguments for a reconstituted NRPB for one or more of the foregoing three major roles, so it is equally easy to marshal arguments against such a new organization. What could a new organization do, in any of these fields, that existing organizations are not doing or cannot do? For instance, what economic or social research could a new organization do that the National Science Foundation, or the National Academy of Sciences, or any one of many private research organizations is not doing? If more money is to be put into such research, is it likely to be more productive if put into an existing organization or into a new one? Likewise, what reason is there to think that a new central federal planning agency could resolve the overlapping, confusion, and often conflict among existing planning and operating federal programs? Why cannot the necessary coordination now come out of the White House executive staff—a staff which has increased greatly in size over the past twenty years, under Republican as well as under Democratic presidents? Is the basic difficulty today one of organization, or lack of it, or is it a president who seems not to know his own mind or to carry out what he says he plans to do? And a range of similar questions could well be raised about any suggestion to establish a comprehensive economic planning and operating unit. Again, there is no lack of federal agencies with at least some role in the national economy; if they cannot solve the nation's economic problems, what reason is there to think that a new agency would be any more successful?

In thus offering arguments for a reconstituted NRPB and in thus raising questions about the value of any such organization, I do not wish to take a position of either advocacy or opposition. My purpose is to raise significant matters for serious consideration. The experience of the NRPB during the ten years of its existence does offer at least the following guidelines, should there be serious consideration of establishing a reconstituted NRPB: (1) The role or roles of the new organization should be clearly defined; (2) The new organization should have a firm legislative base; (3) The new agency should have an administrative structure compatible with its role(s). An administering board may be satisfactory for a research organization, but a board is hopelessly incompetent to manage an active planning and coordinating agency; (4) The roles and the methods of operation of the new agency should be fully compatible; and (5) The methods of operation should be fully compatible with the timing required for the agency's output.

As I study the NRPB experience, I am strongly convinced that no single agency should attempt more than one of the three general roles outlined above. Establish a new research agency if you so choose, but do not expect it also to be a central planning and coordination agency; or, establish a new comprehensive economic planning and operating agency if you so choose, but do not give it either coordination or research functions. A multiplicity of roles in one agency will almost surely guarantee failure at one or all of them.

My final judgment on a reconstituted NRPB is: the value of such an organization depends on the president. If he chooses to establish such an agency as a means of accomplishing his goals, and if he genuinely uses it, then it might be made truly effective; if he is unclear about his goals, or how to reach them, or irresolute in his pursuit of them, then a reconstituted NRPB would be ineffective, would almost surely fail, and would likely be shortlived. To be most effective, an overall planning unit in the executive branch would have to be matched by an overall planning committee in the Congress.

I

ORIGIN AND SETTING

2

The Situation From Which the Board Arose

The origin of the National Resources Planning Board and its predecessor agencies must be analyzed and evaluated in light of their times—the economic times, with its massive and brutal Great Depression; the political times, with its New Deal and its innovative and experimenting president; the social times, with the enormous confusion and despair of the Great Depression gradually giving way to renewed hope; the governmental times, with the federal and state agencies and their capabilities; and the professional and information times, with the kinds of economic and planning studies which the professionals were then capable of making and with the kinds and amounts of data they had to work on. It would be wholly inappropriate to judge the NRPB in terms of 1980 conditions in each of these factors, though the historical perspective which time has provided may enable us better to understand it than the day-to-day participants could.[1]

---

[1] In this chapter I rely heavily on four quite divergent authors, hoping that their differences largely explore the relevant range of experience: Joseph S. Davis, *The World Between the Wars, 1919–39: An Economist's View* (Baltimore, The Johns Hopkins University Press, 1975); George B. Galloway and Associates, *Planning for America* (New York, Henry Holt and Co., 1941); Arthur M. Schlesinger, Jr., *The Age of Roosevelt: The Crisis of the Old Order, 1919–1933* (Boston, Houghton Mifflin Co., 1957); and Rexford G. Tugwell, *Roosevelt's Revolution: The First Year—A Personal Perspective* (New York, Macmillan Publishing Co., 1977).

Back to Normalcy—Post-World War I and the 1920s[2]

World War I had seen an enormous expansion of American industry, a substantial increase of governmental control for war mobilization, an enormous rise in prices generally, and the emergence of the United States as a major world political power.

With the coming of the Armistice in late 1918, the economy expanded and prices rose even more rapidly for a brief period, followed by a sharp, severe, but relatively short economic depression. Although prices in general fell sharply, prices of agricultural commodities plummeted, falling by half or more in some cases within a twelve-month period. Farm debt had risen dramatically during the war, as farm land prices had advanced rapidly, and the sharply lower prices for farm commodities made it impossible for farmers to pay debts which might otherwise have been bearable. Farm foreclosures rose rapidly. Agriculture played a role in the national economy and national life in 1920 which it is difficult for most people to realize today. Nearly half of the total population was "rural," meaning that the people lived on farms, in the open country, or in towns of less than 2,500 population. (Today, only a fourth is rural.) Agriculture contributed a substantial part of the national income, and agricultural distress was, therefore, of concern to the whole nation. But unemployment flared in previous war industries, and the economic depression was general.

Warren G. Harding, Republican, was elected president in 1920; "normalcy" returned; and shortly the nation entered into a period of considerable prosperity, though with pockets of poverty and some depressed industries. During the 1920s, employment and industrial production rose and housing construction boomed; it was the period of the businessman. There was a widespread feeling, not limited to the business community, that the country had entered into a new and permanent form of sustained greater prosperity. The gains in national income were real enough, though somewhat exaggerated in some semipopular literature of the time, but they were most unequally shared among the whole population. In retrospect, it appears that not enough of the increased productivity was passed along to labor and consumers to enable them to buy the increased output from the greater productivity of the economic machine.

---

[2] This section relies primarily on Davis, *The World Between the Wars,* and Schlesinger, *The Age of Roosevelt.*

One activity of the 1920s was to undo the apparent prosperity. This was the frenzied speculation in the stock market, much of it on very slender margins which pushed stock prices upward rapidly, especially in 1928 and 1929, to levels which were not only very high but out of proportion to corporate profits. As long as prices rose, small margins were adequate; at the first breath of the cold air of slightly declining stock prices, the slender margins were inadequate, loans were called, distress sales were made, and prices fell some more. Later investigations revealed much rigging of stock prices, with insiders helping to cause severe swings in prices from which they could benefit. All this was, of course, before national legislation regulating the stock market and stock operations; the Securities and Exchange Commission came much later.

The election of 1928 brought Herbert Hoover to the presidency at almost the peak of the boom. He had had an outstanding career as a private businessman, as organizer of relief after World War I, and as secretary of commerce.

Crash and Depression

Although there had been earlier signs that all was not well, it was the sharp stock market break in October 1929 which began the crash and the Great Depression. Stock-market prices fell, sharply and dramatically at times, with interludes of slight rises or pauses, for more than three years, to levels only a small fraction of their peaks. In the process enormous values were wiped out ("paper," but real nonetheless in a business world) as were hundreds of thousands of stock market speculators. Equally serious, industrial output fell sharply to levels not experienced for decades. Farm output did not decline much (and most of that decline was due to drought, not to lower prices) but farm commodity prices did fall to a small fraction of their level of the late 1920s. Unemployment rose sharply.

It is difficult, at this much later date in history, to fully capture the meaning of these bald statements about the deepening economic depression. There was no federal program of unemployment compensation or of public welfare; to the extent public assistance programs existed at all, they were state or local, and state and local governments were quickly overwhelmed by the magnitude of the economic crash. Individual savings were quickly used up and hardship was severe among many sectors of the population.

In some ways more depressing than the actual economic declines and hardships—serious as they were—was the evident national inability to cope with them. President Hoover was torn between an extreme financial orthodoxy, including a belief in the sanctity of a balanced budget, and humanitarian concerns for the plight of people. At first, he stated publicly, and apparently honestly thought, that only a modest cyclical economic depression was under way, which would cure itself soon without federal interference. Later, some concerns were expressed about accelerated programs of public works, but here he put major responsibility on the states, which were totally unable to finance anything significant, and he resisted any federal program of more than token size. He did accept a compromise federal farm program, much along the lines of one that President Coolidge had vetoed, but its efforts at "orderly marketing," which really meant commodity storage to withhold supplies from markets, were soon overwhelmed by the continuing drop in prices of farm commodities. Late in Hoover's Administration, the Reconstruction Finance Corporation was set up; it had little money and did very little in his term, but it became a major tool in the Roosevelt Administration and, even more, was a major tool for war preparedness later. There was also established by law an Employment Stabilization Board, which accomplished very little in Hoover's Administration but which proved the legal base for much of the National Resources Board activities several years later.

It was not only Hoover and his Administration which appeared helpless as the economy continued to nose dive. At first, business and political leaders other than Hoover asserted the essential economic soundness of the country, arguing that merely a healthy economic corrective period had begun. As conditions worsened, this position became more untenable, of course. At a series of congressional hearings, leading business figures revealed an appalling lack of knowledge and of concern about economic conditions and human welfare in the country, and none were able to suggest means for remedying the evidently worsening economic situation. Hoover was pulled and tugged internally between humanitarian concern and financial orthodoxy, but so was the country, including its intellectuals.

Even more disturbing than the actual conditions, bad as they were, was the philosophical or emotional attitude that began to develop in the country. Despair, hopelessness, and increasing anger and resentment characterized the period—and with scant wonder, as men out of work for months, with no source of public assistance, watched their families suffer hunger and severe privation. There was a good deal of talk about rebellion and some groups armed and prepared themselves for the civil war they thought was coming. Others turned to communism; there arose a good deal of interest in the Russian communistic experience and an almost equal interest in the Italian fascist experience under Mussolini. The United States was increasingly desperate as the bad conditions of 1931 merged into the worse ones of 1932, with the winter of 1932–33 looming as sheer desperation. The economic depression was worldwide.

The New Deal

The foregoing situation changed sharply as a result of the 1932 election. "Roosevelt suddenly became a savior found in the electoral processes Americans believed in. What made this seem strange was that obviously Hoover had been voted out of office and Roosevelt only incidentally voted in. Moreover, the campaign had revealed almost nothing the president-elect actually meant to do."[3]

The election was in early November, but the new administration took office in early March, not in late January as now. The four-month period between election and inauguration was a form of interregnum; Hoover had lost political and popular stature for two years and was clearly repudiated in 1932. He was politically powerless (especially with a Democratic House), and in any case confused and uncertain about what to do. Hence, he did virtually nothing except to watch the economic situation rapidly deteriorate further. He, or some of his close associates, did approach Roosevelt about some sort of joint program but Roosevelt refused to join with him, fearing that under split responsibility he could accomplish little and that he would then be blamed for that lack of accomplishment.

The reason the country had little idea of President-elect Roosevelt's programs, economic and otherwise, was that Roosevelt himself had no real idea of what he was going to do. In his campaign, he had received contradictory advice. There were those who felt he should do very little except simply run, so that Hoover could defeat himself; others advised an activist approach in the campaign, but they were sharply

---

[3] Tugwell, *Roosevelt's Revolution*, p. 3.

divided as to the direction his activism should take. Under advice from
Lewis W. Douglas (who later became Roosevelt's director of the Bureau
of the Budget) and others, Roosevelt made one major speech calling
for a 25 percent reduction in federal expenditures and for a balanced
budget. On other occasions he expressed a humanistic appeal for help
to those unemployed and destitute through no fault of their own; and
still other times he talked of large-scale federal programs in the natural
resources field, each of which would have required large expenditures
and an unbalanced budget.

Roosevelt's inauguration on March 4, 1933, marked the beginning
of a furiously active period in federal government. His first official
acts were to declare a national bank holiday—a period during which all
banks in the country were to remain closed, pending some action which
would assure their continued operation once they were opened—and
to call for a special session of the Congress. An early political action
was his first "fireside chat," the use of the radio (this was, of course,
long before common use of television in the United States) to inform
the people of the United States and to enlist their cooperation. An
emergency banking bill was introduced in the Congress just five days
after the inauguration and just eight hours after its introduction it had
been passed and was on Roosevelt's desk for signature. The Congress
was as desperate for action as was the country, and both were willing
to grant the new president whatever powers he sought. The details of
that act are less important now than the fact that under it most of the
nation's banks did reopen promptly, the power of the federal government
had been used to meet a crisis, and a process of recovery had begun.

There began immediately what was then and since has been called
"the hundred days." In that period, the Emergency Banking Act was
passed, the powers and funds of the Reconstruction Finance Corporation were extended greatly, the Civilian Conservation Corps was established by executive action, the Agricultural Adjustment Act was passed,
the Tennessee Valley Authority was established by legislation, an act
providing for emergency employment relief was passed, a homeowners
loan act was passed, the National Industrial Recovery Act was passed,
and numerous other executive and some legislative actions were taken,
any one of which would have seemed major in less tumultuous times,
and each of which in more normal times would have taken months to
push through the legislative process. Major public works were begun
then or very shortly thereafter. There was even an act declaring beer a

nonintoxicating liquor, opening the way for its legal sale and beginning the process of repeal of the Prohibition Amendment. Roosevelt made extensive use of a "Brain Trust," a group of professors and other intellectuals whom he brought or attracted to Washington.

The numerous, often ill-coordinated, and sometimes contradictory acts of the early New Deal days were, in general, highly popular in the country. People at last had a feeling of hope, a conviction that something was being done, even when they could not always understand what had been done or what might follow from some action, and even when their own personal benefit was slight. As Schlesinger says "even conservatives joined in the applause."[4]

At the same time, there was, naturally enough, criticism—muted at first, but growing in frequency and intensity—as those most shell-shocked by the Great Depression began to regain their courage and to assert their interests. As the New Deal went on, the criticism continued to rise.

In 1932 the Democratic Party was the minority party in the country; worse than its lack of committed members, from a political point of view, was its internal lack of cohesion and its lack of common goals among such members as it had. Part of it was Southern conservative, part was big city political machines, part was labor union support (then vastly less significant than later, since union membership had declined massively during the depression), and a few scattered other groups. One of Roosevelt's greatest political achievements was the creation of a vastly better coordinated party program, the drawing together of basically divergent if not discordant groups, and the enlistment of very large numbers of persons not previously identified with the party, to begin the transformation of the Democratic Party into the national majority party which it has been for the past two or three decades.

Recovery Versus Reform

A basic question for Roosevelt and the New Deal, sometimes explicitly phrased, perhaps more often implicit, and never really resolved was: recovery or reform? The old economic organization had clearly failed to achieve full employment, to produce the maximum volume of goods and services, to distribute its rewards fairly, and to achieve a reasonable

---

[4] Arthur M. Schlesinger, Jr., *The Age of Roosevelt: The Coming of the New Deal* (Boston, Houghton Mifflin Co., 1959) p. 13.

degree of stability in its operations. Should the first and major effort be directed at getting the old economic machine functioning better, or should greater efforts be made to change it because of its demonstrated persistent incompetencies?

In practice, the New Deal did both. The Securities Act was clearly a reform measure, to make illegal many of the stock and money market practices of the 1920s, but the Agricultural Adjustment Act and the National Industrial Recovery Act, as well as the emergency banking legislation, were instituted primarily to get the stalled economy moving again. Many acts and many other actions had elements of both reform and recovery, and Roosevelt's speeches of the day continued to emphasize both, usually not in these simple terms and usually without clear distinction between them.

There was a substantial body of thought in universities, in business, and in government that some basic changes in the whole economic machine were necessary if tolerable performance over the long run was to be achieved. If there was to be fundamental reform, what shape should it take? Had the vaunted virtues of "free" or atomistic competition and of free enterprise, with each producer doing his own thing in his own way, failed to achieve the efficiency and the output which had been claimed? There were certainly many people who thought that some different basis of economic decision making was necessary. Such people generally believed in some sort of collectivist approach —some way for decisions to be made other than by individual producers.[5] But there were major divergences among the collectivists: some favored essentially business cartels, with little or limited government supervision. Few businessmen would have expressed their ideas in these terms but many of them would have welcomed such a change. This was essentially the approach of the National Industrial Recovery Act—an act which was declared unconstitutional in 1935. Others favored a much larger role for government, with essentially government or government–business planning followed by private business implementation within the framework of the plan.[6]

---

[5] Philip W. Warken, "A History of the National Resources Planning Board, 1933–1943" (doctoral dissertation, Ohio State University, 1969) traces these ideas through the 1920s and early 1930s very well with many specific references.

[6] This idea was developed in some detail in Mordecai Ezekiel, *Jobs for All Through Industrial Expansion* (New York, Alfred A. Knopf, 1939). Galloway, *Planning in America,* also suggests the need for a collectivist approach in several chapters.

This question of recovery versus reform affected the NRPB directly throughout its history. While some of its activities were primarily aimed at economic recovery, others were concerned with making the economy work better. While many groups—academics especially, but business and labor to a minor degree—were drawn into its planning, others were more or less excluded from its operations—notably the Congress. Given the NRPB's role, as it saw that role, the exclusion of the Congress was perhaps unavoidable, but it surely played a part in the demise of the organization.

3

Predecessors of the Board

When the National Planning Board, the first direct in-line ancestor of the organizations which led to the National Resources Planning Board, was established on July 20, 1933, by order of the administrator of public works, it naturally had some antecedents. The purpose of this chapter is to describe briefly some of the antecedents more or less directly related to the sequence of organizations which ultimately became the NRPB.[1]

Study of Recent Social Trends

One of Herbert Hoover's early intellectual activities as president was the establishment in September 1929 of a President's Research Committee on Social Trends.[2] The committee included some of the most presti-

---

[1] When I was a graduate student at Harvard more than forty years ago, one of my favorite apocryphal stories concerned the professor who lectured three times a week all fall and all winter, laying the background for the history of the French Revolution, so that by the time the spring vacation arrived he was ready to build the first Egyptian pyramid. This chapter clearly deals only with a more recent past of the National Planning Board.

[2] This section rests primarily on Barry D. Karl, *Charles E. Merriam and the Study of Politics* (Chicago, University of Chicago Press, 1974); and on the President's Research Committee on Social Trends, *Recent Social Trends,* volumes I and II (New York, McGraw-Hill Book Co., 1933).

gious social scientists of the day, and Hoover took a personal role in its meetings and in the preparation of its report. A series of monographs was prepared by individual authors under the auspices of the committee. All in all, this was an attempt to capture the best thinking of the "wise men" of the day, on social trends and problems.

The effort was a private one, in the sense that the committee was composed of private citizens and that most of the contributors were also private persons. The committee's work was financed by the Rockefeller Foundation and the report was privately published. But the deep personal involvement of the president, and the relationship of this project to some activities Hoover had undertaken while secretary of commerce, surely gave it a semiofficial air or blessing.

Viewed as purely a scholarly enterprise, the resulting two-volume report was very impressive, especially in light of the development of social sciences in that day and in light of the information available. The report included chapters on population, mineral and power resources, agricultural and forest land, influence of invention and discovery, agencies of communication, trends in economic organization, occupational patterns, education, social attitudes, metropolitan communities, rural life, racial and ethnic groups, vitality of American people, family and its functions, activities of women outside of the home, childhood and youth, labor groups in the social structure, people as consumers, recreation and leisure time, arts in social life, religious organizations, health and medical practice, crime and punishment, private social work, public welfare activities, growth of governmental functions, taxation and public finance, public administration, law and legal institutions, and government and society.

Every effort was made by Hoover, the committee, and the individual authors to make the separate chapters and the report as a whole as accurate, as objective, and as free of political bias as possible. The committee (p. xciv of the report) indicated its hope that "its work will prove useful to many groups engaged in practical efforts to promote the general welfare of the nation."

If the committee's work was an impressive display of contemporary social science, in two other respects it was a disaster. With few and unimportant exceptions, the base period for all the chapters was 1929 and analyses ended with 1929. Much of the analysis was based on 1930 census data covering 1929. The need for a common historical reference point made the 1929 date reasonable from a research point of

view, but, by virtually ignoring the 1929 crash and the ensuing Great
Depression, the resulting report in early 1933 was totally out of touch
with social and political reality. The other major disastrous effect was
also a matter of timing. The committee was formed in late 1929 and
perhaps its work progressed as fast as such studies could reasonably go,
especially in light of the fact that so many contributors were academic
or other persons with important continuing responsibilities which could
not easily be laid aside. By March 1932 the committee held its final
meeting; a report could have been issued in the fall, just before the
presidential election in November. But

> . . . a sudden bombshell in October or even September would do
> no one any good. From the president's view, it would look like a
> last minute gambit and only confirm the criticisms of those who saw
> similar motives in his various commissions and conferences. From the
> point of view of the social scientists, they would all be called politicians,
> which regardless of the fact that some of them were still ardent sup-
> porters of Hoover, would have violated totally the very scientific
> objectivity they were struggling to achieve.[3]

Although Hoover's foreword is dated October 11, 1932, the books themselves carry a January 1933 first printing date. To a very substantial
degree, then, the reports were ancient history by the time they were
printed. The timing of this study in relation to the political cycle reveals
an unbelievable naivete on political matters, not only by the committee
and the contributors, but by the president. If such reports were to
influence Hoover in his first term, they should have been available to
him by mid-1930 at the latest.

For the purposes of this book, the *Recent Social Trends* effort was
significant in considerable part because of the personalities involved.
The chairman of the committee was Wesley C. Mitchell of Columbia
University and the vice chairman was Charles E. Merriam of the University of Chicago. Both became members of the National Planning
Board when it was established in 1933; although Mitchell left the successor agencies in 1935, Merriam stayed on the committee or the board
of each of the agencies right to the end of the NRPB's existence. His
experience on the Committee on Social Trends almost surely greatly
affected his concept of what the NRPB should do and how it should
do it.

---

[3] Karl, *Charles E. Merriam*, p. 216.

Studies of America's Capacity

Somewhat similar to the *Recent Social Trends* inquiry, but under different auspices and with a narrower but sharper focus, were a series of four books published by the Brookings Institution in 1933: *America's Capacity to Produce; America's Capacity to Consume; The Formation of Capital;* and *Income and Economic Progress.* In a foreword to the first volume listed above, it is stated that, "Only on the basis of real understanding of the motivating forces in economic progress can the nation's accomplishments in the years ahead be commensurate with the opportunities within our reach. The task of arriving at such an understanding is not easy. . . . Each of these volumes sets for itself a severely limited objective," which is then described.[4] Their main conclusion was that our industry was capable of an added production of 19 percent above 1929. "Certainly our findings do not bear out the contention of those who, in the midst of the present depression, say that we were living in a fool's paradise in 1929—that we were 'living beyond our means,' and that disaster had to follow. . . . Finally, the 19 percent . . . would have constituted a very substantial achievement."[5]

The Brookings studies, like the *Recent Social Trends* project, were privately financed and privately conducted; they did not have the participation of the president—at that general period, he was highly critical of Brookings—and they did not have the direct link to public policy which it had been hoped the *Social Trends* studies would have—but which, in fact, they did not have. There was no direct carryover of personnel from the Brookings studies to the National Planning Board and its successors, although Frederic A. Delano (whose activities for the NRPB are discussed in later chapters) was chairman of the board of trustees of the Brookings Institution. John C. Merriam, a brother of Charles E. Merriam (whose relations to the NRPB are also discussed in detail in later chapters) was a member of the board of trustees. None of the authors of the Brookings books played a major role in the NRPB studies. Such evidence as I could find suggests that communication between the NRPB staff and the Brookings staff was limited, perhaps minimal. Nevertheless, the existence of the Brookings studies,

---

[4] See foreword to *America's Capacity to Produce* (Washington, D.C., The Brookings Institution, 1933) pp. 14–15. Harold G. Moulton, Edwin G. Nourse, and several other Brookings' staff were involved on a group basis.

[5] *America's Capacity to Produce*, pp. 422–429.

their careful use and appraisal of available information, and their conclusions undoubtedly influenced the NRPB studies in a large way. The technological and economic potential of the United States, as revealed by these studies, surely was a finding of immense policy importance and offered major hope to a national planning organization.

In a sense, the Brookings studies suffered from one of the major timing problems of the *Social Trends* studies: they too were based on 1929 or 1930 data, with only scant attention to the crash and the Great Depression. However, since their objective was the rather narrower one of measuring economic potential for the longer run, this unfortunate timing was less serious than it had been for the *Social Trends* reports, whose major purpose was to provide a base for government policy.

Agricultural Planning

Throughout the 1920s agriculture was in a somewhat depressed condition—at least in comparison with its pre-World War I position, which came to be considered the norm for "agricultural parity." A large number of studies of agriculture were made during the 1920s, mostly under private auspices. An agricultural program was undertaken, during Hoover's administration, by the newly created Federal Farm Board; and one of the earliest and most dramatic of the New Deal's programs was embodied in the Agricultural Adjustment Act. Crops were plowed up and little pigs were killed, to the accompaniment of much publicity.

A National Land Use Committee, consisting of agricultural college representatives and federal government employees, was created in late 1931. It was paralleled by a National Advisory and Legislative Committee on Land Use—a lobbying arm—composed of representatives of agricultural organizations and some professional and university persons from outside of the land grant college group. These committees issued at least six reports, the last of which was printed.[6]

National Capital Park and Planning Commission

Several major cities of the United States, including notably New York, Chicago, and San Francisco, and literally hundreds of smaller cities

---

[6] National Land-Use Planning Committee and National Advisory and Legislative Committee on Land Use, *The Problems of "Submarginal" Areas and Desirable Adjustments with Particular Reference to Public Acquisition of Land,* Publication no. 6 (Washington, GPO, 1933).

have been rather intensively planned, sometimes from the colonial period into the present. The planning of Washington, D.C., has special significance for the NRPB, in part because of the roles played in it by some of the major actors in the NRPB, and in part because it is an outstanding example of one form of planning.

Washington is a prime example of a planned city that developed into a major metropolis.[7] Established by congressional acts in 1790 to be the national capital, it was initially planned by a French architect and planner, Pierre Charles L'Enfant. Various other planning and development efforts proceeded throughout the 19th century. A new formal and elaborate plan was developed by the McMillan Commission in 1901 and 1902. Following a delay of some years, the National Capital Park and Planning Commission (NCPPC) was established by special legislation in 1926. Frederic A. Delano became chairman of the commission from the beginning, and Charles W. Eliot, 2nd, was appointed as "city planner" immediately. These two men remained at these roles and were active in Washington planning efforts from 1926 until the National Planning Board was established in 1933, when Eliot became executive officer of the latter. Delano was chairman of the NPB and the NRPB and also continued as chairman of the NCPPC. His two roles were sometimes confused. Once, when Senator Carter Glass of Virginia denounced him and the NRPB for refusing planning permission for a structure in Virginia, across the Potomac River from downtown Washington, it was an NCPPC action to which he was objecting.

The NCPPC developed quite specific plans for public works and public improvements of all kinds. In a sense it was physical planning, because it dealt mainly with physical structures, but it was also social planning in the sense that full consideration was given to the potential use of the structures planned.

Governmental Measures During the Hoover Administration

In chapter 2 I pointed out the general inactivity and helplessness of the Hoover administration as the United States slid deeper and deeper in the Great Depression from 1929 to 1933.[8]

---

[7] National Capital Planning Commission, Frederick Gutheim, consultant, *Worthy of the Nation* (Washington, Smithsonian Institution Press, 1977).

[8] See Joseph S. Davis, *The World Between the Wars, 1919–39: An Economist's View* (Baltimore, The Johns Hopkins University Press, 1975)

There was, however, one major step taken during this period which was important—indeed, critical—for the NRPB and its predecessors. Senator Robert Wagner (D) of New York sponsored legislation for an expanded program of federal public works to help relieve some of the distress caused by the depression. Hoover was unwilling to go along with Wagner in any large way, but he did agree to the passage of a law establishing a Federal Employment Stabilization Board (reproduced in its entirety as the first item of appendix A). The act led to nothing significant during Hoover's administration but it did provide the legal precedent for new legislation that became the basis for a greatly expanded program of public works under Roosevelt.

This act also provided that the board should "advise the President from time to time of the trend of employment and business activity and of the existence or approach of periods of business depression and unemployment" and also provided for advance planning of public works by federal agencies, copies of whose programs, plans, and estimates "shall be submitted to the board." It also authorized appropriations of "annually such sum as may be necessary for the expenses of the board." In the appropriation for the NRPB for 1940, Congress attached the provision that the Board could perform only functions authorized by this act. Thus at a time when the NRPB was under severe attack in the Congress, the provisions of this 1931 act were decisive in its legal capabilities.

Conclusion

None of the activities discussed in this chapter, nor all of them taken together, necessarily led to the creation of a National Planning Board or into its evolution into the National Resources Planning Board. These activities did provide some grist for the Board's mill, once it was established, and they did provide some intellectual rationale for at least some of the NRPB's activities. Moreover, some of the people who had developed professionally in this earlier period became major figures in the NRPB sequence of organizations. And, as we have noted, one legislative act did become basic to the NRPB's functioning at a critical date in its history. For all of these reasons, this immediately pre-New Deal history is relevant. With the inauguration of the New Deal Administration of Franklin Delano Roosevelt in March 1933, the stage was set for a wholly new line and magnitude of planning operations.

II

HISTORY, ORGANIZATION, OPERATION

4

The Evolution of the Board and
Its Predecessor Agencies

The organizational history of the NRPB is complex and somewhat confusing, especially to one reading about it for the first time. Four different organizations, with four different but highly similar names, over a ten-year period, combined with a nearly constant set of personalities and with a similar but not identical set of functions, inevitably produce a degree of confusion. The changes which occurred over the ten years are summarized in table 4-1.

By modern federal agency standards, the NRPB and its predecessors were always relatively small. The total expenses of the four agencies over ten years were slightly less than $10 million.[1] Dollar figures in those years can be compared with dollar figures today only by a major upward revision, to reflect differences in prices and salaries, but even if a tenfold adjustment is made, these costs are still not large. More revealing are data on numbers of employees. The NRB had a total of only seven employees; this crept up over the years until, in June, 1943, there were 261 employees on active duty in Washington and in the regional offices, plus almost as many more on military leave or on a per diem employment basis.[2] The last were mostly consultants whom

---

[1] Charles W. Eliot, 2nd, assisted by Harold A. Merrill, *Guide to the Files of the National Resources Planning Board and Predecessor Agencies—Ten Years of National Planning, 1933–1943* (Mimeograph, December 31, 1943).

[2] Charles W. Eliot, 2nd, *Final Report—Status of Work National Resources Planning Board* (Mimeograph, December 31, 1943).

Table 4-1. Summary of History of National Resources Planning Board and Predecessor Agencies

Item	NPB	NRB	NRC	NRPB
1. Full name of organization	National Planning Board	National Resources Board	National Resources Committee	National Resources Planning Board
2. Date established	July 20, 1933	July 1, 1934	June 8, 1935	July 1, 1939
3. Date terminated	June 30, 1934	June 7, 1935	June 30, 1939	August 31, 1943
4. Established by	Order of Administrator of Public Works	Executive Order 6777	Executive Order 7065	Presidential Reorganization Plan No. 1 (53 Stat 1423)
5. Terminated by	Executive Order 6777	Executive Order 7065	Presidential Reorganization Plan No. 1 (53 Stat 1423)	Independent Offices Appropriation Act 1944 (57 Stat 170)
6. Governing board	3 citizen members	5 secretaries plus Administrator of Emergency Relief Administration plus 3 citizen members	5 secretaries plus Administrator of Emergency Relief Administration plus 3 citizen members	3 citizen members
7. Chairman of board	Frederic A. Delano	Harold L. Ickes	Harold L. Ickes	Frederic A. Delano
8. Board reported to	Public Works Administrator Harold L. Ickes	President Roosevelt	President Roosevelt	President Roosevelt
9. Source of funds	Allocation of public works funds	Allocation of emergency relief funds	Allocation of emergency relief funds	Appropriations plus allocations of emergency relief funds
10. Basic difference from predecessor		Reports to President	Different legal basis	No longer cabinet board
11. Basic legal authority	National Industrial Recovery Act of 1933	National Industrial Recovery Act of 1933	Emergency Relief Appropriation Act 1935	Reorganization Act of 1939, for existence; Employment Stabilization Act of 1931, for funds

the Board used frequently. This, too, is small by modern federal agency standards, when consideration is given to the range of activities in which the NRPB engaged.

Beginnings

In a purely bureaucratic and legalistic sense, the NRPB began under President Hoover with the passage of the Employment Stabilization Act of 1931. This act produced almost nothing of a substantive nature during Hoover's Administration, but after 1939 it was the sole legal base upon which the work of the NRPB rested. The act provided for a board composed of the secretary of commerce as chairman, and the secretaries of treasury, agriculture, and labor as members. "No record of meetings of the Board or of joint activities by its members has been found."[3] The board had a small staff, consisting of D. H. Sawyer, director; H. R. Colwell, assistant to the director; Fred E. Schnepfe, principal engineer; and Corrington Gill, principal economist. The last made some studies later for the NRPB but the others seem to have had no connection with it.

This board was abolished by Executive Order 6166, June 10, 1933 (see item 2, appendix A); that order was partially revoked by Executive Order 6221, July 26, 1933 (see item 5, appendix A) when the effective date of the earlier order was postponed until sixty days after the convening of the Congress. It was "abolished" again by Executive Order 6623, March 1, 1934 (see item 6, appendix A), and its functions transferred to a newly established Federal Employment Stabilization Office in the Department of Commerce, without, however, loss of the legal authority to make the studies originally authorized by the 1931 act. This last agency was abolished and its functions transferred to the newly created National Resources Planning Board by Presidential Reorganization Plan No. 1, April 3, 1939 (see item 10, appendix A). By this somewhat tortuous route, the NRPB gained the legal authority to make the kinds of studies of public works and other matters authorized in the 1931 act.

A more important direct ancestor of the NRPB was the National Industrial Recovery Act of June 16, 1933 (reproduced in all parts which directly concern the NRPB as item 3 in appendix A). The important part

---

[3] Virgil E. Baugh, *Preliminary Inventories, Number 50, Central Office Records of the National Resources Planning Board* (Washington, National Archives, 1953, Mimeograph) p. 9.

of this act, for our purpose, is that, in Title II, Section 201, it established a Federal Emergency Administration of Public Works. Section 2(b) in its entirety read: "The President may delegate any of his functions and powers under this title to such officers, agents, and employees as he may designate or appoint, and may establish an industrial planning and research agency to aid in carrying out his functions under this title." Section 2(a) authorized him to employ persons without regard to the civil service laws, to prescribe their duties, etc., and to fix their compensation without regard to the Classification Act. Harold L. Ickes was appointed administrator of the Public Works Administration, in addition to his duties as secretary of the interior, less than a month after the act passed.

National Planning Board

Charles W. Eliot, 2nd, while planning officer for the National Capital Park and Planning Commission, in 1931 tried unsuccessfully to interest then Secretary of the Interior Ray Lyman Wilbur in the creation of some kind of a unit to develop plans for the management and use of the public domain.[4] When Harold L. Ickes became secretary of the interior under the new Roosevelt Administration in 1933, Eliot tried unsuccessfully to be named as an assistant secretary in that department.[5]

A memorandum written by Eliot, on March 4, 1933, to the new secretary of the interior says, in part: "National planning means a consistent policy . . . towards the highest and most efficient use of our resources. The place to start is with physical matters. . . . Here is an opportunity for a practical demonstration of the planning idea. . . . What is needed is a Director of Planning similar to the Director of the Budget. . . ."[6] On the other hand, the same author argues that Louis Brownlow, then director of the Public Administration Clearing House in Chicago and an intimate friend of both Ickes and Merriam, not only suggested the

---

[4] Interview with Charles W. Eliot, 2nd, October 2, 1978; and personal correspondence, December 1979.

[5] Ibid.

[6] Albert Lepawsky, "Style and Substance in Contemporary Planning: The American New Deal's National Resources Planning Board as a Model," *Plan Canada,* vol. 18, nos. 3/4 (September/October, 1978). Lepawsky was the first to call attention to this record.

creation·of a planning committee but also suggested the very persons named to the NPB. Ickes does not acknowledge either in his *Diaries*.[7]

At any rate, the NPB was established by an order issued by Ickes on July 20, 1933 (see item 4, appendix A). The main duties of the new Board were "1. The preparation, development, and maintenance of comprehensive and coordinated plans for regional areas. . . .; 2. Surveys and research concerning (a) the distribution and trends of population, land uses, industry, housing and natural resources; and (b) the social and economic habits, trends, and values involved in development projects and plans. . . .; 3. The analysis of projects for coordination in location and sequence in order to prevent duplication and overlaps and to obtain the maximum amount of cooperation and correlation of effort among the departments, bureaus, and agencies of the Federal, State, and local governments." This broad charter launched the organization which was later to evolve into the National Resources Planning Board.

The Board consisted of three members: Frederic A. Delano, chairman, Charles E. Merriam, and Wesley C. Mitchell. Charles W. Eliot, 2nd, was appointed executive officer. "Assistance in the organization of the Board was loaned from the PWA by assignment of Harold A. Merrill as assistant to the Executive Officer and of Dorothy Jackson as secretary. Additions to this group came slowly, and during the life of the National Planning Board only five more employees were appointed."[8]

> . . . in the field the NPB operated at first through regional and State advisers of the Public Works Administration and later through district chairmen of its own appointment. In the year of its existence the NPB set the pattern followed by its successors, initiating and engaging in four major lines of activity: planning and programming public works; stimulating local, State, and regional planning; coordinating federal planning with respect to the conservation and wise use of natural resources; and conducting a research program. The NPB contributed to the public works program by advising the Public Works Administrator on the allocation of funds and by establishing criteria for the selection of projects. It encouraged planning on the regional level and below by direct financial assistance; by sponsoring Federal projects to gather economic statistics on a community level; by assigning consultants to State planning agencies; by collating and disseminating information on planning programs and techniques. It acted as a clearing house for planning activities of Federal agencies.[9]

---

[7] Harold L. Ickes, *The Secret Diary of Harold L. Ickes: The First Thousand Days* (New York, Simon and Schuster, 1954).

[8] Eliot and Merrill, *Guide to the Files,* p. 22.

[9] Baugh, *Preliminary Inventories,* p. 1.

By far the most important product of the NPB, as far as this book is concerned, was its final report, often called "A Plan for Planning" since that was the title for Section II of the report.[10] Section I reviewed planning activities of the NPB; Section II was the conceptual, historical, and logical basis for planning in the United States; Section III discussed the role of science in planning; Section IV was a review of national planning in the United States and in several other countries; and a brief appendix considered the matter of the geographical distribution of public works projects. The report was, in terms of the day, an outstanding planning report.

National Resources Board

The National Planning Board lasted less than one full year. It was abolished on June 30, 1934, and the National Resources Board was established on the next day by Executive Order 6777 (see item 7, appendix A). At the same time the Mississippi Valley Committee, which had been established by Ickes to advise him on public works projects in that area and which had completed its report under the chairmanship of Morris L. Cooke, became the Water Planning Committee for the new NRB.

Schlesinger's version of the basis for the change from NPB to NRB is as follows:

> What was necessary now, he [Roosevelt] believed, was to 'put the physical development of the country on a planned basis.' To this end, he was thinking in terms of a 'permanent long-range planning commission' which could lay out a twenty-five or a fifty-year program for national development. Such a commission already existed in rudimentary form in the PWA's National Planning Board. Here Frederic A. Delano, Wesley C. Mitchell, and Charles E. Merriam were charged with keeping track of public works projects and helping fit them into a national plan. The Board, chafing perhaps under Ickes' tight reins, was more than responsive to Roosevelt's idea of a permanent commission.[11]

---

[10] National Planning Board, *Final Report, 1933–1934* (Washington, GPO, 1934).

[11] Arthur M. Schlesinger, Jr., *The Age of Roosevelt—The Coming of the New Deal* (Boston, Houghton Mifflin Co., 1959) p. 350. No source is given for the quote from Roosevelt.

The NPB in its *Final Report* set out its position as follows: ". . . the temporary planning board appointed by the Administrator of Public Works recommends that the Federal Government create a permanent National Planning Board, directly responsible to the country's Chief Executive."[12]

Again to quote Schlesinger:

At a meeting with Roosevelt in June 1934, the planning group discussed how its mission could best be defined. The President groped for a phrase like "land and water planning." Eliot suggested natural resources, and Mitchell commented that human beings were perhaps America's most important resource. Merriam then suggested the phrase "national resources." The President repeated the phrase several times, liked its sound and remarked, "That's right, friend Eliot, get that down, because that's settled."[13]

Thus, at this very early stage, the differences in scope of work for the NRB and its successors, which will be discussed in later chapters, had been identified by this discussion of the most appropriate name for the organization.

The first draft of the executive order had been dictated by Roosevelt at the meeting and put into final words later by Eliot.[14] It provided for a National Resources Board as an independent agency. When Ickes heard of this from Eliot and the next day from Delano, he objected violently in his *Diary* for that week.

The plan as outlined would have made this Planning Board, consisting of Mr. Delano, Charles E. Merriam, and Wesley C. Mitchell, supreme in its field, without any Cabinet responsibility, although the proposal named several Cabinet officers, myself included, in a consultative capacity. Charles Eliot, 2nd, would be the Executive Secretary, and, of course, considering all the circumstances, he would really run the whole show. I hit the ceiling when I learned of this plan. In the first place, I don't believe in establishing any more independent agencies; in the second place, I think planning should be attached to the Interior Department; and in the third place, I think Eliot would just run amuck if he were given such power and authority as is contemplated.[15]

---

[12] National Planning Board, *Final Report*, p. 35.

[13] Schlesinger, *The Age of Roosevelt*, p. 350. Barry D. Karl, *Charles E. Merriam and the Study of Politics* (Chicago, University of Chicago Press, 1974) corroborates this; see pp. 245–246. Each relied on materials in the National Archives containing both Eliot's and Merriam's notes of the meeting with Roosevelt.

[14] Interview with Charles W. Eliot, 2nd, October 2, 1978; and personal correspondence December 1979 and January 1980.

[15] Ickes, *The Secret Diary*, p. 171.

Had he been alone in his objections to the draft order, Ickes protestations might not have prevailed. However, Frances Perkins, secretary of labor, Henry Wallace, secretary of agriculture, and Harry Hopkins, relief administrator, joined with Ickes in protesting their exclusion from the Board.[16]

The result was a compromise; the cabinet officers were named to the Board, but Delano, Merriam, and Mitchell were made members of the Board and were also established as an advisory committee, which Delano chaired. "It was plain to see that this new setup did not please Eliot at all, but he couldn't break through the line and he left the White House a wiser but sadder man."[17] This struggle over the place of the Board in the whole executive establishment and over its membership was a forerunner of later struggles over the same matters.

The executive order establishing the National Resources Board provided that "The Board shall submit a report on land and water use on or before December 1, 1934." In the five months from the date of the order until this report date, the Board did prepare a most outstanding report, discussed in more detail in chapter 8.

National Resources Committee

The National Resources Board (NRB) was abolished and the National Resources Committee (NRC) established by Executive Order 7065 on June 7, 1935 (see item 8, appendix A). The NRB, like its predecessor, thus lasted for slightly less than a year. The change to the NRC was in form, not in substance. The NRB had existed under the legal authority of the National Industrial Recovery Act; with the imminent end of the NIRA, which was declared unconstitutional by the Supreme Court, the Emergency Relief Appropriation Act of 1935 provided a new legal basis for the planning activity. The Board was continued unchanged, as was the Advisory Committee. The work of the committee was extended and the staff was strengthened.

While there was a clear line of continuity from the NPB to the NRB to the NRC, and thus to the NRPB, there were nevertheless some changes in each transition; but these were least in the change from the NRB to the NRC. There were probably no more changes under the National Resources Committee than would have taken place had the National Resources Board continued over the same period.

---

16 Karl, *Charles E. Merriam*, pp. 247–248.
17 Ickes, *The Secret Diary*, p. 172.

National Resources Planning Board

The change from the National Resources Committee to the National Resources Planning Board was a change of a very different kind. To understand what happened here, we must consider briefly some other changes then going on or proposed in the executive branch as a whole. President Roosevelt stated the need for reorganization as follows:

> The plain fact is that the present organization and equipment of the executive branch of the Government defeats the constitutional intent that there be a single responsible Chief Executive to coordinate and manage the departments and activities in accordance with the laws enacted by the Congress. . . . There are over 100 separate departments, boards, commissions, corporations, authorities, agencies, and activities through which the work of the Government is being carried on. Neither the President nor the Congress can exercise effective supervision and direction over such a chaos of establishments, nor can overlapping, duplication, and contradictory policies be avoided. . . .[18]

The desirability of a special committee to deal with reorganization of the executive branch was proposed by the Board of the National Resources Committee in meetings with the president.[19] Roosevelt accepted the idea and in 1936 appointed a Committee on Administrative Management, consisting of Louis Brownlow, chairman, Charles E. Merriam, and Luther Gulick. Brownlow was then director of the Public Administration Clearing House in Chicago, active in the affairs of the Social Science Research Council, and an old friend and associate of Ickes and Merriam. The committee reported to the president at the beginning of 1937 and its report, with a forceful message, was transmitted by the president to the Congress within a week of his receipt of it. The report attracted much attention at the time, both by its friends and by those opposed to it, and continues to be regarded by professional workers as a truly major document.

The report has an introduction, including some background on the history of planning in the United States; a section on the White House staff; a section on personnel management; another on fiscal manage-

---

[18] Report of the President's Committee, *Administrative Management* (Washington, GPO, 1937). The quotes are from FDR's transmittal letter to the Congress, pp. iii–iv.

[19] Charles W. Eliot, 2nd, in personal correspondence December 1979 makes this statement; Charles E. Merriam corroborates it in "The National Resources Planning Board: A Chapter in American Planning Experience," *The American Political Science Review*, vol. XXXVIII, no. 6 (December 1944).

ment; a section on planning management; a section on administrative reorganization; a section on accountability of the executive to the Congress; and a conclusion. Each section is briefly analytical but the focus is upon recommendations. The printed report, or at least one version of it, had an extended part on special studies.

In the section on planning management, the case is made briefly but strongly for a permanent national organization. The recommendations of direct importance for the purpose of this book were:

> 1. It is recommended that a National Resources Board, consisting of five members appointed by the President, without salary and with indefinite terms, be created to serve as a central planning agency under the President.
> 2. It is further recommended that there be a director appointed by the Board, in general charge of the staff, and an executive officer, in the classified service; and that the further organizations of divisions of work be left to the determination of the Board.
> 3. It would be necessary for the Board to have ample provision for the maintenance of a staff equal to the performance of the heavy tasks imposed upon it. In general, the equipment of such a Board as is proposed would consist of:
> a. A permanent skeleton staff of career men of undoubted competence, with their assistants.
> b. Other governmental personnel with special skills detailed from time to time for the work of the Board.
> c. Experts and assistants brought in from time to time to deal with special problems as they arise. A contingent fund for this purpose should be available, but inevitably the amounts required would vary widely from one period to another, as different types of assistance were required.[20]

The intent of these recommendations, and almost surely their effect if they had been adopted in the form proposed, was to strengthen the presidency as an institution or as an arm of government. This was both their major strength and the source of the greatest opposition to them.[21]

Any proposal for an effective act or a significant grant of powers to the president for reorganization authority arouses opposition at any time, of course, both from those opposed to the general idea and those opposed to the president. Opposition to Roosevelt's proposals quickly surfaced. The extent and the vehemence of the opposition were even greater

---

[20] Report of the President's Committee, *Administrative Management,* p. 29.
[21] Richard Polenberg, *Reorganizing Roosevelt's Government, 1936–1939* (Cambridge, Massachusetts, Harvard University Press, 1966).

because, at the same time, FDR was pushing for a major reorganization of the Supreme Court. Much of his New Deal legislation had been declared unconstitutional by the admittedly conservative Court. FDR interpreted his sweeping reelection in 1936, when he carried all but two states, as a popular mandate to push his program actively and he thought Court reform—"packing," his opponents called it—essential. After a long and bitter political battle in the Congress, the Court reform bill was defeated. Fears were raised in many quarters that FDR sought truly dictatorial powers, and these fears carried over into stronger opposition to reorganization bills than otherwise would have existed.

At the same time, Secretary Ickes made many injudicious statements about his desire to have the Forest Service transferred to the Department of the Interior and about what he would do when it was. This also aroused more opposition than otherwise would have existed. There were, naturally enough, still other aspects of reorganization which aroused one interest group or another. The legislative struggle over a reorganization act continued through 1937 and 1938, with an act finally approved in April 1939. In order to get any act passed, FDR had to make very substantial concessions on his original proposals.

Under the powers for reorganization which the president did get in the act, he established the National Resources Planning Board by Presidential Reorganization Plan No. 1 on April 3, 1939, effective July 1, 1939; and, in the same order, terminated the National Resources Committee (see item 10 in appendix A). This plan was accepted by the Congress on June 7. The existence of the NRPB was thus legally established, but its legal powers to carry out activities were those created by the Employment Stabilization Act of 1931. The role of the National Resources Planning Board in the activities of the Office of the President were spelled out in more detail in Executive Order 8248 on September 8, 1939 (see item 11, appendix A); and its procedures were prescribed in Executive Order 8455 on June 26, 1940 (see item 12 in appendix A).

The Reorganization Plan called for a board of five persons, but only three were ever appointed; Delano continued as chairman and Merriam continued as a member. Since Mitchell's departure in 1935, his place had not been filled. It was now filled by the appointment of George F. Yantis, a lawyer and a former state legislator from the State of Washington, who had been active in the NRC's Pacific Northwest regional commission. In addition, Beardsley Ruml and Henry S. Dennison were

appointed as "advisers." Persons familiar with the workings of the
NRPB have told me that, to almost all intents and purposes, Ruml and
Dennison were members of the Board—they sat in on Board meetings,
took part freely in discussions, and, although they could not vote, very
few things ever were put to a vote at the Board. All of these people
were part-time. The Board typically met two days each month. Charles
W. Eliot was continued as director.

Very shortly, the staff of the Board was substantially augmented.
Three rather formal divisions were set up. Division A, under Thomas C.
Blaisdell, Jr., was responsible for current reporting of trends in business,
special trend studies of relief and relief policies, science activities, and
general studies in economics and government. Division B, under Ralph
J. Watkins, was responsible for technical studies of transportation, industry, land, water, and energy. And Division C, under Frank W. Herring,
was responsible for the planning of public works and project review.
With this change in organization came a number of gradual shifts in
content of the work and in the way it was organized.

Karl puts the good side of this reorganization as follows:

> The creation by the Reorganization Act of 1939 of the National
> Resources Planning Board in the Executive Office of the president
> brought Merriam and the board the independence they had wanted.
> Although it formalized within a structure of governmental operations
> a staff which has been working together for six years, it also continued
> the more widespread set of academic contacts which the organization
> of the Social Science Research Council had set up for Merriam many
> years earlier.[22]

But even Karl recognizes the shortcomings and weaknesses of that reorganization:

> From the beginning of the board's elevation to independent status in
> the executive office of the president—indeed, as part of the fight to
> achieve that status—the board's continued existence had never been
> more than precarious, although Merriam's intense ambition for it
> seems to deny that. Congressional hostility, particularly in the House
> of Representatives, could easily be mobilized to trim appropriations,
> if not to threaten their cutoff entirely. Roosevelt liked Merriam; he
> trusted Uncle Fred Delano; and he enjoyed reading the board's
> reports. . . . Nonetheless, the reorganization fight over the creation of
> the NRPB had begun to make it clear to FDR that the cost of his
> advisory board was going to be high.[23]

---

[22] Karl, *Charles E. Merriam*, p. 270.
[23] Ibid, pp. 271–272.

It is evident that Karl was thinking primarily of the social studies function of the NRPB, in which Merriam was especially interested, although Karl does mention opposition to water and other physical resource planning.

There was at least one other tangible consequence of the reorganization: in getting freed from any restraints Ickes may have placed on the Board, it also lost the fighting support Ickes could and did give it on occasion. After the NRPB was set up and Ickes was no longer chairman of the Board, there are no further entries in his intimate and detailed diary about the NRPB or about any of its chief actors in their NRPB roles. Ickes' interest may have been more bureaucratic than a reflection of a profound or understanding consideration of the National Resources Committee's functions and role, but he was indeed a fighter and a protector of what he regarded as his.

A less tangible but perhaps basically more serious consequence of the reorganization was that the Board came to be regarded as less an ally and coordinator of various agencies and interests, and—as an arm of the president—more of a rival to other federal agencies. It is very difficult to describe this shift in relationship accurately and without exaggeration.

With the understanding of current events that sometimes comes from hindsight, it seems that the ultimate demise of the NRPB as it was organized and as it functioned after the reorganization, could have been foretold in 1939. A drastic change of course and of organization might have preserved it indefinitely, but possibly those responsible for it would not have chosen to change. There is nothing I can find in the record to indicate that a different path was debated at the highest policy levels of the NRPB.

5

Actors in the Board's Operations

The National Resources Planning Board and its predecessor agencies had a number of strong personalities associated with them, and these personalities made a difference in what the NRPB did and, quite probably, in its demise. A substantial number of persons were involved in the NRPB to some degree or another, but five may be designated as major participants: President Franklin Delano Roosevelt; Secretary of the Interior Harold L. Ickes; Chairman Frederic A. Delano; Vice Chairman Charles E. Merriam; and Executive Officer and Director Charles W. Eliot, 2nd.

President Franklin Delano Roosevelt[1]

Supporters, opponents, and participants in the NRPB agreed on one point: that both in law and in fact the NRPB was advisory to the presi-

---

[1] I presume literally hundreds of books have been written about Roosevelt or the New Deal. I have drawn heavily on Arthur M. Schlesinger, Jr.'s, two books, *The Age of Roosevelt: The Crisis of the Old Order, 1919–1933* (1957) and *The Age of Roosevelt: The Coming of the New Deal* (1959), both published by Houghton Mifflin Co., Boston; and Rexford G. Tugwell, *Roosevelt's Revolution: The First Year—A Personal Perspective* (New York, Macmillan Publishing Co., 1977). I have used to a lesser degree: Frances Perkins, *The Roosevelt I Knew* (New York, Viking Press, 1946); Samuel I. Rosenman, *Working With Roosevelt* (New York, Harper and Co., 1952); and Harold L. Ickes, *The Secret Diary of Harold L. Ickes,* 3 volumes (New York, Simon and Schuster, 1954 and 1955). I have not sought to go to original documents about Roosevelt's life or presidency;

dent. Hence the personality of the president, on whose support the NRPB was totally dependent, is critical to the evaluation of its operations. Even when the NRPB had been the National Planning Board in 1933–1934, and, as such, advisory to Ickes, its ultimate customer was the president; in its final status as the National Resources Planning Board, from July 1, 1939, to the end in 1943, it was totally dependent upon the president.

Roosevelt was a man of unusual personality who aroused strong feelings of love and admiration from millions of constituents and equally strong feelings of hostility, often extending to actual hate and fear, from other millions of constituents. He brought to the presidency new concepts of the role of the federal government in the life of the nation, and new methods of using the vast potential powers of the presidency.

Frances Perkins knew him well from the time he began his political career as state senator in New York in 1910 until his death in 1945. He appointed her to important offices in New York government and she served as secretary of labor during his entire incumbency as president. In addition, she knew the Roosevelts well socially. Her appraisal of the man is made out of great respect and deep affection, yet she tried hard to see him accurately, and her position is well summed up in the following:

> Franklin Roosevelt was not a simple man. That quality of simplicity which we delight to think marks the great and noble was not his. He was the most complicated human being I ever knew; and out of his complicated nature there sprang much of the drive which brought achievement, much of the sympathy which made him like, and liked by, such oddly different types of people, much of the detachment which enabled him to forget his problems in play or rest, and much of the apparent contradiction which so exasperated those associates of his who expected "crystal clear" and unwavering decisions. But this very complication of his nature made it possible for him to have insight and imagination into the most varied human experiences, and this he applied to the physical, social, geographical, economic, and strategic circumstances thrust upon him as responsibilities by his times.[2]

Roosevelt was 51 years old when he assumed the presidency in 1933. His family was very well to do, though not really rich; his father had numerous business interests. The family owned an estate on the Hudson

---

the account in this section is as brief and basic as possible, of those aspects of Roosevelt which I thought were essential for an understanding of his role in the NRPB.

[2] Perkins, *The Roosevelt I Knew*, p. 3.

which has since become a national historical site. Raised as an only child of his parents (there was a much older half brother, who seems to have played only a minor role in his life), with a fine home, many distinguished family friends, no concerns over economic position or security, with considerable travel, and education at Groton and then at Harvard, he was a fairly typical product of families of modest wealth and assured position of the times. He was not an outstanding student, though he did tolerably well; at Harvard he was editor of *The Crimson,* the student newspaper. He married young, after which he went to law school and for a few years practiced law in New York City.

His political career began in 1910 with his election to the New York State Senate, where he served with distinction, but for only a brief time. In 1913 he went to Washington as assistant secretary of the navy (in those days a federal department had but a single assistant secretary and no under secretary, so that he was second in command), where he stayed through the eight years of the Wilson administration. In 1920, he was the Democratic candidate for vice president, going down to defeat with the ticket. He was elected governor of New York in 1928, which position he occupied when nominated for the presidency in 1932.

In 1921, Roosevelt contracted polio; after a period of intense illness, he began a long slow recovery, but never regained full use of his legs. While he could stand with the aid of leg braces and could barely walk unaided by his son or another person, most of the time he had to use someone to help him or manuever him in a wheelchair. Much has been written about the psychological effects on Roosevelt of this long and severe illness, during much of which the ultimate outcome was far from assured, and of his subsequent physical handicap. During the early years of his presidency, his handicap did not much, if at all, constrain his activities, including his travels, but such a long and severe illness and its resulting handicap can hardly have failed to affect his outlook upon life.

Accounts of his biographers and his school officials seem generally to agree that Roosevelt had a good but not profound mind, that his mind was not deeply probing in an analytical way, and that he was not introspective. He liked people, was excellent at meeting and talking with them, and was especially good at drawing them out—when he wanted to; he was also very skillful in bottling them up when he chose. His outstanding characteristic during his presidency was his ability to maneuver and manipulate people, to persuade them to his position or to his end in many cases, or to box them in and blunt their opposition if he could not win them over.

When Roosevelt talked with someone, he would often seem to nod his head in agreement, or to say "yes, yes" in ways that led the person concerned to think that Roosevelt had agreed with him, when more likely what he meant was that he heard and understood what the other was saying. Time and again this led to misunderstandings. Those who knew him well often realized that they had no firm commitment from him when they had sought it, but others often misunderstood, sometimes with emotional reactions when later events showed a lack of such agreement. Roosevelt repeatedly and deliberately encouraged competition between individuals and organizations in his Administration, letting the contest between and among them work out a course of action for himself. He was always determined to keep his options open as long as he could, to avoid premature commitment to some line of action or to some person, so that he could change his course with a minimum of retraction if later this seemed desirable.

Schlesinger, an obvious admirer, sums up his views of Roosevelt (as well as two long and detailed books can be summarized in a single brief quotation):

> It was this astonishing instinct for the future which above all distinguished Roosevelt, his extraordinary sensitivity to the emergent tendencies of his age and to the rising aspirations of ordinary people—a sensitivity housed at the same time within a personality and intelligence sufficiently conventional to provide in itself a bridge holding together past and future. Indeed, his very position on the breaking point between an old world and a new one gave him a special freedom and spontaneity which only a man can possess who is nourished by older values. When Roosevelt accepted the inevitability of change, he did so, not by necessity, but by conscious choice. He had made a deliberate decision, both temperamental and intellectual, in favor of adventure and experiment.[3]

But even Schlesinger said ". . . what was he really like underneath?"[4]

Harold L. Ickes

Harold Ickes was 59 years old in 1933 when he became Roosevelt's secretary of the interior. Ickes was a Chicago lawyer who had been

---

[3] Schlesinger, *The Age of Roosevelt: The Coming of the New Deal*, p. 587.
[4] Ibid., p. 574.

active in politics as a Progressive or as a Progressive Republican, supporting Theodore Roosevelt in his 1912 candidacy for the presidency as a Progressive. He managed Charles Merriam's unsuccessful campaign for the mayoralty of Chicago in 1911; and, because of his unwillingness to deal with powerful political bosses whom he disliked and distrusted, he very possibly was responsible for Merriam's defeat.[5] Like most other Progressives, he found the 1920s a discouraging time, and he gradually became disenchanted with Republicans. He had never met Roosevelt until after the latter's election to the presidency; the story then current was that he had sought to head the Bureau of Indian Affairs and had been Roosevelt's choice for secretary of the interior only after Roosevelt had concluded that George Dern, an earlier choice, would fit into the cabinet better as secretary of war and only after Senator Bronson Cutting of New Mexico had turned down the secretaryship in order to remain in the Senate.

Ickes' widow, speaking out of intense admiration and respect, has described him as follows in her preface to his *Secret Diaries:*

> This is not a balanced or a reflective study. It is the intimate history of two of the most fateful decades in American history, written in heat and under pressure by a turbulently active man who changed his mind many times both as to men and affairs and who never hesitated to express himself fully and pungently. It is also the personal history of Harold Ickes. Here is a man who was passionately alive and earthy, yet remote and essentially detached. He had few intimates, but to those whom he called friend he gave himself warmly and generously. He may have seemed forbidding to some, and yet no one in distress was too obscure to claim his attention and his help. One knew where Harold Ickes stood. There was no deviousness in him. He believed profoundly in the constant upward progress of the human race, and it was for this ultimate conviction that he battled to the end of his life. Under the burden of his massive responsibilities, he grew in strength and understanding until, as the years passed, he came to be regarded as the catalytic agent of the New Deal: the point of fusion of the boldness, the vigor, the passion of its early years.[6]

Harold Ickes was one of the more newsworthy members of the New Deal. Tugwell described him in 1933:

> Ickes measured at least fifty inches around and was of no more than average height. He was fifty-nine years old and might have been thought beyond the age of driving ambition; but it was not so. He

---

[5] Barry D. Karl, *Charles E. Merriam and the Study of Politics* (Chicago, University of Chicago Press, 1974).

[6] Preface to Ickes, *The Secret Diaries,* vol. I.

was acutely conscious of being the only cabinet member with authentic progressive credentials and felt strongly his responsibility to those who had been sponsors of his unexpected selection. He valued the power he had and wanted more. He never gave an inch in controversy and produced on occasion the most cutting characterizations of those he disapproved.[7]

He was a self-styled curmudgeon.[8] His intense scrutiny of public works proposals and his strong determination that there would be no scandals attached to them earned him the popular title of "Honest Harold"—a title which he apparently both relished and despised, but one which some people outside of his department, but close to it, thought inappropriate because of his unabashed use of political power.

In addition to being secretary of the interior, Ickes was head of the Public Works Administration (PWA) through the New Deal. His slowness in acting there, due to his concerns for honesty and the value of proposals, was largely responsible for the establishment of the Works Progress Administration and other agencies for quick employment of unemployed persons, under the direction of Harry Hopkins. Ickes served as chairman of the National Resources Board, 1934 and 1935, and as chairman of the National Resources Committee, 1935 to 1939. In 1939, when the president took the National Resources Committee away from Ickes and established it as the National Resources Planning Board in his own executive office, Ickes protested long, loudly, and vainly—in the same terms he protested his loss of the PWA, the Office of Education, and the United States Housing Administration.[9] Ickes was always a jealous defender of his turf. In the early days, he clearly saw the Planning Board and Resources Board as valuable instruments of national policy, but, after 1939 when the NRPB was set up without his participation, he seems to have lost interest in it.[10]

Ickes was clearly intelligent, dedicated, ambitious, and intolerant. He was supersensitive; in his diary he cites numerous instances when he thought of resigning or told FDR that he would resign—his diary has been characterized as strictly a psychiatrist's couch. He was also loyal to FDR, had the latter's ear and confidence, and was a most effective public servant, given the limits within which he operated.

[7] Tugwell, *Roosevelt's Revolution,* p. 176.

[8] Harold L. Ickes, *The Autobiography of a Curmudgeon* (New York, Reynal Hitchcock, 1943).

[9] Ickes, *Secret Diaries,* volume II, pp. 664–669.

[10] Ickes, *Secret Diaries,* volume III, beginning in 1939, contain no reference to the NRPB or to any of its chief actors in their NRPB roles.

Frederic A. Delano

Frederic A. Delano was an uncle to President Franklin Delano Roosevelt. This might seem, and indeed at the time to the uninformed often did seem, to be nepotism. In fact, it was not. Schlesinger describes Delano briefly and forcefully:

> Few Americans had had more impressive experience in city and regional planning than Delano. Chicago, New York and Washington all bore his mark in their programs for urban development. In 1927 the Committee on the Basis of a Sound Land Policy under his chairmanship had drawn up a basic report on the development of land use policies.[11]

Warken describes Delano at more length:

> Delano, who was the President's uncle, had been born in 1863 in Hong Kong, graduated from Harvard in 1885, and followed a successful career in railroading. In 1914, with his best earning years still ahead of him, Delano left the business world to accept President Wilson's appointment to the Federal Reserve Board, leaving the Federal Reserve in 1918 to become the War Department's Deputy Director of Transportation in Paris. In 1927, he became chairman of a commission of the League of Nations investigating the opium trade in Persia. The commission recommended construction of a railroad to give the people the ability to market other crops (the Trans-Iranian Railway was completed in 1937). His long service in promoting planning went back to the development of the Chicago Plan in 1908; he was also Chairman of the Regional Plan of New York from 1924 to 1939 and later of the Park and Planning Commission of Washington, D.C., a position he held at the time of his appointment and throughout his tenure on the NRPB. Those who worked with Delano on the NRPB remember him variously as a grand, brilliant old man with a remarkably agile mind who was hesitant to use his family connection with FDR and liked to talk of childhood memories. He furnished quite a bit of leadership but sometimes in the late afternoon would run out of gas. He was the cohesive force who held the strong and sometimes antagonistic personalities of the NRPB together.[12]

Delano's relationship to the president might seem to have been a great asset to the NRPB. In some degree, it was. The president was genuinely fond of his uncle and respected him. The president's interest in the NRPB was surely stimulated by the fact of his uncle's chairmanship or

---

[11] Schlesinger, *The Age of Roosevelt: The Coming of the New Deal*, p. 351.
[12] Philip W. Warken, "A History of the National Resources Planning Board, 1933–1943" (doctoral dissertation, Ohio State University, 1969) pp. 44–45.

membership on the Board. His trust in his uncle surely helped to avert any suspicion that the Board was moving in ways hostile to him and his Administration. But in another sense, Delano's relationship to the president was a severe handicap to the NRPB. He was so concerned *not* to take advantage of his personal relationship to the president that he leaned over backward to avoid any suggestion of it. He was vastly less active or aggressive in pursuing matters with FDR than were other members of the Board or staff or some committees of the Board, and almost surely less active than another man would have been in his place. Likewise, he was far less active in pressing Board matters before congressional committees or with individual congressmen than many another would have been for the same reason.

There are two other facts about Delano which are very important to our study. One was his age; he was 69 years old in 1933, and thus 79 years old in 1943. As time went on, his physical energy waned. Alumni of the NRPB have told me of Delano's alertness in the mornings, and of his difficulties of keeping fully abreast of discussions in the late afternoons. But all agree that he remained mentally alert and keen throughout his NRPB experience. The other specific point about Delano is that he had been a fraternity brother of Charles W. Eliot's father at Harvard, and that, when Eliot first went to Washington in 1926 he had briefly lived at Delano's house.[13] Eliot had served as the director of planning of the National Capital Park and Planning Commission, which Delano chaired, and was thus to a substantial degree, a protege of Delano's. This personal relationship between Delano and Eliot was surely a major factor in NRPB history, especially in Eliot's role there.

Delano was known widely and affectionately by the NRPB staff, and indeed by many others, as "Uncle Fred." He was highly respected and loved by the staff, and generally easily accessible to its members. Although employed by the NRPB only part-time, as were the other directors, he was the only director who lived in Washington. Although he continued as chairman of the National Capital Park and Planning Commission throughout the NRPB's life, and had to spend some time on the affairs of that commission, most of the time his office was in the same general quarters as that of the NRPB. He came to his office regularly, and was available for conferences or discussions with staff members, including, of course, Eliot. He surely spent more time on NRPB affairs than he was paid for.

---

[13] Personal interview with Charles W. Eliot, 2nd, October 2, 1978.

Delano was also respected by others in the executive branch, and by the Congress. He may not have been taken very seriously by some cabinet members and others, but they appreciated him both for what he was and for his relationship to FDR. When the Board was under severe and often unfair criticism in 1942 and 1943, as its end approached, Delano was offended and deeply hurt—but he did not act effectively or vigorously in counterattack. By then, he was not only old but unwell to a degree few people realized, and Mrs. Delano was dying (died on June 1, 1943).

Charles E. Merriam

Charles E. Merriam, 59 years old in 1933 when he was appointed to the National Planning Board, was a professor of political science at the University of Chicago. He spent virtually his entire professional life at that university, first joining its staff in 1904 when he was 30 years of age, and remaining until the compulsory retirement age.

Karl, a former student of Merriam's and now professor of history at the University of Chicago, in his biography of Merriam, says:

> Charles E. Merriam is generally acknowledged to be the father of the behavioral movement in political science. . . . Merriam was an academic entrepreneur whose extraordinary sensitivities to the ideas of his times were combined with a willingness to govern the resources available for the development of those ideas to produce a phenomenon rare even in its day: a genuine school of thought.[14]

He certainly enlisted a large corps of devoted followers and disciples in his many years at the university, where his role gradually evolved and where he was a major factor in the development of the whole field of political science as a separate intellectual discipline. He was particularly successful, according to Karl, in his ability to enlist foundation and rich donor funds for the Social Science Research Council, which he helped to create and to manage. According to Karl, Merriam was a most active strategist and politician within the university, building and solidifying his own position, advancing his ideas, enlisting allies, and countering opposition.

He was also an active politician in the local governmental scene. He ran successfully for alderman in 1909 and again in 1913. He ran unsuccessfully for mayor of Chicago in 1911, but lost by only a small margin. These were the only offices for which he ran, although he and his friends

---

[14] Karl, *Charles E. Merriam;* see Preface.

considered the possibility of his entering other races. He was a Progressive or a Progressive Republican in those years, rather closely associated with Ickes and with others of similar views but, like Ickes, shifting to the Democrats when Roosevelt won. Ickes said of Merriam:

> One thing about my old friend Charles E. Merriam is that he has been the most consistent liberal of them all. I have always known where to find him. There have been times when he and I seemed to be all that was left of the old Progressive movement.[15]

Karl presents a picture of a man who emphasized ideas and feelings in his teaching and research more than quantitative evidence, statistics, and certainly more than economics. He engaged in many debates, even controversies, with colleagues at the university and with other professionals at other universities. Some of these, at least to one not much concerned with their apparent content, seem to have been as much personal jousting for position as strongly ideological or conceptual in content. He frequently found himself on the opposite side of arguments with William F. Ogburn, the university sociologist.

Merriam played a very major role in the President's Research Committee on Social Trends. He also played an important role on the President's Committee on Administrative Management, which was chaired by his close friend and collaborator Louis Brownlow. He was particularly close personally to Harold Ickes; the latter's diaries are full of references to conversations with Merriam on subjects other than the NRPB.

Charles S. Ascher, who did important research for the NRPB, has written to me of Merriam as follows:

> On the train to some western meeting of NRPB, I sat next to Charles Merriam in the club car. Over drinks he told me that he considered his life a failure. In the academic world, he was treated as a man of action. In the world of action he was considered a good academe. When he ran for mayor of Chicago in 1912 [sic], he was convinced that he had won, but had been counted out by manipulation of the ballot boxes by the Machine. The manager of his campaign was a Bull Moose lawyer named Harold Ickes. So when the Chicago reform group—the social scientists at the University and the associations of public officials at "1313"—wanted to sell an idea to the Public Works Administrator Ickes, it was Merriam on whom they leaned. . . . Merriam was, of course, the master of the ambivalent statement.[16]

---

[15] Ickes, *Secret Diaries,* volume II, p. 77.
[16] Personal letter from Charles S. Ascher, November 2, 1979.

Merriam has written of his experiences on the NRPB and his appraisal of it. As a Board member he was typically in Washington two days a month for Board meetings but he spent substantial additional time in Chicago, reading reports and otherwise engaged on NRPB business. Writing about the Board in 1941, while it was still most active and, although under attack, still strong, he generally described and seems to have fully endorsed the Board's organization, its functioning, and its results.[17] Writing again more than a year after the NRPB had been killed by the Congress, he was equally strong in his defense of the Board's organization, its methods of operation, and its results.[18] In each he emphasized the purely advisory role of the Board. While he does not say so explicitly, one clearly infers that he more strongly supported the role of idea stimulation and development than he did the role of program coordination.

Karl has expressed his judgment of Merriam's role on the NRPB as follows:

> Congress could never be a symbol of national purposes; the president had to be, and their dependence on each other hung on his capacity to symbolize something which only they in their chaotic compromises of local interests and national needs could define. In those respects, and very importantly, Merriam and the National Resources Planning Board were as close to a philosophy as such a system could get. They could present to the president the logical rationalities which were scientifically and technologically possible and he could present to the congress whatever of them he thought politically possible. Congress in turn could present him with what it considered consistent with its own collective conception of the national interest and he would have to decide whether he would reject it, allow it to become law quietly and without fanfare, or celebrate it as what he had wanted all along.[19]

Karl assigns a major role to Merriam in the thinking and operations of the NRPB. So does Lepawsky, a former student, understudy, and assistant of Merriam's: "When the Planning Board was being established in the spring of 1933, its most influential member, the Chicago professor–politician–planner, Charles E. Merriam . . ."[20]

---

[17] Charles E. Merriam, "The National Resources Planning Board," *Public Administration Review* (Winter 1941) pp. 116–121.

[18] Charles E. Merriam, "The National Resources Planning Board: A Chapter in American Planning Experience," *The American Political Science Review*, vol. XXXVIII, no. 6 (December 1944) pp. 1075–1088.

[19] Karl, *Charles E. Merriam*, p. 270.

[20] Albert Lepawsky, "Style and Substance in Contemporary Planning: The

Merriam enjoyed good relations with FDR; the latter apparently found him stimulating, informative, and interesting. Merriam was widely respected by the staff of the NRPB and by others in the executive branch for his intellectual ability and achievements.

To one who must judge Merriam by the record of what he did as well as by what he wrote, he appears a complex and somewhat contradictory figure.[21] The Committee on Administration Management, of which he was one of three members, and an influential one, came out against boards or commissions which attempted to administer any program, even a research program, and especially against boards of part-time members; it strongly favored single administrator agencies, with advisory boards not in the line of operation.[22] Yet on the NRPB, the committee (apparently with Merriam's full concurrence) took exactly the opposite stand, insistent upon a board to manage the NRPB, a board of part-time persons, with only limited powers to the executive director. As a politician and university staff man, he had been active in university and city politics, not only running for office but also manuevering, planning, even scheming; yet on the NRPB he was adamant that the Board and its staff remain aloof from the Congress. He seems, as I personally found some other political scientists of his generation to be, convinced that the separation of powers between the branches of government was real, that it actually existed or that it should exist and that people should behave accordingly. To anyone familiar with the workings of the federal government, this is nonsense—the executive branch writes more legislation than does the legislative branch, and the legislative branch administers at least as much as does the executive branch. Again, one can understand his taking a position against NRPB staff going to the Congress, if Merriam distrusted Eliot and/or other staff members, but this does not explain Merriam's own reluctance, amounting to almost a phobia, to make personal appearances before the Congress.

American New Deal's National Resources Planning Board as a Model," *Plan Canada,* vol. 18, nos. 3/4 (September/December 1978).

21 I never knew Merriam personally. I recall once being at a meeting of perhaps 100 persons where he spoke. I do not recall what he said. To the best of my recollection, that is the only time I ever saw him. The discussion in this whole section, and more particularly in this paragraph, is based upon the available public record.

22 The President's Committee on Administrative Management, *Administrative Management in the Government of the United States* (Washington, GPO, 1937). The committee consisted of Louis Brownlow, chairman; Charles E. Merriam; and Luther Gulick.

Charles W. Eliot, 2nd[23]

Eliot is the fifth and last of the major actors on the NRPB, as I identify them. When chosen as the executive officer of the National Planning Board in 1933, he was only 33 years of age—a full generation younger than Delano, who (as we noted above) was a contemporary of Eliot's father and of Ickes and Merriam. Eliot came from a distinguished New England family; his grandfather was one of the great presidents of Harvard University, his father was a well-known minister. Eliot was raised in Cambridge and knew many distinguished people as he grew up. He went to Harvard and, while still in his mid-twenties, became the city planner for the National Capital Park and Planning Commission, which was headed by an old family friend, Delano. It was in part this association which led him to the NRPB.

But in early 1933 Eliot, as we noted in chapter 4, seeing the need for some coordination in the many new New Deal programs affecting land, water, and resources, had urged upon Ickes the creation of something like the National Planning Board, and naturally enough wanted to play a major role in it.[24] It is not clear from the public record just how influential Eliot's proposal was in what actually happened, but, at any rate, he was associated from the beginning with the Board as actually established, and he remained its chief executive officer or director until the end. When the Congress terminated the work of the NRPB, Eliot, together with his chief assistant Harold Merrill and a few others (some serving voluntarily for weeks), continued until the end of 1943 to organize the files for turnover to the National Archives, to dispose of furniture and other materials, to terminate the staff, transfer records, and the like—all the steps essential when a federal agency goes out of existence.[25]

---

[23] Eliot, in an enclosure in a personal letter to me, December 12, 1979, says: "All my life I've lived with inevitable confusion of my name with those of my uncle Charles Eliot—the famous landscape architect—and with my grandfather Charles W. Eliot. Because I followed the same profession as my uncle, I've always asked for inclusion of the middle initial W. (for William) to distinguish my name from his; and because of the fame of my grandfather, I was always 2nd, until we moved to California—seventeen years after his death." In this book, since it deals with the NRPB period when Eliot always used 2nd to describe himself, I have also done so.

[24] See footnotes 6, 7, and 8 in chapter 4. Also my interview with Eliot, October 2, 1978.

[25] Charles W. Eliot, 2nd, assisted by Harold A. Merrill, *Ten Years of National Planning, 1933–1943, Guide to the Files of the National Resources Planning Board*

Eliot was in Washington all the time when not on official travel or on vacation. Naturally enough, the responsibility for day-to-day functioning of the NRPB fell on him; so did a great deal of the responsibility for planning its larger operations. At the same time, the Board, especially Merriam, was loath to give him much leeway in his operations. Merriam's insistence that staff should maintain as distant a pose toward the Congress as possible surely restricted Eliot from doing what he otherwise might have in building a knowledge of and a confidence in the NRPB among congressmen who might have been friendly. Eliot might not have been an ideal congressional contact man; too many congressmen regarded him as a Harvard snob, but he surely would have been better than none, which is what the NRPB mostly had.

Eliot's relations with the NRPB staff seem to have been very good on the whole. He was young, ambitious for himself and for his organization, and believed in what he and it were doing. He was eager to do better and listened to staff members, including younger ones, was generally pleasant and considerate. Some staff members who liked and respected him may have had some doubts about the quality of his leadership, although this is not certain.

Merriam–Eliot Differences

There were major and serious differences between Merriam and Eliot, which affected the operations of the NRPB in many ways, and quite probably were a major factor in its ultimate demise. The men were different in several personal respects: age, background, and professional interests. There was clearly a personal antagonism; they did not socialize together. Merriam usually had a social session and a postmortem in his hotel room on the afternoon of the second day of Board meetings, with enough Scotch whiskey available after the meeting was concluded; Eliot was never present or invited. While their mutual distrust had its good side, in that it led to more careful review by each one of the proposals made by the other, on balance it was a liability. If Merriam had been made chairman of the NRPB, he almost surely would have replaced Eliot by a man of his own choice.

More serious than these personal differences were differences in concept of what the NRPB should seek to do. In general, Merriam wanted

---

and Predecessor Agencies, December 31, 1943; and Charles W. Eliot, 2nd, *Final Report—Status of Work, National Resources Planning Board,* December 31, 1943. The second report is labeled "confidential."

the NRPB to be primarily a social planning organization—a President's
Committee on Recent Social Trends continued, extended, brought up to
date, and made a little more specific in conclusions and recommendations. He wanted to be the intellectual power behind the president but
not to be a participant in action. Eliot wanted the NRPB to make social
studies, but he also wanted plans that could be put into practice soon.
He wanted the NRPB to take a vigorous and active role in the coordination of national planning, and wanted to involve a good many people in
it, and in fact did so. It is not clear that Merriam wanted either of these
things. Eliot wanted to communicate with people, including Congress;
Merriam's attitude toward Congress has been noted.

Schlesinger has offered his appraisal of the Merriam–Eliot relationship
as follows:

> On the committee, Merriam's doubts focused with particular intensity
> on Charles Eliot. The tension between them, mounting through the
> thirties as Delano's advanced age weakened his leadership, handicapped
> the committee's work. The personal tension both reflected and aggra-
> vated differences in approach. Merriam and Mitchell, the scholars,
> tended to favor long-term research projects; Delano and Eliot, the
> planners, wanted to shape current policies and programs.[26]

The major differences between Merriam and Eliot were never fully
articulated and spelled out during the NRPB's life. Although there may
have been some veiled exchanges, each man strove, with success, to "act
as a gentleman."

In the later winter and spring of 1943, when the NRPB was under
serious attack in the Congress, and perhaps to some degree as a result
of the emotions aroused by the impending doom, relations between
Merriam and Eliot worsened sharply, more perhaps under the surface
than openly. Philip White has recounted one episode:

> On February 23, Eliot, without authorization of the chairman, and
> despite a standing prohibition from the board members, secured an
> interview alone with the president. Apparently he presented the case
> for his type of organization—the budget bureau, single administrator
> type—and offered his own resignation in token of his lack of self-
> interest. He declared further, in a memo of March 2 to the president,
> that "The experience of the last ten years has demonstrated the need
> and value of planning as an arm of administrative management and
> for the formulation of policy. That need is now so generally recognized

---

[26] Schlesinger, *The Age of Roosevelt: The Coming of the New Deal,* pp. 351–
352.

that congress now wants to have a major share in the work. . . . The problem is one of organization, not justification."

The President took no action.

Informed of the event, Merriam in Chicago wrote to Delano:

"I note the circumstances under which the director has his interview with the president, but for myself I do not at all approve of such action, particularly in view of your instruction to him. There is such a thing as insubordination. There are other aspects of this situation which I can discuss with you when I come to Washington."

He was angry.

Apparently Eliot by this time was past caring what Merriam and Delano thought. He was fighting for planning and for his own future.[27]

Eliot's account of this episode is rather different.[28]

I went to the president to express my very great concern over Uncle Fred's sickness, depression, and reaction to attacks in congress and the press . . . F.D.R. appreciated my telling him, shared my concern and got in touch with Uncle Fred. Of course, I couldn't say all that in the memo for the board which I dictated on my return to my office. So Merriam blew his top. White's "without authorization" is irrelevant and there was no "standing prohibition" (except possibly in Merriam's imagination). I did *not* "present the case". . . . My memo says "since he had done me the honor to appoint me as director. . . . I wanted him to know that if he thought it would help the cause in any way, my resignation was at his disposal."

In view of events during the next two months, it seems probable that Merriam did not believe this explanation, if it was made to him by Eliot. On April 20, 1943, Merriam wrote a "personal and confidential" letter to Delano at the latter's home, saying:

Now that it has been definitely determined to choose some successor to Mr. Eliot as director, I cannot refrain from telling you how great a burden it has lifted from my shoulders and my soul both. I may confess that sometimes our struggle to get things decided upon and then to get them carried out has been almost too much for me. I can now see my way clear to greater service by the board than ever before. In case our appropriation is finally approved by the congress, and I believe it will be, we will face quite a different job from what we have had.

27 White, "The Termination of the NRPB," pp. 148–149. White cites File 1092 (Franklin D. Roosevelt Library [National Archives], Hyde Park, New York) as the source for these communications. The Merriam–Delano letter is dated February 27, 1943.

28 Personal letter to me from Charles W. Eliot, 2nd, January 11, 1980, commenting explicitly on the quotation from White.

We have already made a very notable report in my judgment, but the implications of this report are far-reaching. It will now be necessary for us to make practical contacts with a wide variety of public and private agencies. I have always believed that the quality of our work was far more important than the quantity of it. A great variety of suggestions on post-war planning will be springing up on every hand and it is all the more necessary that we show great discrimination and distinction in what we undertake. The complications and intricacies of these contacts demand a director of very great tact—a diplomat as well as an administrative director.

If we can find a truly competent director, and I am sure we can if we do a thorough job of searching, we can render very great service to the president directly and to the country indirectly. For my part, I am willing to give more time than I have thus far, if we can get an effective working setup on the administrative side.[29]

Taken at face value, this letter suggests that Merriam had won Delano and Yantis over to his position. It clearly implies that Delano had agreed to the replacement of Eliot, but I have not found a confirmation from Delano of this position.

As matters turned out, all of this shortly became irrelevant, for within little more than a month the Senate had taken the action on the NRPB appropriation which was to lead to its early demise.

Two Old-Boy Networks

One might, with only modest exaggeration, characterize the situation described in this chapter to this point as one of two old-boy networks. Ickes, Merriam, Ruml (whom we discuss below), and others were the Chicago Progressive network. FDR, Delano, and Eliot were the New England, or at least the Northeast old family network. One should not overplay this analysis. The named persons had many friends within the groups named, but they had many other friends from other groups as well. There were, however, undoubtedly strong and numerous personal ties within each of these networks.

---

[29] Folder 10, box CCXVIII, "N.R.P.B." library, University of Chicago files on Merriam correspondence and papers. I am indebted to Philip L. White for alerting me to the existence of these files. I have been unable to find any published account which carefully analyzes Merriam's papers and describes his role at the NRPB as he saw it at the time. Philip White's present researches, described in the preface, may provide a vastly better understanding of Merriam's role than anything now available. His inquiry may shed light, not only upon the Merriam–Eliot relationship, but also upon Merriam's relationship to NRPB staff members.

Supporting Actors

Many persons, in addition to those named above, played a fairly direct role in the NRPB and its predecessors. Indeed, several hundred persons were involved in study committees, regional committees, and the like, as well as on staff. It is impossible even to note them all, much less to describe them, and one hardly knows where to stop.

Cabinet members other than Ickes were involved: Henry Wallace from Agriculture, Frances Perkins from Labor, Daniel C. Roper from Commerce, George Dern from War (until his death in 1936, after which Harry H. Woodring succeeded him), and Harry Hopkins (not in the cabinet, but as director of WPA at least as important as a cabinet member) served, or at least they were named, on the NRC and the NRB. Harold Smith, director of the Bureau of the Budget, was both influential and helpful to the NRPB. There were Board members other than Delano and Merriam: Wesley Clair Mitchell in the early days, a well-known professor of economics from Columbia University who had served as chairman of the Committee for the Study of Recent Social Trends; and George F. Yantis, a former state legislator from the State of Washington and a former chairman of the NRPB's Northwest Regional Council in the later days. The latter had a real interest in regional planning, had some contacts with members of Congress, and had a few hobby topics at the NRPB, but he was not a forceful Board member, though he did seem to have some idea or intuition that the Board's aloofness from the Congress would lead to disaster.

Beginning with the National Resources Committee in 1935, Beardsley Ruml and Henry S. Dennison were appointed as "advisors." Ruml had had a distinguished career in public affairs in Chicago, was an old associate of both Ickes and Merriam, and during and after the NRPB experience had a very distinguished career in private business and in various private associations. Alumni of the NRPB tell me that Ruml was a most stimulating person, full of ideas, and very helpful to staff people. His published record at the NRPB and elsewhere, they say, understates the intellectual capabilities and importance of the man. Dennison was a successful New England businessman, with more connections to academia (including Harvard) than was customary for businessmen at that time. Each was part-time, in the same way the Board members were part-time. While each took a role in suggesting Board studies and in reviewing Board reports, neither seems to have tried, or at least effected,

a major change in Board policy—including a resolution of the Merriam–
Eliot differences, a clearer direction for Board efforts, and the building
of a more solid political basis for Board support.

The staff of the NRPB and its predecessors gradually expanded from
its tiny beginnings at the NPB, but major additions to the staff were made
in 1940, when the work of the NRPB was largely divided into three
divisions. Ralph Watkins had been an economics professor at various
universities; he came to the NRPB from the University of Pittsburgh.
Somewhat similar had been the careers of Glenn E. McLaughlin and
Wilbert G. Fritz, who also came from the University of Pittsburgh. These
men and others constituted division B of the staff. Thomas C. Blaisdell,
Jr., a noted economist and political scientist, headed division A. Frank
W. Herring headed division C. These divisions will be discussed in
greater detail in chapter 6. But there were many other able men and
women connected with the NRPB, especially after 1939 and 1940, and
before people began to be siphoned off for the war effort. The names
of many of them will show up in later chapters where the substantive
content of the NRPB studies is discussed.

One of the most remarkable achievements of the NRPB in personnel
recruitment and development was its ability to attract and to identify
young men of outstanding competence and promise. Most of these were
in their twenties or early thirties when attracted to the NRPB; since it
has been out of existence for more than thirty-five years, these men are
now mostly in their 60s, but the following are still active: Joseph L.
Fisher, research organization president and congressman; Milton Friedman, professor, outstanding economist, and Nobel Prize winner; J. K.
Galbraith, professor, outstanding economist, and U.S. ambassador to
India; Lincoln Gordon, university president and U.S. ambassador to
Brazil; Wassily Leontief, university professor and Nobel Prize winner;
Paul A. Samuelson, professor and Nobel Prize winner; Malcolm Toon,
career diplomat and U.S. ambassador to several countries; and Gilbert
F. White, college president and university scholar. Three Nobel Prize
winners, two college or university presidents, several ambassadors, and
a congressman are an outstanding lot of alumni, especially from a
relatively small organization.

The 1930s were a time when jobs were scarce and the NRPB, like
other government agencies, was operating in a buyer's market for labor.
But it also offered intellectual and other opportunity to these young men.
They saw in NRPB employment not only much-needed income but also

a chance to develop professionally, often to travel (which was much less common in those days than today), and to acquire much broader professional experience. The NRPB—and, I assume, Eliot personally—must be given great credit for attracting such people, employing them, and giving them opportunities.

Many distinguished persons served on NRPB committees: Abel Wolman, Harlan H. Barrows, and Thorndike Saville on the Water Committee; William I. Myers, Milton Eisenhower, and others on the Land Committee; Edwin B. Wilson, William F. Ogburn, Warren S. Thompson, and Charles H. Judd on the Population Committee; Owen D. Young on the Transportation Committee; and C. A. Dykstra on the Urbanism Committee. In these modern days, when government is held in such low esteem by so much of the citizenry, when government employment attracts so few of the ablest young people, it is not easy, especially for younger people, to realize that it has not always been like this.

6

Organization, Structure, and Functioning

Although there were some changes, including much expansion of staff during the life of the National Resources Planning Board and its predecessor agencies, the general organization, structure, and method of functioning of the NRPB remained fairly similar if not entirely constant over the ten years of its existence.

Policy or Directing Boards

Throughout its history, the NRPB always had an overall policy or directing board, although the makeup of this board changed considerably. The National Planning Board in 1933 and 1934 had a citizen board with Frederic A. Delano acting as chairman; the National Resources Planning Board from its creation in 1939 until its demise in 1943 was solely a citizen board, also with Delano as chairman. The two intermediate organizations, the National Resources Board in 1934 and 1935 and the National Resources Committee from 1935 to 1939, each had a board consisting of five cabinet officers (or others of essentially cabinet rank) and three citizen members. The cabinet members of the National Resources Board were Harold L. Ickes, secretary of the interior and also public works administrator; Henry A. Wallace, secretary of agriculture; George H. Dern, secretary of war; Daniel C. Roper, secretary of commerce; Frances Perkins, secretary of labor; and Harry

L. Hopkins, administrator of the Works Progress Administration; and their successors on later NRPB organizations.

These boards were, of course, only one—and probably far from the most important—of the many responsibilities of these cabinet officers. Eliot and Merrill tactfully describe the role of these members of the boards as follows:

> The Membership of Cabinet Officers in the Resources Board and Committee secured for the Board the hearty cooperation of bureau chiefs and subordinate officials. It also provided for interpretation of the work and proposals of the Board in meetings of the Cabinet and Executive Council. The disadvantages proved to be: first, the difficulty of getting the attention of such important officers of the Government for meetings or review of reports, and, second, the apparently inevitable delegation of the duties of such Cabinet Members for attendance at meetings, etc. to subordinates and often not the same subordinate. It was sometimes difficult to get continuity of policy and action because of these shifting delegations of authority.[1]

According to Eliot and Merrill, "In the whole five-year period, the Board and Committee met formally only fourteen times (seven times in the first year), primarily to delegate powers to the Chairman and Advisory Committee or to modify, approve, and transmit reports to the president."[2] It is impossible, from the readily available record, to know just how seriously these cabinet members took their responsibilities on the Board and Committee; one may reasonably assume that much of their participation was pro forma but the possibility always existed of a protest or of preventing an action with which they did not agree.

The citizen members of the National Resources Board and the National Resources Committee were also listed as an "advisory committee." They were the same persons who had been citizen members of the National Planning Board: Frederic A. Delano, Charles E. Merriam, and Wesley C. Mitchell. The last left in 1935 and his place was not filled until 1939. When the National Resources Committee was set up in 1935, Beardsley Ruml and Henry S. Dennison were added to the advisers. When the National Resources Planning Board was set up in 1939, it consisted of Delano and Merriam and a new member, George F.

---

[1] Charles W. Eliot, 2nd, assisted by Harold A. Merrill, *Guide to the Files of the National Resources Planning Board and the Predecessor Agencies, Ten Years of National Planning, 1933–1943* (December 31, 1943).

[2] Ibid, p. 13.

Yantis; and Ruml and Dennison were continued as advisers. There was thus, throughout the ten-year life of the NRPB and its predecessors, an extremely high (for government) continuity of personnel. According to Eliot and Merrill, there were seventeen meetings of the National Planning Board, 1933–34; eighty-seven meetings of the National Resources Board and Committee, 1934–39; and seventy meetings of the National Resources Planning Board, 1939–43.[3]

The two advisers to the NRPB, Beardsley Ruml and Henry S. Dennison, were on a full footing with the Board members in practice and legally except that they had no right to vote—an empty difference, since the Board almost never put anything to a vote. As Eliot and Merrill say: "All actions of the central group throughout the ten years were unanimous, but only one or two 'votes' in the whole period were written or finally phrased in the meeting or were ever 'put to a vote.' This informality had certain advantages, but left the Executive Officer or Director to interpret the wishes of the Board."[4]

All the citizen members of the Board or central group were part-time, and all except Delano lived elsewhere than in Washington. They met about three times every two months, ordinarily for two or at most three days per meeting. While membership on the Board was undoubtedly a larger part of the lives of the citizen members than it was of the cabinet members, it was still only one of several interests for each of them. Board members drew no salary as such, but their expenses to meetings were paid and a daily honorarium was given for the days actually spent in meetings. Partly because he was chairman, and partly because he lived in Washington and was thus more accessible to the staff, Delano played a more frequent role in the operations of the staff, but he had other activities demanding of his time and attention. As Eliot and Merrill describe it: "Mr. Delano's residence in Washington made it possible for him to be in the office regularly. He was regarded as 'head of the office' in all inter-governmental communications, budget instructions, etc. Although long association of Mr. Delano and Mr. Eliot provided close working relations and understanding between them, there never was any clear line of delegation of authority from the board to the executive officer or director."[5]

---

[3] Ibid, p. 12. But elsewhere, p. 19, they refer to 174 meetings, or "almost regularly seventeen meetings per year."

[4] Ibid, pp. 19–20.

[5] Ibid, p. 20.

It is difficult at this distance in time to evaluate exactly the role of the Board. As Eliot and Merrill say: "The board or advisory committee formally approved budget allotments and amended them, and the members participated actively in the selection of committee members, research consultants, and key officials."[6] My interviews with surviving alumni of the NRPB seem to suggest that the Board played a major role, not only as suggested by the quotation from Eliot and Merrill, but also in approving the initiation of research and other projects and in approving the reports emanating from such projects. However, the intensity of such review and approval seems to have varied considerably among the various projects, as one would expect. Possibly the most important role of the Board is the negative one suggested. If it never established a clear line of delegation to the executive office, this was important. In large part, this probably reflected Merriam's distrust of Eliot, as well as the generally relaxed administrative style of Delano, but the effect upon the Board's operations may have been substantial.

One of the Board's chief functions was to serve as the chief (but not only) contact from the NRPB and its staff to the president. Again to quote Eliot and Merrill, "Projects and proposed activities of the board were submitted to the president directly by the board and through various cabinet members or other officials, like the Director of the Budget."[7]

Central Office Staff

The NRPB central office staff, on whom the responsibility for the actual operations of the organization naturally largely fell, underwent many changes during its ten-year life, but it had a single head throughout its life. Charles W. Eliot, 2nd, was the staff leader, first with the title of executive officer, later with the title of director, but with essentially the same responsibilities throughout.

The administrative officer of the NRPB and predecessors throughout their history was Harold Merrill, at first with the title of assistant executive officer and later, when Eliot's title was changed to that of director, with the title of executive officer. He was responsible for personnel matters, travel and other expenditures, budgets and accounts, property, and all the other necessary administrative matters of a federal agency.

---

[6] Ibid., p. 20.
[7] Ibid, p. 20.

He performed his job zealously. Although some people thought he was too restrictive in his attitudes, in general he gets high marks from former associates. The continuity of service of these two men, in essentially the same roles throughout, was a major asset to the NRPB.

During the one-year life of the National Planning Board, it had only five employees other than Eliot and Merrill.[8] The staff gradually expanded as the NPB became the National Resources Board and the National Resources Committee, but the largest expansion took place after it became the National Resources Planning Board in 1939. By 1935 the staff had expanded to 50 and in 1943 had reached 261.[9] Although there had been some grouping of workers into units before 1939, the relatively small size of the organization and the generally informal and relaxed methods of operations had not given such groupings major importance as far as the daily operations of the organization went. In 1940, however, three major divisions were established as was noted earlier. Division A was responsible for current reporting of trends in business and unemployment; special trend studies of relief and relief policies, technology, unemployment, population, and youth; science committee activities in connection with business and industrial research; and certain studies in economics, finance, and fiscal policy. By 1942 this division had a half dozen units dealing with one or more of these special topics. Division B was responsible for technical studies on transportation, location of industry, and land, water, and energy resources. By 1942 the division had four units or sections. Division C was responsible for a federal six-year program of public works; the study of federal indirect aids, grants, subsidies, and guaranteed loans as stimulants to private development and construction; keeping abreast of state and local programs of public works and encouraging the formulation of such programs; and aiding in planning large-scale and long-range development of capital budget expenditures of railroads, public utilities, and industry in general. By 1942, this division had four or five sections or units.[10] In addition, there were several units in the office of the director in 1942: one on postwar planning, one on urban conservation and development, a publications unit, a field service section (more about

---

8 Ibid, p. 22. See also p. 25a.

9 Charles W. Eliot, 2nd, *Final Report—Status of Work, National Resources Planning Board* (December 21, 1943).

10 Virgil E. Baugh, *Central Office Records of the National Resources Planning Board*, Preliminary Inventories, no. 20 (Washington, General Services Administration, National Archives and Record Service, 1953).

Table 6-1. Authorship of Reports Published by the NRPB
(percentage of total)

Authorship	July 1933 to June 1939	July 1939 to August 1943
NRPB staff, including temporary staff, with little or no committee participation	33	53
Primarily NRPB staff, with advisory committee	9	10
Committee or commission, including regional commissions, usually with NRPB secretariat or staff; includes reports of conferences	56	34
Other, not easily assigned to one of the above	2	3
Total	100	100

whose relation with regional offices is presented later in this chapter), and the administrative units.

By 1943, when the NRPB was terminated, there were 154 employees on active duty in the Washington office, including Eliot and Merrill, and 72 on active duty "in the field."[11] The NRPB had followed a normal bureaucratic evolution, toward more employees and a more formal organization, as its need for expanded work became apparent and as it was able to get the funds necessary for such expansion. Far more important than this expansion in number of employees was a gradual but significant shift in methods of operation, from one of heavy reliance on committees of persons not on its payroll to a much greater utilization of its own staff (see table 6-1). Throughout its history, the NRPB made extensive use of short-term or temporary employees, as well as of outside consultants.

Committees

The NRPB and its predecessors made extensive use of committees to aid it in various ways. Typically, a committee's members were drawn from other federal agencies and from outside of government. The latter were often university professors but sometimes included businessmen and others. Extensive use was made of committees in the NRPB's

---

[11] Eliot, *Final Report.*

regional operations also. Scores of persons were involved in these committees; the famous 1934 NRB *Report on National Planning* includes the names of 200 persons as members of committees or contributors, and I know from personal experience that many persons contributed to that report who were not named. Some of the committees operated during almost the whole life of the NRPB, being organized early in its existence and continuing to the end.

One outstanding feature of these committees, then relatively uncommon if not previously unknown in government, was the admixture of government officials and nongovernment experts. Some of the committee members were the most outstanding experts in the country; the water committee, for example, included Abel Wolman, Harlan H. Barrows, and Thorndike Saville, among others—the ablest water specialists in the country at the time. They, in turn, drew upon experts in all parts of the country to mobilize the very best talent the country had for their particular task. While the water committee was one of the most outstanding, due in large part to the great ability and dynamic personality of Abel Wolman, its chairman, several of the other committees were also outstanding both in their membership and in their output. In 1939, the National Resources Committee had eight major subject matter committees.[12]

The role of the committees varied considerably, from being the dominant force in planning in a particular field, as water, to being largely an advisory group to an essentially NRPB research operation, as perhaps with energy or population. Moreover, the role of the committees seemed to have changed over the decade, gradually becoming less important but still significant up to the end. Some committees were chaired by government employees, others by outside experts. In all cases, the NRPB provided an employee to serve as secretary to each committee, and in many cases this person was a major factor in its operations. The make-up of the committees resulted in a substantial degree of agency and program coordination that could not as readily have been achieved otherwise.

In retrospect, the NRPB's use of committees was one of the more outstanding features of its successful operations. The committees mobilized talent, knowledge, and experience which would otherwise have been unobtainable—and at very moderate costs. There were, of

[12] Baugh, *Central Office Records.*

course, some disadvantages to such committees: it was often hard to get members to meet at times when all could be present, because each had other demands on his time; and it was often hard to get members to deliver their contributions on time, for the same reasons. Committees for any organization have a way of reaching their own conclusions, which did not necessarily square with those of their sponsors. It surely was easier for the NRPB to prepare a report or a plan on some subject by its own staff, especially as the latter became larger and more able, than it was to get a report prepared by a committee, and this was doubtless a major factor in the gradual shift away from committee reports and toward staff reports. But committees, because of the diverse experience and knowledge of their members, could often produce a report and a plan more nearly comprehensive than could even the ablest staff, and the participation of committee members surely went a long way toward general acceptance of the conclusions of each report.

Although committees of experts from within and from outside of government are still widely used in federal government operations—at the National Academy of Science/National Research Council operations in particular—the opportunities for use of such committees and their value are less today than in the NRPB's lifetime. Then, experts often lacked good means of getting their knowledge and their studies recognized, and the NRPB could often perform a real service here, so that outside experts (and even those in government) were more eager to participate in the NRPB projects than might be the case today. On the other hand, the level of knowledge and the amount of factual information were so much less then, that the personal knowledge of experts was more nearly indispensable. Thus, the heavy reliance and successful use of diverse committees may have been more important and more productive in NRPB days than it would be today.

Use of Consultants

The NRPB made extensive use of consultants. "As specialists were needed on research or other projects, it was found that more often than not they were available only on a part-time basis. The board sought the help of leading figures in various fields, and was able to secure for the public and the government the fruits of research over many years at very slight cost. Once on the payrolls, the board made it a policy to keep a

number of these specialists 'on call' or on a 'panel' of consultants."[13]
This practice began in 1933 and 1934, when many of the consultants
contributed their time. Later, consultants were generally paid $25 per
day, with a few receiving as high as $50 per day. When the employees
of the Board were "covered" into civil service in July 1940, a ceiling
of $25 per day for consultants was imposed, with new appointees limited
to $22.22 per day.[14] By the time the NRPB was abolished, there were
over 230 names on its panel of consultants.

The use of consultants is generally good business for a federal agency.
This practice enables it to tap pools of expertise which would otherwise
be unavailable. While most such experts may come from universities
and other nonprofit organizations, some may well come from industry
and other private business, since specialized knowledge is often to be
found there. Some experts may have private interests which conflict
with their role as advisers to a government agency but it is, generally
speaking, better to have such possible conflicts laid out in the open, as
modern appointment practice requires, than to have the same person
offering information and advice on a less formal basis.

The NRPB's use of consultants reached a high point in 1937 and
declined considerably thereafter. This was part of the general shift
toward internalizing the activities of the NRPB, noted previously. In
1937, total employment of consultants was approximately the equivalent
of fifty full-time man-years but, as noted, most of the employment was
part-time, so that considerably more persons than this were involved in
such employment.

The NRPB's Field Organization

Throughout their history, the NRPB and its predecessor agencies made
extensive use of regional planning organizations. Indeed, "prior to or
coincident with the organization of the National Planning Board, the
Administrator of Public Works appointed ten regional advisers for as
many districts or regions. . . ."[15] These regional advisers were later
replaced by district chairmen, who were part of the NRPB organization
rather than part of the Public Works Administration, but in many cases
the regional chairman had been regional adviser. "The new title was

---

[13] Eliot and Merrill, *Guide to the Files,* pp. 29–30.
[14] Ibid., p. 30.
[15] Ibid., p. 84.

chosen as something different from regional adviser and as an indication of the desire of the board that the 'chairmen' should serve as impartial heads of regional planning groups. . . ."[16]

". . . there were 11 regional offices, each consisting of a chairman, a small technical staff amplified by consultants, and clerical employees. Each of these offices developed its own organization and cooperating committees of federal and state agencies and had its own research projects. . . . a state section was set up in the headquarters office to administer these field offices and this later became the field service section."[17] As this suggests, the headquarters staff of the NRPB provided technical help to these regional offices. The purposes of the regional offices were to provide the headquarters office with information about conditions in each region, including attitudes of state and federal agencies and influential persons, to focus attention on regional, as contrasted with both national and state, problems and opportunities, and to promote regional and state planning. Several regional offices prepared reports, apparently on their own initiative or in response to suggestions or directives from Washington, which were extensive and of high professional quality; some of these reports had circulation in a processed form within their region or elsewhere, and were replaced later by printed reports issued from Washington. Partly to focus attention on regional problems and its efforts to deal with them, the Board itself held some of its meetings within some of the regions—Eliot and Merrill note seven such meetings outside of Washington during the first year of the NPB's existence alone.[18]

The range of activity—and, one may add, the quality of work carried out—varied considerably from region to region, depending in large part upon the regional chairman and his committees. By 1943 all the regional organizations seem to have been functioning quite well, and, had the NRPB continued permanently, the regional offices would probably have all become major factors in national planning.

Relationships to State and Local Planning Organizations

The NRPB and its predecessor agencies did not have subsidiary state planning boards but they did encourage the states to form such boards,

---

16 Ibid., p. 87.
17 Baugh, *Central Office Records*, p. 5.
18 Eliot and Merrill, *Guide to the Files*, p. 85.

assigned and paid planning consultants, and helped the boards get
W.P.A. assistance and other federal financial help for their staffing.

> A proposal for financing federal assistance to state and local planning
> groups was . . . adopted by the board and submitted to the administrator
> (of Public Works) on October 23, 1933. . . . At the same time, nego-
> tiations were undertaken with the W.P.A. . . . These negotiations pro-
> ceeded so satisfactorily that on November 16, 1933, the chairman of
> the board, Mr. Delano, addressed a letter to all city, state, and regional
> planning agencies announcing the availability of such assistance. On
> November 24, the executive officer, Mr. Eliot, in a speech before the
> New England Council in Boston, and with the approval of the admin-
> istrator and the board, offered the assistance of the National Planning
> Board to new state planning agencies. . . . Governor Winant of New
> Hampshire, . . . immediately after the meeting, announced his intention
> of setting up the New Hampshire State Planning Board.[19]

Those who in 1980 believe that government always moves slowly and
hesitatingly should note these dates and the brief time that elapsed
between initial decision and first decisive action.

The states which did not already have planning boards (a few did)
moved quickly to set them up (or similar organizations with other
titles), either by law or by executive action. Eliot and Merrill note that
thirty states had done so by June 15, 1935; and, in the end, nearly
every state established such boards, although one or two states very
shortly abolished the boards they had recently set up.

> There have been many explanations for the rapid growth of the state
> planning movement. Presumably, many governors and leaders of legis-
> lative groups saw in the establishment of a planning agency a logical
> and useful service to their states. The fact that this new agency would
> cost the state very little because of the help available from the National
> Planning Board or the National Resources Board and from the Relief
> Organization, certainly did not deter them. In some states there was
> doubtless also the feeling that compliance with the suggestions from the
> administration in Washington might help the position of the state in
> seeking public works allotments or other help in the war against depres-
> sion. Whatever the reasons might have been in the early days of the
> movement, there was extraordinary unanimity of support from all kinds
> of sources without regard to political party or economic group.[20]

---

[19] Ibid., pp. 93–94.
[20] Ibid., p. 95.

This was one example of the stimulating role that federal agencies and programs can provide for state or local action.

The quality of the work done by the state planning boards varied greatly, from basically pro forma endorsements of state agency projects to high-quality, imaginative, and incisive plans for the physical, economic, and social development of the state. Again, had the NRPB continued, these state boards might well have developed into major forces in the national planning scene. As it was, most such agencies withered and many died after the NRPB was abolished and after federal financial help for their staffing was discontinued, when the war led to the cessation of federal relief expenditures. Others changed their focus to economic development. In the South, the state planning agencies were gradually replaced by state development agencies—the emphasis shifted from planning to economic development, often stimulated by special tax treatment, but nevertheless there was considerable continuity of action.[21] Some state planning agencies have gained substantial strength in recent years, in these new functions or in the older ones.

The NRPB did not play as active a role in the stimulation of city planning as it did in state planning. It did undertake some special studies, including one on lack of coordination of federal projects with city plans.[22] An innovative urbanism project was undertaken by the National Resources Board in June 1935. Various reports about city planning were made by the NRPB (see, for example, item #50 in appendix B).

The interest and activity in regional, state, and local planning on the part of the NRPB and its predecessors reflects much more the background, interests, and viewpoints of Delano and Eliot than those of Merriam. The former two, with their extensive backgrounds in city planning, clearly saw the need for coordination of public works at all levels, to avoid contradictory and conflicting actions and to achieve the maximum complementarity among various public works. While they encouraged regional, state, and local agencies to make social and economic studies, they were much less interested in such studies than was Merriam, with his background in the Committee on Recent Social Trends and the Social Science Research Council.

---

[21] Albert Lepawsky, *State Planning and Economic Development in the South,* National Planning Association, Committee of the South Report, no. 4 (1949).

[22] Eliot and Merrill, *Guide to the Files,* p. 101.

Summary and Evaluation

From my background as a one-time federal administrator and long-time observer of federal agency organization and operation, I draw certain conclusions from the information presented in this chapter about the organization, structure, and methods of operation of the NRPB and its predecessor agencies:

1. The NRPB with its part-time governing board, its full-time staff, its extensive use of committees of diverse membership, its own field organization, and its extensive cooperation with state planning agencies represented an unusual organization and method of operation for federal agencies at that time. Although none of its features was wholly novel, since something like each of them could have been found somewhere in the federal establishment, the combination of these features was most unusual.

2. Over the years, the NRPB shifted its method of operation, from very heavy reliance on committees to much more use of its own staff. This shift was not abrupt but is apparent when operations before establishment of the NRPB in 1939 are contrasted with operations after that date (see table 6-1). The shift may have been, to some extent, a subconscious bureaucratic evolution, as much as an explicit policy decision. In later chapters, I document its nature further and argue that, on the whole, it was a mistake.

3. The weakest link in the whole NRPB structure was the Board itself. As a part-time group, it could not well serve as a directing body, though it strove to do so. At the same time the Board was unwilling to delegate adequate powers to its executive director or to provide him with clear and unequivocal policy guidelines.

4. There was a considerable divergence in interest between the NRPB's Washington office and its field organization. The regional offices and the state planning boards were more concerned with public works planning while the Washington office, although concerned with the same subject, gave much of its emphasis to research on socioeconomic problems; the regional and state offices were concerned primarily with planning for *natural* resources, the Washington office primarily with *national* resources, to revert to the distinction made when the National Resources Board was created in 1934. Tensions between the field and Washington were no more than normal for federal agencies and I do not mean to imply that conflict or controversy raged, but only that the

primary focus of each was different, while at the same time each gave some attention to the interests of the other.

5. The NRPB built a large, influential, generally effective, and generally popular field organization, of which it made little political use until it was under its final attack in the Congress. To any federal bureaucrat, this reluctance to use the power one possesses is curious indeed—and, for the NRPB, fatal. One judges that this lack of effective bureaucratic response was due largely or wholly to Merriam's insistence that the NRPB was solely advisory to the president, should play no other role, and should hold itself aloof from the Congress.

7

The Roles Played by the Board

·

The NRPB and its predecessor agencies engaged in a great many different kinds of activities. They played various roles during their lifetimes. At the first meeting of the National Planning Board in 1933, it decided to group its work or activities under four headings:

1. Planning and programming of public works,
2. Stimulation of city, state, and regional planning,
3. Coordination of federal planning activities, and
4. A research program.[1]

A similar classification of its activities continued throughout its life, but the original scope of activities was somewhat extended and enlarged. In 1940, after the staff reorganization following the creation of the National Resources Planning Board in 1939, the periodic reporting of economic trends was added as a specific function. About the same time the NRPB began to be involved in planning for defense programs and, after war broke out in late 1941, planning for the war effort, although

---

[1] These are described in Charles W. Eliot, 2nd, assisted by Harold A. Merrill, *Guide to the Files of the National Resource Planning Board and Predecessor Agencies, Ten Years of National Planning, 1933–1943,* December 31, 1943. The same classification of activities is reported by Virgil E. Baugh, *Central Office Records of the National Resources Planning Board,* Preliminary Inventories, no. 50, The National Archives, National Archives and Records Service, General Services Administration, Washington, D.C., 1953. Each is quoting from the minutes of the National Planning Board.

86

most of the war planning was soon taken over by other organizations. Shortly after that the president assigned the NRPB the responsibility for postwar planning.

Any classification of the roles played by the NRPB inevitably leads to considerable overlapping. This is not only unavoidable but, to a large degree realistic and desirable, for the activities of the NRPB were numerous and do not fit neatly into any classification, including its own. I find it useful, for the purposes of this book, to group the NRPB's roles into two broad categories, each with several subdivisions: (1) idea development and stimulation, and (2) planning and coordination in general.

Idea Development and Stimulation

The NRPB and its predecessors were the source or the means of propagating many new ideas during the 1933–43 period. These were years of intellectual ferment, especially at the federal governmental level; the despair and apathy of the Great Depression gave way to excitement and confusion as the New Deal experimented with many new governmental programs. The NRPB was surely one of the major sources of ideas at the governmental level in those years.

The NRPB exercised its idea development and stimulation role in several ways:

1. It conducted research with its own staff, including research by persons employed by it just for a specific research project; in making such research studies, it may, or may not, have used an advisory committee. If an advisory committee was used in this research by staff, its role was minor relative to the role of the agency's own researchers. Research includes the collection, analysis, and interpretation of facts and the development of concepts or theory. The research might, or might not, produce a policy recommendation; but, if a policy recommendation was produced, this was at least somewhat incidental to the research results themselves.[2]

---

[2] While there are several studies that might fit this general category, a few may be cited as representative of it: item 52 in table B-1, *Technological Trends and National Policy Including the Social Implications of New Inventions* (1937); item 120 in table B-1, *The Structure of the American Economy: I, Basic Characteristics* (1938); item 170 in table B-1, *The Economic Effects of the Federal Public Works Expenditures, 1933–1938*, by J. K. Galbraith, assisted by G. G. Johnson (1940); item 179 in table B-1, *Research—A National Resource, II. Industrial Research* (1940); item 273 in table B-1, *Transportation and National Policy* (1942); and item 315 in table B-1, *Industrial Location and Natural Resources* (1942).

2. It financed out of funds available to it or arranged for the financing or for the provision of staff paid for out of WPA funds, of essentially research studies which were then carried out by nonstaff persons or by persons only temporarily on its payroll. There is not a clear sharp line between this role and the previous one; the activities are generally similar but the financial role is different.[3]

3. Primarily by means of its committees, the NRPB assembled and synthesized existent but scattered information, producing well-rounded and comprehensive reports which had a vastly greater intellectual impact than the scattered source materials from which they were constructed.[4]

4. The NRPB had a very influential role as a publisher and disseminator of reports. One of the most curious reports in its list, at least to me, is item 157 in table B-1, *Production and Utilization Techniques— Coal*, by A. C. Fieldner and W. E. Rice (1940). These two men were employed by the Bureau of Mines, the research they reported had been financed by that Bureau, and the publication could well have been issued by it. Instead, the authors or their agency, or both, chose to have the report published by the NRPB, even as a mimeographed report. I interpret this as evidence of the fact that the NRPB could publish more quickly, with less delaying and less debilitating reviews, and with wider impact, than could an old-line federal agency. Anyone who experienced the typical federal review and publication process of that period, as I did, can well understand this choice by the authors and their agency. The NRPB's location in the Office of the President helped it get quick publication. While the coal report is the most extreme example I have noted, and is not a very important report, something of the same thing could be said for many other NRPB reports. The land part of the classic 1943 report might have been assembled by the Departments of Agriculture and the Interior and published by one of them. Instead, it was the NRPB which galvanized the federal agencies into action and which gave the report a quicker publication and a greater impact than would have been possible under standard governmental procedures.

---

[3] Illustrative of this category are item 88 in table B-1, *Problems of a Changing Population* (1938); item 99 in table B-1, *Consumer Incomes in the United States— Their Distribution in 1935–36* (1938); and item 107 in table B-1, *Consumer Expenditures in the United States* (1938).

[4] The classic example here was item 5 in table B-1, *A Report on National Planning and Public Works in Relation to Natural Resources and Including Land Use and Water Resources with Findings and Recommendations* (1934).

These idea development and stimulation roles of the NRPB were much in the tradition of the Committee on Recent Social Trends, described in chapter 3, and of the work of the Social Science Research Council, both of which were private efforts. Those private organizations would have had great difficulty enlisting federal agency and other cooperation on the scale necessary for some of these studies; hence the NRPB played an indispensable role. One may reasonably assume that Charles E. Merriam must have found these roles of the NRPB much to his liking.

To be effective, idea development and stimulation require wide dissemination of the results of whatever studies or projects are undertaken. Moreover, they require the putting of ideas into terms readily understood by relatively diverse and relatively large audiences—clear, stimulating, sometimes controversial statements. But the latter are likely to alienate some influential but conservative persons, including some members of the Congress. If the ideas are ever to be translated into action, they must command widespread public support. They are likely to be far more effective in the long pull than in the short run; and, by the time they are translated into action, they must undergo considerable modification from their original statement. Hence, it may be difficult for the originator of these ideas to claim or to receive much credit. These are characteristics of all research and idea development, not limited to the NRPB.

Planning as a Governmental Activity

Planning is a widely used word of many meanings, so that its meaning in a specific situation must be defined or the word qualified by a modifying addition. "If planning is everything, maybe it's nothing."[5]

[5] Aaron Wildavsky, "If Planning Is Everything, Maybe It's Nothing," *Policy Sciences,* 4, (1973). Wildavsky goes on to argue that planning in all countries at all times has been unsuccessful on a national scale, in the sense that plans are not followed or that actions do not conform to plans. "If formal planning fails not merely in one nation at a time but in virtually all nations most of the time, the defects are unlikely to be found in maladroit or untalented planners . . . If governments persevere in national planning, it must be because their will to believe triumphs over their experience. Planning is not so much a subject for the social scientist as for the theologian." While Wildavsky is not alone in his skepticism of planning, his views are at one end of the spectrum of professional opinion about planning.

Government planning differs in (1) content, (2) process, and (3) decision and implementation, and in combinations of these three aspects.

As to the content of planning and of plans, there exists a continuum from the simplest to the most complex. At one extreme, there is a simple compilation of facts—demographic trends, or business trends such as establishment of new industrial enterprises, data on available water and sewer capacity, or the like—in each case with nothing more than a mere presentation of these facts. A next step toward a more nearly complete plan would be some analysis to point to the significance of these facts, the probable consequences of past trends, and the interpretation of different facts in relation to each other. A third step would be a weighing of the facts and a formulation of alternative plans of action based upon them. This step would consist of presentation of the alternative plans, leaving for others a choice among them. A fourth step would include a choice by the planners and the recommendation by them of the most desirable among the alternatives described in the previous step. A fifth step would be an actual choice of or decision by an implementing body on a plan to be implemented. And the last stage of the planning process, or the first stage beyond it, would be the actual implementation of the plan, with necessary modifications as it was actually carried into operation. Clearly, these stages described separately would tend in practice to merge, with various intermediate steps possible.

The planning process likewise exhibits a continuum from relatively simple to more complex. At the simplest, the plan is prepared by a staff of technicians, utilizing data and concepts available to it. The next stage would consist of technicians operating with a lay advisory board or a board made up of ex officio government officials serving in an advisory role only. At its simplest, this second stage would leave primary planning responsibility with the technicians. The third stage would be similar in the sense that a board, either of lay persons or of government officials or both, would work with planning technicians, but now the board would be the responsible agency, the technicians serving as the staff for the board. A fourth stage in the planning process arises if the plans are formally approved by some general governing person or body —a mayor or a city council, a county board of supervisors, a governor or a state legislature, the president or the Congress—which is elected and thus responsible to the general electorate of the unit of government.

The degree of public involvement in the planning process may vary greatly with each of these four stages of complexity of process. Public involvement may be sought at all stages, through publicity, informal meetings, formal hearings, and by other means; or the public may be informed only when the plan is submitted for formal approval by the elected governing body; or may vary in numerous ways throughout the process.

Whatever may be their content and whatever may be the process by which they are drawn up, plans may also differ substantially in the degree to which they represent effective decisions and in the way in which they are implemented. Wildavsky's criticism, noted above, is that national plans are rarely actually implemented. Again, there is a continuum, from the simplest to the most complex. At the simplest stage, a plan is advisory only; it sets forth a scenario of what might be, leaving all public agencies and private groups or firms free to act as they see fit, taking into account the plan as far as they choose to do so but also taking into account whatever else they choose to consider. The next stage in implementation is to make the plan binding on the governmental unit concerned. For instance, the plan might be the basis on which all manner of public works, transportation facilities, schools, and the like are based. While these would be public actions, clearly they would affect private actions also and to this extent would be plans for private action. A third stage would be to make the plan effective or restrictive on at least some private actions—zoning for land use, pollution control requirements, and the like. Lastly, the plans might be implemented by the extension of subsidies, such as direct subsidy payments; credit for specific purposes, perhaps at subsidized rates; and other direct incentives to private action in accordance with the plan.

There are also great differences in the time period or time horizon of plans. At one extreme, the plan may be for actions which must be taken, if at all, within a few days; at the other extreme, the plan may be long range, for twenty years or more into the future.

In my view, speaking as one not identified with any school of planning, any of the above stages in content, process, or implementation, or in combinations of them, is legitimate. That is, I do not insist that planning must conform to some specific definition of mine. Each of the briefly described forms exists somewhere in the United States. I regard it as unproductive, even hopeless, to propose one specific definition and try to conform all discussion to that definition. In the sections which follow, I look briefly at the definition or definitions of planning as the term was used by the National Resources Planning Board and its predecessors, and also at how the term seems to have been interpreted by the opponents or enemies of the NRPB; and in the concluding chapter, I consider how planning has been interpreted in more recent years, by various units of government. It will be evident from the context that different definitions of planning are used at different places in this book.

Planning as the NRPB and Its Officials Saw It

In several reports or articles the National Resources Planning Board or its predecessor agencies and various of its officials defined or described planning as they saw it. Some of the most descriptive statements follow; others could be added but the views expressed would be similar. The actual operations of the NRPB should be examined in light of its concept of its job.

In the summer of 1934 the National Resources Board submitted the final report of the National Planning Board; the latter had by then been superseded by the former. The report prepared by the National Planning Board described planning as follows (p. 30):

> Planning consists in the systematic, continuous, forward-looking application of the best intelligence available to programs of common affairs in the public field, as it does to private affairs in the domain of individual activity. In every well-directed home, in every business, in every labor or agricultural group, in every forward-looking organization, social planning goes on continuously, and in the world of government there is also opportunity for its exercise.
>
> Several considerations are important in looking at plans for planning:
>
> (1) The necessity and value of coordinating our national and local policies, instead of allowing them to drift apart, or pull against each other, with disastrous effect.
>
> (2) The value of looking forward in national life, or organizing preventive policies as well as remedial, of preventing the fire rather than putting it out.
>
> (3) The value of basing plans upon the most competent collection and analysis of the facts.
>
> At the same time, it may be pointed out:
>
> First. In any case, not all planning is or should be national planning . . .
>
> Second. Planning does not involve setting up a fixed and unchangeable system, but on the contrary contemplates readjustment and revision, as new situations and problems emerge. Planning is a continuous process . . .

Third. It is false and misleading to assert that all planning involves wholesale regimentation of private life . . .[6]

Later on, in the same report, (p. 31), the Board says: "The truth is that it is not necessary or desirable that a central system of planning actually cover all lines of activity or forms of behavior. Such planning overreaches itself . . . Wise planning is based on control of certain strategic points in a working system—those points necessary to ensure order, justice, general welfare . . . A totally unplanned nation is as impossible and undesirable as a totally planned economy . . ."

Still later (on p. 33), the Board says: "American planning will be brought about within the general framework of the American Nation, the democratic system of government, and an evolutionary system of social and economic change."

Charles E. Merriam described the functions of the Board and defined planning as follows:

The first function of the National Resources Planning Board is to serve as a clearing house of planning interests and concerns in the national effort to prevent waste and improve living standards. Another function is to cooperate with the departmental, state and local agencies, in general, to use the Board's good offices to see that planning decisions are not made by one group in ignorance of relevant undertakings or research going on elsewhere. Obviously much of this is a matter of diplomacy and intelligent interest rather than of legal authority and high command. Another function is that of collecting and analyzing data relating to our national resources, both human and physical, and of shaping advisory plans for the better use of these resources.

Briefly, planning involves (1) the collection of elaborate basic data from original inquiry; (2) careful analysis of these data by skilled technicians; (3) a look around in order to see that various plans or efforts are not ignoring or working against each other; (4) a look backward to learn as far as possible from trends in what way we are moving; (5) a look forward, projecting either a particular plan or trend, an alternative, or a positive recommendation of a particular plan.[7]

Charles W. Eliot, 2nd, writing in a final report as he was winding up the affairs of the NRPB in 1943, after its liquidation had been decreed by the Congress, said:

---

[6] National Planning Board, Federal Emergency Administration of Public Works, *Final Report—1933–34*, (Washington, D.C., GPO, 1934).

[7] Charles E. Merriam, "The National Resources Planning Board," *Public Administration Review*, Winter 1941, p. 116.

It seems to me that the efforts to formalize or organize national planning work should aim at getting the process of planning recognized as non-political and essential to orderly and efficient government. The planning process is the organization of facts and research materials as the basis for the formulation and selection of policies. This process goes on anyway, and the issue is whether it shall be carried on openly by an established agency or out of sight and inefficiently behind the scenes. . . .

Coordination of Federal planning is the specific responsibility of the Chief Executive under the Constitution. It cannot be done anywhere else than by the President however much Congress may participate, influence, or finally control the purse strings. It is primarily an administrative-executive function which by its very nature the Legislative Branch is not organized to carry on effectively. It is the most important planning activity for immediate and vigorous attention.

Better coordination, better administration does not, of course, mean any kind of threat to the authority or prestige of the Legislative branch or to the democratic method.[8]

The Board and its staff believed planning was good and was American, that facts are needed for good planning, that coordination of government activities is desirable and can be furthered by planning, that research is desirable as a basis for development of plans, and that planning is an aid to efficiency with which economic and social goals may be attained. The Board and staff had strong convictions, amounting to dedication, for its positions. These and other statements often implied but rarely stated explicitly that facts and planning would largely or wholly resolve disputes and divergent actions among government agencies. These and other statements tended to ignore or minimize the fact that conflicts of interest, often irreconcilable, existed among interest groups and within government; and they rarely explicitly faced the fact that opposition to plans and planning are almost inevitable. A statement by Eliot that planning should be "nonpolitical" (he may have meant "nonpartisan") is particularly revealing.

Planning as the NRPB's Opponents Saw It

The Board and its planning had critics, as all governmental agencies and programs inevitably do, but the violence and the emotionalism of

---

[8] Charles W. Eliot, 2nd, *Final Report—Status of Work, National Resources Planning Board,* December 31, 1943. See pp. 24–25.

the opposition to the NRPB and to planning in general was so great, and the determination to do away with the NRPB was so strong, that many of these individuals and groups can fairly be called enemies.

In early 1936 President Franklin D. Roosevelt established a Committee on Administrative Management.[9] It attempted to work in the strictest secrecy, specifically refusing during the course of its work to confer with Congress or to advise the public of the thrust of its proposals. The president sent its report to Congress in early 1937. The report aimed to strengthen the Office of the President by providing him with six executive assistants, to reinvigorate the civil service, to improve fiscal management, to establish a permanent National Resources Planning Board, to reorganize the federal departments including the regulatory agencies, and to create two new departments. The sweeping nature of the proposals, the language in which they were made, and, above all, the secrecy with which the report had been prepared, culminating in its abrupt presentation to the Congress by the president, all aroused much opposition. The Brookings Institution had been employed by congressional committees to prepare a report also on administrative reorganization. Its report went to the Congress at essentially the same time as did the president's report, so the Congress and the nation had alternative or rival reorganization plans to consider.

Before congressional consideration of the reorganization proposals could get seriously under way, President Roosevelt launched an even more controversial proposal, prepared in even greater secrecy. Carried away by his sweeping electoral victory in 1936, a month after his reorganization proposal went to Congress, Roosevelt proposed to modify the Supreme Court, which had declared many of his programs unconstitutional, by the addition of more justices—the court-packing proposal, as it was generally called. This stirred a hurricane of opposition, not only in the Congress but throughout the country, and among Democrats and New Deal supporters as well as among Republicans. The numerous sources of opposition were spearheaded or focused by Frank Gannett, owner of a chain of eighteen newspapers. He and others formed a National Committee to Uphold Constitutional Government (NCUCG). It

---

[9] This section draws heavily on Richard Polenberg, *Reorganizing Roosevelt's Government, 1936–1939* (Cambridge, Massachusetts, Harvard University Press, 1966). The court-packing and reorganization fights were among the more dramatic episodes in American history; what follows in this section is the barest minimum account of those aspects of the larger struggle which are pertinent to the subject of this subsection—namely, the attitudes of the enemies of the NRPB.

raised considerable funds, built up large lists of leaders in all walks of life to whom it distributed very large numbers of pamphlets and other materials, and encouraged radio programs—all in opposition to the court-packing proposal. The court-packing bill was defeated in the Senate by a combination of forces, of which Gannett's committee was surely a major one, in the summer of 1937.

In early 1938, the Senate took up the reorganization bill in earnest. In an effort to win votes, the bill was watered down, and wavering Senators were given private assurances that their pet agencies and bureaus would not be disturbed. After spirited debates and much political maneuvering, the bill passed the Senate at the end of March. But it effectively failed in the House in early April, when, by a narrow vote, it was recommitted to committee. Many factors, including inept management by the Administration and the bill's sponsors, were responsible for the defeat in the House.

The National Committee to Uphold Constitutional Government mobilized its supporters around the country to send almost 100,000 telegrams in one day to Washington when the Senate had the reorganization bill under consideration. Another flood of letters and telegrams descended on the House when it had the bill under active consideration. Many of these were, of course, pro forma, and charges of deception and false messages were common, but there is little doubt that the NCUCG did stir up a vast amount of popular opposition to reorganization, as it had earlier done in opposition to court-packing. It was widely charged then that many of the persons opposing reorganization had little real understanding of just what was proposed.

A much watered down reorganization proposal did pass in 1939. This drew much less opposition, in large part because it was mostly meaningless.

Opposition to reorganization arose from many quarters and was directed at many aspects of the proposal, but some of the opposition was specifically against the planning board. The opponents of the NRPB or indeed of any national planning board thought that planning was anti-American, perhaps communistic as in Russia or fascist as in Italy; that the Board and its planners sought to regiment and control the lives of Americans; that the planners were impractical in their ideas and proposals; and, more specifically, that they simply did not understand the American system of government and its politics. A great deal of the opposition was directed implicitly, and sometimes rather explicitly, against President Roosevelt personally. Statements were made that he sought to make himself a permanent dictator of the United States, as Stalin was in Russia, Hitler in Germany, and Mussolini in Italy. The efforts of the Board and its staff to counter these arguments of its opponents or enemies were generally not effective in winning them over. There was hostility, hatred, and fear on a considerable scale. The opponents were just as sincere and dedicated in their opposition as the members and supporters of planning were in their support.

NRPB Helps Develop Planning as a Governmental Activity

A major effort was made by the NRPB throughout its history to improve the quality of planning at federal, regional, state, and local levels. Today one must realize that planning as a field of activity or as a body of knowledge and practice was much less fully developed during the 1933 to 1943 period of the NRPB's existence than it is today. There was very much less teaching about planning in universities then than now. The techniques of planning were embryonic, with many planners working out their own techniques to fit their own circumstances. Delano and Eliot were particularly concerned with the quality of planning, because of their own professional experience in city planning. Merriam had had less direct involvement in city planning but he was neither uninformed about it nor uninterested in it. There was a general realization throughout its history that the Board alone could not possibly do all the planning that was needed, even if it had seemed desirable that it do so, and that the active participation of units of government at every level was highly desirable. But, if the plans so developed were to have their maximum national value, they must at least be generally comparable from one city or state to another and it was here that the NRPB could play a major role.

One may reasonably assume that the personal contacts of NRPB staff members with planning officials at every level of government over the years were extremely influential, quite aside from any reports that have survived. One might, from a diligent search of the files of NRPB internal memoranda to be found at Archives, gain some hint of the extent of this influence, but even those records probably would not capture the full extent of this kind of influence. Staff members surely must have served as idea exchangers as they went from one office to another, almost inevitably discussing work and methods at other offices they had visited. They were not the only influence of this kind, of course, but their role must have been significant at a time when the planning field was growing and developing as it was during the decade of the NRPB's life.

The NRPB undertook a number of direct planning activities, by its staff or by its committees:

1. *Water planning.* One of the most active and most effective parts of the NRPB was its water committee, composed of leading engineers and other water specialists from outside of government and of heads or other senior personnel from agencies with major water development responsibilities in the federal government. No fewer than forty-two of the reports listed in table B-1 deal with water. Some of these reports might well be considered primarily idea development and stimulation, but some are clearly planning studies as this term is used here. The water committee made large contributions to the techniques of water resource analysis and planning, which greatly affected the water planning and development of federal agencies during the existence of the NRPB and in the years since its demise.

2. *Public works coordination.* From its beginning as the National Planning Board, the NRPB sought to play a major role as a coordinator of public works for the federal government; and throughout its life it was resisted in this role by one or more of the federal agencies—the Corps of Engineers, in particular. "Coordination" could involve several activities: a direct engineering coordination, to insure that what one agency did was not negated by what another agency did, or that physical interference of one engineering development with another was held to a minimum; or it could mean planning whole river basins as units; or coordination in a fiscal and budget sense, to encourage public works during periods of depression and unemployment and to discourage them in periods of high economic activity; or coordination of public works at federal, state, and local levels of government. The NRPB got into all of these. With the signing of Executive Order 8455 on June 26, 1940, President Roosevelt imposed on the NRPB a detailed continuing responsibility for coordinating the public works program of all federal agencies (in cooperation with the Bureau of the Budget) and for reporting on such programs to the president.

3. *Formulation of national policy.* In one sense, this objective permeated all NRPB activities, but I include here those activities the prime

purpose of which was the development of proposals along lines or for subjects where national policy was unclear. Some of the reports that I would place in this category were prepared by individuals and published by the NRPB without endorsement by the Board—with specific disclaimer of such endorsement in some cases.

4. *Stimulation and aid in obtaining financing from other federal sources of state and local planning.* The NRPB's role in this regard has been described in chapter 6 and need not be repeated. One may simply say that state and local planning generally, and of natural resources in particular, got immense stimulus from the NRPB.

5. *Federal agency coordination other than public works coordination.* The NRPB on occasion tried to coordinate activities or programs of federal agencies other than their public works. It is hard to know how much of this it did or how effective it was; one suspects that its greatest triumphs were not recorded. Eliot and Merrill mention this activity but they are not very informative as to its effectiveness.[10]

Much of what the NRPB did in planning and coordination was more in the tradition of the city planning, with which Delano and Eliot had been identified, than it was in the tradition of the social science research with which Merriam had been identified. The efforts of planning and coordination were directed at more immediate, more specific, and more physical problems than were the efforts at idea development and stimulation. Immediate, practical results to clearly evident problems were sought. While the NRPB, as a federal agency, clearly had to work in a public arena, subject to public scrutiny and criticism, coordination is often best achieved quietly and in some degree of privacy.

Published Reports of the NRPB as a Measure of Its Activities

Much, but not all, of the NRPB's activities resulted in some form of published report. Their numbers, the variety of their subjects, and their length and complexity are a measure of the roles played by the NRPB. Information on the content of the major reports is presented in later chapters.

The pace of publication of major reports from the NRPB quickened throughout its lifetime (see table 7-1). In the days of the National Resources Board (July 1, 1934 to June 7, 1935) and the National

---

[10] Eliot and Merrill, *Guide to the Files*, pp. 103–104.

Table 7-1. Number and Length of Major Reports by National Resources Planning Board and Predecessor Agencies, 1934–43

General Subject[a]	Number and Length (in pages) of Major Reports											
	1934	1935	1936	1937	1938	1939	1940	1941	1942	1943	Undated	Total
Economics, no.	0	0	0	0	2	5	10	15	6	1	1	40
Length	0	0	0	0	381	1,278	680	1,655	1,105	25	60	5,184
Energy, no.	0	0	2	0	0	3	1	2	0	0	2	10
Length	0	0	112	0	0	871	86	88	0	0	275	1,432
General, no.	4	4	1	2	2	5	2	6	14	10	1	49
Length	606	219	61	331	200	745	96	308	1,066	692	111	4,435
Housing, no.	0	0	0	1	0	4	2	1	2	0	0	10
Length	0	0	0	561	0	263	280	20	55	0	0	1,179
Industry, no.	0	0	0	2	0	0	0	2	7	0	0	11
Length	0	0	0	369	0	0	0	259	676	0	0	1,304
Land, no.	0	1	0	0	2	0	4	2	4	0	1	14
Length	0	1,073	0	0	112	0	159	214	553	0	75	2,188

Planning, no.	0	4	8	11	17	14	13	13	16	9	2	107
Length	0	611	1,158	1,387	2,064	1,489	1,144	1,232	2,644	809	502	13,040
Population, no.	0	1	1	3	3	0	0	0	1	2	2	13
Length	0	63	64	219	421	0	0	0	111	263	177	1,318
Public works, no.	1	2	0	0	0	0	0	2	5	1	0	11
Length	182	326	0	0	0	0	0	108	748	90	0	1,454
Research, no.	0	0	0	0	3	1	1	1	1	0	0	7
Length	0	0	0	0	426	30	370	70	122	0	0	1,018
Transportation, no.	0	0	1	0	1	0	3	13	3	1	0	22
Length	0	0	164	0	71	0	227	1,215	608	49	0	2,334
War and postwar, no.	0	0	0	0	0	0	0	6	12	15	1	34
Length	0	0	0	0	0	0	0	452	694	1,052	56	2,254
Water, no.	1	10	5	5	5	2	6	0	3	5	0	42
Length	423	577	821	1,535	927	233	1,027	0	413	844	0	6,800
Total, no.	5	21	18	24	35	34	42	63	74	44	10	370
Length	1,211	2,869	2,380	4,402	4,602	4,909	4,069	5,621	8,795	3,824	1,256	43,938

a See table B-1 (appendix B-1) for more detail.

Resources Committee (June 8, 1935 to June 30, 1939), the number of reports did not exceed thirty-five in any year and in most years was considerably fewer. Under the NRPB, the pace of publication picked up to seventy-four reports in 1942 and to forty-four in the six months of 1943 that the NRPB was really operative. Had all the defense area impact reports been included in the list from which table 7-1 is calculated, this latter rate would have been much higher. The considerable increase in staff after 1939 was one factor in the increased rate of report production. Although the number of reports increased greatly, the quality, in my opinion, remained high.

"Customarily, 5,000 copies of major reports were ordered at the first printing, but this number has naturally varied with our estimate of the probable demand for different kinds of documents. As the supplies available were exhausted, reprints were ordered . . . Congress, itself, ordered reprints of some of the reports . . ."[11]

The NRPB, like many government agencies of that period, maintained many lists of names of persons or organizations with particular interests who had requested copies of reports, either all reports or reports on particular subjects. Eliot and Merrill itemize twenty-five such lists, including the number of names on each.[12] One may be sure that the organization sought to get its reports to persons and groups interested in them.

Table 7-1 gives some hints as to the very wide range of subject matter included in NRPB reports and in its activities as a whole. The most common general subject is "planning," with more than a fourth of all reports, covering a wide variety of subjects. Of continuing major interest were the reports on water, nearly all from the NRPB's water committee. There were many reports included under the general heading "economics" and these too included a wide range of specific subjects. War and postwar became the subjects of reports only in the last three years of the NRPB's life. Transportation, population, public works, industry, and energy were also categories in which several reports were issued at intervals throughout the life of the NRPB and its predecessors.

Nearly two-thirds of the NRPB reports described in table B-1 were mimeographed and only slightly more than a third were printed (table 7-2). In terms of pages, the printed reports were nearly as long in total as the mimeographed reports. While the proportion printed varied from

---

11 Ibid., p. 60.
12 Ibid., p. 71.

Table 7-2. Method of Reproduction and Plan of Publication of Reports of the National Resources Planning Board and Predecessors, by Number and Length (in pages), 1934–43

Year	Method of Reproduction			Total Reports	Where Report Issued	
	Printed	Mimeo-graphed	Other		Wash-ington	Region
1934, no.	3	2	0	5	5	0
Length	997	214	0	1,211	1,211	0
1935, no.	5	8	8	21	19	2
Length	1,827	574	468	2,869	2,791	78
1936, no.	8	10	0	18	16	2
Length	1,377	1,003	0	2,380	2,202	178
1937, no.	13	11	0	24	20	4
Length	1,980	2,422	0	4,402	3,379	1,023
1938, no.	16	19	0	35	25	10
Length	2,412	2,190	0	4,602	3,919	683
1939, no.	19	15	0	34	31	3
Length	2,641	2,268	0	4,909	4,527	382
1940, no.	15	25	2	42	35	7
Length	1,432	2,334	303	4,069	3,470	599
1941, no.	16	44	3	63	48	15
Length	1,641	3,516	464	5,621	4,264	1,357
1942, no.	23	49	2	74	57	17
Length	3,665	4,862	268	8,795	6,731	2,064
1943, no.	14	29	1	44	34	10
Length	1,435	2,364	25	3,824	2,969	855
Undated, no.	1	9	0	10	9	1
Length	12	1,244	0	1,256	1,200	56
Total, no.	133	221	16	370	299	71
Length	19,419	22,991	1,528	43,938	36,663	7,275

year to year, there is no clear trend toward or away from mimeographing. About a fifth of all the reports were issued in the regions; and there is no clear trend either toward or away from regional publication.

Some of the reports published by the NRPB were written by its more or less permanent staff members, and others were written by persons temporarily on its staff. Sometimes there was an advisory committee to aid the author(s), sometimes there seems to have been none, and it is difficult to know how much reliance was placed on such committees when they did exist. A great many of the shorter, often mimeographed, reports were written by NRPB staff. A large proportion of the reports came from committees organized by the NRPB.

The evaluation of the NRPB's performance in these different roles is postponed until chapter 22, but it may simply be said here that these various roles were, to a considerable degree, incompatible, and that no small part of the NRPB's problems arose because of this incompatibility.

III

SUBSTANTIVE FIELDS AND ACTIVITIES

8

NRPB Reports Concerning
Natural Resources

The 1934 Report

One of the earliest and one of the most outstanding reports by the NRPB and its predecessor organizations was *A Report on National Planning and Public Works in Relation to Natural Resources and Including Land Use and Water Resources with Findings and Recommendations.*[1] The report included 455 out-sized printed pages. First was the report of the Board itself; next the long reports of the Land and Water Committees; next the report of the Committee on Mineral Policy; and, finally, the brief report of the Board of Surveys and Maps. Each report contained a great deal of specific information, including many maps and some statistical tables. The writing was serious and sober but clear and not highly technical. This report, like virtually everything else written at this period, ignored the possibility of major war and its effects on demand and supply.

The report of the Board itself began with a relatively short statement of findings and recommendations. The findings and recommendations are numerous, detailed, and specific; there is repeated strong endorsement for continued planning under the National Resources Board or successor auspices to deal with each of the points made in the recommendations. The report of the Board is to a large extent a summary of the reports of its committees, and hence may be considered separately

---

[1] See chapter 4, p. 46.

for each committee. However, the summarization of the committee reports was constructive and their adoption by the Board was its endorsement of them. The report of the Board as a whole was circulated widely and each of its main committee reports was reprinted and distributed separately. The Board's report concluded with an abbreviation of that part of its June 1934 report which was "A Plan for Planning"—a strong statement on the necessity for a permanent national planning organization.

The Land Committee and Its Report

The Department of Agriculture (USDA) had been deeply into land planning before the National Planning Board was first created in 1933, and at the first meeting of that Board, representatives of the USDA appeared to discuss their land planning activity.[2] One result was the creation of a Land Planning Committee of the Board in the fall of 1933, with three representatives from Agriculture and three from Interior, Jacob Baker, and Eliot who also served as secretary. This committee had no chairman but met upon call of the secretary. The committee was formally recognized by the Land Grant College Association in late 1933 as the successor to the joint USDA–Land Grant College land use committee which had been operative for more than two years (see chapter 3).

In the spring of 1934, in one of those innovations not closely correlated with existing organizations for which President Roosevelt was so well known, a Committee on National Land Problems was created, consisting of the secretaries of agriculture and interior and the Federal Emergency Relief administrator. With the establishment of the National Resources Board, only a few months later, on June 1, 1934, this separate committee was abolished.

The Land Committee of the National Resources Board was soon chaired by M. L. Wilson, then an official in the Department of the Interior, later under secretary of the Department of Agriculture, and a well-known agricultural economist. Other members of the committee were major professional persons in the Departments of Agriculture and the Interior. The Director for the Land Section was L. C. Gray, who had been executive secretary of the National Land Use Planning Committee described in chapter 3; he was able to mobilize a large number of persons

---

[2] Charles W. Eliot, assisted by Harold Merrill, *Guide to the Files of the National Resources Planning Board and Predecessor Agencies, Ten Years of National Planning, 1933–1943*, Dec. 31, 1943.

in the USDA to assist in the committee's work and was able to draw upon a great deal of detailed research which had been carried out in the department in the previous decade or more, as well as to draw upon persons and work elsewhere in the federal establishment.

The report of the Land Planning Committee was divided into three major parts: conditions and tendencies influencing major land requirements; land requirements in relation to land resources, for the nation as a whole; and maladjustments in land use and in the relation of our population to land, and proposed lines of action. The first of these was in turn composed of three parts: the outlook for population; the outlook for industrial conditions and employment; and relation of mechanical progress in agriculture to land utilization and land policy. The population analysis was fairly standard demographic analysis of the time; it was clearly much influenced by the substantial decline in the birth rate in preceding years, especially in the preceding decade. "Soon after 1960 the population will have reached its greatest size and will begin to decline" (p. 95).

The short section on industrial conditions faced up resolutely to the severe decline in industrial output since 1929, though written shortly after the report of the Committee on Recent Social Trends and about contemporaneously with the Brookings "Capacity" studies, each of which had largely ignored the Great Depression. The report shows the uncertainty of its authors about future trends. "To the extent that . . . full utilization of our industrial resources and technological progress can be brought about, there will be demand and purchasing power in the cities to justify the use of a much larger area of land in agricultural production than would otherwise be the case" (p. 101).

The section on mechanical progress is very short and very general, yet it does raise significant questions. It will be recalled that, in 1934, American agriculture was still overwhelmingly animal-powered, and that the great majority of the farms lacked central power station electricity. The Land Committee was fully aware of the potentials for increased mechanization although there is nothing in the report to suggest that the committee foresaw the rapid rate of farm mechanization which was to ensue in the next two decades.

The second major part of the Land Committee's report, on land requirements, is notable for the breadth of its interest and concern, even though many of its specific conclusions have proven to be wide of the mark. There is an extended analysis of agricultural land requirements,

balancing up the expected demand for agricultural commodities as estimated from the demographic and other data, with expected future trends
in crop yields per acre. Evidence is presented that crop yields per acre
for important crops had not been trending upward over the past several
decades and may have been trending slightly downward; this was before
the agricultural revolution of the next few decades was apparent at all.
With the aid of hindsight we can now realize that the role of drought
and of expansion onto drier Great Plains and other western lands in
holding down crop yields was much underestimated. There was virtually
no recognition that the imminent rapid trend toward farm mechanization
would free many millions of crop acres from the production of feed for
workstock, so that these lands could produce food for humans, or that
mechanization would increase the demand for fossil fuels. The conclusion was stated (p. 126) "Although . . . it probably will be necessary by
1960 to add considerably to our crop acreage, there is no immediate
necessity for such action. In fact, for the next few years ahead or until
there is a decided improvement in both domestic and foreign demand
for our agricultural products, we shall need to shrink our present crop
area." As it turned out, of course, by 1960 the surplus of crop area was
vastly greater than it had been in 1934.

What was remarkable in the report dealing with land requirements
was its extended treatment of the need for forestland, recreation land,
land for wildlife purposes, and land for other purposes. The analysis of
forestland requirements was made by the Forest Service. While its
authors felt (p. 143) that the long-term productivity of the nation's
forests "would exceed by a safe margin the estimated current normal consumption of timber . . . it must be recognized, however, that at least 40
years would be required to build the forest up to this productivity" and
"this points inevitably to a deficiency of timber supply, judged in terms
of present standards of consumption, during the interim between the
exhaustion of virgin stumpage and the realization of full yields from the
second-growth forests." While this report is less inaccurate in projecting
future timber demands and supply than have been most Forest Service
projections, this relatively better showing was due to the assumption of a
continuation of the extremely low level of consumption of wood products
in the early 1930s.[3] In the years since then, timber growth and timber

---

[3] Marion Clawson, "Forests in the Long Sweep of American History," *Science,*
vol. 204, no. 4398 (June 15, 1979) pp. 1168–1174.

consumption have each risen far more than the committee foresaw, and timber inventories have been built up at the same time.

The sections dealing with land requirements for recreation and wildlife are not very sophisticated by modern standards of land requirement analysis, but in terms of the data and the understanding then available they are very good.

The longest part of the report of the Land Committee is concerned with maladjustments in land use and in proposed lines of action. This also includes analysis of agricultural, range, forest, recreational, wildlife, Indian, public, tax-reverted, and other special land situations. One major adjustment proposed was the public acquisition of five million acres of farmland annually for fifteen years, or 75 million acres in total. The report also recommended the public acquisition of 244 million acres for timber production and an additional 114 million acres for recreation, wildlife, and similar purposes. Although some private land was purchased by the federal government in the following decade, nothing remotely close to this acreage has been purchased. Other specific recommendations were made for soil erosion control. The Land Committee also called attention to the need for better coordination among federal agencies, and to some extent between them and state agencies, in the land acquisition in which many agencies were then engaged. The need for a permanent effective overall national planning agency was developed seriously, and rather more quietly than in those NRPB reports which generally made the same point later.

The Water Committee and Its Report

Even before the Water Committee of the National Planning Board was established, Federal Works Administrator Harold L. Ickes had created a Mississippi Valley Committee, which had reviewed reservoir projects proposed for construction and whose report on water development in that region was submitted to Ickes in October 1934 and sent to the Congress.[4] Concurrently with these activities, the president had appointed, not as a part of the NRPB, a Special Committee on Water Flow, for which Eliot served as secretary and which completed its report by assembling agency projects.[5] Its report is shown as number 4 in table

---

[4] Report of the Mississippi Valley Committee of the Public Works Administration (Washington, D.C., GPO, 1934).

[5] Eliot and Merrill, *A Guide to the Files,* p. 108.

B-1, although it is not, strictly speaking, an NRPB report. The National Resources Board's Water Committee was composed of men who had served on the PWA Mississippi Valley Committee. Both committees were chaired by Morris L. Cooke, a person who played a number of roles in the New Deal Administration and who at that time was a consulting private engineer. Two members of the committee were from the U.S. Corps of Engineers; the others were from universities or other private employment, but represented wide experience with the Bureau of Reclamation, the Miami Conservancy District, and the new Tennessee Valley Authority.

The report of the Water Committee was, in some respects, even more outstanding than the report of the Land Committee. A substantial number of regional and specialized reports had been prepared for the Water Committee by consultants (many or most of them unpaid) in various parts of the country. One-half million words of such specialized reports were summarized into 70,000 words in the committee report.

The water report was divided into three sections: principles and policies of use and control of water resources; inventory and use of water resources; and special aspects of water problems. The report includes a considerable number of maps, many folded (even into these large-size pages), some in color (which in those days was less common and far more expensive than now), and a considerable number of charts and statistical tables. The text is serious in tone but well and clearly written and readily understandable by nonspecialists. Much of the discussion starts at a basic or fundamental level and proceeds quickly to important policy issues. Emphasis is placed on the unity of water development within each river basin or system and upon the use of water for multiple purposes.

The signed report of the Water Committee includes a section of recommendations: for the making of surveys, inventories, and records of conditions fundamental for the use and control of water resources; for an exhaustive study of needed federal and state legislation; for selective experimentation in regional planning; for planning of specific projects; and for an organization for advisory planning of the use and control of water. The last bears great resemblance to the National Resources Board under whose direction the Water Committee had worked.

This part of the Water Committee report is then followed by a long section, inventory and use of water resources, which describes in modest detail each kind of water use—irrigation, water power, recreation, as well as such things as floods, droughts, public water supplies, drainage, waste disposal, and the like. The detail in each section is limited by the overall length of the report, of course, but one is impressed with the scope of the committee's thinking and with the great amount of information conveyed.

The final part of the Water Committee's report consists of six signed essays by consultants: identification of benefits from public works; costs and utilities of water and land transport; conservation and use of water on farms in humid areas; legislative aspects of the use and control of water resources; international aspects of water allocation and use; and government control over water resources in certain European countries. The fourth of these consisted of a summarization of four regional reports on legislation, each compiled by consultants to the committee.

The report on mineral policy was prepared by a committee, of which Harold L. Ickes was nominal chairman, but the committee's report is signed by C. K. Leith, vice chairman, whom one may reasonably assume did most of the directing of the work. Most of the committee's members were federal employees, and the assistance of several federal agencies and members of their staffs is acknowledged. The style of this report is rather different from that of either the Land or the Water Committee; it is shorter, with far less specific data (many major sections or subdivisions are only one or two pages in length), and one has the impression that the committee expected the reader to accept its judgment rather than seeking to inform the reader with data and information. But, especially in view of the state of professional analysis of mineral problems then extant, it is an outstanding report.

There is a short section on the need for a national policy. This is followed by a relatively long section which is divided into many subsections: depletion and the growing handicaps of mining; forecasts of mineral consumption; conservational problems arising from surplus of production or plant capacity for coal, petroleum, copper, lead, and zinc; conservational problems arising from deficiency of domestic supply; minerals and the problem of monopoly; minerals on public lands; extension of government ownership; submarginal minerals and mineral lands; taxation; scrap metals; use of the State's police powers for conservation; scientific and engineering approach to conservation; health and safety; and federal agencies of mineral administration. While this range of coverage is very wide, the depth of analysis in each is less than in comparable sections of the land and water reports. For instance, the section of forecasts of mineral consumption is nonquantitative, and without much apparent economics underlying it, in sharp contrast to the sections of the land report dealing with future requirements.

It is noteworthy that this report of the Minerals Policy Committee does not have a section dealing with energy as such, nor is there such a section in the report as a whole. The Minerals Policy Committee did consider coal and petroleum, but separately, and with no attempt to cover the whole range of energy sources, uses, and demands.

The third major section of the Mineral Policy Committee report is concerned with international aspects. It too is very brief and quite general, without much data and with almost no economic analysis.

The final section of the report as a whole is from the Board of Surveys and Maps, composed of men from many federal agencies but no nongovernmental members. It emphasizes the need for accurate maps for all land, water, mineral, and other programs; describes briefly the current status of mapping in the United States; and presents a program, including budget estimates, for completion of the mapping to a scale and detail which it thought necessary.

We may conclude this consideration of the 1934 report by saying that it would be an outstanding report today, by whoever might compile it and with whatever time the compilers may have had; given the state of knowledge in 1934, given the lack of data on many important matters, and given the short time for its preparation, the result is impressive indeed. In my view, this was the National Resources Planning Board at its very best. It should be noted further that this was done when the Board had only a very small staff—that the report was compiled primarily by consultants recruited from various federal agencies and from nongovernmental origins. How far was the outstanding quality of the report due to its origins? It is true that the NRPB was fortunate in finding many able persons in government and elsewhere who were eager to pool their knowledge into such comprehensive syntheses. But it is equally true that the NRPB was skillful in the way it took advantage of this opportunity.

With justifiable pride and with only slight exaggeration, the Board in the foreword to its report (p. v) says:

> This report of the President's National Resources Board brings together, for the first time in our history, exhaustive studies by highly competent inquirers of land use, water use, minerals, and related public works in their relation to each other and to national planning. The report lays the basis of a comprehensive long-range national policy for

the conservation and development of our fabulous natural resources. If the recommendations contained herein are put into effect, it is believed that they will end the untold waste of our national domain now, and will measurably enrich and enlarge these national treasures as time goes on.

Subsequent History and Work of the Water Committee

In preparing the Mississippi Valley Committee (MVC) and the December 1934 reports, Morris Cooke had been interested primarily in national power policy; the major thrust of the MVC report was the establishment of the Rural Electrification Administration of which he became the first head. Harlow S. Person served as acting director of the water section of the NRB for some months, during which time a number of committees or subcommittees were organized to follow up on recommendations or proposals of the committees just described.

With the establishment of the National Resources Committee on June 8, 1935, the new MVC moved to place its Water Committee on a firmer continuing basis. A senior person from each federal agency with major responsibility in the water field was named to the new committee. In addition, three unusually able men from outside of government were named to the committee: Abel Wolman, professor of sanitary engineering at Johns Hopkins University; Harlan H. Barrows, professor of geography at the University of Chicago; and Thorndike Saville, dean of the College of Engineering, New York University. The first two of these served on the committee until March 1941 and the third served on it until the NRPB was terminated. While there were other nonfederal members, these three were outstanding because of their ability, long association together, and long service on the committee. Wolman was chairman of the committee throughout his tenure on it. Gilbert F. White was made secretary of the committee and was a major factor in its productivity.[6]

In appendix B, I list forty-three reports with about six thousand pages as being primarily concerned with water; in their report, Eliot and Merrill list fifty-nine reports as being concerned with water. Their list is more extensive than mine largely because they include progress reports and other reports of the parent organization, which contained important sections on water but which as a whole were not on water. Many of the reports in each list were only mimeographed, as table B-1 shows, many

---

[6] Ibid., pp. 109–110.

were rather short, many were quite technical, and probably had only limited circulation to water specialists. However, such reports were very influential with this group and made a substantial impact on water planning during that era.

A brief review of some of the reports issued from the work of the Water Committee will show the nature of its work. In December 1936 (two years after the monumental report described in the preceding section), the National Resources Committee published *Drainage Basin Problems and Programs,* consisting of 540 large size printed pages, with numerous maps, charts, and tables (see item 41 in table B-1). In its letter of transmittal to Delano, the committee said as follows:

> These studies were undertaken early in 1936 at the request of the National Resources Committee, with the following objectives:
> (1) To determine the principal water problem in the various drainage areas of the country,
> (2) To outline an integrated pattern of water development and control designed to solve these problems, and
> (3) To present specific construction projects and investigation projects as elements of the integrated pattern or plan, with priorities of importance and time.
> The findings of the investigation are reasonably clear on the first and second items of the assignment. The third item presented special difficulties, particularly since it necessitated review and appraisal by the Committee of thousands of projects, aggregating billions of dollars in estimated cost and relating to water-resources development, during a period of some 10 years. It was impossible in the time available for all members of the Committee to pass on all the projects. Individual responsibility of members of the Committee for final classification is therefore not to be assumed. (p. v)

The latter part of this statement was a delicate reference, fully understood by the principals and all other knowledgeable people, to the fact that the Corps of Engineers was doing its best to deny the legitimacy of the NRPB's work in the water field and to its complete refusal to rank its projects according to any priorities.[7]

The report itself is a most impressive document. There is a short general summary, followed by a discussion of water problems and pro-

---

[7] Interview with Abel Wolman, August 25, 1978, and my discussions with the late Harlan H. Barrows during the early 1940s. See also Philip L. White, "The Termination of the National Resources Planning Board" (master's thesis, Columbia University, 1949); and Philip W. Warken, "A History of the National Resources Planning Board, 1933–1943" (doctoral dissertation, Ohio State University, 1969).

grams for each of the eighteen major water districts into which the whole country was divided; and this in turn is followed by fairly detailed discussion of ninety-four individual river basins which made up the eighteen major districts. Each district and basin report includes a detailed listing of all proposed water development projects in the area, classified as "Group A—for immediate investigation or construction; Group B—for deferred construction; and Group C—time of construction indeterminate."

In response to the president's directive of August 1937, the committee prepared a revision of its 1936 report, which was issued by the NRC in February 1938 (see item 78 in table B-1). About the same time, a series of reports from regional planning commissions, each of which is described on its face as "drafted in the field . . ." were published both separately and bound together (see item 66 in table B-1). These latter clearly involve the participation of large numbers of persons in each region. Although these reports are characterized as material for the 1937 revision, they are almost the same regional and drainage basin reports included in the committee report published earlier in December 1936.

The 1937 revision closely follows the format of the 1936 report but is shorter. The six-year recommended program would cost nearly $900 million in (presumably) then current prices, which would be about twelve times that amount in 1979 prices.

After these comprehensive reports on water problems in different parts of the country, the Water Committee continued to do outstanding work, but its publications were, generally, more highly specialized.[8]

The Water Resources Committee of the NRPB made a major and lasting contribution to the planning of water use and development in the United States. In making that assertion, I am aware of how difficult it is to measure the impact of any organization on the course of history. Nevertheless, taking full account of the difficulties of precise identification of cause and sequence, and realizing full well that many of these items are matters of degree as well as of kind, I list the following major contributions of the Water Resources Committee of the NRPB to water use, development, and policy in the United States:

1. It more accurately and fully defined the data requirements for competent water resource planning than had been done prior to its work

---

[8] Reports dealing explicitly with water, listed in table B-1 are, among others: items 39, 86, 94, 115, 128, 139, 142, 145, 151, 167, 235, 257, 277, 319, 340, and 356.

and it did a great deal to improve the coverage and the quality of water data.

2. It developed, if in fact it did not introduce, the concepts of coordinated or unified and multiple-purpose water development for a whole river basin, cogently pointing out that water development in any part of a basin unavoidably affects water use and water quality in other parts of the same basin and that the same water often has value for several purposes.

3. It assembled a vast amount of data for every river basin in the country—the best data then available. The result was a more accurate and more detailed picture of water resources, water problems, and development possibilities than had ever been available previously.

4. It contributed greatly to a better coordination among federal agencies concerned with water development. One can hardly claim complete success here—the resistance of the Corps of Engineers has been noted—nevertheless significant progress was made, and no longer did each agency operate as if it had the whole river to itself alone.

5. It contributed greatly to the idea of ranking proposed water development projects according to some priority scale. Again, its success was less than complete, and for the same reason as in the foregoing point. But no agency was ever again as comfortable in its efforts to pretend that everything it did was equally and highly valuable.

6. As part of the foregoing, it contributed greatly to the idea of benefit–cost analysis as applied to water development projects. While much of its contribution here was not highly technical, compared with more recent economic analysis applied to water development, the committee's work in this regard was basic and influential.

7. It stimulated the practice of cooperation among the different functional agencies properly involved in water planning at local and state levels.

There have been many studies of water use and development in the United States since the NRPB expired in the summer of 1943.[9] Many of them have been conducted by men active with the NRPB Water

---

[9] For a thorough and detailed history of water resource programs see: Beatrice Hort Holmes, *A History of Federal Water Resource Programs 1800–1960*, (U.S. Department of Agriculture, Miscellaneous Publication No. 1233, Washington, D.C., 1972); and Beatrice Hort Holmes, *History of Federal Water Resource Programs and Policies, 1961–70* (U.S. Department of Agriculture, Economics, Statistics, and Cooperatives Service, Miscellaneous Publication No. 1379, Washington, D.C., September 1979).

Committee. Some have dealt with specific river basins, such as the
Colorado or the Missouri, or otherwise have been less national in their
scope; others have dealt with only certain aspects of water development.
A few have had or sought to have national coverage of water use for
all purposes.[10] Each of these reports owes a debt explicitly, and even
more implicitly, to the work of the NRPB Water Committee. While new
methods have been developed, new data have been made available in
many ways, new demands for water have emerged, and even some new
concepts of resource development have evolved, yet every one of these
and other reports that might be listed is a direct descendant of the work
of the NRPB Water Committee.

Subsequent History and Work of the Land Committee

Following publication of the 1934 report, the National Resources Board
almost immediately published a two-volume back-up analysis, in itself
a significant contribution to the professional literature (see item 20,
table B-1). After that, the Land Planning Committee hibernated, partly
because the USDA participants in the 1934 report, led by Gray, became
deeply and totally involved in that Department's land programs. In addition, M. L. Wilson shortly became under secretary of agriculture, a
post which demanded his full time and energy. Although he remained
chairman of the NRB–NRC Land Planning Committee through 1936, he
apparently was not active. Table B-1 shows that no further reports from
the Land Committee were published until 1938. The feud between
Ickes and Wallace at this time, arising out of Ickes' determination to
have the Forest Service transferred to his department, was a further
inhibiting factor.[11]

In late 1938 the Land Committee was reorganized and members
from outside of government were added; William I. Myers, then or

---

[10] The *Report* in three volumes of the President's Water Resource Policy Commission, in 1950; parts of the report, *Resources for Freedom,* by the President's
Materials Policy Commission, in 1952; USDA Yearbook of Agriculture, *Water,*
1955; *Water Supply and Demand,* Committee Print No. 32, Senate Select Committee on National Water Resources, 86th Congress, 2d Session, 1960; Nathaniel
Wollman and Gilbert W. Bonem, *The Outlook for Water—Quality, Quantity, and
National Growth* (Baltimore, Johns Hopkins University Press, 1971). Wollman
was also the author of the Senate report. See also many publications of the Water
Resources Council, a federal organization created, at least in part, to fill the role of
the NRPB Water Committee.

[11] Personal letter from Eliot, December 21, 1979.

shortly dean of agriculture at Cornell University, became chairman and continued in this role as long as the NRPB continued.

During these later years the Land Committee authored a number of published reports. Eliot and Merrill (pp. 119–120) list seventeen reports involving land, in addition to the reports described above. I list thirteen during the same period: I include some mimeographed reports they omit, while they include some general reports which had important land sections (some of which they also include in their list of water reports) which I omit. All of the reports after 1938 were specialized by topic or regional in scope or both; there was nothing after this date of both inclusive subject matter coverage and inclusive geographic coverage.[12]

While there have been a great many public and private studies of land use in the United States since the NRPB expired, perhaps none of them achieves the comprehensiveness of the 1934 report, discussed earlier.

My judgment is that the Land Committee of the NRPB and its predecessors was, on the whole, less effective and less influential in a professional sense than was the Water Committee. There are several reasons, I believe, why this was so. First, the Land Committee lacked the dedicated kind of chairman the Water Committee had during so much of its life. Wilson was able, but was absorbed in other interests, and his tenure on the committee was limited. Something of the same thing could be said for Myers, and the considerable interval between Wilson's active chairmanship and Myers' assumption of the chairmanship left the Land Committee without much leadership for that period. Second, because there was vastly more research and planning on land than on water in the regular Departments of Agriculture and Interior, the NRPB had a somewhat less distinctive role in land research and planning. We have noted that L. C. Gray and several others who played major roles in the 1934 report shortly ceased to be associated with the NRPB's activities. In 1938, Secretary Wallace reorganized the USDA and gave the Bureau of Agricultural Economics major responsibility for land use planning in agricultural and rural counties throughout the nation. This, at the minimum, siphoned off some of the interest in land planning to which the NRPB otherwise may have drawn. Third, there was no simple theme to unite land use planning such as there was for water. The obvious fact that the water in a watershed ran downhill, and that all water use was therefore inevitably interrelated, made it clear that coordinated

---

[12] The pertinent reports listed in table B-1 are: items 82, 91, 140, 150, 168, 178, 185, 189, 283, 301, 303, and 311.

water use planning was sensible. While there was much talk about multiple land use planning, the logic for it was not as compelling as for water.

Nevertheless the Land Committee did a great deal of excellent work. Its reports merit closer scrutiny than they have received, and fare well by comparison with more recent studies.

Minerals and Energy

The NRPB's work on minerals and energy was, on the whole, less well organized and less voluminous than its work on either water or land. The story of its activities is somewhat confusing because of the formation and operation of several committees, some not directly under the NRPB and its predecessors, and because some of the work relating to minerals and to a lesser degree to energy was published in some of the NRPB reports relating to industries.

In May 1934 President Roosevelt, acting upon a suggestion of the Science Advisory Board of the National Academy of Sciences, established a special Planning Committee for Mineral Policy under the chairmanship of Secretary of the Interior Harold L. Ickes.[13] When the National Resources Board was organized that summer under Ickes' chairmanship, this committee became the Mineral Policy Committee, which prepared the 1934 report discussed earlier in this chapter. Various special projects were undertaken by this committee, but it was discontinued in January 1936 and its functions transferred to the NRC, which by that time had succeeded the NRB.

In the meantime, the NRB had undertaken a survey of energy sources by an Exploratory Committee on Competing Fuels. Also in the meantime, the president in July 1934 had established a National Power Policy Committee. These various committees were composed of federal employees and there was considerable overlapping membership among them. The latter committee underwent name, organizational, and membership changes as time went on, particularly as war drew near and then was actually upon the country. While these committees were closely related to the NRPB, in part because Ickes played a major role in each, they were not formally a part of the NRPB and I do not attempt here to trace their meetings or their output.

---

[13] Eliot and Merrill, *A Guide to the Files*, pp. 122–139.

The National Resources Committee's serious and comprehensive work on energy began in 1938 with the appointment of Ralph J. Watkins from the University of Pittsburgh as chairman of the Energy Resources Committee and also as director of the NRPB's energy research staff. The committee was composed of federal employees. Watkins drew several competent economists to this staff. Under his leadership, a comprehensive report on *Energy Resources and National Policy* was prepared during 1938, transmitted by the NRC to the president and by him to the Congress in early 1939, and very shortly printed (see item 104 in table B-1). Thus energy, three or four years after water and land, became the subject of a comprehensive study.

This report is an impressive document. It begins with a brief summary of the long committee report, which has four main parts: (1) Energy resources industries; (2) Energy reserves; (3) Technology and conservation; and (4) Evolving public policy.

Watkins and some of his staff had economics or business school backgrounds and they sought to introduce economic analysis into the consideration of energy resources and use. A vast lot of information is presented in charts, tables, and text.

This report was outstanding for its time, but seems less so by the standards of present day energy analysis. The economic analysis is more descriptive than conceptual or theoretical; there is no summarization of all kinds of energy into a single balance sheet; and the demand analysis for energy is not developed in the conventional demographic, economic, and technological terms common today. But it surely marked a great step forward in the application of economic concepts to energy problems and was highly influential at the time. The energy committee continued through the life of the NRPB.

One or another of the committees produced several rather specialized or technical reports on minerals and energy for the NRPB, which are listed in table B-1.[14]

It is interesting and probably significant that the NRPB never had a minerals committee as such, nor did it ever produce a report summarizing the national situation for nonfuel minerals in a manner comparable to its major national reports for water, land, and energy. There is consideration of some minerals in the 1934 report and in later reports, but

---

[14] The pertinent reports listed in table B-1 are: items 28, 34, 117, 119, 157, 220, and 233.

it is more or less incidental to other major objectives of the reports in question.

There have been, of course, a great many public and private studies of energy and of minerals in the years since the NRPB was terminated. I shall not attempt to list them, much less to comment upon them. I have the strong impression that the NRPB mineral and energy studies, while important—even path-breaking for their day—have had less impact on developments since the termination of the NRPB than its studies on land and water have had in their respective fields.

Summary and Evaluation of the NRPB's Activities in Natural Resources

As one contemplates the reports discussed in this chapter, and the NRPB activities which lay behind the reports, certain conclusions stand out.

1. The NRPB (and, of course, its predecessor organizations) played a highly important role in the consideration of natural resources during the years of its existence. It may fairly be judged to have been the most important and most influential federal agency with such concerns.

2. The NRPB's role was to summarize and synthesize existing information and to call attention to natural resource problems. From a purely intellectual or professional point of view, and according to the state of knowledge and of professional expertise of the day, its work in these roles was outstanding. Some of its reports even read very well in light of today's knowledge and today's expertise.

3. The NRPB mobilized existent expertise and knowledge very effectively and very efficiently. Its use of committees was particularly effective in this regard. Men from all over the federal government and, especially in the case of the Water Committee, from all over the nation were drawn together, to work at minimum cost to the country and to mobilize a great deal of information and knowledge which they had gained from their experience. The NRPB's success in this regard was perhaps greater at the beginning than at the end of its life.

4. Circumstances, economic and otherwise, in the country much favored this type of committee work during the NRPB's early days. Many professional men were eager to make their input into reports which would be given national circulation, and to do so, in many cases, without direct financial benefit to themselves. There was, in addition,

a great deal of valuable information existent which had not been drawn together and synthesized but which could be so drawn together rather easily. Once the first big syntheses were completed, this type of activity had less utility—there was no need to repeat the 1934 report immediately, for instance, and there was not enough truly new material to justify another such report until a few years had passed. If the NRPB had continued permanently, it is altogether possible that in the immediate postwar years it would have undertaken a new set of comprehensive resource reviews.

5. The various reports of the NRPB discussed in this chapter in almost all cases made recommendations. They were not simply fact-finding and reporting, nor did they content themselves with analyzing alternatives, although there was much of both of these activities. Instead, the writers of these reports had convictions and they expressed them, typically in forthright language. Recommendations were made to the intellectual community at large, to federal agencies, to the business community, and for legislation.

6. Although some of the NRPB's recommendations aroused some opposition in the Congress, among the federal agencies (the Corps of Engineers, in particular), and outside of government, on the whole its reports in these fields commanded substantial approval and support.

As I contemplate this record, and as I think ahead to the story which will be told in the next few chapters, I must speculate on what should have happened had the NRPB largely confined its activities to the kind of studies of natural resources described in this chapter and refrained very largely from at least some of the kinds of activities described in the next few chapters. Its role would have been more limited but might have been fully as effective and the agency might have survived longer. To quote the old Mother Goose rhyme, "Had the boat been stronger, my tale would have been longer."

9

NRPB Reports Concerning People and Their Lives

All NRPB research and reports were concerned with people; we noted in chapter 8 that its concern with natural resources was a concern over how the use of natural resources affected people. But some NRPB reports dealt with people as subjects or objects of the inquiry—their demography, their housing, their research activities, and their welfare and security from adversity. These are the subjects of this chapter.

Population Studies

The 1934 report, in its section on land use and land requirements, considered population factors. In a style which has become very common in the years since then, population projections were made as basic to the analysis of future demand or future requirements for some natural resource. But in the 1930s this method of analysis was much less common. The 1934 report did not employ this approach in considering future demand for water, metals, or energy minerals.

By the early 1930s many intellectuals were informed and concerned about the economic and social consequences of the clearly evident decline in birth rates in the United States. Such persons believed that the rate of population growth, then slowing down, would before long become zero, and then, later, actual declines in total population would occur.[1] However, this knowledge and this concern were not widespread in popular, governmental, business, and professional circles. The United States had grown steadily in total population from its earliest colonial days; the first census in 1790 had shown about 4 million people and the 1930 census showed about 123 million. The general expectation was that population numbers would continue to increase; such continued increase was built into nearly every business and governmental decision, as well as being deeply embedded in the thinking and feeling of ordinary persons. In the early 1930s the idea that population in the United States would cease to grow came as a shock to many people, and, as a consequence, the NRPB's studies on this subject were upsetting to many persons.

The NRPB established a Science Committee in 1935. Three members were designated by each of the National Academy of Sciences, the Social Science Research Council, and the American Council on Education. It, in turn, established a Committee on Population Problems, some of whose members were drawn from the parent committee and others were well-known demographers from universities. The Committee on Population Problems acquired a technical staff of several persons knowledgeable about and experienced in population studies, and drew upon scholars from different fields and different locations to produce a major report, *The Problems of a Changing Population,* in May 1938. The report includes 306 pages, of the large size chosen for NRPB reports. It contained a great many maps, charts, and tables. By any standards, it was a truly major professional inquiry and report.

In a summary the committee presents its conclusions and makes modest recommendations. While the report is primarily a demographic and sociological study of people, it contains a good deal of economic analysis. As the foreword says (p. 5):

> It cannot be too strongly emphasized . . . that this report deals not merely with problems regarding the quantity, quality, and distribution of population, important as they are, but also with the widening of opportunities for the individuals making up this population, no matter how many or where they are. In our democratic system we must progressively make available to all groups what we assume to be American standards of life.

---

[1] I encountered this intellectual position among some of my colleagues in my early days in the Bureau of Agricultural Economics in the years immediately following 1929.

The committee report in its first major section traces the growth of population in the United States, with particular emphasis upon the slowing down in the rate of that growth. Various estimates of future population are given, with population expected to reach a peak sometime between 1955 and 1980 at a peak level of somewhere between 138 and 155 million persons.[2] In fact, of course, population is still increasing in 1980 and has now reached a level of about 220 million. This section of the report concludes (p. 8):

> The gradual slowing down of population growth is due to social changes taking place throughout the whole civilized world. The trend toward cessation of natural increase and toward an increase in the proportion of older people will not necessarily lead to unhappy results, though these changes raise problems that need careful consideration. There is no reason for the hasty adoption of any measures designed to stimulate population growth in this country.
>
> Problems relating to the welfare of persons past middle life are becoming increasingly urgent. In addition to provisions for insurance and other old age benefits, attention should be given to opportunities for and conditions of employment of older workers not ready for retirement. There should be consideration of further possibilities for adult education and other measures for enhancing the usefulness and increasing the joy of persons in the later middle and last years of life.

The second main part of the committee's report is concerned with population distribution and redistribution. It is pointed out that there then existed a substantial imbalance between population numbers and economic opportunity in various regions; the cutover regions of the northern Lake States and the Great Plains are particularly pointed to. Curiously enough, in light of discussions in more recent decades, the Appalachians are not so singled out for mention. This section concludes with a number of suggestions for facilitating population readjustment and for improving economic opportunity in the regions of lowest per capita incomes.

The third main part of the committee's report deals with the conservation of human resources, particularly education and welfare measures for the severely disadvantaged groups. It cautiously concludes (p. 12):

---

[2] Had the committee clearly described its estimates as "projections," based upon certain assumptions as to future birth, death, and immigration rates, they could not have been wrong, even though they missed the mark. While it did not explicitly label its estimates as "forecasts," the language it used to describe them fairly reasonably leads one today, as it led people at the time, to regard such estimates as forecasts of what it actually expected to happen.

Questions relating to qualitative population trends call for more extensive study. There is need for further definition and measurement of physical and mental characteristics influencing health and personality, and study of conditions affecting individual development. There is also need for the systematic investigation of the influence on the size of family of various economic, social, and psychological factors, about which very little is known at the present time.

The fourth main part of the committee's report is rather longer than each of the foregoing and is concerned with opportunity for individual development. This includes particularly consideration of public health programs, educational programs, and cultural development generally. This section of the report concludes, in part, as follows (pp. 15–16):

> The health of the country has been greatly improved by advances in medical science and their application through public health administration . . . More than half the occupied hospital beds in this country are assigned to patients suffering from mental diseases. The social, economic, and medical aspects of these diseases, whereof the causes are still largely unknown, are very serious. They deserve the most intensive study . . . There is clear evidence of gross inequality in educational opportunity in different parts of the country . . . Social forces affecting the life of the people of the United States today are of the greatest complexity. The traditional ways of living of those who comprise the Nation have been in many cases destroyed by migration to new scenes, the conditions of urban living, and the impact of new techniques of production and communication . . . There is need for the coordination, critical interpretation, and dissemination to the whole country of the results of significant advances in educational research and administration.

The fifth and last section of the committee's report was concerned with research on population problems. A number of specific and practical suggestions for improved research and for better data collection were made; some of these are substantially dated and need not be described in detail here.

This population study by the NRPB committee brought together the best knowledge the United States then had about its population. As such, it was a major contribution. It focused intellectual and popular attention in this country on population problems. Its forecasts of future population numbers, however, were woefully in error—an error that consisted primarily of extrapolation into a distant future of trends apparent only for a few past years. In particular, it did not foresee the "baby boom"—

the upsurge in the birth rate that began in the late 1940s and continued into the early 1960s. Joseph S. Davis, in general a severe but just critic of population forecasting, says of the NRPB 1938 report, "Accurate prophecies of the actual growth in the 1940s, and of the rise in birth rates that has contributed most to this growth, would surely have seemed incredible if not fantastic to the able scholars who produced this work, as well as to most of its readers. Even in retrospect it is not easy to account for so extraordinary a change."[3]

The NRPB Population Committee forecasts for various regions were even more markedly wrong. In general, the tremendous growth in population in the West and in the Sun Belt were underestimated and the depopulation of large areas was largely overlooked. For national or regional planning organizations which attempted to develop plans based on expected demand, these errors in population forecasts were serious indeed. Aside from those erroneous population forecasts, the rest of the report stands up very well indeed—the trends and the problems it notes are, in very large measure, the trends and the problems of today also.

This report, *as such,* drew much interest but not severe adverse reaction at the time. There was, however, a great deal of adverse reaction to some other NRPB writings which were, more or less explicitly, based on this population study. One such was the major report on welfare, security, and relief (discussed later in this chapter). Another was a pamphlet produced for the NRPB by Harvard professor Alvin Hansen, which dealt with the role of the federal government in achieving full employment (discussed in chapter 10). Each of these drew major policy conclusions from the judgment that we were rapidly approaching a stable population, which was one of the 1938 population report's main conclusions. But the adverse reaction to these latter two reports was due primarily to the policy conclusions they drew, not to the basic population analysis of the 1938 report.

Both prior to and after the 1938 report, the NRPB issued some rather specialized population studies (see items 22, 23, 57, 58, 59, and 98 in table B-1). In July 1938 the NRPB published a short pamphlet, *Population Problems,* which very well summarized the long report described above. There was virtually no output from the Population Committee thereafter until 1943, when, in August, as one of its very last publications

---

[3] Joseph S. Davis, *The Population Upsurge in the United States,* War-Peace Pamphlet no. 12 (Food Research Institute, Stanford University, December 1949) p. 19.

before its termination, the NRPB published *Estimates of Future Popula-*
tion of the United States, 1940–2000, a 137-page printed report consisting very largely of tables showing estimated future population numbers
by age and sex groups, under different assumptions as to future birth and
death rates. These were projections based on data from the 1940 census,
among other sources. They resulted in considerably higher projected
future populations, with much later dates of population peaking, than
did the 1938 report. However, as a forecast, they are still far too low.
The medium-fertility medium-projection calls for a population that peaks
about 1980 or 1990 at about 160 to 165 million (depending upon
assumptions as to immigration), while even the high-fertility medium-
mortality projection, which does not peak before 2000, contemplates a
population in 2000 of 190 to 200 million (again depending on assumptions as to immigration)—each far below the 220 million population
that actually exists in 1980.

One of the most curious of the NRPB's publishing ventures, which
raises many questions in my mind about its operations, falls in the
population field. In 1942, well after the war was on and when the NRPB
was under attack in the Congress for, among other matters, its lack of
relevance to the war effort, it produced a mimeographed report (item
293 in table B-1), *The Wastage of Human Resources,* by Lawrence K.
Frank. In March 1943, when both the war effort was more intense and
the end of the NRPB was a much more likely possibility, it published a
126-page printed report (item 327 in table B-1), *Human Conservation—*
The Story of Our Wasted Resources, also by Lawrence K. Frank, with
the assistance of Louise K. Kiser. This report is excellent by professional
sociological or demographic standards; it presents a lot of interesting and
useful information, and is well-written as government publications go.

Something of the flavor of the report may be suggested by these brief
quotations from its introduction (pp. 1–2):

> Conservation of natural resources has increasingly been accepted as
> essential to our national welfare and survival. Only recently, how-
> ever, have we begun to realize the magnitude and seriousness of the
> equally vital task of human conservation which the war has now made
> an acute national problem.
> Since we have been so successful in reducing human loss in some
> areas and for some groups, we can now assert not only the possibility
> but the social necessity of making further advances in human conser-
> vation. . . .

This preliminary statement on human loss is offered in the hope of enlisting the attention and earnest endeavor of all those who recognize that our scientific knowledge and resources now make possible what our ethical formulations and human values for so long proclaimed— the conservation of human life and personality as the major social goal of a democratic society. This is the focus of the post-war period by which all social, economic planning for the future must be guided.

I endorse the general thrust of the report's conclusions and recommendations. My reservations about the report, *published at that time,* fall into several groups: (1) it has little relation to planning for any kind of future action; (2) it has no discernible relation to the war effort, at a time when every government agency was under severe public criticism if it was alleged that its work was unrelated to the war; and (3) in peacetime it could just as well have been published by some agency other than the NRPB—the Public Health Service, the Office of Education, or the Census Bureau, for instance. Its publication seems a particularly insensitive action for an agency under political attack—unlikely to win much support, likely to provoke more opposition.

Since 1943, there have been a great many population studies, some by the Bureau of the Census, some by other federal agencies, and some by private organizations. It has become fairly standard, as a research procedure in investigations of particular natural resource use, to start with population projections—as the 1934 report did in its land section. It is not clear to me how great was the NRPB's influence in the subsequent population studies. I have expressed my admiration for the 1938 report. Much of what has been done in the past forty years is similar to some parts of that report, and one could thus draw the conclusions that that report was the origin of many ideas and forms of analysis used since then. My own belief is that the NRPB's population work was influential, though perhaps not decisive, in later development of the field.

Housing

The NRPB never had a major committee devoted exclusively to housing; studies of housing were made by its Industrial Committee and its Urbanism Committee, and some of its economic reports considered housing also. Housing might have been discussed under any of those headings but here it is discussed separately.

There was a long (561-page) mimeographed report in 1937 (item 62 in table B-1), *Some Factors in the Development of Housing Policies in the United States,* the extent of its distribution being unknown. In 1940, the NRPB published a major printed report, *Housing, The Continuing Problem* (item 175 in table B-1), but with a specific disclaimer on the cover page, "The National Resources Planning Board assumes no responsibility for the views and opinions expressed herein." Its letter of transmittal to the president states in fact: "This document summarizes and reproduces a series of technical monographs on varying aspects of the problem. Except for the Summary, these technical papers have been published at intervals during the last 2 years, and in each case the author assumes full responsibility for the views expressed herein."

The Industrial Committee, chaired by Thomas C. Blaisdell, Jr., of the NRPB's staff, in its letter of transmittal to NRPB chairman Delano says in part (p. iv of item 175):

> The Industrial Committee transmits herewith the fourth and last of the series of monographs prepared, at the request of the President, by numerous collaborators and agencies and assisted by a technical staff. A study in this field was originally undertaken in the spring of 1938 in connection with larger problems of the construction industry. The Industrial Committee recommends the publication of this Summary at this late date because it gives some perspective to the materials already made available in the earlier technical monographs.

It would appear that the statements in this latter letter of transmittal refer only to the summary, discussed below.

While much of the specifics of Blaisdell's summary are outdated, much remains as accurate today as when written. "We need more houses," (p. 13); but he sets his sights on 800,000 a year, while in recent years actual building has been mostly in the 1½ to 2 million range and targets have been considerably higher. "We need better houses ... We need more good houses in stable and livable communities ... The housing problem is not one problem, but a combination of interrelated problems ... The solution of the housing problem, therefore, cannot be found in any single or simple formula." (p. 13)

Blaisdell concludes (pp. 19–20):

> When controlled private activity cannot produce the necessary housing, public initiative is called for. It is now generally accepted that it is impossible for a large portion of our population to achieve the mini-

mum standard of housing which the public conscience demands. Hence, the program of public building with subsidy for the lowest income groups has been written in Federal and State law.

The greater part of the 1940 report consists of technical papers, signed by their authors.[4] While they are dated by the passage of time, they may read remarkably well in light of today's conditions.

The NRPB subsequently issued two pamphlets on housing: a summary of the 1940 report (item 149 in table B-1), and one concerned with the role of the house-building industry in the postwar period (item 291).

While the NRPB considered housing as a basic consumption good or service for the population, as an industry which made an important contribution to the total economic output, and as part of the urban structure, its considerations of housing were comparatively less in total volume than housing receives today in actual federal government planning or would receive were an overall national planning organization in operation today. On the other hand, its studies, while only modest in number, were more realistic than much of the housing planning of the postwar years. It is hard to say how much the NRPB advanced the state of the art in housing planning. I would simply say, all housing planners today should be required to read the 1940 report in full; they might get new insights and new perspectives thereby.

Research

The establishment of a Science Committee by the NRPB in 1935 was noted earlier in this chapter. This committee undertook a number of projects, including those of its subcommittee on housing described in the foregoing section; and it also undertook studies of research in the United States. The NRPB published three major reports, or three parts of one report, growing out of the Science Committee's detailed and intensive studies, under the general title, *Research—A Natural Resource.*

---

[4] These include: The Residential Building Process: An Analysis in Terms of Economic and Other Social Influences, by Lowell J. Chawner; Private Housing Legal Problems, by Horace Russell; Legal Aspects of Public Housing, by Leon H. Keyserling; Location Factors in Housing Programs, by Jacob Crane; Site Planning, by Frederick Bigger; The Significance of Small House Design, by Pierre Blouke; Building Materials and the Cost of Housing, by Theodore H. Kreps; Labor and the Cost of Housing, by Mercer G. Evans; and Building Regulations and the Housing Problem, by George N. Thompson.

Part I. Relation of the Federal Government to Research, 255 pages, was published in December 1938 (see item 103, table B-1). The chairman of the Science Committee at that time was Charles H. Judd; he also served as chairman of the subcommittee on research and as director of its rather considerable technical staff, who had been recruited from within and from outside of government. There were also special contributors to the report.

The Science Committee summarized this report in 16 pages. It used restrained terms, as befit dignified scholars, but without real meat. The findings, based on the report, are highly informative about the amount, kind, and problems of federal research at that time. The recommendations include, in part, the following (p. 4):

> 6. That research within the Government and by nongovernmental agencies which cooperate with the Government be so organized and conducted as to avoid the possibilities of bias through subordination in any way to policy-making and policy-enforcing.
> 7. That research agencies of the Government extend the practice of encouraging decentralized research in institutions not directly related to the Government and by individuals not in its employ.
> 8. That the interrelations of governmental research agencies be furthered by the organization of central councils along the lines followed by the existing national councils of research specialists. These interagency councils would serve to systematize the efforts which are now made by various interbureau committees to coordinate the research activities within the Government.

The report of the Science Committee includes a strong defense of the value of research and of the need for the federal government to engage in it; and includes many specific suggestions for better planning and budgeting for research in the federal government. The report as a whole includes signed essays on various aspects of research by federal agencies, on legislative provisions affecting such research, on the legislative branch and its relations to research, on research in universities and colleges, on the special problem of the Bureau of the Census, and on the Library of Congress in relation to research. Each is serious, with substantial supporting information, and the whole is quite an impressive document. It describes the situation as it existed in the middle 1930s; while many things have changed over the more than forty intervening years, some of the problems described have a strangely familiar sound.

Part II. Industrial Research was published by the NRPB in December 1940 (see item 179, table B-1) and also as House Document 234,

77th Congress, 1st Session, with the notation on the cover that the report had been prepared for the National Resources Planning Board by the National Research Council of the National Academy of Sciences. By this time the Science Committee had undergone some changes in personnel, and Edwin B. Wilson was now its chairman. The NRPB and its Science Committee had enlisted the active participation of the National Research Council, and it, in turn, had organized a Committee on Survey of Research in Industry, composed of twenty-six persons, a few from universities, none from the federal government, and nearly all from large industrial firms or associations noted for their research activities. This committee in turn assembled a staff, led by Raymond Stevens, a vice president of Arthur D. Little, the well-known consulting firm.

The main part of the report is a long series of signed essays by industrial researchers conducting research in their own laboratories or familiar with the research conducted by such laboratories. I have not read these essays carefully, in part because I am incapable of judging their technical content and in part because I assume that they are substantially dated by now. I am impressed with the fact that each essay is primarily technical and only incidentally deals with economic or social problems arising out of the research or its application. But, by any standards, the report is an impressive document, not only for the wealth of information it contains, but as a cooperative effort by the large number of contributors. One can easily see that the NRPB gained substantially by its sponsorship of the study; it was thereby associated with leading research organizations and gained an outstanding publication.

There is a very brief summary of findings and recommendations by the Committee on Survey of Research in Industry and endorsed by the Science Committee, but no action by either the National Research Council or the NRPB. The findings are useful but not exciting reading at this date; the recommendations are directed first to industry, urging more and better research efforts by industrial firms; secondly to labor and industry, urging research on worker fatigue and injury; and to government, suggesting means for better cooperation in research between government and industry. All of this, as the report as a whole, in moderately clear writing, calm in tone, and without controversial discussions or recommendations. One surely judges that reports such as this must have helped the NRPB achieve a good reputation among reasonably conservative scholars, businessmen, and legislators.

Part III. Business Research was published by the NRPB in June 1941 (see item 202, table B-1). The Science Committee then had the same membership and chairman as it had had for the Part II report, but now the Social Science Research Council appointed a Committee on Business Research, advisors were appointed by the Business Advisory Council of the Department of Commerce, and a technical staff was assembled. The resulting report is much shorter than either of the earlier reports. The Committee on Business Research wrote the report, which was then forwarded to the president by the NRPB Board without either adoption or disclaimer; the Science Committee endorsed it, but without adding more than a letter of transmittal; and there are no individually signed essays.

The report has a brief setting and summary, without recommendations, in which the difficulty of defining "business research" and of obtaining information about it is discussed, along with a caution that much activity described elsewhere as business research is really only routine data collecting and recording. The report is an excellent statement of the business research activities of private companies and their service organizations. While severely dated today, it is an excellent record of the situation in 1940.

Welfare and Security

One of the most outstanding and one of the most controversial, if not the single most controversial, of all the NRPB's reports was *Security, Work, and Relief Policies* (see item 252, table B-1). Both cover and flyleaf bear a date of 1942, but its actual public release was more than a year later.

This report was prepared by the Committee on Long-Range Work and Relief Policies, which was appointed by the Board in late 1939.[5] In Barry Karl's view the appointment of this committee "marked the beginning of postwar planning."[6] The transmittal letter from the NRPB to the president, dated December 4, 1941, speaks of the committee as having "participated continuously over the past two years both in the research and in the drafting of the report."

---

[5] Philip W. Warken, "A History of the National Resources Planning Board, 1933–1943" (doctoral dissertation, Ohio State University, 1969) pp. 215–216.

[6] Barry D. Karl, *Charles E. Merriam and the Study of Politics* (Chicago, University of Chicago Press, 1974) p. 275.

A committee of nine persons is listed in this transmittal letter; about half were federal employees, the other half from universities and private associations. The chairman of the group was William Haber, professor of economics, University of Michigan. Most of the group would have been considered moderately but not extremely liberal by the standards of the day. The committee retained Eveline M. Burns as director of research; a trained economist, she had studied and been a faculty member at the London School of Economics. Sir William Henry Beveridge was also at this school but she was not a student of his.[7] His name was, soon after the committee's establishment, to be associated with a report about similar programs in Britain. At the time of her appointment as director of research for the committee, Burns was a member of the graduate economics department at Columbia University. In addition to Burns, a substantial staff was assembled and a large number of federal agencies and private persons made significant contributions to the study.

In its letter of transmittal to the president, the Board says:

> The Board Members find themselves in general agreement with the recommendations of the Committee, considered as a whole but not in all detail. We have stated our own position at greater length in the Introduction to the report. In our general program for the stabilization of employment and the development of our national resources, this report holds a peculiarly strategic place. We submit it with the hope that it will be of assistance in the determination of major policies in a series of related fields.

There is no statement or transmittal letter from the committee to the Board; presumably, taking the Board's transmittal letter as evidence, the report as a whole is that of the committee; at any rate, there are no individually signed chapters.

Warken has traced the history of this report in some detail.[8]

> Roosevelt received the security report on December 4, 1941 and the development report on the 16th of the following December. He delayed over a year in sending the security report forward and there was considerable speculation as to the reasons for his delay in sending them to Congress. In October 1942, William Green wrote to the President asking him about the social security report and was told that the report was to go forward within the next few weeks. As late as January 9, 1943, however, FDR was still holding the reports and asking

---

7 Personal letter from Eveline M. Burns, December 23, 1979.
8 Warken, "A History of the National Resources Planning Board," pp. 224–226.

for advice as to what to say in his message of transmittal which he now indicated was scheduled to go to the Hill about the first of February. Even the NRPB must have been in the dark as to the President's exact plans because on February 10, 1943, the day the reports were sent to Congress, Frederic Delano sent a memorandum to the president commenting on the recently released British post-war plan which contained a reference to the possibility of transmitting the two NRPB reports.

There is no definite explanation for the timing of the release of the reports. It is possible that the pressures of the war distracted the President's attention for most of 1942 and that when at the end of the year he received the development report for 1943, he decided to send them forward together and was waiting for the appropriate time. Several publications suggested that release of the reports was deliberately timed to distract attention from the potentially critical second annual report of the Truman Committee. The Truman report did appear on the same day that the President sent the NRPB reports to Congress and they took the front pages away from the Senate Committee. There is no evidence that this was a deliberate action on the part of the administration but Dorothy Thompson, who favored the reports, noted that part of the explanation for the inadequate treatment they received from the press was the administration's not having given them to the press for examination until twenty-four hours after their general release. This might indicate that although the reports were intended for release in February the selection of March 10, 1943 was made for secondary reasons.

While the attempt to swamp the Truman report may have been a factor in the selection of March 10, there were other and very sound reasons for releasing the report in early 1943. The NRPB was in serious trouble in Congress and these reports could conceivably help the agency in its fight to secure appropriations for another year. They would also reassure the country that the administration had post-war plans comparable to those of Britain.

Whatever may have been the president's motives, it is clear that more than a year elapsed between the transmittal date of the report from the Board to him and his forwarding it to the Congress. Before speculating further about the reasons for this delay, a summary description of the report itself is desirable.

In a brief introduction to the report, the Board says:

This report is concerned particularly with making adequate provision for those who have no means of livelihood or only inadequate means . . . Four main points seem to need emphasis:

First, that our economy must provide work for all who are able and willing to work. Included in this is a special responsibility for an adequate youth program which should be an integral part of any governmental undertaking to establish security. This will be particularly true in the postwar period.

Second, that for great numbers whose work is interrupted, the social insurances must carry much of the load of providing adequate income.

Third, that where the insurances or work policies fail to take care of an interruption in income, adequate guarantees of minimum aid and assistance must be given both to individual and families through a general public assistance system.

Fourth, that where adequate services essential to the health, education, and welfare of the population are not available, public provision should be made for the development of such services.

These four points are then elaborated, each in a few paragraphs. Later on in the introduction, and in the nearest approach to an economic justification for the program, the Board says:

If we take these objectives as seriously as we take national defense—and they are indeed a fundamental part of national defense—the ways and means of obtaining the objectives are ready at hand. On the basis of full employment and of a national income at say one hundred billion dollars, all the proposed services can be provided. It is not the provision of these basic services that would threaten the security and prosperity of the nation, but it is, on the contrary, the failure to develop the purchasing power implied in these services that drags down our national income from time to time and everything with it to a lower level. But operating at half capacity or, as we once did, at a level of $43,000,000,000 of national income, we cannot provide these services, nor can the national economy be operated effectively.

Burns has said:

One thing is important. At no time while I was preparing the report was any pressure put on me to change any part of it or to soften any of the recommendations, and as far as I know, my Committee were left entirely alone with only occasional prods to complete the report. As I understood my job it was to survey and evaluate the gamut of income maintenance and work programs, to see how far they met the needs and to suggest ways in which a better coordinated and improved group of programs might be developed.[9]

---

[9] Personal letter from Burns, December 23, 1979.

The conduct of the research and the publication of the report were thus in the best tradition of academic freedom for impartial inquiry and full reporting of the research. Had the NRPB been an academic institution such as a university, or a private organization such as the Social Science Research Council, these actions would have been highly estimable.

The Board, in the introduction to the report, emphasizes its general agreement without endorsing every detail. Taken as a whole, the Board's statement is not only a statement of the report's principles, beliefs, and policy but a ringing defense of them. "Some may urge that such a program must be set aside until the war emergency is ended. But to postpone until the war is over will be too late. We should move now on the major changes needed to set our house in order."

Submission of the report to the president and by him to the Congress was a political act, in the broadest sense of that word. The position of the Board might, or might not, have been good politics for the president with his great prestige and great popular following; for an agency under severe political attack, in wartime, with a president engrossed elsewhere and perhaps not willing to defend the agency in any case, it was foolhardy or worse. By December 1941, when the report was forwarded to the president, the Board may have had little room for choice—the existence and major findings of the study were already well known in liberal intellectual circles, and suppression or modification of the report would have drawn outcries of criticism from those who supported its findings. By 1943, the NRPB was probably irrevocably doomed, no matter what it or its friends might then do; but publication of this report surely won few friends it did not already have, stirred up its enemies to new frenzies, and lost it some of the uncommitted persons who might have been won over by a different course.

The whole report is very long (640 of the large-size pages). While those prejudiced against it from the start might well have found parts or statements to criticize, the first two-thirds of the committee's report impresses me as, on the whole, a high-quality professional job of data assembly and data analysis; some conclusions were drawn, but, generally, there were no recommendations for action in this part of the report. In Part V, however, which is titled "Planning for the Future," there are a lot of policy recommendations. One may assume that it was these— insofar as critics based their objections on what the report said instead of what they chose to believe it said—that drew most of the fire. There is little point in a detailed review of these recommendations at this date;

their flavor is pretty well indicated by the quotations from the Board's introduction, which was, on the whole, far milder in tone than Part V of the report. This part of the report was generally described—and not merely by persons hostile to it—as "cradle to the grave" public assistance. One may note that a very great deal of what was recommended about unemployment insurance, welfare aid, old age assistance, and medical insurance has come into existence in the intervening decades— whether one takes this as exoneration of the report or as confirmation of its critics' worst fears.

The report produced a great deal of public comment, most of it highly critical. Warken cites references to news accounts and editorials in such newspapers as the *New York Times,* the *Wall Street Journal,* the *Denver Post,* and others.[10] White cites critical articles by the *Washington Times-Herald.*[11] The reaction in the Congress was mostly highly critical and hostile. Some of this adverse reaction was crocodile tears, shed by those who were eager to use any device they thought would be popular in attacking President Roosevelt.

The grounds of attack on the report, on Mrs. Burns, and on the NRPB for this report were several. Basic was the rebellion of the critics against the philosophy of the report, which the quotations earlier in this section have set forth. There was a widespread and deep-seated view that the proposals of the report were much too generous—that somehow poor people did not deserve the kind of help that was proposed, although this position was rarely stated so specifically. There was also a lot of criticism of this report (and even more of the Board's proposals for full employment which we will describe in the next chapter) on the grounds that they were repudiations of private enterprise and the opening wedges toward socialism. The Security report was repeatedly criticized, and even its friends were disturbed, because of the lack of economic analysis —could the country possibly afford what was proposed? As noted above, the nearest to a defense of an analysis on this point is the short quotation from the Board's introduction.

We have quoted at length from Warken about the delay in the president's submission of the report to the Congress and of Warken's speculation of the reasons for the delay. The president surely was engrossed

---

[10] Warken, "A History of the National Resources Planning Board, " pp. 226–237.

[11] Philip L. White, "The Termination of the National Resources Planning Board" (master's thesis, Columbia University, 1949) p. 127.

in the war effort, but one may doubt if that was the major reason for the delay. He could hardly have failed—astute politician that he was—to realize that the report would provoke the kind of reaction that it did in fact provoke. He may well have waited for what he thought an auspicious time for the report's release. The release of the Beveridge report in Britain, which covered much of the same ground, brought some pressure on him by those who felt the United States should not lag in its plans for the postwar period. Warken may well have been right in his speculation that the precise timing of the release of the report was dictated by Roosevelt's desire to smother the critical report of Senator Truman's committee. This was a tactic Roosevelt used throughout his many years in the presidency, with great skill and effect. What the president says on an important issue at his press conference pushes other news off the front page, sometimes into very inferior positions within the newspapers. It is important to note that the role of the newspapers was greater than now simply because of the lack of competition from other media. Although Roosevelt used radio with great skill, he did not use it to broadcast news conferences.

There were other NRPB reports that drew adverse reaction at this time (as we shall note later). Those reports, combined with this one, gave weight to those who saw "conspiracy" in nearly everything the NRPB did.

Summary and Evaluation

The NRPB activities described in this chapter drew mixed reactions from various sectors of the whole American public. There was much interest and some support for all of these studies and proposals, but there was also a rising tide of opposition which grew increasingly bitter and hostile, culminating in the reactions to the Security report, described above. Perhaps this tide of opposition was inevitable, given the general social and political trends of the times, including the similar rising tide of opposition and increasing bitterness toward President Roosevelt and his New Deal ideas.

From the perspective of the present, I must regard the strong policy recommendations and the publication of the Security report as essentially political moves, in both the broad and the specific senses of that term. It was not merely a planning report on how to carry out established national policies; it was a policy-forming document of the most specific kind. There could be little wonder that the political opponents of the president regarded it in precisely this light.

This political character of the Security report raises at least two major questions: (1) Was the NRPB really equipped to play a political role? Did it have the kind of personnel, the understanding of the political process, the internal organization, the support from the president, and the facility of getting its ideas before the Congress and the nation which an effective political role required? (2) For those who held the ideas and objectives put forth in the Security report, was the NRPB the most effective political tool, the mechanism most likely to secure national approval of these policies? One is forced, I think, to answer both questions in the negative: the NRPB was not well equipped for this role and it was not an effective political mechanism for the advancement of the policies it espoused. Certainly, the Security report and its contemporaries were instrumental in the NRPB's termination, although by 1942 and 1943 the NRPB was probably doomed, irrespective of these reports.

It is, of course, easier to reach these judgments today than it was in 1942 and 1943, and easier for someone not involved in the actual operations of the NRPB than for the Board and its staff to have reached the same conclusions. Moreover, even if any one or any combination of persons most directly involved had reached these conclusions, it is by no means clear that they could have done anything different than the NRPB actually did. There was a momentum to its operations, a philosophy in its approaches to problems, and a relationship to the president which would have made a drastic change in direction nearly impossible. The Board itself seems not to have considered any such redirection as is implied above. The personal correspondence between Merriam and Delano in April 1943 relative to the replacement of Eliot, cited in chapter 4, suggests that a substantial degree of disorganization and dissension must have existed within the Board or between the Board and its director at this time, thus reducing the Board's power to act in the face of the criticisms it received.

10

NRPB Economic Inquiries and Reports

All NRPB work and all its reports had an economic dimension or connotation. This chapter, however, looks at economics in a much narrower framework: studies and reports whose major focus was upon economic facts, economic relationships, and economic policy. Even so defined, there is no sharp line of demarcation between the subject matter of this chapter and of the two preceding and three following ones.

Many of the NRPB reports which I classify as "economics" or "industry," were reproduced only in mimeographed form and one may assume were circulated only to relatively small audiences. This is not, of course, saying that they were lacking in influence, for at that time much of the most significant thought from federal agencies appeared in mimeographed form, to avoid the lengthy and often enervating review processes required for printed reports. Most of the discussion in this chapter, however, focuses on the major printed reports, as representing the major intellectual efforts and considered positions of the NRPB and its authors.

Lepawsky, a political scientist at the University of California who has conducted extensive research on NRPB, expresses a judgment about the NRPB's economic planning: "Compared to the later CEA, . . . the New Deal's Planning Board, together with its newly collaborating Fiscal Board, constituted a relatively unsophisticated economic planning mechanism." With some justice he criticizes the NRPB for presenting many plans, including plans for public works, "with slight sense of

proportion and little notion of priority." [1] It is true that the NRPB and
its researchers typically did not use the sophisticated economic analytical
procedures of today—no economist did then: It is also true that the
NRPB did not much concern itself with fiscal and monetary policy,
except through its offshoot, the Fiscal and Monetary Advisory Board.
And it is also true that other agencies and other persons, outside of the
NRPB, were highly influential in economic planning and policy during
the New Deal period. However, I think that a careful judgment of the
major reports discussed in this chapter will show that they had solid
economic foundations and that they made significant contributions to
economic policy of the time—perhaps more so than would more sophisticated analyses for a reading public not then ready for them.

Lepawsky has this to say about the Fiscal and Monetary Advisory
Board:

> ... there was the functionally more limited and operationally more
> cautious Fiscal and Monetary Advisory Board. The Fiscal Board was
> proposed and launched by the Planning Board in 1938. By 1939 it
> was located within the Treasury under the chairmanship of Secretary
> Henry Morgenthau. More monetarily than fiscally-minded, Morgen-
> thau was dubbed Henry the Morgue by the ever jocular FDR because
> each New Deal recession made him more discontent than the last.
> Nevertheless, the Fiscal Board learned to function smoothly with the
> Planning Board. This provided the Roosevelt administration with an
> improvised piece of governmental machinery that came closer than
> ever before to the Council of Economic Advisers, established in 1946
> as this country's first full-fledged agency for fiscal policy and economic
> planning. [2]

Public Works

It will be recalled that the National Planning Board, the first agency in
the NRPB series, arose under the Public Works Administration in 1933
because of the need for bringing some order out of the flood of proposals for public works, which were then seen as a chief means of
fighting the severe unemployment and the extremely low personal
incomes when the New Deal began. The very first report, and one of
the only two reports of the National Planning Board, was a mimeo-

---

[1] Albert Lepawsky, "The Planning Apparatus: A Vignette of the New Deal,"
Journal of the American Institute of Planning (January 1976) p. 18.

[2] Ibid., Footnotes of sources in original omitted in this quote.

graphed publication by Russell V. Black, a research consultant to the NPB, *Criteria and Planning for Public Works* (item 1 in table B-1). His focus was explicitly on physical planning—the major interest of Ickes, who was chairman of the NPB, of Delano who was vice chairman, and of Eliot who was then its executive officer. 'The reason I include it in this chapter on economic planning is that Black gives explicit consideration to criteria for selection and programming of public works and to potential needs for public works. While his analysis is, as Lepawsky says, relatively unsophisticated in an economic sense, it is sound economics and full of good common sense. One can well believe that his analysis and his advice, if heeded by proponents of public works projects, would have resulted in a much more economically defensible program. He discusses public works by the federal government, by states, and by municipalities and presents a good deal of statistical data on proposals and needs for highways, water development, buildings, land acquisition, and other kinds of public works.

Black's report is dated June 1934; in May 1935 the National Resources Board, which had succeeded NPB, held a conference on the division of costs of public works (see item 6, table B-1).

The next *published* report of the NRPB on public works was *The Economic Effects of the Federal Public Works Expenditures, 1933–1938,* (item 170, table B-1) by J. K. Galbraith, assisted by G. G. Johnson, Jr. Galbraith, then early in his career as an economist, worked under the sponsorship of the Subcommittee on the Economics of Public Works, of the Public Works Committee, of what was by then the NRPB. Although the report is dated November 1940, a footnote to the introduction states, "The manuscript of this study was completed in substantially its present form during the autumn of 1939. It has not been revised in accordance with subsequent developments." The report is fairly long (131 pages of the large-size pages used by NRPB for its printed reports), and is full of tables and charts. The specifics are highly dated, valuable for the historian but not requiring detailed description here. The analysis shows direct employment on public works by months, and in relation to total employment or output of supplying industries, and on-site and off-site compared. From the vantage point of today, I suspect it seriously underestimates the off-site or secondary employment effects of the public works.

While the report does not include recommendations as such, it does include some conclusions in the final chapter, the spirit of which is reflected in the following (p. 74):

To summarize, the practical problem of public works timing, under conditions as they appear at present, is not that of arranging an on-again-off-again program to accord with the appearance and disappearance of unemployment. Nor, under conditions as they now appear, can it be expected that the total volume of construction employment can be made to absorb all unemployed. Timing of public works consists in having a continuing program (possibly expanded to accord with continuing unemployment) which can be increased or decreased with the broader swings in employment and economic activity.

This view of the role of public works was more moderate and more sensible than was common at the time. The wisdom of this viewpoint was neglected in the immediate post-World War II period, when public works expenditures were tried as a means of coping with the reconversion problems of the postwar transition. The fact, well developed in this report, is that most public works move too slowly to deal with short-term unemployment problems.

The NRPB toward the end of its life (early 1942) issued three mimeographed reports (items 248, 249, and 258 in table B-1) on programs of public works for range conservation, recreational land, and forest conservation. These were apparently looking forward to programs of public works in the postwar period, in an anticipation (quite common then) that there would likely be severe unemployment at that time. At a still later point (May 1943) when the end of the NRPB was really near, it issued another somewhat similar report (item 342 in table B-1), concerned with population relocations required by federal reservoir development or relocation possibilities opened up by federal public works activities. It is impossible at this date to be sure, but one may judge that their impact was very limited—the war was on, the postwar adjustments were in the uncertain future, the reports probably had only modest circulation, and they were not particularly novel. If the NRPB had survived, these reports might have been influential in guiding public policy on public works in the postwar period.

Maynard M. Hufschmidt, who was employed by the NRPB during this period to work on economic and public works matters, has commented as follows:

> NRPB's major impact on public works planning was not so much in its major reports as in its continuing activities of carrying out the procedures set forth in Executive Order 8455, including the technical review of Federal water resource projects by the Evaluation Subcommittee of the Water Resources Committee and the efforts to get Federal

agencies to prepare six-year programs of public works. When the war started and most non-war related public works were halted, emphasis in NRPB and the agencies turned toward building a "shelf" of public works projects for the postwar period.

This activity of NRPB, which was primarily a process activity, was not actively opposed by the construction agencies and their affiliated Congressional committees, and it was one NRPB activity that was picked up by the Bureau of the Budget in July 1943.

However, an attempt by the Bureau of the Budget in 1943–44 to build up a modest public works coordinating staff in the Bureau, to carry out the provisions of Executive Order 9384 which replaced Executive Order 8455, was defeated in the Appropriation Committees, in part, because of opposition of the Corps of Engineers and other Federal construction agencies.[3]

This commentary is particularly valuable, first to show that some of the NRPB's useful activities did not result in publications, and second to show that some of the opposition it encountered would arise against any agency that tried to perform the same functions.

Consumer Incomes and Expenditures

In the early 1930s, information about consumer incomes and consumer expenditures was much less in volume, accuracy, detail, and adequacy of sample than are similar kinds of information today. There was a great deal of interest in consumer incomes and expenditures; several of the chapters in the two volumes on *Recent Social Trends* and the "Capacity" books by the Brookings Institution (see chapter 3 for more detail) had used such information as was available to discuss the income and the welfare situation of important groups in the population. They also discussed the expenditures for and production of various important consumption items. But the data were fragmentary, or suspect as to accuracy, or lacking in detail, or otherwise generally unsatisfactory. One of the NRPB's greatest intellectual accomplishments lay in its sponsorship of two classic reports, described in more detail below.

Ickes in his *Secret Diary,* for the week ending April 9, 1937, says:

I have seen the President two or three times this week. I went in with Merriam and Ruml because they wanted to lay a plan before the President on behalf of the National Resources Committee calling for some-

---

[3] Personal letter from Maynard M. Hufschmidt, January 8, 1980.

thing in the way of a consumption survey, all directed toward the end of a better balanced economy ... We had a long session this morning with the President on Merriam's and Ruml's plan and apparently a group will be set up to do some high economic thinking. I am on this group mainly, I suppose, because I am titular Chairman of the National Resources Committee, but, as always, economics is out of my line. Present in addition to Merriam and Ruml were Henry Morgenthau, Henry Wallace, Miss Perkins, Harry Hopkins, Dr. Lubin, and Marriner Eccles.[4]

Eliot says that the proposal for such a study had been discussed several times in Board meetings in the three months preceding this conference.[5] Delano and Eliot were not present at this conference with the president because when they were in Boston on other business, Delano had fallen seriously ill and had required an emergency operation. Eliot says that the project was not the brainchild of Merriam and Ruml, as Ickes says, but was the product of extensive discussions among all Board members and himself.

This diary entry by Ickes, written at the time, is highly informative on many points. It shows how major NRPB projects were indeed discussed in detail with the president and his major advisors prior to their inauguration. It also demonstrates that Ickes did indeed have a limited knowledge of and interest in economics, and that this particular study had participation from the very highest levels of the administration.

In the end, an impressive number of high-quality persons and organizations participated in the study. The Industrial Committee of the National Resources Committee at that time consisted of Thomas C. Blaisdell, Jr., of the NRC's staff as chairman; Lauchlin Currie; Leon Henderson; Charles Eliot; Isador Lubin, commissioner of the Bureau of Labor Statistics; Harry D. White, of the Treasury Department; Mordecai Ezekiel, of the Department of Agriculture; and Gardiner C. Means—a roster of some of the leading economists in federal service at the time. The project was planned and conducted in large part by the Bureau of Home Economics of the Department of Agriculture and the Bureau of Labor Statistics of the Department of Labor; and the Central Statistical Board cooperated. Funds were provided by the Works Progress Administration, and hundreds, if not thousands, of persons on welfare payments were employed as field enumerators and office clerks. In that

[4] Harold L. Ickes, *The Secret Diary of Harold L. Ickes, Volume II, The Inside Struggle, 1936–1939* (New York, Simon and Schuster, 1954).

[5] Personal letters from Eliot, December 29, 1979, and January 2, 1980.

period of severe unemployment, some very able and industrious people were on public welfare and it was possible to get able, diligent, responsible workers off the relief roles. A competent technical staff worked under the direction of Hildegarde Kneeland.

Over 300,000 families and single person households were interviewed periodically throughout a year for the income study and over 60,000 families for the expenditure study; each sample was chosen to represent as accurately as possible the income ranges, family size, occupation, and regional differences among the population of the United States. Three truly major reports were published from this study: *Consumer Incomes in the United States,* August 1938 (item 99, table B-1); *Consumer Expenditures in the United States,* June 1939 (item 112, table B-1); *Family Expenditures in the United States—Statistical Tables and Appendixes,* June 1941 (item 197, table B-1). Each of the two earlier reports had been preceded by a mimeographed version, issued a few months earlier (items 87 and 107, table B-1), and they were followed a few months later by an NRPB pamphlet summarizing the main conclusions (item 113, table B-1). The reports described in detail the definitions and methods used, the location and nature of the sample, and other relevant facts about the study.

In a sense, the *Income* report produced no new or sensational ideas, but it did produce more accurate figures on the amount and distribution of incomes than had ever been available before—and figures which would seem incomprehensible to younger Americans today. A third of the families and of individuals not in family groups had less than $750 annual income. These included a substantial number of both individuals and families on relief or welfare, but 70 percent of them did not receive such public assistance. While most were in wage-earning or farming occupations, some were clerical, business, or professional. In total, they had only 10 percent of the national income. The upper third had incomes above $1,450 annually. Some were single men or single women, but most were families, of which the model size was three to four persons. A very few families in this income range were on public welfare during part of the year. While a substantial portion of this income class were clerical, business, or professional people, wage-earners were the most numerous group and farmers were well represented. This group had about two thirds of the national income. Even within this group, there was a substantial disparity in incomes—the highest 5 percent of all income units had well over a quarter of the national income. The specific figures for 1935–36 need to be corrected—multiplied by at best ten—to be comparable with figures today. The figures drove home at least two major points: (1) most people in the United States were relatively poor, even by the standards of the day; and (2) most of the income was in the hands of a comparatively small minority of the whole population.

The *Expenditures* study likewise produced few novel ideas that sociologists had not learned from sample studies made in previous years or decades, but its wide coverage, large sample size, and great detail did produce a far more accurate and detailed picture than had ever been available previously. One third of all consumer expenditures was for food, nearly a fifth was for housing, with household operation, clothing, automobile, medical care, recreation, furnishings, personal care, and tobacco following in that order, and with still smaller amounts for other miscellaneous purposes. While there were differences among these expenditure categories, there was a surprisingly similar response in expenditure on each of them, as average income rose. When people had more money to spend, they increased their expenditures for most items in their budget—better food, perhaps more of it, better housing, better clothing, more or better automobiles, better medical care, more recreation, and so forth. Increased expenditures, at least as averages for groups of consumers, did not increase for just a few items in the family consumption pattern, but for each of them, and by remarkably similar patterns of increase. The great exception was the relation of saving to income. When consumer income was very low, deficits were incurred to try to maintain the previous level of living; on the average, savings were negative at incomes below $1,250. Savings rose rapidly, both in absolute amounts and as a percentage of income, as average incomes rose, until the relatively very few families and individuals with $20,000 or more income were saving almost 40 percent of their incomes.

These results applied to the times in more subtle ways than the mere difference in general price level, noted above. The data were collected for the 1935–36 period; while the extreme depths of the depression had passed, incomes generally were still very low. In particular, farm incomes were low and the United States then was far more of an agricultural nation than it is today. Moreover, farming in some of the sample areas had just experienced, or was then experiencing, severe drought, with further reduction in farm incomes. The tendency for people of very low income to have negative savings—to spend more than their income, making up the deficiency by drawing on past capital accumulation—came in part from farm families experiencing lower incomes during the period of study than they had experienced in the past or than they expected to achieve in the future.

These results greatly strengthened the idea that people's expenditures depend more on their idea of their own "normal" income than they do on their income during a particular time period. This concept is often associated with Milton Friedman.[6] It is probably significant that he was on the technical staff for the *Expenditure* study and that his help is acknowledged in the *Income* study.

These two major reports and the statistical addition were enormously useful and influential at the time. I speak from personal experience, having used them as a basis for estimating "normal" farm family expenditures and savings under different settlement conditions, especially in studies I helped to make for the Columbia Basin irrigation project of central Washington. The expenditure patterns revealed by the studies became the basis for the Bureau of Labor Statistics weighting in some of its price series, and in other ways the results were used extensively in government and in private business. The NRPB itself published, in mimeographed form, three studies based largely upon these reports (items 169, 218, and 231, table B-1).

All of the studies were organized in detail, financed, and carried out by other federal agencies. A large share of the professional expertise came from agencies other than the NRPB. The question may well be asked: Why did not these other agencies organize, finance, and conduct the studies without a role by the NRPB? The answer is, it seems to me, that the NRPB played a significant catalyst or entrepreneurial role, one which was critical to the whole result, in the sense that without its efforts the studies would not, in fact, have been made.

Industrial Organization and Location

During its existence, especially during the latter half of its life, the NRPB made and published a substantial number of reports dealing with indus-

---

[6] Milton Friedman, *A Theory of Consumption* (Princeton, Princeton University Press, 1957).

trial organization and location. The first printed report was in 1940 (item 146 in table B-1): *Capital Requirements—A Study in Methods as Applied to the Iron and Steel Industry,* prepared for the Industrial Committee of the National Resources Committee by Louis J. Paradiso under the direction of Gardiner C. Means. It is labeled as a "preliminary edition for technical criticism" and the introduction refers to a still earlier (March 1939) preliminary report for technical criticism. There is neither endorsement nor disclaimer by the Board, except as implicit in the label, and no letter of transmittal from anyone to anyone.

This emphasis on the preliminary and technical nature of the report arose from at least two factors. First, at this stage in the development of economic theory, methodology, and analysis, industrial location studies such as this were relatively new, if not novel, and there probably was a genuine desire on the part of the technical staff to secure the best possible criticism by contemporaries. But, second, studies of this kind, and especially studies of iron and steel, were often regarded with caution, if not distaste and hostility, by the industries concerned. The large business firms were not anxious to have government agencies engage in economic studies of their industry, with the possibility of later government policies that the industries would resist. By calling the report "preliminary" and "technical," at least some of this industry hostility would be muted, if not avoided.

Thomas C. Blaisdell, Jr., then chairman of the Industrial Committee, has commented as follows on the steel report:

> The Capital Requirements study of steel created such a powerful kick-back from the industry that the President appointed a special engineering study by an independent firm. It confirmed the findings but handled the public relations differently. The importance of the study became apparent at a later date when the War Production Board, following much the same logic, set the tonnage goal at exactly the same figure.[7]

In the years which followed, the NRPB published in mimeographed form a number of reports on industrial organization and location (see table B-1), each of which carried the name(s) of its authors and each of which was of modest length (50 to 80 pages usually).[8]

---

[7] Personal letter from Blaisdell, November 11, 1979.
[8] See table B-1, items 166, 184, 188, 192, 194, 199, 219, 221, 247, 264, 275, 296, 312, 313, and 314.

In December 1942 (if one accepts the title page as definitive) or in February 1943 (if one accepts the Board's transmittal letter to the president as conclusive), the NRPB published a long (360-page) printed report, *Industrial Location and National Resources* (item 315, table B-1). The war had been on for a whole year and there was much criticism in Congress and elsewhere of federal agencies which seemed to carry on their usual activities without regard to the war effort. Partly for this reason, perhaps, the Board's letter of transmittal took pains to point out the relevance of this report to the war and postwar governmental and national activities. In fact, several of the authors of this report, notably Glenn E. McLaughlin who had directed the study, had been serving as consultants to various war agencies, particularly to the War Production Board, and the knowledge and data they had acquired in making this study and its antecedents were put directly to use in this way. The report has a brief introduction, presumably though not explicitly written by McLaughlin, followed by twenty chapters signed by one or at most two authors who were staff members or consultants to the NRPB. The report as a whole is a summation or synthesis of the many detailed reports noted above, as well as of others. It is lengthy, detailed, quantitative, not overly technical, but serious.

The report contains relatively little in the way of recommendations. Something of its flavor is expressed in the following brief quotation from near the end of the introduction:

> The Federal Government has never played a neutral part in the determination of industry patterns. Most governmental measures have some influence on the use of resources and the growth of industry . . . when peace returns, we shall be faced with problems of industrial readjustment and relocation hardly less difficult than those involved in mobilization for war. An effective program is likely to call for the employment of varied kinds of governmental action consistent with the spirit of our democracy and our system of free enterprise.

At about the same time as the publication of this report, the NRPB published other reports which aroused a storm of criticism in the Congress and elsewhere (see chapters 9, 11, and 13). The *Industrial Location* report seems to have largely escaped such criticism, perhaps because the others served as a lightning rod to protect it. It was, of course, one of the NRPB's major reports and as such drew general criticism directed at that organization.

General Economic Studies

The NRPB made and published several studies which can most readily be described as general; the major ones are briefly discussed in this section.

In June 1939, the NRPB published a major report (item 120, table B-1), *The Structure of the American Economy: Part I. Basic Characteristics,* a product of the Industrial Committee, authored by Gardiner C. Means. He was assisted by a considerable staff, some of whom (such as Paul M. Sweezy and William S. Vickery) later achieved considerable professional reputations of their own. This was complemented in 1940 by *Part II. Toward Full Use of Resources* (item 155) and by a *Supplement* (item 156 in table B-1).

The rationale for this major report was stated in the preface:

Earlier reports of the National Resources Committee and its predecessors have examined the Nation's material resources of land, water, and minerals; the changing character of the population which seeks to utilize these resources; and the improving engineering techniques whereby resources are used to serve human needs . . . In this report on the structure of the American economy an effort is made to bring the major aspects of the national economy into focus so as to emphasize the organic character of the process whereby the Nation's resources are employed to provide useful commodities and services.

The report is long and detailed, with many tables and charts—a thoroughly professional piece of economic inquiry. It does not lend itself to short and easy summary but a few quotations from the introduction and from the conclusion will capture some of its flavor:

This report attempts to delineate the essential structural characteristics of the American economy. Its aim is to clarify the problem of achieving effective use of resources, not to offer any solution . . . Knowledge of structure becomes imperative when any organization or machine fails to run properly . . . The American people are faced with a basic national problem in the extensive idleness of men and machines. Resources of manpower and materials and skills are available to establish a much higher level of living than now exists. The serious failure to use these resources to the full is placing our democratic institutions in jeopardy.

The report and the activity on which it was based had one major result. In 1938 a special Temporary National Economic Committee

(TNEC) was established by Senate resolution, and its very extensive studies and investigations were published in a long series of reports and monographs, which provided a more detailed and more quantitative picture of the American economy, as it was then, than had ever been available earlier. It was, at least to a degree, stimulated by the NRC studies.

A very ambitious report was published in January 1941, as *Development of Resources and Stabilization of Employment in the United States* (item 180 in table B-1). The whole report was also published in three parts (items 181, 182, and 183 in table B-1), each of which probably enjoyed some circulation on its own. The title of the report is somewhat misleading in that it is almost wholly devoted to a consideration of public works.

The nature of the report and its intended use is well described in the message of transmittal from the president to the Congress:

> National defense is more than a mobilization of a Nation's armed strength. Equally must we focus public thought on the ideals and objectives of our national life. We must seek wider understanding of the possibilities for that future we prepare to defend. Among those possibilities are the larger use, the conservation and development of the Nation's resources. I have from time to time during the past eight years called to the attention of the Congress these possibilities; and during these years several laws have been enacted to promote the orderly development and prudent husbandry of our national resources, human as well as material. The National Resources Planning Board has now completed its report, which I send you herewith, on the Development of Resources and the Stabilization of Employment in the United States. This is the first of a series of such reports which each year I shall transmit to the Congress shortly after submission of the Budget of the United States. The Budget contains the recommendations of the Chief Executive for the financial outlays to carry on a public works program during the next fiscal year. This report places these recommendations within the framework of a long-range policy of intelligent planning for the future.

This message makes clear the president's intention to use the NRPB as a coordinator of public works for the whole federal establishment and, at least to some extent, to coordinate federal public works with those sponsored by states and units of local government. The report itself is divided into three main parts: Part I: The Federal Program for National Development; Part II: Regional Development Plans; and Part III: Functional Development Policies. Each has a substantial amount of detailed information, in the case of Part I for each of the federal agencies with any significant public works program. The material in this report is, of course, wholly dated now and there is little purpose in trying to summarize the findings here.

But the report is significant in other respects. The planning function implicit in it rested solidly on the legal foundation of the Employment Stabilization Act of 1931, which by 1941 was the primary legislative basis for the NRPB's work. The report led the NRPB up to the trough of decision making for actual public works, if it did not quite give it a drink from that trough. This activity was in one sense an extension of the NRPB's general planning function, but it brought the organization closer to actual decisions than it had been earlier; and, by the same token, it took it closer to controversy and opposition from other agencies —most notably the Corps of Engineers. This report surely gave the NRPB more visibility in quarters where it had been less noticed previously. Had the NRPB continued permanently, and had it exercised this function with vigor, and with effect, it surely would have been made into a different organization than it was before this date.

The NRPB made and published several other more or less miscellaneous economic studies. For instance, it or its regional offices made several studies on commodity trade flows into and out of some regions. There was a good deal of interest in this sort of information and analysis in the 1930s. It made at least one study of taxation and another on interest rates.

11

NRPB Concerns With Transportation and Urban Structure

Transportation Studies

Over the years of its existence, the NRPB and its predecessor agencies made a number of rather specialized studies on transportation, each published as a mimeographed report, most signed by one or two individual authors, without either endorsement or disclaimer by the Board. One may assume that these reports were issued in small editions, with limited circulation, and with unmeasured but possibly significant effect.[1]

The NRPB's major contribution to transportation policy was its report, *Transportation and National Policy*, dated May 1942. A printed report, with 513 large size pages, it was a truly major result of the NRPB's long interest in transportation matters. Board chairman Delano, because of his earlier personal involvement in railroad management, was particularly interested in this and other transportation studies. There is a letter of transmittal from the Board to the president which states, in part: "The Board is fully in accord with the view that the building of a superior and more effective transport system is a basic essential to the fuller development of our national economy." This statement might be taken as an implicit endorsement of the report but there is no explicit endorsement.

---

[1] See table B-1, items 40, 100, 159, 172, 177, 186, 190, 195, 209, 211, 212, 213, 214, 215, 226, 228, 234, 309, and 347.

There is also a letter of transmittal from Owen D. Young, chairman of the Advisory Committee, to Delano, which says, in part: "The report consists of a summary statement of findings and recommendations on national transport development policy prepared by Dr. Ralph J. Watkins, Director of the Study, and a series of studies assembled under Dr. Watkins' direction from contributions by a staff of specialists and agencies within the government. . . . Four meetings of the Committee were held. Two of these were concerned with the formulation of plans for the study, and two were for the purpose of reviewing drafts of reports. One of these latter meetings was devoted to a review of an interim report prepared by the staff, and the last meeting was devoted to a consideration of a draft of the final report." It goes on to describe the procedure by which three different drafts of a report were circulated to the committee for review and criticism, and to relate how the pressures of war effort made further attention to the report difficult. "Under the circumstances, therefore, it has seemed wise to submit the Director's summary and the staff and agency studies to you with the recommendation that they be published." The report does not, therefore, have explicit committee endorsement but does have committee support to the extent of urging its publication. The committee consisted of major federal employees in transportation agencies, except for Young, who was at that time president of General Electric Corporation.

The summary report describes the importance of transportation in the economy and life of the country; the role of public action in the development of transportation; the past evolution of the transport system, its present problems, and the possibilities for the future; and the elements of an efficient transportation system. Capital and labor problems are also considered. The summary ends with a series of policy recommendations:

A National Transportation Agency should be established to coordinate all Federal development activity in transportation. . . . The planning and construction of modern, unified terminal facilities to serve a coordinated transport system is a logical public responsibility for which leadership should be undertaken by the proposed Transportation Agency. . . . Logic and necessity suggest that the credit of the Federal Government must, by appropriate fiscal devices and under appropriate safeguards, be made available to the end that the formidable tasks of railway modernization and improvement may be included in public works programs aimed at upbuilding the country and sustaining the national economy in the forthcoming difficult years of transition from

war to peace.... Under appropriate legislation the Transportation
Agency should be empowered and directed to proceed at once with
developing and carrying out plans for the economic consolidation of
operating railroads.... War conditions provide an excellent opportunity
in the highway transportation industry for the redesign of automotive
equipment along functional lines; and for the planning of a modern
interregional highway system and urban express routes to accommodate
the automobile of the future.... Major emphasis in future highway
development must be directed to the provision of express highways and
off-street parking in urban areas.... Immediate authority should be
granted to permit the Federal Government to acquire and finance land
acquisitions at the request of State and local governments, as well as
for Federal promotional agencies.... The proposed National Transportation Agency should be directed to accept the unexampled challenge
of air transportation by planning in the most enlightened manner for
the establishment of the new medium as a major and integral part of
our future transportation system.... The proposed Transportation
Agency should ... undertake continuing evaluation of the economic
results of present regulatory practices, including changes in the rate
level, quality of service, and intensity of competition.... The complexity of the rate structure and of issues involved in the present controversy and the nature of the problem are such that further legislative
treatment appears inadvisable.... The logic of a nation-wide organization of transport employees requires a parallel organization of employ-
ers in each of the several branches of transportation for the conduct of
industrial relations on an industrywide basis ... and the transportation
industries, properly developed and coordinated as contemplated in this
report, offer some of the most promising opportunities for wise investment.

Elsewhere in the summary (p. 9) the suggestion is made that federal
ownership and operation of the railroads may ultimately be necessary
unless sufficient and adequate consolidations and improvements can be
made. A more definite proposal is made that the government should take
over the ownership of the fixed transportation plant for the railroads, as
it has provided the basic transportation plant for highway travel, with
operation of the railroads left in private hands.

The similarity of titles between the sections of this report and the
previously listed mimeographed reports indicates that this printed version
is in large measure a refined and more readily available source than the
earlier ones. The treatment in each section is professional, with tables,
charts, and careful writing.

There is no need for a detailed review of this report. In one sense,
the discussions are dated—air transport was relatively new, the inter-

state highway system did not exist, the railroads, while in financial trouble, still seemed to offer some possibilities for profitable private investment, and other aspects of the national transportation situation were different then than they appear now, nearly forty years later. But in many other aspects the report as a whole was prophetic and far ahead of its time—the need for coordination among forms of transport is still a vital problem, the need for relaxation of former controls over at least some forms of transport is still an active issue, the need for a massive infusion of new capital into railroads is still evident, the case for public ownership of railroad fixed plant is still strong, and in various other ways the analysis of this long book has major relevance today. While some actions in the direction of the report's recommendations have been taken, on the whole its recommendations have not been followed—and the problems are still with us.

While this report is nominally a product of a special advisory committee, in fact it was dominantly an NRPB staff output or the output of consultants from universities and other federal agencies enlisted by the NRPB for this effort. The transmittal letter from Young, to Delano, speaks of the desirability of bringing the report to a conclusion because of the war pressures on the time of the committee members, as noted above. This was undoubtedly a factor, but another and perhaps more important factor was the great difficulty in getting the committee members, each of whom spoke for some special interest or form of transportation, to agree on a report.[2] By the device of making it clear that the Summary Report was strictly that of the study director, and the section reports were those of their authors, the report was cleared for publication by the committee. This illustrates the de facto shift of NRPB report preparation from committees to staff, which we noted earlier. In terms of getting excellent reports published, there is much to say for it; in terms of commanding widespread acceptance and support of the findings of the study, it may be more doubtful as a tactic.

This major transportation report drew some adverse comment in the Congress and elsewhere but far less criticism than some of its proposals might have been expected to draw. The report came out during the war, yet was not primarily concerned with the war, and as such might well have been expected to draw criticism on this ground, as did many other activities, not only of the NRPB but of other federal agencies at this time. Its advocacy of a larger role for government action, including

---

[2] Interview with Ralph J. Watkins, August 8, 1978.

possible ownership of railroad roadbeds and even of rolling stock, or of possible government operation of railroads under some conditions, did draw criticism in the Congress, from Senator Robert Taft and others. But what largely saved the transportation study from severe criticism was that at this time the critics had still better targets in the NRPB than this. The *Security, Work and Relief Policies* report and the NRPB annual report *National Resources Development, Report for 1943* drew so much fire that the transportation report was to some extent passed over.

Urban Structure

The NRPB made one major study (reported in three parts) on urban structure, as well as several smaller studies concerned with one aspect or another of the general urban problem. These were in addition to its studies on housing and to its numerous studies on planning of specific aspects of cities or plans for particular urban areas, all of which are discussed in other chapters.

Some time before June 1, 1936, a Research Committee on Urbanism was organized by the National Resources Committee. The research committee was composed mostly of persons outside of the federal government, although Eliot and M. L. Wilson (then undersecretary of agriculture) were also members. An interim report (item 36, table B-1) was published in mimeographed form in July 1936; a major printed report, *Our Cities, Their Role in the National Economy* (item 50, table B-1), was published in June 1937; two printed supplementary reports (items 126 and 127, table B-1) were issued in early 1939 to present some of the basic data and information which had been collected but not included in the 1937 report; and a small pamphlet was published in September 1937. The discussion which follows relies primarily on the 1937 printed report.

The 1937 report has a foreword by the National Resources Committee which has some brief background discussion, a statement of emerging problems, some eleven specific recommendations, and a closing section on "possible accomplishments." A few brief quotations will capture some of the flavor of this foreword:

> This report . . . is the first major national study of cities in the United States. The Country Life Commission reporting to President Theodore

Roosevelt in 1909 explored the problems of rural living for the first time in systematic fashion, but until now there has been no similar examination of urban conditions. There have been many special studies in particular cities, but none of the place of cities in our national scheme of things. . . . Urban and rural communities have many economic problems in common. . . . The city has seemed at times the despair of America, but at others to be the Nation's hope, the battleground of democracy. . . . The faults of our cities are not those of decadence and impending decline, but of exuberant vitality crowding its way forward under tremendous pressure—the flood rather than the drought. . . . The most drastic inequalities of income and wealth are found within the urban community. . . . Competing forms of transportation have left their disrupting imprint upon the national urban pattern. . . . The unparalleled growth of cities has been accompanied by uncontrolled subdivision and speculative practices and by the most fantastic real estate booms. . . . Urban housing is one of the most burdensome problems the country now has to face. . . . Juvenile delinquency, organized crime, and commercial rackets are among the vexations of the city. . . . Urban public finance is another emerging problem of vast proportions. . . . Our overlapping medley of independent governmental units was intended for a rural and a manorial society but never for the sprawling metropolitan regions of America and the satellite suburbs.

These and other statements in the report are fully applicable and highly pertinent to the cities and metropolitan areas today. The eleven recommendations are more dated. They deal primarily with what the federal government might then do to assist the cities with their economic, governmental, housing, and other problems. While an active federal role is envisaged, the recommendations are for vastly less federal activity than exists today and, as far as I can ascertain, did not provoke adverse reaction from the critics of the NRPB at the time.

The main body of the 1937 report has parts and sections (as was the fashion with NRPB reports at this juncture) with such headings as the following: The Facts About Urban America; The Process of Urbanization—Underlying Forces and Emerging Trends; The Problems of Urban America; Special Studies of the Urbanism Committee; and Statements of General Policy and Recommendations. There are many maps, some in color, some folded in; many charts and statistical tables; and, on the whole, a scholarly and professional job of analysis and writing.

This report was a truly major intellectual undertaking for the time, and well merits its claim to be the first truly overall national survey of urban problems. One can reasonably conclude that it was the forerunner from which other studies and action have followed, culminating in the establishment of a federal Department of Housing and Urban Development in 1965.

Conclusion

The NRPB's activities in transportation and in urban problems are important for themselves, and they illustrate, when taken in conjunction with the other reports described, the very wide range of the NRPB's interests and activities.

12

NRPB Reports on Planning

The NRPB issued some reports that dealt directly with the quality of planning as a function or activity. In December 1936, the National Resources Committee published *Public Works Planning,* a 221-page printed report (item 42, table B-1). While much of the report consisted of a detailed review of drainage basin problems and programs, including a detailed listing of specific projects by drainage basins, prepared by the Water Resources Committee, the first part, the report by the National Resources Committee, is almost a primer of planning public works. There are sections on such subjects as "planning and selection of projects," "planning organization," "making the plans," "selection of projects," "state and local inventories and programs," and the like. This must surely have been very helpful to state and other planning organizations at the time, anxious as most of them were to obtain federal funds to employ people in their localities in the construction of needed public works.

In 1937 the National Resources Committee issued a preliminary mimeographed report which even then was a revision of some earlier report, and in 1938 it issued a final printed report on *Suggested Symbols for Plans, Maps, and Charts* (item 93, table B-1). This was very much a "how to" report, the purpose of which was to attain a much greater degree of comparability between reports prepared by different planning organizations. Such things as the accepted color for different land uses, or the accepted symbols for different kinds of structures, were explained and illustrated in detail. A somewhat different but generally very similar report was issued in 1939, *County and Municipal Planning: A Statement of Improved Practices and Procedures* (item 114 in table B-1).

There were also various reports describing sources of information available to and useful for local planners.[1] The NRPB also either sponsored or played a major role in conferences of planners where the major concern was development of expertise in planning, and sometimes these conferences resulted in publications, usually mimeographed and with modest distribution.[2] There were also reports, mostly mimeographed and perhaps with modest yet important circulations, on planning in other countries.[3]

These reports are not very impressive in 1980, in light of the many changes which have occurred during the ensuing 40 years. Much more significant, at the time, than these reports were the numerous papers given and personal participations of NRPB staff in national, regional, and state planning conferences.

The NRPB Promotes Regional Planning

In the 1930s there was much interest in many professional circles in regional planning.[4] The states were seen as too numerous and too small to cope with many serious economic and social problems, and state boundaries frequently did not conform to boundaries of natural units. On the other hand, the nation was too large and too diverse to deal with important problems and situations which might affect large areas and considerable numbers of people and yet not be nationwide in scope or at least not nationwide in form and content. It was evident that many problems were interstate. But it was also evident, even to the most

---

[1] In 1936, *Classified Guide to Material in the Library of Congress Covering Urban Community Development* (item 29); in 1940, *Federal Aids to Local Planning* (item 148); and in 1942, *Bibliography of Reports of State, Territorial, and Regional Planning Agencies* (item 246).

[2] See 1938, *Proceedings of the National Zoning Conference,* Chicago, Illinois, December 1937 (item 79) and *Planning Technicians' Conference* (item 101).

[3] In 1940, in Latin America (item 161), in Germany (item 171), in Sweden (item 173), in Germany again (item 187), and in selected countries (item 217).

[4] Earle S. Draper, "Regional Planning," in George B. Galloway and associates, *Planning for America* (New York, Henry Holt and Company, 1941), is one good example.

enthusiastic regional planners, that there existed no unit of regional government. There had been some development of interstate or regional compacts, but these were often difficult to negotiate, typically limited to a few activities, and often presented serious problems of internal government and operation. The Tennessee Valley Authority, established early in the New Deal, was a major regional development, often seen by both friends and opponents as a precursor of other regional authorities. During the NRPB's life there was some attempt to establish additional regional authorities. In the later 1940s and early 1950s, after the NRPB no longer existed, there were strong but unsuccessful efforts by various groups and persons to establish such regional authorities, built around river basin systems—the Missouri and the Columbia, for instance.

During the period of its existence the NRPB was in the forefront of promoting and developing regional planning. Among the difficult problems, never fully resolved then or later, were how to define a "region"— by natural features, such as river systems, or by economic interests; whether to follow or to disregard state boundaries; whether to have regions for all purposes follow the same boundaries, and other problems. In its own work, the NRPB used "flexible" boundaries, the exact contours depending upon different activities.

One of the earliest major expressions of its interest in regional planning was the December 1935 report of the National Resources Committee, *Regional Factors in National Planning* (item 25, table B-1). The report consists of a relatively brief foreword, findings and principles, and recommendations by the committee. The letter of transmittal to the president states, in part, "The members of the Committee have not all had an opportunity to give full consideration to all of the points involved. However, they endorse the recommendations and desire to indicate to you their belief in the great importance and value of this study." The report itself is long (223 large-size pages) and is by a Technical Committee on Regional Planning.

Some flavor of the thinking of the National Resources Committee, or at least of its staff, concerning regional planning, can be conveyed by some brief quotes (p. v):

> The Problem. The consideration of what are called regional problems is thrust upon the attention of our Nation by a number of urgent situations. Among these are: 1. The increasingly clear realization of the inadequacy of single states to carry out all planning programs necessary for conserving our natural resources. . . . 2. The development

of an extensive interstate cooperation movement. . . . 3. The rise of interstate metropolitan planning. . . . 4. The emergence and activity of two group-of-states planning regions—the Pacific Northwest Regional Commission and the New England Regional Planning Commission. 5. The establishment of more than 100 types of Federal regional areas dealing with field administration and departmental planning. 6. The creation of the Tennessee Valley Authority and the proposals for the establishment of other like authorities. 7. The pressure of economic distress and unbalance in various agricultural-industrial areas of the United States, and the corresponding necessity of establishing subnational administration in the regions served by the several economic groups. . . .

The Committee went on to say (p. ix) :

It has been suggested that regions—perhaps 10 or 12 in number— be organized as new political units, combining and regrouping states, as a basis of congressional representation and as independent authorities. Quite aside from the constitutional questions involved, however, such groupings would not be flexible enough to deal effectively with the rapidly developing and changing regional activities of our governments, such as power, water, minerals, industry, agriculture—and might even obstruct the function they should serve. The proposed grouping and coordination of administrative or other agencies, on the other hand, would be flexible and adaptable, and would make possible all that may wisely be attempted in subnational situations and problems. . . .

A regional organization, whatever its varied form, should not be considered a new form of sovereignty, even in embryo. It need never develop to the stage where it will have elected officers, a legislative body, and the power to tax. Consequently, the region need not have fixed boundaries. By the same token the region need have no definite body of citizens.

The Committee went on to make a number of specific recommendations for the establishment and functioning of the regional bodies it had described and proposed, including the following:

We recommend pointing Federal policy toward regrouping the field districts used by the numerous United States agencies (now involving some 108 different arrangements of districts with as high as 73 agencies in some centers) in the direction of achieving a limited number of regional centers, say 10 to 12. (p. xi)

The report of the Technical Committee is a first-class professional document. It starts with a discussion of the regional "problem," proceeds to a description and analysis of "some attempts at solution of the problem," and then discusses "geographic factors and criteria." The final section of its report is "The integration of administrative and geographic factors in regional planning." The report as a whole is not only a good factual account of regional planning as it then existed in the United States but is also a good conceptual discussion of the elements of regional planning which are still reasonably accurate for the United States.

The NRPB issued a long series of printed reports, from its Washington office, which were typically final reports that had been prepared in the regional offices, mimeographed there, and distributed primarily within the region.[5]

These reports were of varying degrees of specificity and some contained concrete recommendations, many of which were translated into action promptly. Many of the reports were summarized and published together, with some updating of at least some of them, in an NRPB report of February 1942, *Regional Resources Development, Report for 1942*.

Even a brief summary of each of these reports would be longer than is appropriate for this chapter, but the New England report (item 35, table B-1) may be briefly characterized as somewhat typical of the group. There is only the briefest letter of transmittal from Ickes to the president, and only a two-page foreword by the committee. The report is from the New England Regional Planning Commission, one member of which is from each of the six New England states, plus the chairman, plus two members-at-large. In addition to these commissioners, there was an extensive list of consultants and two technical advisory committees, one on water and one on aviation. The report of the commission is six pages long, with eleven recommendations, mostly to the effect that regional planning should proceed in New England. The bulk of the report is by the commission staff and is divided into sections on population, land resources, recreation, water resources, transportation, industry, publicity, and planning agencies in New England. The report has several tables, many maps, and many photographs—an attractive and thoroughly professional job. One of the striking features at the beginning is a graphic diagrammatic map of New England—on which no state lines appear! One can readily imagine that this map must have upset those (and I know from personal experience they were many,

---

[5] See table B-1, items 30, 31, 35, 55, 63, 65, 80, 110, 135, 278, 279, 355.

and that they were emotional) who thought regionalism was a threat to the integrity of the states. This and other regional reports were, in a great many ways, similar to NRPB central office reports on similar subjects—and not necessarily any less outstanding than the central office reports.

The regional planning commissions were highly variable in the amount and timing of their activities. The New England and Pacific Northwest commissions were the earliest, the most active, and the most prolific in their reports. The other regions to a degree followed the lead of these two. The pace of regional activity, or at least of reports emanating from regional activity, seems to quicken in 1940 and later years. If the NRPB had continued indefinitely, the regional organizations might have come to play a much larger role in the planning and even in the development of natural resources.

One interesting offshoot of the NRPB's concern with regions or areas different in size than states was its promotion of "area analysis." Organizationally within the NRPB, this was the interest of a special sub-committee of the Land Committee. The concept of area analysis was a methodology developed by Charles C. Colby, a professor of geography at the University of Chicago. The focus was a kind of regionalism—not always the grand regions established by the NRPB, but more geo-graphically determined areas, often smaller but sometimes larger than states. Had the NRPB survived, this type of analysis might have had a considerable impact in planning of smaller regions. Two reports, both listed as Technical Paper Number 6, *Area Analysis—A Method of Public Works Planning,* were published, the first in July 1942 and its revision in April 1943 (items 287 and 322 in table B-1). The preface to the latter states: "This document is not an end product in itself, but a tool for implementing two major planning responsibilities: (1) plan-ning for the postwar period, and (2) securing better programming and planning of public activities." Each report is essentially a manual for planners, telling them what kinds of information to look for, how to assemble and analyze it, and how to apply the "method." Perhaps the most significant aspect of this concern with area analysis is the con-siderable number of reports that were prepared by NRPB staff persons.[6]

---

[6] See table B-1, items 196, 236, 244, 245, 253, 254, 255, 256, 259, 266, 268, 274, 322, and 361.

The NRPB Stimulates and Helps State Planning

The NRPB's role in helping to stimulate state planning is one of its success stories, which was described in chapter 6. The NRPB issued several reports concerned with state planning, of which we pick the three largest and most important for a brief review.

In June 1935, the National Resources Board issued a 310-large-size-page report, *State Planning, Review of Activities and Progress*. On pp. iv and v it says:

> This volume and account of State Planning Progress has been compiled from circulars of the National Planning Board and National Resources Board, from reports of state planning and land planning consultants, official publications of state planning boards and from special statements and reports prepared for this purpose. . . . The meaning of the state planning boards which have recently sprung into life is the expression of a desire to . . . (1) Take a comprehensive view of the resources and planning problems of the several states; (2) To relate the work of the local planners, already under way in many cities and in a number of counties, to the work of the state as a whole; (3) To relate the work of the states to each other by better cooperation and coordination, as in the case of water users; (4) To relate the work of the state planning agencies to that of the national government; and (5) Finally, to relate the work of the several public planning agencies to that of private and semipublic agencies within the state, as in the development of transportation and power.

The report has brief findings and recommendations, both of which are an endorsement and encouragement of state planning. There is also a brief historical section. The greater part of the report is given over to an account of planning, first in each of the states, then by general subject matter groups. It contains a good deal of highly useful reference material about the boards of that time. This material is, of course, highly dated, and there is no purpose in a detailed review of it. The report does not give a critique of state planning as it then existed—perhaps, in view of the delicate politics of the situation, no federal report could. There is only the slightest hint of any shortcomings.

In March 1938 a special committee of the NRPB, composed in part of state planning officials, in part of NRPB staff, and in part of consultants from universities and other outside organizations, submitted a report which the National Resources Committee published as *The Future of State Planning* (117 large-size pages). As one might expect, this group was sympathetic to state planning, thought it should go forward, and offered a number of suggestions for strengthening it. Given that general stance, the statements of the special committee are not abrasive or contentious, although those opposed to planning might well take issue with them. There is a good discussion of the organization and the "bewildering variety" of activities of the state boards. There are only veiled suggestions that some boards were not strong and that the commitment of some states to planning was not very great. More than half of the report is taken up with a listing of members of the various state boards and with a bibliography of board reports.

In June 1942 the NRPB issued a 134-large-size-page report, *State Planning,* which was in many respects patterned after the two earlier reports described above. There is only a very brief foreword: "A decade of State planning has proved the utility of State planning boards as arms of planning management for State functions in our Federal system. . . . State appropriations and allotments rapidly increased. . . . Increasing staff work as an arm of planning management for the Governor and in wartime planning has brought the State planning boards into day-to-day contact with the problems of our changing economic and social life. . . . Many of the boards are devoting almost full time to war problems while others have limited their general activities to completion of reports which are already under way." A large part of the report is concerned with an account of the status of the planning boards in each state but there are also two appendixes, one on state legislation on planning, zoning, and platting, and the other on state conservation legislation.

The NRPB Helps Make City Plans

City planning, interpreting the words in the broadest possible sense, is very old in the world. Rulers, legislatures, and others have developed plans for their cities and undertaken public works to carry them out, from the earliest walled villages to the present. In the United States, major plans have been developed for New York, Chicago, and Washington, among other cities.[7]

---

[7] Russell Van Nest Black, *Planning and the Planning Profession—The Past Fifty Years, 1917–1967* (Washington, D.C., American Institute of Planners, 1967); and Mel Scott, *History of City Planning in America Since 1890* (Berkeley, University of California Press, 1969).

City planning, as an organized and continuing activity of city government in the United States gradually became established in the early twentieth century and, by World War I, zoning as a means of enforcing public plans on private parties was invented and began to be applied.[8] Both city planning and zoning were actively promoted by the federal government during the 1920s, particularly by Herbert Hoover, then secretary of commerce. A model zoning ordinance was developed in 1928 under his direction. Zoning as a legal means of private land control was authenticated by the Supreme Court in 1926, in the famous Euclid zoning decision.

Frederic Delano had had a long experience in city planning when the first National Planning Board was established in 1933. He had been involved in the Chicago Plan in 1908, was chairman of the Regional Plan of New York from 1924 to 1929, and chairman of the Park and Planning Commission of Washington when the NPB was established and throughout the history of the NRPB. Charles Eliot had joined the Park and Planning Commission as city planner in 1926 and was the director of its small staff in 1928, a position which he held when the NPB was established in 1933. With this deep personal involvement in city planning, it was only natural that both Delano and Eliot sought to encourage city planning by the NRPB and its various predecessors. Charles Merriam, although not so specifically in city planning as the other two, had been involved in city politics in Chicago and was thus familiar with planning in that city, and there is no reason to believe that he was any less convinced of the desirability of the NRPB's encouragement of city planning.

To the old arguments in favor of organized planning by cities, the Great Depression added the important consideration that this was often the best way to get much needed federal public works and the local employment they brought. The New Deal was in this way the beginning of a system of federal encouragement of local planning which continues on an increasing scale to the present—such plans are often required as a condition to receipt of federal funds. We have noted in chapter 6 that the NPB played a major role in getting federal funds allocated to cities for their planning activities. By early 1937 there were about a thousand city or town planning agencies and half as many metropolitan or county

---

[8] Seymour Toll, *Zoned American* (New York, Grossman, 1969). For a recent statement of urban land use planning, including a history of its development, see F. Stuart Chapin, Jr., and Edward J. Kaiser, *Urban Land Use Planning,* third edition (Urbana, Illinois, University of Illinois Press, 1979).

planning agencies in the United States.[9] Perloff estimates that there
had been only about 200 planning commissions in the early 1920s.[10] By
1968 more than 10,000 local governments had planning boards; this
included about 6,600 city governments, nearly 1,600 counties, and
over 2,400 New England-type townships.[11] These different sources employ somewhat different definitions and hence are not precisely comparable, but a marked increase in numbers of local planning organizations
has surely occurred. Three-fourths of the 1968 planning boards had
no full-time employees, working instead with part-time or with volunteer
help. Nevertheless, they made plans and/or enacted zoning ordinances.
It is difficult to estimate the role that the NRPB played in this development of local planning. Much of it would likely have taken place if the
NRPB had never existed. On the other hand, the NRPB clearly gave an
immense stimulus to local planning during the years it existed, and some
of its techniques and its impetus almost surely carried over into later
years as well.

The NRPB provided help to city planning agencies beyond its role
in the provision of federal funds, important as this was. For instance,
on December 15, 1939, it issued an extensive mimeographed report,
Federal Relations to Local Planning, which described the services, including information, various federal agencies were prepared to provide
to local planning organizations. There seems little doubt that the NRPB
stimulated a large amount of city planning and helped to improve its
quality.

In a few instances, the NRPB or its staff entered directly into the
making of city plans. Examples are its publications on city plans for
Anchorage and Sitka (items 294 and 295, table B-1).

Summary

For the ten years of its existence, the NRPB and its predecessors
epitomized planning in the United States—both to those who feverently

---

[9] Ladislas Segoe, "City and County Planning," in Galloway and associates,
Planning for America; NRC Circular X, *Status of City and County Planning in the
United States,* May 15, 1937.

[10] Harvey S. Perloff, *Education for Planning: City, State, and Regional* (Baltimore, Johns Hopkins University Press for Resources for the Future, 1957).

[11] Allen D. Manvel, *Local Land and Building Regulation—How Many Agencies? What Practice? How Much Personnel?* Research Report no. 6, National
Commission on Urban Problems, (Washington, D.C., GPO, 1968).

believed in planning and to those who violently opposed it, and to the masses in the center between these extremes. In addition to its work on substantive issues, the NRPB helped greatly to stimulate and to improve planning at regional, state, and local levels. It was not only the practitioner of planning in its own studies, but the stimulator and the instructor for planning by others, and it helped other agencies get other federal funds or manpower. In these various roles, its efforts were important and surely left a permanent legacy for planning as a profession.

13

The NRPB as War and Postwar Planner

Much of the NRPB's work, as described in the foregoing chapters, had utility for the war and postwar efforts of the United States. In particular, its industry location, transportation, energy, and area analysis studies assembled information which could have been highly useful in planning the war programs. Partly because many of those studies were undertaken before the defense or war efforts became dominant in federal affairs, or because they were undertaken primarily for other purposes, I have chosen to discuss those studies under other headings. In this chapter, I consider only those NRPB activities directed specifically to the defense, war, and postwar efforts.

The United States entered World War II in early December 1941, immediately following the Japanese attack on Pearl Harbor on December 7. But the possibility—indeed, the probability—of war had been evident for many months and defense programs had come to dominate activities of the federal government well before Pearl Harbor. U.S. involvement in war had been more or less foreseen as early as fall 1937, when President Roosevelt made his famous "quarantine" speech in Chicago, denouncing Hitler for aggressive actions and arguing that other nations had to quarantine themselves against such actions as they would quarantine against the plague.[1] When Germany invaded Poland in early

---

[1] Harold L. Ickes, *The Secret Diary of Harold L. Ickes, The Inside Struggle, 1936–1939* (New York, Simon and Schuster, 1943) pp. 221–222. With characteristic modesty, Ickes claims credit for suggesting the term.

September 1939, the war actually began in Europe and American involvement in it became vastly more probable; the United States immediately began defense mobilization.

In Defense and War Planning

As the defense efforts unfolded, the NRPB was called on for advice, information, and even special studies.

> When the Second World War began the NRPB found itself caught up in the rush of events and an increasing amount of its time and effort was directed toward the war effort. The Board and members of its staff made valuable contributions to more effective resource use, improved industrial location, transportation, and to the relief of urban congestion caused by rapid expansion of the war making potential. The major job of coordinating the conversion, however, was left to the specially created emergency agencies. The role of NRPB was largely limited to furnishing data and expert advice. Even this contribution was of declining value. As the war agencies accumulated knowledge and gained experience they were able to rely on their own staffs and files and to function without the aid of the NRPB.[2]

When the defense effort began the United States was totally unprepared for war. Not only was its war machine at a low ebb and its military manpower limited, but the military agencies had simply not planned for a worldwide war. Members of the NRPB staff who were quickly drawn into the defense and war planning effort have told me how appalled they were at the primitive level of planning in the defense agencies.[3] The military forces had assumed they could go into the markets and, on a priority basis, buy what they needed—an assumption perhaps reasonable for a much smaller scale of war effort but totally unrealistic for the worldwide war into which the United States entered.

In typical fashion, Roosevelt did not assign the defense responsibilities to existent agencies but created new ones, beginning with the Office of Emergency Management in September 1939.[4] These agencies underwent many changes, with confused and overlapping responsibilities.

---

[2] Philip W. Warken, "A History of the National Resources Planning Board, 1933–1934" (doctoral dissertation, Ohio State University, 1969) p. 248.

[3] I am indebted to Wilbert G. Fritz for information on this point.

[4] Herman Miles Somers, *Presidential Agency: OWMR, The Office of War Mobilization and Reconversion* (Cambridge, Mass., Harvard University Press, 1950). See especially chapter 1.

Some of the NRPB staff—Watkins, McLaughlin, Blaisdell, Fritz, Gordon, and others—were drawn into the defense and war planning effort while yet on the NRPB staff, in some cases being detailed part-time or full-time to one of the new agencies for periods of months, or transferring out of the NRPB to one of these agencies. Their experience in making studies for the NRPB had made them some of the most informed persons in the nation. Often one of the benefits of federal programs, additional to their main purposes, is the training and development of men.

Far more important than the specific knowledge they had acquired was their broad understanding of the American economy in general and their experience with developing broad national plans. All of these personal abilities and knowledge were used in a major way in the war effort.

But it is far from clear how influential their voices were in the agencies to which they were detailed or transferred. Time and again, their advice, proven by events to have been sound and perceptive, was disregarded. For instance, in early 1941 Robert Janeway, an NRPB staff member, prepared a report pointing out the coming crisis in railroad cars. Ralph Budd, director of rail activities in the defense agency, speaking out of his experience as a railroad man, rejected the NRPB analysis, only a few months later being forced to concede that the supply of railroad cars was indeed insufficient and that action must be taken to overcome the deficiency.[5] This is but one of several incidents in which the NRPB or its members were accurate and perceptive, but in which their advice was generally disregarded.

If NRPB staff members were used (at least to some degree) in the defense and war effort, the NRPB as an *agency* was used scarcely at all, especially after the defense effort got really under way. Somers, in his very fair and analytical book (see footnote 4), scarcely mentions the NRPB's contributions. The official history of the War Production Board and of the whole defense and war mobilization effort mentions the NRPB only once and in an incidental way.[6] One might expect such an account of an agency by its successor to be biased and to exaggerate its own role, but it hardly deems the NRPB worthy of even a back-of-the-

---

[5] Warken, "A History of the National Resources Planning Board," pp. 137–138.

[6] Bureau of Demobilization, Civilian Production Administration, *Industrial Mobilization for War: History of the War Production Board and Predecessor Agencies, 1940–1945, volume I, Program and Administration* (Washington, D.C., GPO, 1947).

hand brushoff. Millett gives the NRPB a small role in federal policy generally (which I discuss in more detail in a later chapter) and implicitly says it played little or no role in the defense and war effort, and that as that effort progressed it gradually lost touch with the president.[7]

If the Board and staff of the NRPB had sought to play a major role in the defense and war effort—and there is reason to believe that at least some members did—its organization and personalities were totally unsuited to the task. A part-time board, with an aged chairman (Delano) determined not to take advantage of his relationship to the president, and who had no stomach for a rough and tumble political fight; a vice chairman (Merriam) who came to Washington only at monthly intervals, and had a curious distaste for active political involvement; a third member (Yantis) who also came to Washington only infrequently and who was not very aggressive at any time; and an executive officer (Eliot) who may have been eager enough to get into the fray but was held back by his board—these are hardly the stuff of which an active and successful agency is made in the political jungles of Washington. Had any effort been made to use the NRPB as the chief defense and war planning agency, its staff would have had to be expanded greatly and its organization and operations modified greatly to meet such expanded responsibility.

Although the NRPB was not at the center of defense and war planning, it did carry out some activities directly related to defense and war, some of which were quite successful and so recognized at the time. One of these was its role in the development of a national roster of scientific and specialized personnel.[8] Beginning in 1940, the NRPB took the leadership among federal agencies and professional organizations in the development of such a roster. A questionnaire was agreed upon and sent to a half million persons, using lists of members of scientific and professional organizations and other lists. The replies were coded onto punch cards—this was well before the days of modern computers, but the punch card coding and sorting system evolved was unusually innovative for the times. Its rate of operation was as slow as an ox cart, compared with the modern computer—the sorter could handle 400 cards a minute and the tabulator 80 cards a minute, but these were

---

[7] John D. Millett, *The Process and Organization of Government Planning* (New York, Columbia University Press, 1947) pp. 137–152.

[8] *National Roster of Scientific and Specialized Personnel* (National Resources Planning Board, June 1952). This 47-page publication does not include any names, but does describe the process in detail and does include some tables showing numbers of persons by professional category.

lightning fast compared with hand sorting of the questionnaires. During the period in which the activity was centered in the NRPB, but with the help of many other federal agencies and private professional associations, over 1,500 requests for names had been received and over 135,000 names had been certified to the requesting agencies. The roster was transferred to the War Manpower Commission in April 1942.

The NRPB took the leadership, at the urging of a number of other federal agencies and of private organizations, in another defense and war effort, which, through no fault of any of the participants, was much less successful. This was a program to preserve the cultural resources of the nation from damage or destruction in the event the war actually reached into the United States. From the vantage point of 1980, the idea that the United States might have been invaded by German, Italian, or Japanese armies or have been bombed by their air forces in the early 1940s may seem unrealistic or even absurd; but it was taken seriously at the time, and in fact the Japanese did make a symbolic shelling of the California coast and did release incendiary bombs, a few of which reached the Pacific coast. Inventories of public records and of cultural treasures were undertaken and proposals were made for the development of safe storage centers away from Washington, but the progress of the war and the demands for materials and men for the war effort made an actual program of removal and storage impossible. It must also be recalled that this was before microfilming of records was common and practical, hence the proposals were for removal of the records themselves. As far as any program for protection of the identified cultural resources is concerned, this NRPB effort came to nought. It probably was important in the extent to which it stimulated public interest in such resources and in their later care and protection.

The regional offices of the NRPB engaged in one activity directly related to the war effort. In cooperation with the Office of Defense Health and Welfare Services, the NRPB regional offices made a number of studies of the impact of the war upon communities in which a good deal of war effort was concentrated. Smith lists eighty such studies.[9] They were mostly made in early 1942; they range in length from a single page to 100 pages or more; they were all mimeographed; their distribution is unknown; so is the relative contribution of the

[9] Lester W. Smith, *Preliminary List of Published and Unpublished Reports of the National Resources Planning Board, 1933–1943,* Record Group No. 187, Records of the National Resources Planning Board, The National Archives, SR 3 (46-3), March 1946.

Defense agency and the NRPB. Far more seriously, it is impossible now to know what impact, if any, they had then. Alumni of the NRPB have told me that in their judgment, these reports did have some impact.[10] Certainly, the situations around military bases and in cities of heavy war construction were appalling. The military then was highly impervious to outside intellectual influences, and almost all its energies were directed to building up the war machine. I have selected only a few of the larger of these reports for inclusion in table B-1 (items 263, 267, 280, 284, and 366). It is unclear from the record whether these cooperative studies were an effort by the NRPB to hitch onto the war programs or an effort by the Defense agency to ride on the coattails of an established federal agency.

In Postwar Planning

The NRPB played a larger role—indeed, the dominant role among the federal agencies—in postwar planning until it was abolished in mid-1943, less than halfway through the war. The NRPB not only undertook postwar planning itself and through its committees, but it actively stimulated such planning by other federal agencies. All postwar planning by federal agencies during that period had limited impact upon what actually transpired once the war was over. I speak from some personal experience in this activity.

In November 1940, slightly more than a year after the war had begun in Europe but more than a year before the United States became involved in the war, Roosevelt instructed the NRPB to begin what was then called postdefense planning.[11] Warken says, quoting NRPB file materials, that President Roosevelt had instructed the agency more than a year previously not to be directed exclusively to war activities but to continue its long-term planning efforts.[12] One may credit FDR with sincerity in these directives and yet see in them a typical pattern of Roosevelt's shifting power and favoritism away from NRPB and toward the new agencies he was creating, without making explicit what he was doing. FDR may well have understood the NRPB's limitations for defense and war planning.

---

[10] I am indebted to John Miller for information on this point.

[11] National Resources Planning Board, *After Defense—What? Full Employment, Security, Up-Building America, Post-Defense Planning* (Washington, D.C., GPO, August 1941).

[12] Warken, "A History of the National Resources Planning Board," p. 182.

In August 1941 the NRPB published a brief pamphlet, describing its work on postdefense planning and appealing for help from other federal agencies and from other groups and agencies around the country. It classified its plans into seven general categories: plans for demobilization; plans for public works and activities; plans with industry; plans to expand service activities; plans for security; plans for financing; and plans in the international scene. In its discussion, the NRPB referred frequently to the studies it had made and the reports it had issued on the same subjects in earlier years. "This outline of possible post-defense activities is far from complete. It is presented to direct attention to post-defense planning problems, to indicate the areas which are in need of exploration, and to invite the cooperation of public and private agencies in this important and intricate task."

In January 1942, immediately after the United States had entered the war, the NRPB published another brief printed pamphlet, *After the War—Full Employment*[13] (item 243, table B-1). This was an essay written by Alvin H. Hansen, then a professor of economics at Harvard. This pamphlet drew on Hansen's research and other writings. He had previously presented some of this material at Temporary National Economic Committee hearings. Preparation of the pamphlet had begun some months earlier and a draft had been circulated rather widely for criticisms. Hansen was one of the rather close and direct followers in the United States of Keynes, the English economist, and in this pamphlet he endorsed and explained Keynes' theories of using the federal budget as a balancing mechanism to the fluctuations in general economic activity. "It is the responsibility of Government to do its part to insure a sustained demand. We know from past experience that private enterprise has done this for limited periods only. It has not been able to insure a continuous and sustained demand. . . . The public debt is something very different from the private debt of an individual. . . . a nation may make itself poor by repayment of the public debt. . . . A public debt internally held has none of the essential earmarks of the private debt of an individual. A public debt is an instrument of public policy." These brief quotes may convey the general flavor and thrust of Hansen's essay. His position may be questioned in some of its details but it is near economic orthodoxy today, whereas in 1941, 1942, and 1943, this pamphlet, almost as much as any NRPB publication, aroused fierce and

---

[13] Alvin H. Hansen, *After the War—Full Employment* (Washington, GPO, January 1942).

emotional criticism, in the Congress, in the business world, and in at least part of the press. Senator Robert Taft, then the leading Republican intellectual and a powerful figure in the Senate, was particularly incensed by it.

Also in January 1942, the NRPB published its *Report for 1942— National Resources Development*. This was a continuation of the report on the same subject a year earlier; each described public works planned for the ensuing year or longer, as well as some of the policy issues as seen by the NRPB. The introduction briefly traces some of the history of defense, war, and peacetime planning, including some of the history traced in this book. In his letter of transmittal to the Congress, Roosevelt described it as a "companion document to the Budget of the United States." The introduction also states "new objectives," which we describe below in the discussion of the next report. Part I of the report consists of eleven large-size pages devoted to a discussion of postwar planning, in terms similar to those of the earlier pamphlet. The greater part of the report (over 200 pages) is a more detailed backup and description of planned public works. I characterize this report as a vigorous and positive exposition of the NRPB's concepts of the American economy and society and of the steps needed to achieve its objectives. This report, along with others about the same time, was also widely criticized in the Congress and elsewhere.

In September 1942, the NRPB issued a 32-page pamphlet, *Post-War Planning—Full Employment, Security, Building America* (item 300, table B-1) which restated its goals for the postwar period, described the planning activities under way in about the same grouping of subject matter employed in earlier reports, and again sought to enlist other groups in the activity. A few quotes may capture its flavor: "There are those who contend that we should not plan now, but should wait until the end of the war and then begin to plan. To wait until the war is over will be to wait until it is too late. . . . In all these fields work is under way. It is not glamorous or headline activity. But if patiently and steadily the steps of formulation, discussion, and revision and blue-printing can be pursued, the end of the war will find us ready to implement the ideas and ideals of our people in positive post-war action. . . . Of course the claims of men and materials for victory should and must have priority, but there is still room and need for careful preconsideration of the problems that are certain to come with peace, before the armistice brings that battling to a close."

On the last page of this pamphlet, the NRPB made a statement of faith and belief, to which there is every reason to believe that its members and staff were deeply and sincerely committed. That statement in full is as follows:

OUR FREEDOMS AND RIGHTS

We look forward to securing, through planning and cooperative action, a greater freedom for the American people. Great changes have come in our century with the industrial revolution, the rapid settlement of the continent, the development of technology, the acceleration of transportation and communication, the growth of modern capitalism, and the rise of the national state with its economic programs. Too few corresponding adjustments have been made in our provisions for human freedom. In spite of all these changes, that great manifesto, the Bill of Rights, has stood unshaken 150 years. And now to the old freedoms we must add new freedoms and restate our objectives in modern terms:

FREEDOM OF SPEECH AND EXPRESSION, FREEDOM TO WORSHIP, FREEDOM FROM WANT, AND FREEDOM FROM FEAR, these are the universals of human life.

The translation of freedom into modern terms applicable to the people of the United States includes, as the National Resources Planning Board sees it, the following declaration of rights:

1. THE RIGHT TO WORK, usefully and creatively through the productive years;

2. THE RIGHT TO FAIR PAY, adequate to command the necessities and amenities of life in exchange for work, ideas, thrift, and other socially valuable service;

3. THE RIGHT TO ADEQUATE FOOD, CLOTHING, SHELTER, AND MEDICAL CARE;

4. THE RIGHT TO SECURITY with freedom from fear of old age, want, dependency, sickness, unemployment, and accident;

5. THE RIGHT TO LIVE IN A SYSTEM OF FREE ENTERPRISE, free from compulsory labor, irresponsible private power, arbitrary public authority, and unregulated monopolies;

6. THE RIGHT TO COME AND GO, TO SPEAK OR BE SILENT, from the spyings of secret political police;

7. THE RIGHT TO EQUALITY BEFORE THE LAW, with equal access to justice in fact;

8. THE RIGHT TO EDUCATION, for work, for citizenship, and for personal growth and happiness; and

9. THE RIGHT TO REST, recreation, and adventure; the opportunity to enjoy life and take part in an advancing civilization.

Although this pamphlet had been designed to reach a wide audience, in November 1942, the NRPB issued a large single sheet, printed on both sides and folded into a pamphlet-type publication, further summarizing in graphic form the contents of the September pamphlet and some other NRPB materials. One must conclude that the NRPB was thus striving vigorously, not only to establish its own role in postwar planning but to popularize the whole concept and to prepare the American public for some of the anticipated postwar readjustments.

In early 1943, the NRPB submitted to the president, and he forwarded to the Congress, the third of its annual reports, *National Resources Development, Report for 1943.* This one is similar to the two preceding ones in its restatement of the goals for the postwar period and in its statement of public works planned for the year ahead. It also contains a rather detailed account of postwar planning by the federal government up to that date.

In June 1943, after Congress had passed the legislation which ended the NRPB's life, the NRPB published a longish pamphlet, *Demobilization and Readjustment.* At the authorization of the president, the NRPB had established a "conference" on postwar readjustment of civilian and military personnel. Members of the conference were high-ranking federal officials from civilian and war agencies. The group met twenty-seven times, had materials prepared by a number of federal agencies, and issued an excellent report. In these respects it was reminiscent of the early NRB and NRC studies which had so successfully mobilized talent from all over the federal government. The NRPB recommended early demobilization after the war ended—a recommendation which was followed with a vengeance, but mostly as a result of public pressures to get the boys and girls home by Christmas. Various proposals were made to help the readjustment problem, not only for members of the armed services but for civilians working in war plants. One of the major recommendations, largely followed, was to avoid a war bonus to veterans and instead provide funds for their education. The process of reconversion turned out to be as disorderly as the process of mobilization for war had been, with many conflicting voices within the Administration.[14]

What did the NRPB's postdefense and postwar planning actually accomplish? It is difficult to say. Its direct contribution may have been small, in part because the agency no longer existed when the postwar period actually arrived. Its indirect contribution may have been con-

---

[14] Somers, *Presidential Agency.* See especially chapter 6.

siderable, both in the actual demobilization and reconversion processes and in legislation enacted after the war. The men who had served in its demobilization conference mostly continued in important governmental posts, and their experience on the conference group may well have influenced their later thinking and action. Wartime price controls were abandoned soon after hostilities ended, in a way that doubtless the NRPB would not have approved of. The specific plans for transitional employment were mostly not carried out, but in part because the private economy adjusted so rapidly to meeting the pent-up civilian demand for goods of all kinds. The Employment Act of 1946 set forth national policy to achieve maximum employment and production, in a way that the NRPB would surely have approved of, and that did, at least to a large degree, embody some of the NRPB's postwar goals. The Council of Economic Advisers was instituted and now is an accepted tool of both Republican and Democratic administrations, to perform some of the economic analyses and reporting the NRPB sought to do or felt should have been done. One can find other legislation or other governmental programs in the years since the NRPB's demise which might, with some ingenuity, be traced back to the NRPB's postwar planning efforts.

IV

THE NRPB IN THE STRUCTURE OF AMERICAN GOVERNMENT

14

The NRPB in Relation to State and Regional Planning Organizations

The relationship of the headquarters of the NRPB to its own field organization and of both to state and regional planning organizations is one of the success stories of the NRPB's history. Perhaps these relationships were more under its control than were its relationships with other branches of government—notably with the Congress—or perhaps the Board and staff had a greater unanimity of objective and procedure in these relationships than in others. Whatever the explanation, the relationships here were generally cordial, effective, and productive.

Washington, Regions, and States

The seat of the national government is in Washington, of course, and, with few exceptions in peacetime, the national headquarters of federal agencies are also in Washington. But a great deal of the domestic work of any federal agency takes place "in the field," nearer where people live and work. A comparatively few federal programs can be and are conducted wholly from a Washington office, but more require local offices as well. Typically, nowadays, a federal agency has regional offices to serve a group of states; it may or may not have state offices as well. Many federal agencies have county or local offices also. Some federal agencies have large numbers of local offices, others comparatively few.

In general, there are many difficult relationships between Washington and "the field," about which there is a substantial body of professional literature. A federal agency administers a national program, under applicable law, and its operations at all levels must conform to that law, and to agency policy to the extent that the agency has legal discretion in establishing policy. But, especially in a large and diverse country such as the United States, there are many local situations which differ from the general national situation to which the law was directed. Flexibility in administration of the law is necessary and desirable, as well as a convenient service to local citizens, and it is for these purposes (among others) that offices at all levels below Washington are established. But where does desirable flexibility to meet local situations, within the broad limits of the national legislation, end and divergence from national purposes begin? When does friendliness and service to local people end and identification of the federal employee with the local interests, to the neglect or perversion of the national interest, begin?

The NRPB as a federal agency faced some of these typical Washington–field relationships, but in a considerable measure its Washington–field relations did not fit this typical pattern. It is true that the NRPB had its own regional offices, each with a small staff, and between these persons and Washington there were more or less the typical problems. But the NRPB from the beginning promoted the formation of regional planning committees or commissions, composed of leading citizens from the region, over whom it had no legal or administrative control except in their roles as NRPB bodies. That is to say, every member of such regional commissions had many other interests and much prestige in his or her own right—that was why they were asked to be members of the regional bodies—and these people rightly felt that they were not beholden to the NRPB for their personal or professional positions. As a matter of fact, the NRPB encouraged its regional commissions to develop independence, initiative, and regional responsibility. Thus the regional offices of the NRPB were much less directly under its control and domination than were the regional offices of many another federal agency at that time.

The NRPB exercised, and sought to have, very little direct control over state planning offices. Strictly speaking, the state planning offices were not legally a part of the NRPB. They were established under applicable state law or administrative action, and could be abolished or their personnel changed without NRPB approval. The NRPB did help the state offices obtain federal funds or federal allocation of manpower, primarily from emergency relief sources, which provided much, and sometimes all, of the resources available to a state planning office.

Legally independent, the state offices at the outset were heavily financially dependent on the federal government, but this dependence steadily decreased as more state funds became available. The NRPB provided a planning consultant to each state planning office, at least part of the time, and in some cases these were the chief full-time personnel of such offices. The NRPB helped the state planning offices obtain state funding and it explicitly urged them to innovate and experiment in developing plans to meet each state's own particular problems.

It is fairly evident, as I examine the record, that the NRPB deliberately set up a "non-Washington" structure that its Washington office did not closely control. In this respect, the NRPB differed from many if not all the other New Deal agencies. Prior to the New Deal, the federal government had had comparatively few local offices. It had post offices, local offices of the Forest Service, and some others, but it typically dealt with individual citizens through state governments. Prior to the New Deal there were no federal unemployment, welfare, Social Security, or other similar programs of direct help to individuals. When the New Deal agricultural programs began, the Agricultural Adjustment Administration for the very first few years operated largely through the Agricultural Extension Services, which received some federal funds but were basically state and local in their government. When the soil conservation programs began, the Soil Erosion Service (later changed to the Soil Conservation Service) also tried to operate in part through extension services. In each case, these federal agencies shortly established their own field organizations, which they could directly manage and control. The welfare and other New Deal programs increasingly also established their own field organizations, each an integral and immediate part of the Washington-based agency. A comparatively independent field organization may be permissible, even desirable, in a research and planning agency such as the NRPB, when it would not be tolerable in a direct action agency, which had a clear directive from the Congress and the president that it could not be sure would be carried out by field organizations it could not control.

How the NRPB Sought to Influence Regional and State Planning

Although the NRPB did not seek to control, nor did it in fact control, the regional and state planning offices, it did seek to influence them.

To this end it used several major devices: provision of funds and man-power, under specific conditions; a flow of information from the Wash-ington office to the field offices; close and frequent contact from NRPB regional offices to state planning agencies; a flow of information obtained from each state, compiled and circulated to the other states by the Washington office; and in some cases by publication of regional reports.[1]

In its fifth circular letter, dated December 11, 1933—just after Eliot had made the first announcement to the states that federal funds would be made available to aid in state planning (see chapter 6 for details)—six conditions were established for NPB support of federal funding of state planning:

1. The governor of the state agreed to appoint a state planning board. While its membership was up to him, it was suggested that a board might well consist of four heads of state departments plus three outstanding citizens.

2. The governor agreed to sponsor legislation to make his state planning board permanent.

3. The state agreed to make drafting and stenographic help available to the board; such help might be recruited from welfare rolls and paid for by federal welfare or relief funds.

4. The state agreed to develop a state planning program.

5. The state agreed to suggest a qualified planner to direct the work.

6. The governor expressed his willingness to name a member to any regional planning organization that might be established.

The actual amounts of money made available to the states for these planning boards were small even by the standards and price levels of the day, and ridiculously so in comparison with present day amounts of funds transferred from federal agencies to various state programs. In the fiscal year 1935, for instance, less than $200,000 was thus made avail-able for state planning, including for the Washington office of the NRPB's

---

[1] The NRPB and its predecessors sent a confusing lot of circulars and circular letters from the Washington office to the field; many of these were revised and updated, some several times, hence the name or number of either circular or circular letter is insufficient without its date also. What follows in this section is a brief distillation of the file of these circulars and circular letters at the National Archives.

state planning services.[2] Steadily increasing state funding was promoted and obtained. In Circular III, dated February 11, 1935, there is the suggestion that $25,000 to $40,000 of federal funds annually are necessary and sufficient for an adequately functioning state planning office. Even if these sums are multiplied by ten or more, to bring them from the very low salaries of that day up to modern salary levels, they are clearly still small in the federal context. However, they were critical at the time and they enabled the state planning offices to do a great deal of excellent work.

Beginning with its second circular letter, dated September 30, 1933— even before the state planning agencies were formed under NPB encouragement—suggestions were made to field offices and local agencies on how to proceed with the development of regional plans. Over the years, many of the other circulars and circular letters contained information, suggestions, or proposals from the NRPB Washington office to its own regional offices or to the state planning offices or to both. For instance, its seventh circular letter, dated March 23, 1934, is addressed to the state planning consultants and contains rather detailed suggestions of what a state plan should contain and how one should be made. The first item of this, incidentally, was that a preliminary state plan should be completed within six months of the appointment of the planning consultant. Clearly, Eliot and the others at the NRPB did not wish planning to be the excuse for delay. The twelfth circular letter, dated May 22, 1934, had been prepared by the U.S. Geological Survey, listing the USGS information, especially on river basins, that might be helpful to state planning boards. This is an excellent example of the NRPB's enlistment of other federal agencies to provide information to state planning organizations. Circular XIII, dated September 28, 1939, summarized federal activities that in the opinion of its author (Melville C. Branch, Jr.) might affect local planning.

Perhaps more important than this flow of information and suggestions from the NRPB to the field were its circulars and circular letters which reported to the same people what they, in effect, were doing. That is, the NRPB obtained information from each state planning board about its basic legislation, about the membership of its board, and about its activities; and this material was then assembled into a publication for

---

[2] Charles W. Eliot, 2nd, assisted by Harold Merrill, *Guide to the Files of the National Resources Planning Board and Predecessor Agencies—Ten Years of National Planning, 1933–1943*, December 31, 1943.

distribution back to the organizations which had provided the information, as well as to others. This was a clearinghouse function of great value. Especially when a program is going well, as state planning was during the NRPB years, there is nothing more stimulating and useful to one part of it than reports on what others are doing. It was not only the information directly so exchanged which was useful, but also the feeling of comradeship and, to some extent, of rivalry among the states which these reports stimulated.

There was a long series of these circulars and circular letters, including updates, which described the work of the state planning boards. Some of these reports express interest, even amazement, at the scope of work of these state boards, and as I read even these summary reports I too am much impressed. It is evident that the state boards, while perhaps following in a general way the suggestions of the NRPB, did indeed take fully the NRPB's urging to develop their own programs in their own ways, and did not hesitate to innovate.

The NRPB helped its own regional organizations more directly than it helped the state planning boards, gave them more specific tasks to carry out, assembled national reports on some subjects based on what the regional offices had done, and in some cases published regional reports. The NRPB employed part-time consultants for special tasks in its regional offices and sometimes these consultants made direct contributions to the state planning offices.

Where and How the Field Organization Fitted into the Overall NRPB Structure

During most of its existence, the NRPB and its predecessors had a special field unit in the Washington office, at first under Robert W. Randall, later under John Miller. After the enlargement and reorganization of the NRPB's staff in 1940, the field unit was not assigned to one of the three divisions but was directly under the director, Eliot, and Harold Merrill, the executive officer, on the organization chart. Every survivor of the NRPB with whom I have talked, and every NRPB document I have examined, gives at least pro forma endorsement to the field organization, including the state planning boards, as part of the whole NRPB structure. The Board itself, especially in its early days, held many of its meetings in different cities around the country, to stimulate planning in those areas and to give national coverage to its activities. However, it does seem that the various staff people in the three divisions, or elsewhere in the Washington office, except the field section, had only modest interaction with the field. The relationships were cordial enough, with perhaps less than normal federal agency Washington–field frictions; no major controversies or feuds developed, as far as I can ascertain. But there is some doubt in my mind that the field and the Washington staffs were always operating closely together.

The field organization tended, especially at first, to consist of persons with city planning, architectural, or engineering backgrounds. The primary concern of the regions and states, especially at first, was public works and natural resource planning. To some extent, the field organization was Eliot's "baby," although both Delano and Yantis strongly supported the idea of regional and state planning organizations. To some extent, Miller was able to get both regions and states interested and involved in the kind of social planning that Merriam was more directly interested in.

I have noted in other chapters how little use the NRPB at the Washington office level made of the potentially powerful political force that its regional commissions and state planning bodies presented. It would have been improper and, during most of that time, illegal as well for the staffs to have engaged in political activities in support of the NRPB, but these limitations did not apply to the individuals who made up regional and state boards. As I have noted, Eliot apparently did make some political use of these bodies late in the NRPB's history, but such efforts were too late.

The regional offices of the NRPB played an important role in their encouragement of state planning and in their aid to state planning offices. If there had been no regional offices, presumably the NRPB's relations with the state planning offices would have been conducted out of Washington. The closer physical proximity of the regional offices, the closer personal ties between regional and state personnel, the feeling of the state personnel that they were dealing with federal employees who knew and understood their problems, and other factors were all most important assets of the regional offices. There were rather frequent formal and informal meetings between regional and state personnel, all of which helped greatly in the furtherance of the work of the state offices.

It is unclear how much, if at all, the regional offices of the NRPB and the state planning offices may have affected or influenced the decisions of the Washington office as to policy on kinds of studies to be made, methods of operation, general role of the organization, relations with the Congress, and the like. A detailed search of all the correspondence from state and regional offices to the Washington office of the NRPB might have revealed something, but this is by no means clear. If the field had criticisms of Washington, these might easily *not* have gotten into written form—many a person would hesitate to put into writing what he would say verbally, fearing that such criticisms would get into hostile hands to his disadvantage. In any case, I have not made any such detailed search through the correspondence files.

Role of State Planning Agencies in Their States

Various of the NRPB reports emphasize the wide variety of studies made by state agencies. Circular VI, dated May 19, 1935—about a year and a half after state planning boards got started with federal help—states that about 200 state planning reports had been prepared; most were only typed and their circulation is unknown but must have been limited. They may, however, have been influential. Circular IV, dated February 12, 1935, reported on the reactions of governors in nineteen states to planning reports by their state agencies. The reports and the quotes of governors' reactions were all favorable, some very much so; there is no evidence of unfavorable reactions, if any. Circular VIII, dated December 2, 1935, reported on newspaper reactions to state planning reports. Some 300 clippings from a survey of 400 leading newspapers of the country show a considerable and generally highly favorable press reaction to the state planning reports.

It is highly probable that the state planning boards differed greatly in their competence and effectiveness. Federal agency records are unlikely to dwell on limitations of state agencies unless limitations are very severe, and NRPB reports on state planning are not explicit about the shortcomings of specific state planning boards.

All of this suggests that the state planning reports were significant in their content and in their effect, but one cannot be sure that this was truly the case. On the surface, and in a pro forma way, the state planning reports surely were important. I had some personal contact with some of them at the time and that was surely my personal reaction. But the real test of such state reports would have been: How far were any governmental or private actions actually changed by such reports, from what they would have been without the planning reports? It would have been extremely difficult to have answered this question with any assurance at the time and it is impossible to do so now, largely because one would have to compare actual developments with some unknown and hypothetical developments that otherwise would have occurred.

A still more intriguing question is: How far, if at all, did the state plans influence, affect, or guide decisions by federal agencies, including the Congress and the president? Perhaps this question should be matched by another: How far *should* state attitudes affect national decisions? If a state planning agency developed a plan proposing the siting of some federal facility in some location, or proposing that it not be located in some other location, how far should the federal government pay attention to such state plan? To be specific, and using a present-day rather than an NRPB-day example, how far should the federal government today depend on state plans as a basis for the development of a national program for sites for disposal of atomic waste? Can sound national policy ever come out of a mere compilation of state interests and local plans? How far should national policy require conformity in state plans and state actions? Questions such as these were rarely if ever raised during the NRPB period, as far as I have been able to determine from the record. It might be argued that state planning was too new, too unsure of itself, and too poorly accepted to have served in answering such general questions at that time. Of course, in the end federal decisions, as in fact state decisions, would be made primarily by a political process, but this does not necessarily mean that the state planning process was without influence—even politicians get their ideas somewhere.

If the NRPB Had Become Permanent

If the NRPB had survived and become a permanent agency, how would its own regional offices and the state planning offices have evolved? Would they have been built, over time, into stronger, more effective, and more independent (at least in the case of the state) agencies? Or might the state planning agencies have become more nearly branches of the Washington office of the NRPB, or might the latter have established its own state offices? Or might the whole regional–state structure have been liquidated?

In one sense it is futile to imagine what would have happened, had the course of history been different. But in another sense it may be very useful to do so, if any consideration were to be given in the future to the establishment of a reconstituted NRPB, as we discuss in a later chapter. A great many federal agencies today have their own local planning efforts or require the preparation of local plans as a condition to the receipt of federal grants of various kinds. Many federal agencies encourage citizen participation in their planning, either because of their genuine conviction of the value of such citizen involvement or because they are required by law to do so. The present federal planning and federally stimulated planning are at best functional, concerned with the operations of some particular program, and only rarely integrative or comprehensive, although often called the latter.

15

The NRPB and Other Executive Branch Agencies

In this chapter I explore the interrelationship between the NRPB and other agencies in the Executive Branch. It is fairly easy to show those interrelationships on an apparent or surface level. But it is very difficult to know now the real nature of those relations—how far did the other agencies cooperate because they really wanted to do so, how far because they thought the president expected or demanded that they do so, how far was there concealed resentment or foot-dragging, and how far was there open opposition to the NRPB? Some facts are ascertainable and some relationships can be inferred, but some can only be speculated about. Beckman, speaking of the NRPB, says: "Its most challenging problems of administration, for example, its relations with other federal agencies and with Congress and the technical obstacles to national planning which it encountered, are not well documented."[1] Eliot and Merrill say: "The membership of Cabinet officers in the Resources Board and Committees secured for the Board the hearty cooperation of bureau chiefs and subordinate officials."[2] One might surely infer from the latter that, without such endorsement from "on high," at least some of the bureau chiefs and subordinate officials might not have been so coopera-

[1] Norman Beckman, "Federal Long-Range Planning—The Heritage of the National Resources Planning Board," *Journal of the American Institute of Planning*, vol. XXVI, no. 2 (May 1960) p. 89.

[2] Charles W. Eliot, 2nd, assisted by Harold A. Merrill, *Guide to the Files of the National Resources Planning Board and Predecessor Agencies—Ten Years of National Planning, 1933–1943*, December 31, 1943.

tive, but it is not clear that Eliot and Merrill mean to so imply. It is highly probable that the NRPB met some of the normal bureaucratic reluctances to be cordial to other agencies.

What might be called the accepted doctrine is that the other federal agencies cooperated very well with the NRPB. That is the general tone of the Eliot and Merrill report cited above. Merriam expresses a similar view.[3] It is true that a great many of the NRPB reports, especially the early ones, listed the names of many cooperating persons in those agencies. The classic 1934 report, for instance, lists a score or more federal agencies and several hundred individuals from those agencies as having contributed specifically and significantly to the report.[4] Some of the later reports, as some of those from the Water Committee, listed an equal or larger number of persons, including many persons from outside of the federal government. Typically, every federal agency with an interest in a subject was included on committees studying various problems, but, of course, mere inclusion on a committee is no evidence of the nature of the relationship. It is altogether possible that the NRPB was able to get better cooperation from other agencies in its role of idea development, where the agencies would be less inclined to see a threat to their established positions, than it was able to get in program coordination, which in practice often meant that some agency had to give up something it cherished.

Eliot and Merrill describe Ickes' relationship to other agencies as follows:

> The work gained greatly by the continuous and vigorous support given to it by the Secretary of the Interior. The fact that the Chairman was a cabinet officer had only one disadvantage: in relations of the Advisory Committee and staff with other branches of the government. The differences which developed at different times between Secretary Ickes and Secretary Wallace or Relief Administrator Hopkins, or the Chief of Engineers, etc., sometimes limited the usefulness of the Board in its efforts for coordination of policies. Whether or not the Secretary participated or influenced the work of the Committee and staff on these

---

[3] See, for example, Charles E. Merriam, "The National Resources Planning Board," in George B. Galloway and Associates, *Planning for America* (New York, Henry Holt and Company, 1941); and Charles E. Merriam, "The National Resources Planning Board: A Chapter in American Planning Experience," *The American Political Science Review,* vol. XXXVIII, no. 6 (December 1944).

[4] National Resources Board, *A Report on National Planning and Public Works in Relation to Natural Resources and Including Land Use and Water Resources with Findings and Recommendations* (Washington, GPO, 1934).

problems, the mere fact of his chairmanship affected the attitude of cooperating agencies.[5]

Ickes, in his *Secret Diary,* relates his side of an admittedly heated quarrel with Secretary of Agriculture Henry Wallace in January 1937, on the matter of the location of the Forest Service, as between the two departments. And he mentions another equally heated quarrel in early May 1937, with Secretary of War Harry H. Woodring on the operations of the Water Committee of the National Resources Committee. So the delicate Eliot–Merrill reference to "differences" had plenty of experience underlying it.[6] Although such quarrels were not specifically or wholly on NRPB matters, they surely must have affected in some degree the NRPB's relations with the agencies concerned. Ickes believed that Eliot and others connected with the National Planning Board sought to get it out from under his chairmanship, and no doubt they did to some degree.[7] His chairmanship may indeed have cost the Board something, in its relations with other agencies, as Eliot and Merrill suggest.

There are some specific evidences that other federal agencies welcomed, even sought, cooperation with the NRPB. Warken relates that Secretary of Agriculture Henry Wallace in 1935 requested the Board to undertake a study of federal land drainage programs and methods. He also relates how, in 1942, the Division of Civilian Supply of the War Production Board asked the NRPB to prepare a report on energy resources, and, in 1941, the Office of Production Management asked the NRPB for a rating of various public works projects for which allocations of scarce materials were requested.[8] White relates how, in 1943, when the NRPB was under attack in the Congress—the attack which proved fatal—several federal agencies submitted letters of commendation of the Board's work.[9] There was at least one instance when Bureau of Mines researchers apparently preferred NRPB publication of their

---

[5] Eliot and Merrill, *Guide to the Files,* p. 14.

[6] Harold L. Ickes, *The Secret Diary of Harold L. Ickes, The Inside Struggle, 1936–1939* (New York, Simon and Schuster, 1954).

[7] See footnotes 7 and 10 in chapter 4, and the discussion in the text regarding them, for evidence on this point.

[8] Philip W. Warken, "A History of the National Resources Planning Board, 1933–1943" (doctoral dissertation, Ohio State University, 1969). The references are on pages 69, 143 and 144.

[9] Philip L. White, "The Termination of the National Resources Planning Board," (master's thesis, in the Faculty of Political Science, Columbia University, 1949) p. 145.

report to its publication by their own agency. One could doubtless find other explicit evidence of favorable relationships—relationships not dictated from above, but arising out of genuine conviction of the persons and agencies involved—between various federal agencies and the NRPB.

There was one federal agency with which it would not have been surprising had there been some jealousy and rivalry, especially for the attention and favor of the president, but with which there was, in fact, quite a good cooperative relationship. This was the Bureau of the Budget. The Budget and Accounting Act of 1921 established that bureau in the Treasury Department.[10] In 1939, as part of the reorganization of the Office of the President, it was transferred to his Executive Office. In recent years it has been named the Office of Management and Budget and its duties somewhat expanded. The Committee on Administrative Management in 1937 had recommended the strengthening of the White House staff, the reorganization of the civil service system with a single administrator as part of the president's staff, the transfer of the Bureau of the Budget from Treasury to the Executive Office and its strengthening, and the establishment of a permanent National Resources Planning Board as part of the president's office.[11] As we have noted, the proposals of this committee for administrative reorganization were only partly implemented, some of the opposition in the Congress being the result of the bitter fight over the "packing" of the Supreme Court.[12] The first reorganization bill was defeated in 1938 and a greatly watered down version passed in 1939. Under it, Reorganization Plan No. 1 established both the Bureau of the Budget and the NRPB in the Office of the President.

Beckman has described the relations between the NRPB and Budget as follows:

> The Bureau of the Budget did not have its interests as directly impinged upon by NRPB as did some of the line agencies, because the Bureau's program and project review prerogatives were not impaired. The NRPB was most concerned with long-range planning of the six-year type whereas the Bureau of the Budget was concerned with the more

---

[10] Harold D. Smith, *The Management of Your Government* (New York, McGraw-Hill, 1945).

[11] President's Committee on Administrative Management, *Report with Special Studies* (Washington, GPO, 1937).

[12] See footnote 5, chapter 1, for reference to Richard Polenberg's book, *Reorganizing Roosevelt's Government, 1936–1939* (Cambridge, Harvard University Press, 1966) for a detailed account of the fight over these proposals.

immediate future. Older, larger, with definite responsibilities, the Bureau of the Budget was not displaced. Agency projects approved by the NRPB were reviewed de novo by the Bureau.[13]

A somewhat different view is provided by Warken, quoting internal memoranda of the NRPB: "There are other indications that while relationships between the two agencies of the Executive Office were cordial, the NRPB found it difficult to establish a regularized procedure for the joint activity."[14] There is considerable evidence that Harold D. Smith, director of the Bureau of the Budget, strongly supported the NRPB, both because he believed in the existence of such an agency and because, as a loyal lieutenant of the president, he wished to help a sister agency in the Executive Office. Smith had long been associated with Brownlow and Merriam in Chicago, and this may have helped achieve harmonious relations between the two agencies. Had the NRPB been able to resolve its problems, a healthy and productive relationship between it and the Bureau of the Budget might well have developed and continued into later administrations. As it was, with the termination of the NRPB, some of its functions of review of public works were transferred to Budget.

There was one federal agency, or more accurately, one interest group with which was allied a federal agency, that was opposed to the NRPB throughout its history. This was the Rivers and Harbors Congress with which were allied a good many congressmen and the Corps of Engineers of the War Department. This federal agency had authorization from the Congress to report its projects directly to the Congress, in an earlier day completely bypassing the president and yielding only gradually, reluctantly, and partially to Roosevelt's efforts to bring it in line with overall programs. Although Corps personnel were generally cooperative with the NRPB's Water Resources Committee on a purely technical level, the top Corps staff, the most deeply concerned congressmen, and the Rivers and Harbors Congress (which was to a large extent composed of congressmen) all very much opposed the NRPB's efforts to correlate their water development projects with the water development projects of other agencies or with other public works programs. This triumvirate had built a powerful lobbying and legislative "pork barrel," carefully insuring that all or most congressional districts got a little pork in each appropriation

---

[13] Beckman, "Federal Long-Range Planning," p. 91.
[14] Warken, "A History," p. 121.

act so that it was difficult for any congressman to oppose the program as a whole.

Rivers and Harbors' opposition to the NRPB continued throughout the latter's life, waxing and waning from time to time. It opposed the Presidential Reorganization Bill in 1938 and 1939, fearing that this would reduce the Corps' role. In various attempts by the Administration to get enabling legislation for the NRPB, the Rivers and Harbors bloc either opposed the legislation entirely or sought to have navigation and flood control work excluded. There is reason to believe that the bloc encouraged members of the Congress, who would have been opposed to the NRPB in any case, to oppose appropriations for it, after 1939. The history of relations between the NRPB and the Rivers and Harbors bloc is long, detailed, and involved with, one suspects, many of the most significant actions by the latter not revealed by the public record. There seems no need to try to trace all these relations in detail here. When the Rivers and Harbors bloc sought legislation in 1937 which would have given the Corps complete authority over all water planning, the president vetoed it. Later, its opposition to the NRPB seemed to wane, at least temporarily, but the opposition of this interest group was surely one factor in the demise of the Board.

The NRPB's relations with the Tennessee Valley Authority (TVA) are somewhat unclear. It will be recalled that TVA was established by Act of Congress in the New Deal's "Hundred Days," at the beginning of Roosevelt's term in 1933. The TVA clearly had legislative authority for comprehensive planning and development of the whole Tennessee River system including land and other resources in the river basin. During the period of the NRPB's existence, TVA took these comprehensive planning duties seriously; later it became, or at least its critics charged that it became, more nearly a public power agency which made only token efforts at comprehensive natural resource planning and development. For a long time, TVA tried to keep other federal agencies out of "its region"; for instance, it insisted that the Soil Conservation Service not work on the problems of soil erosion and not organize soil conservation districts within the Tennessee basin, because the TVA was doing all that was necessary in this field. I have found no clear evidence in the published record of serious conflicts between the NRPB and the TVA, although some alumni of the NRPB have told me they believed at least some conflicts did arise. Apparently the NRPB respected the TVA's claims to dominance within the Tennessee basin and did not overtly challenge it on this issue. The Water Committee of the NRPB, in its studies of drainage basins, surely recognized the existence and the legislative mandate of the TVA.

Struggles over federal water developments obviously did not end with the end of the NRPB; anyone even moderately informed about recent natural resource policy issues in the United States is aware of President Jimmy Carter's struggles against the authorization and appropriation of funds for water development projects which he considered economically unsound. The history of water policy development since the NRPB period is long and complex and I make no attempt to trace it even summarily.[15]

Not unexpectedly, the NRPB had some problems of a different kind with some federal agencies, in spite of efforts to avoid them. Eliot and Merrill say, in speaking of NRPB committees:

> We always insisted that the members from the various government bureaus were not representatives of their several agencies but appointed from them by the board and not by their department heads. As a matter of courtesy, we asked the consent of the department heads to have Mr. X or Mr. Y give time to the work of the committee, and we assumed that the committee members would keep their chiefs informed of what was going on; but a determined effort was made to maintain the freedom of action of the members as individuals. . . . These committees were not the old style interdepartmental committees which are well known to be primarily "back-scratching parties"; nor were there good opportunities for "leg-rolling" because of the presence of outside members.[16]

One need not question either the sincerity of this statement nor the seriousness of the effort to implement the views expressed, but one may judge that success was sometimes less than perfect. At best, the men from some agencies were asked to play two roles: as employees (usually senior staff men) of their agencies, and as subject specialists working for a national planning organization. At times some men found it difficult to keep these two roles separate. For instance, the advisory committee for the transportation study, which, in 1942, produced the major report, *Transportation and National Policy,* had seven members, each a major official of a federal agency directly concerned with one

---

[15] See footnote 8, chapter 9, for a reference which does trace these policy conflicts in detail.

[16] Eliot and Merrill, *Guide to the Files,* p. 27.

form or another of transportation. As we reported earlier, the chairman
of the committee, Owen D. Young, justified the publication of the report
at that date because of the difficulty of getting committee members to
work further on it due to the pressure of war duties. Watkins has
suggested that one further reason for the chairman's position was the
difficulty of getting the committee members to budge from their agency
policy positions.[17] One of the most natural bureaucratic tendencies is
for each agency, and every representative from each agency, to defend
the agency's turf, to resist any compromises with other agencies which it
is feared may not be matched by equal compromises from others, and
generally to be defensive and possessive. The NRPB made serious efforts
to avoid this sort of situation and generally was more successful than
most government efforts in doing so, but the problem simply could not
be avoided wholly.

One of the devices used by the NRPB to deal with this situation, as
well as its other advantages, was the use of an outside, or impartial,
chairman. As Eliot and Merrill say: "The 'impartial' chairman was
another feature of this committee organization which was an important
factor in its success."[18] The Water Resources Committee, for instance,
had several very able and influential chairmen, of whom Abel Wolman,
a professor at Johns Hopkins University, served the longest and probably
had the greatest impact upon the committee's work. Some of the other
committee chairmen were also quite influential in the work of their
respective committees. It is a significant commentary on the times and
the role that the NRPB played as a synthesizer of information and as
an effective publisher, that these men from universities, industry, or
elsewhere, typically very able and very busy, were willing to devote time
and energy to NRPB committee work.

We have noted in other chapters, how the NRPB gradually shifted
away from reliance on committees for its reports and toward greater
reliance on its own staff. This was probably a normal bureaucratic
evolution. It was surely easier to manage staff activities than to work
with committees, but this shift undoubtedly weakened the NRPB's
relationships with other federal agencies. Oftentimes the best way to
get a person or an organization committed to the findings of a report
and the lines of action to which those findings lead is to get that person
or organization directly involved in the preparation of the report. When

---

[17] Personal interview, August 8, 1978.
[18] Eliot and Merrill, *Guide to the Files,* p. 28.

there are several organizations, it may be difficult to get agreement among them on the nature of the report, but their varying ideas and policy positions must be dealt with sometime and often this is easier in the committee room than it is later when the report has been widely circulated and agency positions have been publicly announced.

We may conclude this brief chapter by saying that, on the whole, the NRPB seems to have been reasonably successful in its relations with other federal agencies. There was some outright opposition, most probably a degree of foot-dragging at times, which is not reflected in the official records, and some relationships that were less than perfect. But these seem not to have dominated the situation or even to have been truly major problems. In contrast, there seem to have been a large number of working relationships which ranged from satisfactory to very good. Some frictions among units are inevitable in any governmental structure, whether federal, state, or local, and in any large private organization; the NRPB and the various federal agencies seem to have had about as little of this as one could reasonably expect.

16

The NRPB and FDR

In earlier chapters we have pointed out that the NRPB was dominantly an advisory agency to the president, and we have to some extent considered its relationships with him. In this chapter we explore those relationships more explicitly and in more detail.

FDR and Conservation

One of President Franklin D. Roosevelt's marked personal characteristics was his deep personal interest, emotional at times, in forests, parks, rivers, soil, and other natural resources and conservation matters. On his family estate he had trees of different species planted in commercial forest plantations, and his correspondence files contain many quite explicit letters about what should be done in the management of those forests. On his tours around the country while president, he made many speeches at dams, parks, conservation camps, and other locations with a conservation or natural resource popular interest. These places were generally very effective locations for political speeches but he also loved them for what they meant to him personally.

> Franklin D. Roosevelt's biographers all agree that he held a lifelong belief in the necessity for conservation. His interest in this field had the natural result of producing among the Roosevelt papers an extraordinarily large and rich volume of documentation, all of which can now

208

Table 16.1 President Roosevelt's Papers on Conservation and Share Relating to the NRPB or Predecessors, 1933–1945
(number)

Calendar Year	All Printed and Numbered Papers on Conservation[a]	Papers Referring to the NRPB or Predecessors
1933[b]	76	0
1934	103	10
1935	140	16
1936	125	19
1937	157	23
1938	115	21
1939	121	25
1940	65	14
1941	47	7
1942	21	1
1943	17	2[c]
1944	35	0
1945[d]	24	0

[a] In addition, there were many items referred to in the footnotes to these papers. These data are thus more of an index than a measure of total numbers of all papers.
[b] Roosevelt inaugurated March 4, 1933.
[c] NRPB terminated by congressional action August 31, 1943.
[d] Roosevelt died April 12, 1945.
Source: *Franklin D. Roosevelt and Conservation, 1911–1945*, compiled and edited by Edgar B. Nixon, General Services Administration, National Archives and Record Service, Franklin D. Roosevelt Library, Hyde Park, New York, 1957 (Washington, GPO, 1957).

be published. The difficulty lay only in selecting from the huge mass those papers that are of sufficient significance to warrant publication.[1]

I have reviewed the two volumes of Roosevelt's papers on conservation rather quickly, seeking to identify and count all references of any kind to the NRPB and its predecessors. Some of the documents included were letters to or from Delano or other NRPB personnel; some made only passing reference to the NRPB, yet whoever prepared the document for the president's signature or for his attention thought it worthwhile to include the NRPB among the agencies referred to. FDR initiated some of the documents; the originals of some of them are in his own handwriting. One may assume that the great mass of these documents,

---

[1] Herman Kahn in the Foreword to *Franklin D. Roosevelt and Conservation, 1911–1945*, compiled and edited by Edgar B. Nixon, General Services Administration, National Archives and Records Service, Franklin D. Roosevelt Library, Hyde Park, New York, 1957 (Washington, GPO, 1957).

even those which FDR signed, were actually prepared by someone else—with all the demands on his time, he could scarcely have written the longer and more involved ones. But it would be a mistake to assume that he did not know what was in the various documents or that he did not understand what he signed or agreed to.

The total number of "conservation" documents printed in this source exceeded 100 annually from 1934 to 1939 inclusively (table 16-1). This comparatively large volume of documents is at least one measure of FDR's interest in resource and conservation matters. In 1940 and 1941, as the war drew nearer, the number of documents fell off greatly, and in 1942 and later years, up to FDR's death, the demands of the war effort pushed resources and conservation to a much smaller role. In the later years, many of those included dealt specifically with the war effort. The percentage of all the documents that at least mentioned NRPB (or its predecessor agencies) also rose and fell in a similar pattern. That is, when the total number of documents was high, the NRPB portion ranged from 10 to 20 percent; when the total number declined, the portion referring to the NRPB declined also, to less than 5 percent in 1942.

These data are not proof but they are suggestive of the interest which FDR attached to the NRPB in peacetime and also of his willingness to push it aside when war came.

The 1934–1939 Period

FDR took a major hand in the conversion of the National Planning Board from a group advising the Public Works administrator to the establishment of the National Resources Board, directly advisory to him. The National Planning Board and some of its senior staff had met together for a few days, then met with FDR in June 1934.[2] Whereas Eliot had suggested the name, Natural Resources Board, Merriam objected that it should include human as well as natural resources, and suggested the name "National" rather than "Natural" Resources Board, and FDR accepted this idea with enthusiasm. Therein, as we have noted in other chapters, arose no small part of the NRPB's subsequent

---

[2] The account which follows owes a great deal to my interview with Charles W. Eliot on October 2, 1978, and to a letter from him January 2, 1980. It is corroborated by Barry D. Karl, *Charles E. Merriam and the Study of Politics* (Chicago, University of Chicago Press, 1974) pp. 245–247, and by other accounts of the same events. See also chapter 4 of this book.

opposition. FDR initially agreed that the new NRB should report directly to him, and be independent of Ickes. The latter objected so strenuously that the Board was made to consist of cabinet officers plus Delano, Merriam, and Mitchell who had constituted the NPB, and Ickes was made chairman of the new Board.

Eliot and Merrill say over the ten years of its existence the Board met some fifty times with FDR, but the frequency of such meetings declined from a high of nine in 1940 to a low of two in 1942. The trend in these meetings thus parallels the trend in FDR conservation documents relating to the NRPB.

> Projects and proposed activities of the Board were submitted to the President directly by the Board and through various Cabinet members or other officials, like the Director of the Budget. The Board customarily avoided asking affirmative action by the President in writing, and relied on conversational clearance of work programs. In several cases, letters or memoranda signed by the President and addressed to Mr. Delano or to the chairman of committees, carried requests for the cooperation of other Federal agencies, and these informal brief papers were reproduced and circulated to those concerned. From time to time, brief notes from the President referred reports and papers to the Board for comment and recommendations.[3]

Later on in their report, Eliot and Merrill make it clear that customary White House procedures in the handling of presidential transmittal of reports to the Congress were followed. In addition to Board meetings with FDR, Board members or Eliot met informally with FDR or with major White House staff.

Beckman has graphically described the NRPB's relations with FDR:

> The Board was in all things loyal to the President. . . . At the formal meetings an agenda was presented to the President. . . . The meetings were marked by broad-ranging discussions rather than by attempts to resolve specific issues. Insofar as contributing to day-to-day operating decisions was concerned, the Board was not an indispensable part of the President's office. Records indicate that the President gave few specific assignments to the Board. It is probably fair to say that the President looked upon the Board as an "intellectual spearhead" which contributed to the development of public policy and to the coordination

---

[3] Charles W. Eliot, 2nd, assisted by Harold Merrill, *Guide to the Files of the National Resources Planning Board and Predecessor Agencies—Ten Years of National Planning, 1933–1943* (December 31, 1943) p. 15.

of federal agency activities. In solving immediate national problems he generally looked elsewhere.[4]

Millett, who was employed by the Board for about a year and a half about the time of the beginning of the war, takes a rather different view.[5]

> The Board simply did not function effectively as a management device. It was infrequently consulted by the President on various problems coming to his attention. In a twelve-month period only one important piece of paper on a current problem came directly from the White House to the Board for recommendation. . . . It is difficult to decide just how far the deficiencies in Board operation resulted from the temperament of Mr. Roosevelt, from personality conflicts within the Board, or simply from the administrative device of a board itself. Certainly the Board saw the President only occasionally. Even these meetings apparently were more characterized by jovial reminiscences and broad-ranging and indecisive conversations than by discussion and decision on immediate problems. The board insisted upon seeing the President as a board. Each meeting was then a conference rather than a business session. Mr. Merriam has indicated that an agenda was regularly presented to the President; failure on his part to voice specific disapproval of a project was construed as authority to proceed.

Millett's views must be judged in part because he was at the NRPB after FDR's activities on conservation matters had declined markedly, as noted in table 16-1. His reference to "personality conflicts" should be considered in light of Merriam's efforts to displace Eliot (see footnote 29, chapter 5, and the discussion incident thereto).

The president customarily sent to the Congress, for its attention, the reports coming from the NRPB, and to this extent he was a public champion of it. During the 1935–1939 period, the National Resources Board and the National Resources Committee operated on funds allocated to them by the president, from emergency relief or other funds at his discretion. Thus, the president had to take no position with Congress in defending the agency's budget during these years, nor did the agency itself have such a responsibility. But during the 1935–1939

---

[4] Norman Beckman, "Federal Long-Range Planning—The Heritage of the National Resources Planning Board," *Journal of the American Institute of Planning,* vol. XXVI, no. 2 (May 1960) p. 91.

[5] John D. Millett, *The Process and Organization of Government Planning* (New York, Columbia University Press, 1947) pp. 140 and 141. It is not clear how far these statements reflect Millett's personal experiences and how far they reflect his analysis of the available records.

years FDR did, on at least one occasion, come most strongly to the defense of the NRC before the Congress. White quotes extensively from FDR's message when he vetoed (August 13, 1937) a resolution which would have placed in the Corps of Engineers all responsibility for water planning, thus in effect removing responsibility for such planning from the NRC.[6] FDR's message was most vigorous in defense of the kind of planning the NRC was supposed to be doing. While this may have been one of the more outspoken evidences of support for the NRC, in the years here under consideration, FDR seems to have looked upon the NRC as a useful but not vital part of his office.

1940 to Near the End of the NRPB

The years after 1939 were, generally speaking, a period of the NRPB's diminishing role with FDR, as table 16-1 shows. War was impending or actually under way, and resources and peacetime planning had to yield. Even Eliot and Merrill more or less concede this. Other writers were, on the whole, more inclined to think that the Board was gradually losing influence with FDR, even before the final attack in 1943.

With the perspective that time brings, I judge that the Board and staff members misjudged their relationships with FDR in these later years. He remained as cordial to the Board as an agency and to its individuals, as he had been earlier. But, as Karl says, "the reorganization fight over the creation of the NRPB had begun to make it clear to FDR that the cost of his advisory board was going to be high."[7] Even if FDR was gradually aware of this, he did not let it intercede directly in his relations with the Board or with its members.

The years after 1939 were years when the NRPB engaged in great activity, issued many publications, and received increasing public attention. FDR no doubt gloried in its activities and in the attention it received. When it was useful to him, he used it and supported it. When war came or was imminent, he turned to other instruments which he judged—rightly, I think—could better meet his needs.

---

[6] Philip L. White, "The Termination of the National Resources Planning Board," (master's thesis, Columbia University, 1949) p. 46. Also see Nixon, *Franklin D. Roosevelt.*

[7] Karl, *Charles E. Merriam,* p. 272.

17

The NRPB and Congress

In contrast to its relations with the president, other executive agencies, and its own field organization, which on the whole were very good, the NRPB's relations with the Congress ranged from poor to simply awful. (I use the word "awful" in its literal sense—to a one-time federal bureaucrat, the NRPB's abysmal or nonexistent relations with the Congress are indeed awe-inspiring.) Its relations with the Congress were poor in the sense that they were distant and infrequent; poor, in the sense that Charles E. Merriam insisted and the rest of the Board agreed that Board and staff should hold itself as aloof from the Congress as possible; poor in the sense that the NRPB did not keep its actual or potential friends in Congress informed; and poor in the sense that it made no real attempt to win over its critics or to nullify their opposition. Continued controversy in the Congress and opposition from important members of the Congress were exacerbated by the NRPB's words and actions. It made no real effort at conciliation.

These judgments about the NRPB's relations with the Congress are reached in spite of some lack of clarity and detail in the record. But what there is in that record seems unequivocally to point in this direction. Beckman says: "Members of the NRPB believed, as a matter of policy, that it was inappropriate for a staff arm of the president to develop close relationships with Congress as a whole or with individual members. Contacts tended to be formal and infrequent."[1] Even Eliot and Merrill,

---

[1] Norman Beckman, "Federal Long-Range Planning—The Heritage of the

in their official description of the NRPB's operations say: "Practically the only contact of the members of the board and advisors with members of Congress was at appropriation hearings before the House and Senate committees. The senators and congressmen whom the members interviewed outside of appropriation hearings, or conferred with on board business, probably did not exceed twenty in the first nine years . . . no joint meetings or regular channels were opened for communication and conference."[2]

Relations of the NPB, NRB, and NRC with Congress Prior to 1939

The National Planning Board, the National Resources Board, and the National Resources Committee had very limited relations with the Congress primarily because their operating funds were allocated by the president, from emergency relief and other funds at his disposal, rather than from the normal appropriation process. "It is important to bear in mind that until 1939 Congress had had almost no direct concern with the planning organization no matter what its name. The authorization for the establishment of a planning agency and the appropriation for its work were never specifically made, but were always included in the large, general grants of power and money which Congress provided for executive action to meet the 'relief emergency' situation of the depression."[3] This statement is somewhat of an exaggeration, as White's own subsequent analysis and as the rest of this subsection show, but there is a substantial degree of accuracy in it too. No necessity to seek an annual appropriation may have seemed a great advantage to a federal agency in those years as well as later, because it spared the agency the necessity of devoting so much time to budget preparation, so much critical questioning at appropriation hearings, and probably some rebuffs and reductions in amounts requested. But it was then—as always, I would argue—an advantage dearly bought. Whatever may be the prob-

National Resources Planning Board," *Journal of the American Institute of Planners,* vol. XXVI, no. 2 (May 1960) p. 92.

[2] Charles W. Eliot, 2nd, assisted by Harold Merrill, *Guide to the Files of the National Resources Planning Board and Predecessor Agencies—Ten Years of National Planning, 1933–1943,* December 1943.

[3] Philip L. White, "The Termination of the National Resources Planning Board" (master's thesis, Columbia University, 1949) p. 12.

lems arising out of the budget-appropriation process, the attitudes and the criticisms arising in that process must be faced somewhere, sometime, in some way, and postponement may only exacerbate them—as the NRPB experience clearly shows.

In fact, as Rockwell shows (and as White agrees, in general) :

> . . . some seventeen bills or amendments thereto have been introduced into Congress, the intention of which has been to establish a permanent national planning agency of one kind or another. Only five of these bills had as their single objective the creation of a National Planning (or Resources) Board. Four others had as their principal objective the establishment of regional planning authorities throughout the nation, with the creation of a national planning board as a secondary objective. Three bills providing for the reorganization of the executive branch of the government and two bills relating to the construction of public works provided for the establishment of a national planning board. A water pollution control bill, a flood control bill, and finally, a routine appropriation bill account for the remaining attempts to secure a planning agency with permanent status.[4]

Rockwell goes on to say: "Such a hodge-podge of proposals reflects attempts on the part of individual planning enthusiasts to append planning legislation as a rider to any bill related to public works, rather than a concerted and persevering effort on the part of any large groups of legislators."

Eliot and Merrill provide a generally similar account of these bills.[5]

Rockwell goes on to show how these various bills were supported primarily by their authors and by persons directly involved in the planning process, and by almost no one else. The opposition in the Congress was considerable, although neither as extensive nor as virulent at this time as it was to become later. The criticisms in the Congress were against the vagueness and the sweeping character of the proposals and against the inclusion of "human resources" as part of the subject matter for planning. When Rockwell illustrates and documents these bills, including the defenses for them, one is impressed with the amateurishness and naivete of the sponsors. At no time did the Administration officially throw its weight and influence behind any of these bills.

---

[4] Landon G. Rockwell, "National Resources Planning: The Role of the National Resources Planning Board in the Process of Government" (doctoral dissertation, Princeton University, May 1943) p. 131.

[5] Eliot and Merrill, *Guide to the Files,* pp. 32–39.

White shows that the most serious of these efforts, the one originating from the Administration, was made in 1936 but was unsuccessful.[6] One episode during these years was the effort of the Rivers and Harbors Congress in 1937 to place all water planning in the hands of the Corps of Engineers. Roosevelt vetoed this in August 1937, thereby keeping at least some of this function in the NRPB, but the passage of the resolution which he vetoed was evidence of the power of the NRPB's enemies and of the lack of support for it in the Congress. Throughout these years, at various times and in various ways, the Rivers and Harbors Congress opposed the NRPB. Both White and Warken document this and there seems little need to explore the details.[7]

In 1939 there was an episode which interests me considerably, in part because I later knew well the chief figure involved and partly because my present judgment is that a completely different attitude on the part of the NRPB and the Administration as a whole have led to a greatly different subsequent history for the NRPB. Senator Hayden of Arizona, a very influential senator especially on resource matters, and a long-standing champion of permanent status for planning, had sought legislative support for the NRC in 1937. In 1939 he introduced S. 19, to create a permanent National Resources Board. He would have limited its concern to natural resources and he would have preserved the cabinet membership on the board. The NRPB and the Administration apparently did not actively oppose Hayden's efforts, for he was too influential and too good a supporter of the Administration, but their support was lukewarm, to put it most kindly. Eliot and Merrill say: "This measure was vigorously opposed by Dr. Merriam and Mr. Brownlow, who were already at work on the proposals of the President's Committee on Administrative Management."[8] Their chief objections to Hayden's bill were its limitation to natural resources, omitting human, and to the form of the Board's organization. His bill got nowhere, at least partly as a result of the Administration's attitude.

When I personally worked closely with Senator Hayden about ten years later, I formed the judgment that he would never knowingly carry a banner for a hopeless cause and that any measure he actively promoted, with full Administration support, would have passed at this time, though perhaps modified in the process. Merriam was strongly

[6] White, "The Termination."

[7] Philip W. Warken, "A History of the National Resources Planning Board, 1933–1943" (doctoral dissertation, Ohio State University, 1969).

[8] Eliot and Merrill, *Guide to the Files*, p. 37.

opposed to the limitation to natural resources, yet once the reorganization of 1939 was made (discussed below), the Board's legal authority was enormously smaller than this—confined in their annual appropriations to those functions authorized previously to be performed by the Federal Stabilization Board.

Under the authority of the Hayden bill one could study supply and demand for natural resource commodities, including many economic and social factors related thereto, if one did not overemphasize the human resource research. My present judgment, from the vantage point of forty years more history, is that failure to support the Hayden bill in 1939 really sealed the ultimate doom of the NRPB.

Relations of the NRPB and Congress, 1939 to 1942

The relationship of the NRPB to the Congress became more direct and even less cordial after 1939. Roosevelt, acting on the advice of his Committee on Administrative Management and on his own convictions in 1937, sought legal authority for the establishment of a permanent planning unit in his office. His general plans for reorganization were in considerable part thwarted by the Congress in 1938, in large part because of the fears and antagonisms FDR had aroused at this time, especially by his attempt to "pack" the Supreme Court. They were accepted in a watered-down form in 1939. The situation as to a planning organization has been well described by White:

> On the President's specific recommendation that a permanent planning agency be established on a statutory basis, Congress provided in the Emergency Relief Appropriation Act of June 30, 1939 only that the National Resources Planning Board should be composed of three members "from widely separated sections of the United States" appointed by and with the advice and consent of the Senate. Neither the Reorganization Plan nor the Emergency Relief Appropriation Act made specific provision for annual appropriations for the Board. Whether or not appropriations could have been justified on the general authority of these acts is conjectural. Acceptance in 1940 of the "Clark Amendment" limiting the board to the functions authorized in the Employment Stabilization Act of 1931 made that question moot. Thereafter, the legal thread of the board's existence was its combination with the Federal Employment Stabilization Board for which the Act of 1931 had authorized "such annual appropriations as may be necessary."[9]

9 White, "The Termination."

The Clark amendment to which White alludes was a provision in the Independent Offices Appropriations Act of 1941, as follows:

> Provided, that no part of the funds appropriated under this item shall be used for the performance of any functions or duties other than the functions heretofore authorized by law to be performed by the Federal Employment Stabilization Board.[10]

The Administration accepted this amendment, probably judging (rightly) that an appropriation would not otherwise be forthcoming; but this clearly limited the scope of the NRPB's work, or at least the Congress intended that it should.

Thereafter, the NRPB was subject to the annual appropriations process, including questioning and criticism in the appropriation committees but also on the floor of each house when the appropriations came up for vote. This questioning grew increasingly critical, even hostile. White, Warken, and Galloway each quote a number of statements by congressmen in criticism of the Board.[11] To some extent, they quote the same persons in the same speeches. Some of the criticism was simple, though often deeply felt, antagonism to planning as such; some was indirect criticism and antagonism to the president; some was genuine belief that the work of the Board was unimportant or duplicative of the work of other agencies; some arose from a genuine concern over economy; and some was to specific actions or reports of the Board. Some were emotional and extravagant even by the standards of political, especially southern political, oratory of the day.

Although a full account of congressional statements about the NRPB seems unnecessary for the present purpose, a few sample quotes from the debates in the House on April 12, 1940, may give some sample of congressional attitudes.[12]

Mr. Warren of North Carolina: "The record of this agency, to say the least, is very unimpressive and I am eternally opposed to seeing it made a permanent agency of the government." Mr. Wigglesworth of Massachusetts: "Every one of the activities of this agency is in a field which other agencies of the government are either performing or capable of

---

[10] Independent Offices Appropriation Act of 1941, Public Law No. 459, 76th Congress, 3rd Session, approved April 18, 1940.

[11] For White and Warken, see previous references; for Galloway: George P. Galloway and Associates, *Planning for America* (New York, Henry Holt and Company, 1941) chapter 3.

[12] These and other quotes are found in ibid., pp. 74–77.

performing. . . ." Mr. Knutson of Minnesota: "There is a feeling that
this organization is a sort of wet nurse set up by President Roosevelt
to nurse along those bureaus which he promised in 1932 that he was
going to abolish." Mr. Mott of Oregon described it as "extravagant and
useless" and also as "harmful and even vicious . . . it has held back
proper legislation by improper and unauthorized methods." At that
same time, Senator Byrd of Virginia described the NRPB as "one of
the 80 new agencies which in accomplishment shows less for the actual
money expended than any other agency of the government." There
were other criticisms and also some defenders, the latter generally
Administration supporters on all matters, at this time and later.

The appropriation acts from 1939 forward used similar language to
the Clark amendment quoted above, in authorizing the NRPB to carry
out the functions of the Employment Stabilization Act of 1931. (The
relevant parts of that act are quoted as number 1 in appendix A).
While Section 3(a) does authorize the Board created under this act
"to advise the President from time to time of the trend of employment
and business activity and of the existence or approach of periods of
business depression and unemployment . . . ," the main thrust of this
act is the preparation of a long-term program of public works. I think
it reasonable to believe that the Congress, in enacting the Clark amendment intended to limit the NRPB to this function. The NRPB surely
interpreted its charter, under these appropriations, far more broadly.
Merriam, in particular, took the view that one could not sensibly plan
public works without national plans for the whole economy, and on
this basis he justified the NRPB's extensive and widening range of
activities.[13] Regardless of the logical accuracy or inaccuracy of this
position, this stance on the part of the NRPB—like any other attempt
by a federal agency to stretch its authorization beyond what Congress
clearly intended—ultimately led to disaster.

Some of NRPB's Chief Actors—Again

In considering this matter of the NRPB's relations with the Congress,
it is essential to consider again the chief actors in the NRPB. After
all, the relations with Congress were as much a reflection of these men
as they were of the Congress—it was a *relationship,* not merely the
nature of the Congress which was involved.

---

[13] White, "The Termination," p. 147.

By the later NRPB years, Frederic A. Delano, chairman of the NRPB, was old, beginning to lack energy for effective action, and in any case regarded a direct political fight as beneath his dignity. He was most determined not to trade upon his relationship to his nephew. He would present to the appropriate committee the case for an appropriation to the NRPB and he would talk with members of the Congress at their request. But he would not engage in the kind of intense, sometimes difficult, lobbying for the agency without which its chances for an appropriation were bleak indeed.

Charles E. Merriam, the vice chairman of the NRPB, was primarily an academician. He thought it was simply improper for a member of the president's staff to have any relations with the Congress except the most necessary formal and distant ones. He appeared before congressional committees only rarely—as rarely, apparently, as his position as vice chairman would require him to go.[14] There is no evidence and little reason to believe that he had any informal relations with individual members of the Congress. All of this would have been serious enough, but in addition Merriam distrusted Eliot and specifically forbade the latter to deal directly with the Congress.

Charles W. Eliot, the director of the NRPB, at least recognized the need for some meaningful communication with the Congress, but he was totally restrained by the Board from anything effective. He might not have been the best emissary in any case, because his background and mannerisms might have offended or alienated many congressmen, but at least his best efforts would have been vastly better than what did exist.

A few of the NRPB employees did have some personal contacts with individual members of the Congress or did at times appear before congressional committees on specific issues.[15] While these were almost surely useful to the NRPB, they did not begin to compensate for the other deficiencies in congressional relations.

---

[14] Eliot in a personal letter, January 2, 1980 says: "I can't find a single time when he even attended a Congressional Hearing. Even when Mr. Delano was sick, he made Yantis read the opening statement at the April 1943 Appropriation Hearing."

[15] Personal interviews with Ralph J. Watkins and Glenn E. McLaughlin in 1978.

The NRPB's Field Organization in Relation to the Congress

We have noted how little the NRPB seems to have used its field organization as a political force—using this term in its broadest meaning. One would have expected any federal organization with a large and distinguished field organization to have used that organization in its support at crucial times.

In making the foregoing statement, one must be tentative. The written record seems to show little use of the field organization, at least until the very end. But one would doubt that any use of the field organization for basically political ends would have shown up in the written record in any case—no sensible federal bureaucrat would have put such matters on the record. But there is also no evidence in terms of what members of the Congress did or said to show that their constituents had given them any reaction to the NRPB.

Contemplating this situation, and bearing in mind the personalities described briefly above, one suspects strongly that Merriam played a dominant role here, quite possibly giving strong but verbal directions to the NRPB Washington and field staff to make no efforts whatsoever to convey information or attitudes to members of the Congress. It surely would have been consistent with his other attitudes for him to have taken some such position. One can hardly believe that the near total lack of use of the field organization to support the NRPB in the Congress arose by accident, without any such strong action by Merriam, directly or indirectly.

V

DEMISE AND LEGACY

18

Why and How Congress
Killed the NRPB

To fully understand the events that are described in this chapter, one must recall briefly the general situation in the United States at the beginning of 1943.

1. The United States had been at war for slightly more than a year, and at this stage the war had not gone particularly well. Following the surprise attack at Pearl Harbor in early December 1941, the Japanese had overrun the Philippines and a number of the Pacific islands. While the United States had won some striking naval battles, it was still primarily on the defensive in the Pacific. On the European front, no significant victories had yet been achieved. The national effort was in the build-up of war strength—men, ships, airplanes, and war weaponry in general. There was an enormous emotional appeal to direct all national energies to the war effort, and to abolish or set aside everything not working to that end.

2. President Roosevelt was directing virtually all his personal energies toward the war effort also. As we have noted previously, in 1942 he saw the National Resources Planning Board but twice, instead of more or less monthly as he had done some years earlier. He was increasingly willing to trade his interests in various matters for support for the war program, in the Congress and elsewhere.

3. At the same time, the Congress as a whole was growing increasingly hostile toward President Roosevelt. The members of the Congress were under great pressure to support the war effort, including

FDR's proposals to this end. In this regard, their position in 1943 was not unlike what it had been in 1933, when the enemy was economic depression. Congress in those early war months was reduced to little more than a rubber stamp in a number of important ways. As a result, it attacked with venom those targets which were open to attack, including many New Deal peacetime programs, the NRPB among them. Over the years a considerable number of congressmen had been hostile to the NRPB, and their numbers now increased, as did their opportunities to attack the NRPB. There was a substantial "hate Roosevelt" feeling and one way to hit the president was to hit his uncle, Frederic A. Delano, chairman of the NRPB.

4. The 1942 elections had seen a substantial swing of the electorate to the right. In the House, there had been a net swing of over forty seats to Republicans, and in the Senate a new swing in the same direction of eight or nine.[1] In addition to this general swing, a number of prominent liberal Democrats had been defeated, generally replaced by conservative Republicans, so that the tone of the whole Congress changed in a direction clearly disadvantageous to the NRPB.

5. Perhaps most serious from the NRPB's point of view was the fact that the country as a whole had lost interest in the kind of planning the NRPB was set up to do and in the kind of programs it proposed. The general public was also caught up in the war spirit and the war program. The New Deal was dead, even by the president's admission, or at least set aside until after the war. Whatever degree of popular support NRPB planning had had during the later 1930s waned during the early 1940s.

Publications in 1942 and 1943

Although earlier chapters have discussed in more detail the NRPB publications, it is helpful to recall again a few of the more important and more controversial ones which appeared about this time. In the summer of 1942 there had appeared *Transportation and National Policy*. Although prepared about the same time, *Security, Work, and*

---

[1] Philip L. White, "The Termination of the National Resources Planning Board" (master's thesis, Columbia University, 1949) not only provides these statistics (p. 110) but also quotes from a number of prominent newspapers and news magazines, emphasizing the general nature of this political shift. The Democrats lost eight seats in the Senate while the Republicans gained nine, one of which had been held by an Independent.

Relief Policies was not publicly released until early 1943, as we have pointed out previously. The *National Resources Development Report for 1943,* Parts I and II, came out in early 1943. In addition, there were several popular or semipopular pamphlets prepared and released, based on these and other major NRPB reports. Of the pamphlets, the one by Alvin H. Hansen, *After the War—Full Employment,* was particularly noteworthy in the attention and criticism it drew.

These reports in general were vigorous, not to say aggressive, expressions of the ideals and conceptions of the NRPB and its staff. Considered purely as professional inquiries and writings, they were, in general, good quality jobs. Many of them were ahead of their time, in the sense that the country was not yet ready to accept their findings, but did so, with more or less modification, in the following decades. But many of these reports were not directly relevant to the war effort and drew criticism on this ground.

More serious than all this, however, was the fact that the timing of these reports could hardly have been worse. At a time when the nation was engrossed in war activities and when there was clearly evident a substantial political shift to the right, these were strong statements of the kind of liberal social planning which had already drawn so much criticism upon the NRPB. The release of these reports at this time fed the flames of opposition. As the old farmer said after his Jersey bull charged the railroad freight engine head on, with anticipatable results, he admired his courage but deplored his judgment. The NRPB in effect flung down the gauntlet to its opponents at a time when the tide of battle was running against the agency. As with the bull, a little more caution might have prolonged its life.

In 1940, Franklin Delano Roosevelt had run for an unprecedented third term as president of the United States, and had been elected. In late 1942 and early 1943, it was widely expected that in 1944 he would run for still another term, his fourth, in part because the war effort was clearly in midstream. Many actions of the government in those years were popularly perceived, and with some accuracy, as part of his drive for this fourth term. This attitude carried over to the NRPB reports as well. *Business Week,* on the cover of a March 1943 issue, showed two NRPB reports, with the notation: "For the 1944 campaign, Roosevelt gives potential candidates . . . something to shoot at".[2]

---

[2] Philip W. Warken, "A History of the National Resources Planning Board," (doctoral dissertation, Ohio State University, 1969) p. 236.

Appropriations for Fiscal 1944
in the House of Representatives

The final battle arose over the NRPB appropriation request for fiscal 1944 (the year which began on July 1, 1943). As White put it: "In 1943 the wall fell in. It did not fall in rapidly with resounding reverberations, but it crumbled slowly under somewhat mysterious pressures. The board died as it had existed, hesitantly and uncertainly."[3] And later he says: "In reality it is quite surprising that the National Resources Planning Board lasted as long as it did. Until late in its life it could claim virtually no Congressional support won to it by its activities. Those who carried the ball for the board in Congress did so in all but a few cases because the President wanted it. They had no comprehension of its functions or conviction of its worth. When support was won to a degree in later years, it was largely for the physical planning activities carried on at the regional, state, and local levels."[4]

Warken has put the same idea in somewhat milder terms: "The NRPB was already in serious trouble on Capitol Hill when FDR sent the post-war reports forward. The Board for a number of years had experienced difficulties in securing its annual appropriations and 1943 was no exception."[5] Millett has briefly described what happened as follows: "In 1943 the House of Representatives refused to provide any additional appropriations for the National Resources Planning Board. ... The only explanation given to the House at the time was that the board duplicated the work of other agencies."[6] Karl, after describing some of the opposition to the NRPB, said: "What killed the NRPB was the same opposition that had hampered its activities all along. What that opposition had in 1943 was the margin for victory it had lacked in previous battles."[7]

In its budget request for the 1944 fiscal year, the NRPB (with, obviously, the approval of the Bureau of the Budget) had asked for $1.4 million, an increase over the $1.0 million it had for fiscal 1943, and an increase in the number of employees from 252 to 350. The

---

[3] White, "The Termination," p. 27.

[4] Ibid., p. 159.

[5] Warken, "A History," p. 237.

[6] John D. Millett, *The Process of Organization of Government Planning* (New York, Columbia University Press, 1947) p. 150.

[7] Barry D. Karl, *Charles E. Merriam and the Study of Politics* (Chicago, The University of Chicago Press, 1947) p. 278.

Appropriation Committee Hearing in early January was, as White puts it, "not notably unfriendly." There were the usual criticisms, from opponents of the president, that the Board duplicated the work of other agencies, that it was too far left or even communistic in its studies and reports, that it was too much an effort by the president to dominate the country, and the like. In addition, there was resentment that in the previous fiscal year the Board had augmented its funds, over the amount appropriated to it, by an allocation from the president's emergency funds; and Eliot refused or was unable to give unequivocal assurance that this would not happen again in fiscal 1944. Yet, in executive session, the committee voted against the appropriation of any sum for the NRPB.[8] The vote in the committee had apparently been close, somewhat along partisan lines but with some Democrats teaming up with enough Republicans to defeat the NRPB.

A determined fight to save the NRPB appropriation was not made on the House floor. Then Congressman, later Senator, Warren G. Magnuson of Washington offered a floor amendment to give the NRPB an appropriation of $415,000 (less than half what it had asked of the committee); but Congressman Everett Dirksen of Illinois raised a point of order that no statutory authority existed for such an appropriation.[9] Dirksen had been one of the most consistent anti-Roosevelt members of the Congress. He was wrong in this statement, but Magnuson was too ill-informed to refute him, and the matter was allowed to drop. This was another example of the poor level of communications between the NRPB and its potential friends in the Congress. When the NRPB needed friends in Congress to defend it, it had few informed friends— it reaped the harvest of its long policy of aloofness from the Congress. It might have made little difference if Magnuson's amendment had been put to a vote—it probably would have failed in any case. And so the appropriation bill passed the House with no appropriation for the NRPB, and the action shifted to the Senate.

Appropriations for Fiscal 1944 in the Senate

The extended fight, first in the Appropriations Committee and later on the floor of the Senate, over the NRPB appropriation for fiscal

---

[8] White cites as authority for this statement letters from Representative Clarence Cannon, Chairman of the House Appropriations Committee, to President Roosevelt, February 19, 1943, and another to Frederic A. Delano on February 14, 1943.

[9] *Congressional Record*, 78th Congress, First Session vol. 89, part 1, p. 1072.

1944, has been well described by White, relying on the record of the Senate Appropriation Committee *Hearings,* the *New York Times,* and the *Congressional Record,* as follows:

The Senate Committee hearing of 1943 was one of the most exhaustive and generally favorable in the board's history. Senators Reed (Republican, Kansas) and Bankhead (Democrat, Alabama) both indicated that they had opposed the board in 1942, but now, as a result of "reports" from home, felt inclined to look much more favorably on it. Senator McKellar (Democrat, Tennessee), who had in the last year expressed grave misgivings about the duplication of effort in which he felt the board engaged, now stated that his attitude was "very kindly." Senator Glass was absent, but a letter to him from the President urged the committee to give due consideration to the needs of the executive office. The President, through his executive office, always gave Congress his full support in regard to the appropriations for its office functions; therefore, it was felt that the President should receive something like the same consideration from Congress.

Despite these expressions of good will, an appropriation of workable size was not forthcoming. Throughout one whole afternoon the subcommittee tied at five to five on an amendment to appropriate $534,000 for the board. Finally, it was agreed to, six to four. Then in the full (appropriations) committee the deadlock recurred. One entire session was consumed in a ten to ten impasse. A recommendation from the committee would probably see the appropriation through the Senate floor and into conference with the House subcommittee upon whom strong public and administration pressure would then be brought to bear. This was the course of action which had saved the board from elimination in 1940 when, as now, the House had made no appropriation. This same strategic maneuver, in reverse action (House to Senate) had only last year helped to avert the crippling financial blow of the Senate's $400,000 appropriation. It was not to be possible again.

The ten-ten tie in the Senate Appropriations Committee meeting was finally broken by a compromise recommendation of $200,000. This was patently insufficient for the board's operation. It served primarily to indicate to the Senate that if the committee in its deadlock tended to lean in either direction, it was against the board. This was perhaps the decisive moment. Until that decision there had been a fighting chance. After it, though some hope still existed, it proved entirely vain.

On the Senate floor the situation was explained by Senator McKellar who then offered an amendment to increase the amount of appropriation to $534,000. An issue so narrowly decided in committee is customarily referred to the full legislative body for decision. This was the effect of Senator McKellar's amendment. This was to be the "acrimonious debate" which Budget Director Smith had mentioned, which the President, his supporters in Congress, and the board members and staff had always sought to avoid. Their appraisal of its nature and result was accurate.

The Senate rejected the McKellar amendment after six hours of deliberation in which the *New York Times* characterized the opposition as "largely sarcasm and denunciation." The vote was 31 to 43. A few moments later the committee amendment authorizing a $200,000 appropriation was adopted 44 to 31. Both the pro-board and anti-board factions maintained a solid nucleus of 31. The decisive middle-of-the-roaders who voted against the McKellar amendment and for the committee amendment were McNary (Republican, Oregon), Burton (Republican, Ohio), Capper (Republican, Kansas), Chavez (Democrat, New Mexico), Danaher (Republican, Connecticut), Davis (Republican, Pennsylvania), George (Democrat, Georgia), Lodge (Republican, Massachusetts), Maloney (Democrat, Connecticut), Vandenberg (Republican, Michigan), VanNuys (Democrat, Indiana), and Wiley (Republican, Wisconsin).

The conference still remained, but its action was limited to a compromise within the ranges of the completely inadequate Senate appropriation and the complete absence of appropriation by the House, between $200,000 and zero. The board was finished. The conference had merely to decide the detail of the termination. This it did with a vengeance.[10]

During the Senate debate on the appropriation, the NRPB and some of its reports were criticized at length and sometimes in strong terms. Senator Taft made an extended, careful, and sensible critical commentary on the Board's work, especially the *Security* report by Eveline Burns and the *Full Employment* pamphlet by Alvin Hansen. The general grounds of his opposition are evident in his statement at this time:

In my opinion, they [the NRPB reports] are based on two policies and theories. The first is the theory of unlimited public spending and con-

---

[10] White, "The Termination," pp. 28–31. White relies on and to some extent quotes U.S. Congress, Senate Committee on Appropriations, *Hearings,* vol. 38, 78th Congress, First Session, Subcommittee on HR 1762, Independent Offices Appropriation Bill for 1944, pp. 189–240; *New York Times,* May 28 and May 30, 1943; and *Congressional Record,* 78th Congress, First Session, vol. 89, part 1, pp. 2965–2966. My own research yields essentially the same analysis, including the voting cited by White, but from *Congressional Record,* vol. 89, no. 97, May 27, 1943, pp. 5031–5078.

stant increase of the public debt after the war. A policy of deficit spending is implicit in the measures the board proposes and in its attitude toward the spending of government money. In the second place, the board's plans are based on unlimited government interference in and regulation of all business activity, plus a very large amount of government regulation of what is now private industry.[11]

In Taft's view, these characteristics of the Board, as he saw them, were enough to damn it entirely. Just a few moments before speaking the quoted statement, he said ". . . as a practical matter I am correct when I say the Congress has never passed a planning law, has never created a planning agency, and has never given the board authority to do the kind of things it is doing. . . ." Senator Byrd, Senator Tydings, and Senator Hill also joined in criticism of these reports.

A revealing episode showing how poorly informed were the NRPB's supporters took place during these debates.[12] Senator Taft had taken particular exception to the proposal for compensatory governmental spending to alleviate unemployment which Hansen, following Keynes, had advocated in the *Full Employment* pamphlet. McKellar denied any such thing had been said by the NRPB—on page 5063 of the *Congressional Record* he is reported as saying: "Of course, as I said a little while ago, I have never read the pamphlet, indeed I never heard of it, it is something new to me." Senators Taft and Tydings were able, on the spot, to show him specific language which McKellar rejected as expressing his beliefs. McKellar, defender of the NRPB on this day, was thus made to look foolish, while the NRPB's critics or enemies were obviously better informed.

The action in conference between House and Senate was to deny the NRPB the use of any funds not appropriated, so as to forestall any allocation from the president; to require that its work be terminated by August 31, 1943; to provide for a liquidation period up to the end of 1943; to provide that its records be transferred to the National Archives; and to provide that "the functions exercised by such board shall not be transferred to any other agency, and shall not be performed after such date except as hereafter provided by law or as authorized in the ensuing proviso of this paragraph with respect to winding up the board's affairs." The president accepted this legislation and thus the NRPB was brought to its end.

---

[11] *Congressional Record,* Senate, May 27, 1943, p. 5037.
[12] Ibid., pp. 5062–5066.

Immediate Consequences and Attitudes

Liquidation of a federal agency is always a difficult operation, more so in this case because of the limited time allowed and because the NRPB's functions could not be transferred to another agency. Eliot has described in fair detail what was done.[13] Including Board members, staff, consultants, those on active and inactive duty, and those on military leave, there were over 500 names on the personnel lists at the beginning of June. These people were mostly placed on terminal leave immediately. Vigorous and generally effective efforts were made to help displaced persons find other employment if they wished it. Bills were paid, records packed and shipped to Archives—a myriad of important but often tedious details, which we need not examine in detail here. In my research, I have caught no hint that all this was done in anything but a competent and thorough manner, especially in view of the short time available and the inevitable trauma of defeat.

When termination became definite and final, Eliot held a farewell meeting with the staff. The NRPB had been an organization with a high morale and it was small enough that the Washington office employees were well acquainted with one another. Termination of the agency under these conditions was as emotional as the death of a loved friend or relative, and the final staff meeting was an emotional one.

There were a few instances of recrimination and conflict among the NRPB staff and/or Board, but, given the circumstances, these incidents were relatively uncommon. There is no evidence in the Eliot–Merrill account, in other documents released by the Board then, or in discussions I have had with NRPB alumni about this period, of the efforts Merriam had exerted to have Eliot replaced. Those efforts were obviously meaningless once the NRPB was killed. But it may be instructive to examine briefly some of the attitudes of persons informed or involved, as far as these have been revealed in writings.

Landon Rockwell, who was never employed by the NRPB, but was well informed about and highly sympathetic to it, writing in early 1942, concludes his long report as follows: ". . . despite the lack of legislative status, the work of the National Resource Planning Board and its predecessors has been responsible for the development of a well-defined planning function within the Federal Government. It appears, then,

---

[13] Charles W. Eliot, *Final Report—Status of Work, National Resources Planning Board* (December 31, 1943).

that the functions of the National Resources Planning Board have become firmly established in the structure and process of government. As the specific agency responsible for the exercise of the planning function, the National Resources Planning Board itself may or may not be permanent; that depends upon congress and future administrations." [14] While Rockwell had traced some of the NRPB's appropriation problems, there is no hint in this report that the agency's demise was imminent. Rockwell was not, at that time, an important figure on the American intellectual scene, but his written attitude, as expressed above, was typical of the attitude of a great many other people whom I knew personally at that time, who felt that the agency's work was highly important and likely to continue.

As I read Eliot's *Final Report,* I feel that, even some months after the NRPB had been officially terminated, he could hardly bring himself to believe that it had actually happened. He concludes his report with a section on "Need for Coordination" from which a few sentences may be quoted to give the general flavor of his attitude:

> I believe that the growth of power in governments at all levels makes it more important than ever before that we develop whatever techniques or tools we can find for coordination of policy and that this need is more evident in the Federal Government today than in any other organization in the world. It seems to me that the efforts to formalize or organize national planning work should aim at getting the process of planning recognized as non-political and essential to orderly and efficient government. The planning process goes on anyway, and the issue is whether it shall be carried on openly by an established agency or out of sight and inefficiently behind the scenes. . . . Coordination of Federal planning is the specific responsibility of the Chief Executive under the Constitution. It cannot be done anywhere else than by the President however much Congress may participate, influence, or finally control the purse strings. . . . I believe that the major effort to establish national planning should be in this field of Federal coordination of plans and programs. It involves the establishment, through appropriate legislation, of a Bureau of Planning or a Bureau of National Development as part of the White House staff or Executive Office.[15]

He goes on to append to his report the draft of a bill to accomplish his recommendation.

---

[14] Landon G. Rockwell, "National Resources Planning: The Role of the National Resources Planning Board in the Process of Government" (doctoral dissertation, Princeton University, May 1942) p. 217.

[15] Eliot, *Final Report,* pp. 23–25.

One may reasonably wonder if Eliot meant "nonpartisan" rather than "nonpolitical." As a widely experienced planner he surely knew that planning was political in the broadest sense of that term, and that it could not be otherwise. Whether it could be nonpartisan is problematical but at least possible.

Eliot had suffered a traumatic blow to his strongest and most deeply held convictions; but he did not abandon those convictions as a result. While his experience with the NRPB may have led him to somewhat modify his procedures, if a new planning agency had been established, I have the feeling that he would have tried to proceed along essentially the same lines as the NRPB in any new public planning body.

If Eliot had difficulty accepting the fact that the NRPB was in fact terminated, Merriam almost pretended it never happened. In an article in a professional journal, published a year and a half after the NRPB's termination, he describes NRPB history, with no hint of congressional and other criticisms and appropriation problems. That might have been excusable, as putting the best possible face on an unpleasant experience, but then he says, "I shall not undertake to unsnarl the tangled threads of the liquidation of the board . . . difficulties [which] have been almost forgotten already and the sounder view now prevails."[16] He goes on to blandly assert that almost everything it sought to do is being carried on in the federal government or by state planning organizations. "As a result of past experience, I am more thoroughly convinced than ever that they [members of the Board] should serve on a part-time basis, rather than as a part of the regular staff." There is no hint in this article that Merriam had sought actively, but behind the scenes, to have Eliot replaced.

Who Was Responsible for the NRPB's Demise?

The NRPB's demise in 1943 naturally leads to the question, Who was basically responsible for what happened? My view, as I survey the whole NRPB history from the vantage point of thirty-five years, is that the end was inevitable as early as 1939, when the first problems in getting appropriations arose. Certainly nothing effective was done in the ensuing four years to neutralize or to overcome the opposition expressed

---

[16] Charles E. Merriam, "The National Resources Planning Board: A Chapter in American Planning Experience," *The American Political Science Review,* vol. XXXVIII, no. 6 (December 1944).

in 1939 or to remedy the basic deficiencies in the NRPB's organization and staffing. On the contrary, many studies were made and reports issued which exacerbated an already difficult situation. One may deliberately follow a hazardous policy, if one has strong convictions, but then one should not be surprised at the result—as Eliot and Merriam, each in his own way, seems to have been.

Nineteen forty-three was a year full of exciting incidents for the NRPB but, if my thesis is correct, all of these had limited importance, in the sense that the ultimate outcome would have been the same, whether or not these particular incidents arose. If the NRPB had survived 1943, it almost surely would have gone under in 1944.

Stressing that the die seems to have been cast in 1939 and that nothing effective was done in the succeeding four years to rescue the NRPB raises the question: Why not? Again, who was responsible? My guess is that no one connected with the NRPB would have reached the same conclusion during the 1939–1943 period which I now reach in 1980; and if I had been connected with the agency then, I probably would not have reached my present conclusion either. Problems with Congress were evident; their seriousness could easily have been misunderstood; no crisis seemed to require drastic actions; and the NRPB continued along its established, if not preordained, lines.

White puts the matter very well: "It has been mentioned that there was never any appreciable support of the board in congressional circles, though it was winning for some of its activities a greater degree of tolerance late in its life. This lack of support is not entirely to be laid to the unpopularity of its work. The board failed dismally in its lobbying obligations. Responsibility falls chiefly on Merriam for almost prohibiting this sort of activity. Delano was also reluctant about lobbying, but less so, and more justifiably so. Eliot, on the other hand, must bear a considerable responsibility for the unfruitful nature of much of the lobbying he was permitted to undertake."[17]

---

[17] White, "The Termination," p. 168.

19

How Hard Did FDR Fight
to Save the NRPB?

When the NRPB was under its fatal attack in early 1943, how hard did President Roosevelt fight to save it? Did he do everything that any president could possibly have done, or was his defense of the agency largely pro forma because he recognized that it could not be saved no matter what he did? These questions are impossible to answer unequivocally and in a manner that will be convincing to everyone. White recognizes that there are at least three schools of thought on this point: those who believe FDR thought the NRPB was a political liability he could not afford in wartime; those who insist that his attitude in 1943 was just what it had always been; and those who frankly admit they cannot tell.[1] White identifies the second view with Merriam. Karl is the most positive of the authors I have encountered. "Contrary, also, to a good bit of commentary then and since, Roosevelt recognized the value of the board and fought to keep it. It seemed to no one that he was doing enough, and in the press of affairs at that late stage in his career, that is probably true."[2] Like many another Karl statement, this one seems internally contradictory. It probably reflected Merriam's ideas. Beckman says: "Although it cannot be definitely established, it

---

[1] Philip L. White, "The Termination of the National Resources Planning Board" (master's thesis, Columbia University, 1949) p. 152.

[2] Barry D. Karl, *Charles E. Merriam and the Study of Politics* (Chicago, University of Chicago Press, 1974) p. 279.

seems conclusive that at some time early in 1943 the President became resigned to the Board's impending demise."[3]

After weighing such evidence as I can find, of actions more than of words, I come to the conclusion that FDR's defense was something more than pro forma, but considerably less than all-out, and that even at the beginning of 1943 he was reconciled to the loss of the NRPB.

In earlier years, FDR's intervention had been decisive in the NRPB's efforts to get appropriations. This had been true every year, beginning with 1939. Without his direct help, and without the general support in Congress which every president can rely on for his program, the NRPB would have been cut off or drastically whittled down much earlier. In addition to his support on appropriations, FDR had also allocated substantial sums to the NRPB each year from his emergency funds. While this was a major short-range gain for the NRPB, giving it substantially more money with which to operate, the long-run effect of such allocations was negative, for in the 1943 appropriation fight one of the objections that weighed heavily with otherwise somewhat uncommitted congressmen was that the NRPB had augmented its appropriation in this way. No congressional appropriation committee ever accepts such augmentation gracefully and the agency concerned is likely to lose in the end.

It must be stressed again that in 1943 the United States was at war and that essentially all of Roosevelt's efforts were directed to winning that war. We have noted that he saw the National Resources Planning Board but twice in 1942. It is more evident in retrospect than may have been apparent at the time that Roosevelt was unwell and that his energy was not as great as it had formerly been. He died in the spring of 1945, and his last year, at least, was one of seriously declining personal energy.[4]

On the usual formal front, Roosevelt surely supported the NRPB strongly. In mid-February, after the House had passed the Independent Offices Appropriation with no funds for the NRPB, FDR wrote Congressman Cannon, chairman of the whole Appropriations Committee, strongly defending the NRPB. In March, he wrote Senator Glass, chairman of the Senate Appropriations Committee, again strongly de-

---

[3] Norman Beckman, "Federal Long-Range Planning: The Heritage of the National Resources Planning Board," *Journal of the American Institute of Planners,* vol. XXVI, no. 2 (May 1960) p. 91.

[4] Jim Bishop, *FDR's Last Year, April 1944–April 1945* (New York, William Morrow and Company, 1974).

fending the NRPB. These were the sort of actions one would expect from a president defending a unit of his own office.

But there were other events of this period which suggest that FDR had little time for the NRPB. On February 6, 1943, Delano wrote to General Watson, the president's confidential aide, asking for a meeting of the Board with the president; and it was the president, not Watson, who replied, "No, sorry."[5]

It was on April 20, 1943, that Merriam wrote his confidential and personal letter to Delano concerning the replacement of Eliot.[6] This letter clearly implied that Delano and Yantis had agreed to Eliot's replacement. There is nothing in the record to indicate whether or not FDR was a party to whatever agreement had been reached. Merriam and Yantis had seen FDR on March 11, 1943, but Merriam's memo for the file does not include anything about Eliot's replacement.[7] Even if that had been discussed with FDR, the written record might well have omitted any reference to it. But it may well have been that Merriam felt emboldened by what he thought FDR's attitude would be.

This combination of an unauthorized visit by the director to the president, his explanation which may have been doubted by a suspicious Board member, a visit by the two Board members (Delano presumably being ill) to FDR, and the personal-confidential letter from one Board member to another suggest many behind-the-scenes maneuverings or even intrigues during February, March, and April 1943, aimed at trying to involve the president on their side. The surface relationships were hardly smooth and cordial but actions unrevealed at the time may have reflected far more disharmony underneath.

Karl says the Board met with the president on May 2, in an attempt to plan strategy on the appropriations.[8] Eliot says his records show no such meeting.[9] On the other hand, Eliot says the Board met with FDR on June 30, in Eliot's absence, to discuss disposition of confidential materials.

At the end of May, Eliot proposed to the Board that they all resign, in the hope that this might enable the Board to continue under other leadership; but no one was willing to resign and thus nothing came of

---

[5] White, "The Termination" p. 153. White cites File 1092, Franklin D. Roosevelt Library (National Archives), Hyde Park, New York.

[6] See footnotes 27, 28, and 29, in chapter 5, and the discussion based on them.

[7] Personal letter from Eliot, January 11, 1980.

[8] Karl, *Charles E. Merriam*, p. 281.

[9] Personal letter from Eliot, January 11, 1980.

his proposal.[10] Whatever might have been the merit of this proposal, it was far too late for such action to be effective in saving the NRPB.

The Board sought to meet again with the president in August, to deliver its final report, but "he was not available."[11] He did send friendly letters to the Board members at that time—letters drafted by Eliot. Still later, in December, he wrote Eliot a kindly farewell letter.

At the end of August, when Eliot was in the process of liquidating the Board's affairs, he sought instructions directly from the president on how he should proceed on various matters. But his request was rejected by General Watson, the president's aide; the latter sent some of Eliot's proposals to Delano, who responded, for the first time, rather sharply critical of his protege.[12] One can understand Eliot's desire for direction from someone in higher authority, but FDR clearly had more important things to do.

In a letter to Congressman Cannon in February, Delano had said: "If I go down, I will go down with colors flying."[13] This would suggest that, at this fairly early date, Delano foresaw the probable outcome of the congressional struggle and was resigned to it.

By June, the president was conferring with various persons, apparently including Delano, about Administration support for what was then known as the Mead-Lynch bill, which would have provided large sums for state and postwar planning.[14] While this bill seems never to have come to anything, the fact that FDR, or persons fairly close to him, were considering such a bill at this time is further evidence that FDR had lost hope for the NRPB and was directing his efforts elsewhere.

Admittedly, the evidence in this chapter is not wholly conclusive as to FDR's waning support for the NRPB, although I think that on balance the available facts do support this viewpoint. But I base my conclusion on one additional factor: FDR's personality and his mode of working with others. In chapter 5, I described some major aspects of FDR's personality, including his reluctance to give a definite answer, especially

---

10 White, "The Termination," p. 150.

11 Karl, *Charles E. Merriam,* p. 282.

12 White, "The Termination," p. 151. White gives File 1092, Franklin D. Roosevelt Library, Hyde Park, N.Y., September 9, 1943, as source.

13 Ibid., p. 142. White gives File 203, Franklin D. Roosevelt Library, Hyde Park, N.Y., February 22, 1943, as source.

14 Among the materials I inherited from Robert W. Hartley was a folder on this bill, including typed copies of several memos. Since this history is after the NRPB demise and since the bill never passed, there is little point in considering it further here.

a negative one, to any person, and his habit of turning to new persons or new agencies without dismissing old ones. My reading is that FDR gradually lost faith in the NRPB and gave up support for it, without being willing unequivocally to say so to anyone—probably not even to himself. His general friendliness was misunderstood by those most directly concerned as strong support, when in fact it was not.

It would also have been in character for FDR, even if he had become disillusioned with the NRPB, to have done nothing decisive either to abolish it or to reform it during the years between 1939 and 1943. He may not have realized how seriously disorganized it was and he surely had many other things on his mind all those years. He may have vaguely felt that all was not well and yet not have realized how unwell it really was, and in any case not been prepared to do something decisive.

20

The Legacy

Although the NRPB was ended as an agency in 1943 the congressional action did not wipe out all memories of it and all its results. It is probable that some of its congressional enemies hoped that ending the agency would indeed erase all influence its work may have had, but this was not the case.

The function of this chapter is to briefly describe the major legacies that the NRPB left. These legacies are tangible in some respects and intangible in others. For the latter, it is hard to disentangle the NRPB's effect from those of other agencies and actors, especially as time went on.

Published Reports

One of the most tangible of the NRPB's legacies was its printed reports. Eliot and Merrill say that the usual print run of these reports was 5,000, with further printings when demand for a report so required.[1] These reports went to many libraries and individuals, as well as to public agencies and public figures, federal and state. The mimeographed reports had an unknown but much smaller distribution, but may have been quite important in the development of professional thinking among workers at various levels and locations.

---

[1] Charles W. Eliot, 2nd, assisted by Harold Merrill, *Guide to the Files of the National Resources Planning Board and Predecessor Agencies—Ten Years of National Planning, 1933–1943* (December 31, 1943).

The impact of these reports at the time of publication is impossible to measure in any quantitative way but must have been substantial. Today their impact seems disappointingly small. One can read recent reports by other agencies or authors on land, water, transportation, energy, minerals, housing, population, welfare, or other subjects on which the NRPB issued one or more major reports, and rarely find a specific reference to the NRPB report, which in some cases was the basic document in the field.[2] The published reports, though part of the intellectual heritage of this country, simply are not widely used today.

As I ponder this record, several possible explanations rise to mind. In the first place, the termination of the NRPB stopped further citation by the agency of its own work. That is, had the NRPB continued to operate, it would undoubtedly have frequently cited its own reports, and would have carried on further research which would have built on them, thus keeping the reports fresh in the minds of its professional and public audience. Second, the awkward size of the reports as well as their mostly paper bindings made many librarians less than enthusiastic to shelve them. Finally, I suspect there was some vague feeling among librarians, researchers, and planners that, the NRPB having been killed, the reports were no longer relevant. Such an attitude would have been illogical but I suspect it existed.

NRPB reports are long since out of print. They are also not easily available in most libraries. Had it not been for the personal collection of the late Robert W. Hartley, who had been a major staff member of the NRPB, I would have been severely handicapped in my research for this book.

NRPB Functions Taken Over Elsewhere in the Federal Government

Abolishing the NRPB did not abolish the problems with which it had sought to cope, and over the years many of its functions were taken over, to a greater or lesser degree, by other federal agencies, under

---

[2] I speak from some personal experience. In my numerous writings on various aspects of land use over the past twenty-five years, I have rarely if ever cited an NRPB report; yet when making this study, I encountered a number of NRPB reports which had direct relevance to what I had done and could well have been used effectively. As I talk with middle-aged and younger professional workers in any of the fields where the NRPB published reports, I find them largely unaware of the NRPB's reports and indeed often uncertain as to what the NRPB was, when it existed, and what it did.

either preexisting or new authorizing legislation. Beckman made a careful analysis of the extent to which he thought the NRPB's functions had been taken over elsewhere in government by 1960 (see table 20-1).

If one completely accepts Beckman's description of functions and of the federal agencies performing them in 1960, it adds considerable weight to the view expressed in Congress and elsewhere that the NRPB was in fact doing what other federal agencies were equipped, or could easily be equipped, to do as well or better. A defender of the NRPB might well argue that these specific functions were not as well carried out when scattered among many agencies as they would have been had such functions remained in a permanent NRPB. It is note-worthy that Beckman's analysis does not include the general coordina-tion function which the NRPB always placed high on its list of func-tions and responsibilities. Beckman supplies no evidence and makes no statement that this general coordinating function for the whole of the federal government was performed anywhere in the federal establishment in 1960.

Beginning about 1950, a number of special committees or commis-sions were created, and were quite significant in the studies they made. Among these there was the President's Materials Policy Commission (the Paley Commission), the Senate Select Committtee on Water Policy, the Outdoor Recreation Resources Review Commission, the Public Land Law Review Commission, the National Advisory Com-mission on Food and Fiber, the President's Commission on National Goals, the National Commission on Urban Problems, and the Com-mission on Rural Poverty. Several others might also be cited, including the first and second Hoover commissions on administrative organization of the executive branch. This same general device has been used in more recent years. In three aspects these committees or commissions were different from the NRPB: (1) they were congressional, or joint congressional–executive, or at least congressionally accepted, rather than purely presidential, as the NRPB had been; (2) they were temporary, rather than designed as permanent as the NRPB had been; and (3) they were for a specific task, sometimes a rather broad or general one, but not for analysis and planning over the entire range of economic, social, and political problems, as the NRPB had been. My judgment is that both the specific nature of their tasks and their limited life were critical to their endorsement or acceptance by the Congress. Temporary com-mittees or commissions have problems of getting organized and staffed

Table 20-1. Former NRPB Functions and Performances as of 1960.

NRPB Functions	Present Administering Agency
Stabilization and Trends	
Quarterly reports on trends of business and unemployment; development of long-range work relief, stabilization, finances, and fiscal policies.	The Council of Economic Advisers, created in 1946, appraises economic developments and the economic policies of the federal government; prepares periodic economic reports for the President.
Science and Research	
Roster of scientific and specialized personnel; studies of federal, industrial and business research. Study of conservation of cultural resources.	The National Science Foundation, set up in 1950, maintains registers of scientific personnel; encourages and supports basic research; fosters interchange of scientific information. The President's Special Assistant for Science and Technology is concerned with coordination in the fields of science, technology and missiles. National Park Service preserves American historical properties.
Industrial Location	
Studies of location of industrial plants, especially defense plants.	The Office of Civil and Defense Mobilization, since 1953, has been responsible for the strategic relocation of industries, services, government and economic activities. The Department of Commerce is responsible for long-range industrial preparedness and programs for the mobilization of industry.
Transportation	
Formulation of a comprehensive national transportation policy.	Since 1950 the Office of Under-Secretary of Commerce for Transportation has been concerned with establishment of a more integrated transportation program.

(Table continues on next page)

245

Table 20-1 (continued)

NRPB Functions	Present Administering Agency
Energy Resources	
Plans for meeting emergency problems in the coal and oil industry and long-range program of conservation and wise use of energy resources.	The Department of the Interior is responsible for programs of development and utilization of minerals and fuels, including defense minerals activities.
Land Planning	
Urban and rural land planning; development of improved planning techniques, more adequate planning data, and integrated regional programs.	The Housing and Home Finance Agency makes grants for planning and development of urban areas. The Bureau of Land Management, Department of the Interior, is concerned with identification, classification, use, and disposition of public lands. The Forest Service, Department of Agriculture, is responsible for conservation and use of the nation's forest lands.
Water Planning	
Review of federal water-resources projects; promotion of improved basic data, water-planning techniques, and integrated water programs.	The Bureau of the Budget reviews water resources project reports. The Flood Control Act of 1944 requires Corps of Engineers project plans to be submitted to the states concerned and to the Interior Department for their views and recommendations. The Interagency Committee on Water Resources and its five field committees seek to coordinate water and related land resource policies of federal agencies.
Public Works	
Compilation of federal six-year program of public works, encouragement of state and local programming of public works; analysis of economic aspects of federal construction expenditure.	The Bureau of the Budget compiles a six-year program of public works. The Special Assistant to the President for Public Works Planning assists the President in coordinating planning in the general field of public works. The Council of Economic Advisers analyzes economic aspects of federal construction expenditure.

Security, Health, Education

Development of work, relief, and social-security policies, studies of youth, education, nutrition, health, and libraries.

The Department of Health, Education, and Welfare is responsible for improving and coordinating administration of federal programs in the fields of health, education, and social security.

Regional, State, and Local Planning

Clearinghouse on plans and methods; technical assistance; demonstrations; grants; studies of urban housing.

HHFA administers planning advances for community facilities and makes urban renewal grants for comprehensive statewide, metropolitan-area and community planning.

Source: Norman Beckman, "Federal Long-Range Planning—The Heritage of the National Resources Planning Board," *Journal of the American Institute of Planners*, vol. XXVI, no. 2 (May 1960).

but they do not threaten the creation of a permanent ongoing bureaucracy. While some of the special committees or commissions did stir
some controversies, these were nothing like as severe as those which
engulfed the NRPB. While the results of these special groups were not
invariably translated into action or into legislation, their record is at
least as good as that of the NRPB. For the specific task, but not for the
general overall coordinating function, the special committee or commission has many advantages, not the least of which is acceptability.

The NRPB and Regional, State, and Local Planning

As we have noted in earlier chapters, the NRPB promoted planning at
regional, state, and local governmental levels, by various means, including financial assistance. In 1943, the NRPB regional offices folded. In
much later years, various regional planning or regional action groups
have been established under federal sponsorship and financing, but these
seem to have owed little directly to the NRPB. The subsequent history
of state planning organizations varied greatly from state to state. A good
many of the states did continue some form of state planning organization, often renamed and often redirected as to function, and today
virtually every state has some kind of an organization that could be
considered a state planning office, though not always so designated.
Lepawsky has shown how the southern states within a few years had
designated their planning organizations as development organizations,
with a change in focus appropriately described by the change in name.[3]
The functioning and operation of the state organizations that could be
considered planning agencies is variable today; it is difficult to say to
what explicit extent their present organization and operation is influenced
by the NRPB experience.

Local planning in the United States has gone forward very actively
since 1943, in considerable part stimulated and financed by federal
programs in housing, public roads, public health, community planning,
and other fields. By 1968 there were 10,000 local governments with
planning boards. The extent and the form of planning is highly variable
today from one county to another and from one city to another, but
virtually all middle-size and larger cities have active planning organiza-

---

[3] Albert Lepawsky, *State Planning and Economic Development in the South,*
NPA Committee of the South, Report no. 4, National Planning Association (Washington, 1949).

tions, as do nearly all counties near larger cities or metropolitan areas. These local planning organizations are, for the most part, strongly entrenched in the local political and bureaucratic scene. They develop transportation, public service, land use, environmental, and other plans. Some of them are closely identified with the zoning authorities or other licensing or approving organizations in their areas, such as building, health, and subdivision code enforcement; but others are largely separate from such implementing organizations. Even their critics must acknowledge that they exist in large numbers and that they do have substantial effect on private decisions. While the NRPB's stimulus to local planning may, to some degree, underlie the existence of these numerous local planning organizations, the personnel of most of them today are quite unaware of the NRPB's activities in this field.

The NRPB's Influence on U.S. Planning of the Late 1970s

The foregoing paragraphs have briefly noted the increase in local planning in the United States in the past decade or two. The great increase in planning at federal, regional, state, and local levels has been prompted by and dominated by the whole matter of grants-in-aid, which in the total U.S. governmental structure have reached a level of $80 billion annually from the federal to the state governments and almost $27 billion annually from states to local governments. Each of the many granting organizations and each of their many programs has its own brand of planning, its own brand of accountability to its constituency, with little or no correlation among them, and with very little comparability in the plans made.

How far is the NRPB responsible for this enormous proliferation of granting and planning in the thirty-six years since its demise? My judgment is: directly, little or not at all; indirectly, a good deal. I think that the NRPB did exert a substantial influence on what has happened. Not the least of its influences may have been the role it played in training planners, whose knowledge and experience has been transferred in turn to another generation of planners.

One agency deserves special mention in connection with planning in the 1970s. This is the Advisory Commission on Intergovernmental Relations, which was established by act of Congress in 1959. The commission's membership includes representatives of the executive and legislative branches of government from federal, state, and local government, and also some representatives of the general public. While authorized by the Congress and operating on federal appropriations, it is an independent commission—not federal or state. It makes studies on many aspects of governmental operations, including appraisals of various ongoing programs. While its reports are only advisory, they have had substantial influence if not effect on governmental operations at all levels. ACIR is perhaps unique in that it typically carries its studies to the point of suggesting draft legislation to put its recommendations into effect.

The NRPB's Alumni

The NRPB left a legacy of able, trained, and experienced analysts and planners whose personalities and capabilities owe at least something to their experience with the Board. We have noted how many of these men and women were drawn into the war programs, often for some months filling a role with one of the war agencies as well as a role at the NRPB. We have also listed some of the most outstanding NRPB alumni still professionally active. In addition to this latter group, there were many other very able professional workers among NRPB alumni who attained high professional recognition, even if not Nobel prizes, but who have died or retired some years ago. Many mature scholars and professional workers were associated with the NRPB on a part-time or consultant basis.

In all of these cases, one may reasonably judge that the NRPB experience was an important part of the professional and personal development of the persons concerned.

Federal agencies are almost never established explicitly to develop mature professional workers further in their professional careers, but such professional development is always one by-product of federal programs established for other purposes. The NRPB and its predecessors were planning agencies, but they were also professional-development agencies. The country was surely enriched by this aspect of the NRPB experience.

NRPB Functions Taken Over by Private Groups

Some private groups which coexisted with the NRPB have since expanded and strengthened their work. The Brookings Institution, for instance, had been created more than a decade before the NRPB, and has been a research, educational, and planning institution ever since. But, beginning about 1950, its program has been greatly expanded and strengthened, and some of its recent studies are similar to the kinds of work the NRPB did. Indeed, a few former NRPB staff members joined Brookings during this period. The National Planning Association (NPA) was established in 1934; it has always sought to have substantial, if not equal, membership from labor, business, and agriculture. It has made studies, primarily by committees representing its general interest groups, and its publications have been widely circulated and undoubtedly have had substantial influence on policymakers and others. Some of its studies are similar to those the NRPB made earlier. Again, some of the former NRPB personnel joined NPA.

Some new private or semiprivate organizations have been created since the NRPB's demise, which carry on functions or activities at least somewhat similar to those of the NRPB. The Committee for Economic Development, composed primarily of businessmen, has operated somewhat like the NPA in its use of committees and in its publications. It began about the time the NRPB died and in some degree grew out of the NRPB experience. The Potomac Institute is another private group which has made studies and published reports, again with some similarities to the NRPB as far as subject matter is concerned. The Rand Corporation was formed under the aegis of the Air Force, has had a lot of federal funds, but has operated somewhat as a private organization, again making studies and publishing reports. The American Assembly of Columbia University periodically draws together groups of persons of varying interests and backgrounds, to discuss some major policy issue of the day, thus making a substantial contribution to national thinking on the matter. This is not, of course, a complete accounting of all private groups which have some degree of similarity to the NRPB.

Special mention must be made of Resources for the Future, since it is, in some sense, a direct descendant of the NRPB. Charles Eliot played a major role in proposing the creation of what became RFF, and in bringing it to the attention of the Ford Foundation.[4] He proposed the Mid-Century Conference which really launched RFF. Over the years since 1952, Resources for the Future has made a large number of studies of natural resources, energy, and the environment; its publications

---

[4] Resources for the Future, *The First 25 years, 1952–1977* (Washington, Resources for the Future, 1977).

number over 200, with total sales in excess of half a million. To a substantial extent, it has taken over the research function of the NRPB in the same fields.

It is difficult to estimate just how important the NRPB's example was in these various organizations, but I judge not unimportant for any of them, and not the only influences on any of them. But the extent of this influence was often indirect and is often not understood today.[5]

It is noteworthy, I think, that these private groups have each operated primarily in the idea-stimulation role that I have ascribed to the NRPB. Some have operated broadly, covering most or all of the subject matter range that the NRPB included, while others have defined a narrower range of subject matter for themselves. They have not done nearly as much in the planning-coordination role as I have described the latter for the NRPB. It would, of course, be extremely difficult for an outside private organization to serve as a planning coordinator for the president, as the NRPB was supposed to do. Lack of direct access to the president and lack of inside but basic information would alone severely impede it.

Some of the private organizations have, however, played a role as "post-auditors" of federal programs. That is, they have critically examined some federal program and offered criticisms and suggestions regarding it. This role of private organizations might well be expanded. Some private organization, such as the National Planning Association, might take on the function of regular review and audit of federal programs, across the whole spectrum of the latter. This would, of course, require substantial staff, either full-time or on a consultant basis, and correspondingly sufficient funds. The Brookings Institution does something like this annually in connection with the federal budget.

Later Public Programs Proposed in NRPB Studies

A substantial number of federal programs adopted since 1943 were, at least to some extent, foreshadowed or proposed in NRPB reports, but it is impossible to say to what extent such programs owe their existence or their form to the NRPB studies, since many other forces and personalities were also at work. The Employment Act of 1946 in its endorse-

---

[5] Only a few of my older colleagues at RFF are reasonably informed about the NRPB and what it did, or its influence on RFF's creation.

ment of national efforts at maximum employment surely is compatible with earlier NRPB thinking. The many social service and social welfare programs enacted or extended since 1943 have substantial resemblance to the recommendations of the report on *Security, Work, and Relief Policies*—a report, which, as we have noted, stirred up enormous and emotional criticism at the time. Some of the proposals and actions for deregulation of transportation organizations in the later 1970s have at least some similarities to NRPB recommendations. And the list could go on and on.

The NRPB reports dealt with what then seemed like major issues of public policy. The subsequent legislation also dealt with the same basic and long-standing issues. To this extent, there is an obvious overlap or continuation. It seems highly probable that the NRPB reports influenced the thinking of some of the major actors in the later legislative action—indeed, in some instances the same persons were involved. But it would be a mistake to assume that the NRPB reports were *directly* responsible for what happened later—there were too many new forces and too many new actors for the relationships to have been direct.

Intellectual Attitudes Toward Planning and Social Action

Possibly the most important, and surely the hardest to measure, of all the NRPB's legacies has been its impact upon intellectual attitudes in the United States toward planning in general and toward social (mostly governmental) action on economic and social problems. Surely no involved analysis is necessary to demonstrate that there have been great changes in intellectual attitudes toward both planning and social action from the 1930–33 period until the present (1980). The United States today directs enormously more intellectual effort into its analysis of economic and social problems of all kinds than it did fifty years ago. The typical answer to almost every problem today is to seek a new law or a new governmental program to deal with it. One need neither endorse all these efforts as wise and effective nor condemn them all as useless and wasteful, nor adopt an intermediate judgment, to agree that such a wide range of intellectual activity and such a variety of governmental programs exist.

How far have these developments been due to the NRPB? Some of what has happened since 1943 is undoubtedly a consequence of the

NRPB's having existed and operated for ten years. Its reports were enormously stimulative at the time. But equally, I judge that not all that has happened in these intervening years can reasonably be credited, or charged, to the NRPB. There have been too many other influences—wars, changing age distribution of population, increased economic output, new ideas about the desired society and the desired private life, and many others. I believe the United States today is different, in some degree and in some ways, because the NRPB existed; but I do not attempt to estimate precisely how much or in which ways this difference exists.

One of the NRPB's intangible but highly important contributions to American history was to make "planning" more respectable. The NRPB's kind of planning was bitterly denounced by the conservatives in the Congress yet some of them went out of their way to endorse planning as a general concept. In more recent times, "planning" is less likely to be the descriptive word than is "public policy analysis," but the processes are the same or closely similar. Many of the studies of private organizations, described above, have included projections (of what would happen under specified assumptions) or forecasts (judgments of what was most likely to happen) for some future date, often a moderately distant one. This type of analysis is much more common today than forty to fifty years ago, and I judge that the NRPB played a role in making it intellectually more acceptable.

21

An Appraisal

How do I rate the NRPB in an overall appraisal? Clearly, such an appraisal is difficult and necessarily subjective in the sense that my personal viewpoints and attitudes may lead me to judgments which someone else, using the same facts, might not reach. Moreover, any responsible social scientist hesitates to classify any organization as "good" or "bad"; life is too complex for such simple judgments. The final judgment must rest somewhere between these extremes and may well differ on different aspects of the NRPB totality. But, with all the difficulties and all the limitations of an overall appraisal, I would be remiss, as a student of the NRPB, if I did not make some kind of an overall conclusion about it. That is the purpose of this chapter.

How Important Was the NRPB?

We may well start by considering how important the NRPB was. If it was unimportant, then the quality of that unimportance does not much matter. The persons involved in the NRPB, as far as I can judge from the written record and from interviews with survivors, felt that the NRPB was important. This comes through in the writings of Eliot, Merriam, and Gilbert White, to cite but three of its major figures.[1] On the other

[1] Charles W. Eliot, 2nd, *Final Report—Status of Work, National Resources Planning Board,* December 31, 1943; Charles E. Merriam, "The National Re-

hand, Samuel Rosenman, who served as a major speech writer for Roosevelt and was very close to him personally, both before and during his presidency, mentions the NRPB only briefly and incidentally; and Frances Perkins, who had worked closely with Roosevelt while he was governor of New York and who served as his secretary of labor throughout his administration, never once mentions the NRPB or any of its major actors in their NRPB roles.[2] Harold Ickes, in his *Secret Diary,* includes a good many items about the NRPB's predecessors, when he was chairman, but this seems to have been more a matter of defending his turf than of genuine understanding. Once the NRPB was organized as an agency directly reporting to the president and Ickes was no longer part of its governing board, he never again mentions it.[3] These slight references and omissions are not conclusive but they suggest that the NRPB, however much it was noticed by both friends and enemies in some quarters, was not a commanding force in the New Deal as a whole.

Others, writing in later years after the NRPB no longer existed, have explicitly or implicitly expressed different judgments about it. Millett, who had been employed by the NRPB for about one and a half years toward the end of its life, seems to feel that it had some good points and accomplished some worthwhile things, while at the same time it was seriously flawed in its basic organization, its staffing, and its operations.[4] Karl takes a position on the whole more favorable, even laudatory, of the NRPB, but one has the impression this is primarily due to his admiration for Charles Merriam, whose biography he was writing and whom he considers to have been the dominant intellectual force on the NRPB.[5] Lepawsky, a former graduate student under Merriam and a great admirer, takes a generally favorable view of the NRPB but, as

---

sources Planning Board: A Chapter in American Planning Experience," *The American Political Science Review,* vol. XXVIII, no. 6 (December 1944); and Gilbert F. White, "Land Planning," in George B. Galloway and Associates, *Planning for America* (New York, Henry Holt, 1941).

[2] Samuel I. Rosenman, *Working with Roosevelt* (New York, Harper and Co., 1952); and Frances Perkins, *The Roosevelt I Knew* (New York, Viking, 1946).

[3] Harold L. Ickes, *The Secret Diary of Harold L. Ickes: Volume I, The First Thousand Days, 1933–1936; Volume II, The Inside Struggle, 1936–1939;* and *Volume III, The Lowering Clouds, 1939–1941* (New York, Simon and Schuster, Vols. I and II, 1954, Vol. III, 1955).

[4] John D. Millett, *The Process and Organization of Government Planning* (New York, Columbia University Press, 1947).

[5] Barry D. Karl, *Charles E. Merriam and the Study of Politics* (Chicago, University of Chicago Press, 1974).

with Karl, one has the feeling this is largely on the basis of his attitude toward Merriam:

> Planning under the New Deal became, for the first time in United States history, government-wide and nation-wide in extent, trans-governmental and socio-economic in impact, and top-level in political influence. It radiated outward from the White House itself where the New Deal's prestigious but vulnerable National Resources Planning Board (NRPB) maintained a foothold throughout the "Planning Decade." In its quality, moreover, New Deal Planning was—at least for its own day—generally compelling if not always convincing. More often than not, it was basic in content, suitable in kind, foresighted in vision.
>
>   However, this is not the image uniformly accorded New Deal planning in either professional or popular circles, neither at that time nor today. For, despite their definitive character or exemplary status in general, the specific New Deal plans were sometimes defective and often disappointing. They were, at times, irrelevant and tangential, impractical and utopian, shortsighted and expedient, diffused and discursive. Like the New Deal itself, the National Planning Board (successively retitled National Resources Board, National Resources Committee, and finally National Resources Planning Board) was born in crisis and embroiled in dispute; and, after an arduous decade of experience, it was abolished in 1943 at the climax of the Second World War following a warm Congressional debate which reflected a controversial rather than ineffectual record.[6]

Beckman, writing some years after the NRPB's demise, takes a more balanced view of its accomplishments and shortcomings:

> A completely objective evaluation of whether the National Resources Planning Board successfully met the requirements of a central planning agency is probably impossible. Standards or criteria against which to measure its performance would be difficult to find, and subjective values attached to alternative approaches and goals prevent agreement on an ideal role for such an agency. The description . . . of NRPB goals, history, organization, and relationships provides at least some basis for evaluation. It reveals that, in achieving goals, the Board was more successful in conducting research on public-policy questions and stimu-

---

[6] Albert Lepawsky, "The Planning Apparatus: A Vignette of the New Deal," *Journal of the American Institute of Planners,* vol. 42, no. 1 (January 1976); and "Style and Substance in Contemporary Planning: The American New Deal's National Resources Planning Board as a Model," *Plan Canada,* vol. 18, nos. 3/4 (September/December 1978). The quotation is from the latter source.

lating state and local planning than it was in coordinating federal planning and programming of public works.[7]

Rockwell, writing while the NRPB was still in existence, on the whole regards it as highly important and as successful.[8] Philip White is generally affirmative in his attitude toward the NRPB while at the same time pointing to serious weaknesses in its organization and operations.[9] Warken takes a somewhat similar though also somewhat different position:

> The National Resources Planning Board made a significant contribution to planning in the United States. Originally created to assist in the ordered development of public works, it constantly expanded its areas of concern during the ten years of its existence. Moving first into the use and conservation of natural resources such as water, land, and minerals, the agency was by the late 1930s involved with problems of population, production, and social welfare. In the course of its involvement, the agency developed three primary interests: basic research, coordination of the activities of federal and non-federal action agencies, and the promotion of planning as an administrative concept. The efforts of the NRPB to convince people that a permanent planning body, independent of action agencies, should be created within the federal government achieved only temporary success.[10]

Quite possibly the most eloquent and most reliable evidence of the NRPB's importance comes from the statements and actions of its enemies. One may be fairly sure that members of Congress would not have devoted so much time and energy to the destruction of the NRPB unless they had felt it was important—and, in their view, undesirable, even vicious.

I conclude that the NRPB was highly important in the New Deal, more as a stimulator of ideas than as a coordinator of government action, but that it was not the sole or even the dominant influence in either sphere.

---

[7] Norman Beckman, "Federal Long-Range Planning—The Heritage of the National Resources Planning Board," *Journal of the American Institute of Planners,* vol. XXVI, no. 2 (May 1960).

[8] Landon G. Rockwell, "National Resources Planning: The Role of the National Resources Planning Board in the Process of Government" (doctoral dissertation, Princeton University, May 1942).

[9] Philip L. White, "The Termination of the National Resources Planning Board" (master's thesis, Columbia University, 1949).

[10] Philip W. Warken, "A History of the National Resources Planning Board, 1933–1943" (doctoral dissertation, Ohio State University, 1969).

How Well Did the NRPB Play Its Roles?

I have divided the NRPB's roles into two broad groups: idea development and stimulation, and planning and coordination in general, with subdivisions for each.

I would give the NRPB a fairly high grade for its role as an idea stimulator. It surely had ideas, as the description of its reports in earlier chapters shows; and those ideas surely stimulated many people. Its ideas stimulated not only those who found them agreeable but also those who opposed them—or opposed the NRPB itself. I have formed the strong judgment that the NRPB was more successful in getting acceptance of its ideas prior to 1939 than it was after that date; and I attribute this difference to two factors: (1) in the earlier period, the NRPB had a cabinet governing body—a largely pro forma one, but still its members had to accept some responsibility for its operations—whereas later it had only its own board of directors; and (2) in the earlier period it operated primarily through committees, often committees of diverse governmental and other membership, whereas in its later years it increasingly operated through its own staff. Perhaps the most telling testimonial to the influence of the NRPB's ideas was the fact that they, more than any other single factor, stirred up the opposition that killed the Board.

In exercising its general planning and coordination function, the NRPB's record is spottier. It did very well in developing water planning, its accomplishments in that field having been continued in essentially the same intellectual form until today. It did much less well in land, or mineral, or energy programs; and it scarcely touched agricultural programs. Its achievements in coordination of public works was distinctly limited, due in very large part to the stubborn and largely successful opposition of the Corps of Engineers. Its role in formulating welfare, transportation, industrial location, and other ambitious policies was often exciting, but generally unsuccessful during the period of its existence—perhaps for reasons wholly out of its control. But its role in these respects surely had a major impact upon current thinking and probably upon subsequent action.

Could Some Other Federal Agency Have Filled These Roles Equally Well or Better?

The National Planning Board was created in 1933 to deal with clearly evident problems, and its successors through the life of the NRPB continued because the problems continued. But, if the NRPB and its predecessors had never been created, could some other federal agency have played the roles NRPB sought to play, equally well or perhaps better? For instance, might the Bureau of the Budget have served as the public works coordinator? It will be recalled that after 1943, when the NRPB no longer existed, the Bureau of the Budget did indeed take over this function. The National Science Foundation was not in existence during the period of the NRPB's life but was created not many years afterwards; it might have been created earlier and taken over the roles of research stimulator and financer which the NRPB played. Or some private agency, perhaps with public funds, might have played the research role—the Social Science Research Council, perhaps. Or there might have been some direct congressional activity in one or more of the roles NRPB sought to play; it will be recalled that Congress did indeed make some moves in this direction during the last days of the NRPB.

In one sense, it is futile to speculate on what "might have been" and yet it is vital, I think, to realize that the NRPB was *not* the only mechanism that could have been created to deal with the problems it sought to deal with.

Why Did the NRPB Not Do Better?

The NRPB clearly failed, in the biological sense of failing to survive. It may fairly be considered to have failed to some degree earlier and in different ways; at the least, it did not fully perform all the roles it established for itself. In retrospect, it clearly was not an indispensable arm of the president, although it was useful to him. Its studies either created or exacerbated some difficult political situations and it surely heightened controversy on many issues which were at the best controversial. It did not serve either the president, itself, or the country as a mechanism for the resolution of such controversial issues—the basic and elemental political roles of finding common ground and achieving maximum agreement among divergent forces.

What factors were responsible for this absolute failure to survive and this relative failure to achieve objectives? How far was its part-time board a major factor? How far was Merriam with his quaint ideas of the separateness of the executive and the Congress, and his consequent unwillingness to let the Board win any friends in the Congress, in some degree responsible for the NRPB's demise? How far was Delano's age and his determined posture not to trade upon his relationship to the president a major factor in the NRPB's failure? How far did the shift in the NRPB's major emphasis from coordinating other federal agencies, prior to 1939, to its functioning more largely as a separate agency after 1939, operate to weaken its support in the federal establishment? Would a lower public profile, with less publicity about its work, have led not only to continuation but to larger results?

The thrust of these rather specific questions is: how far were the NRPB's problems peculiar to *this* NRPB, with its particular actors and its particular times, and how far would the basic problems it faced have plagued *any* NRPB, then or later? It surely is not difficult to point to shortcomings of the NRPB which actually existed; they are implicit in the foregoing questions and they have been discussed in some detail in earlier chapters. Had President Roosevelt or anyone else moved successfully to have cured these particular difficulties, how much difference would this have made in the final result? Were the difficulties that the NRPB faced so basic that any other planning organization would have come to essentially the same end?

Might the NRPB Have Survived, Had It Been Different?

Let us speculate with one scenario of a possible NRPB considerably different from the one which actually existed.

In chapter 1 we traced how FDR, drawing on the recommendations of his Committee on Administrative Management, had sent a sweeping reorganization bill to the Congress in 1937; how this had been first postponed and then in 1938 defeated, largely because of the fight over the "court packing" bill; and how a greatly modified and reduced reorganization act was passed in 1939. Under the latter, FDR, by executive order established the National Resources Planning Board. In a strictly legal sense, it thus had legitimacy; in a broader political sense, the NRPB did not have political support or endorsement from the Congress. The debates over the reorganization bill had clearly revealed much opposition to FDR in general and to his planning board in particular. The executive order guaranteed a life for the NRPB but at the same time went far toward assuring that that life would be a limited one. This was clearly an important juncture in the life of the NRPB and should have been a warning that a substantially different approach was needed if it was to survive. The lack of real congressional endorsement of the NRPB surely was a major handicap in the remaining years of its life.

Nineteen hundred and thirty-nine was also the year in which Senator Hayden introduced his bill to establish a *natural* resources planning agency. Suppose, for the moment, that the Administration had gotten strongly behind this bill, and that it had passed. It would have limited the new board to studies of natural resources, but economic and social factors could have been brought into consideration, to the extent that they affected the use of the natural resources. Suppose further that this bill had abolished the board, as a governing body, replacing it with a single "strong" administrator, who might or might not have had an advisory board. Suppose still further that, after the act passed, President Roosevelt had terminated all the top personnel of the NRPB, including the members of the Board and the director, and replaced them with a new and different type of administrator. Suppose still further that the new agency had sought the maximum cooperation from the federal agencies and that it had maintained a low public profile, encouraging others to claim public credit for studies made or actions taken. Suppose still further that the new agency had sought to work closely with its friends in Congress, explaining its work and seeking to win acceptance of its results. Suppose still further that the new administrator had been the kind of person who would have commanded respect and cooperation from the Congress.

The foregoing is one alternative scenario to the NRPB after 1939. I regard it as a practical alternative, if President Roosevelt had supported it. But other scenarios could be devised, which would have been directed to remedying the NRPB's obvious shortcomings. Of course, a new organization might have developed weaknesses of its own. Curing one set of deficiencies, even if this succeeds, does not guarantee that new and unexpected deficiencies will not appear.

Had this, or any other plausible, scenario been adopted, would it have enabled the NRPB to survive (perhaps under a different name and surely with changed functions)? Or was the opposition to the president so deep in the Congress that no planning organization he devised could have survived longer than the NRPB in fact did survive? Or was the opposition to planning, as an activity, so deep and so strong that no national planning organization could have survived? One may surely doubt the last; a number of the NRPB's opponents in the Congress went out of their way to endorse the idea of planning even while strongly criticizing the NRPB. It is impossible to give a firm answer to these questions but in my judgment it is at least possible that a *natural* resource planning agency could have survived.

In this connection, it is helpful to recall briefly the history of the Council of Economic Advisers. Created in 1946, it was a major implement in economic policy for President Truman. It was controversial; when the Republicans captured the White House in the election of 1952, the first intent of the new Eisenhower Administration was to abolish the council, and actually it was dismantled down to only a very few employees. But then it dawned on someone close to the president that the council could be a very useful instrument for *his* policies. It was restaffed and it functioned, not only through that administration, but in every administration since then, and it is highly doubtful if any man gaining the presidency in the future will liquidate the council as an organization. Had the NRPB been recast, as suggested above, and had it become firmly established and widely respected in the Congress, might it have continued through changes in administration also?

Would a different NRPB, reorganized along the foregoing or any other lines of major change, have been worth preserving? Its role would surely have been different; would it have been worthwhile? I judge that Eliot would have answered in the affirmative but Merriam might have answered in the negative. Eliot was deeply committed to the NRPB as a career and as the center of his professional life; he would have been gravely disappointed if he had been displaced from it but he would have been glad to see at least some of his ideas continued. Merriam had many interests, of which the NRPB was but one; while he may have been as committed as Eliot was to the idea of a planning organization, he could bear the loss of the NRPB with less personal disturbance.

Whatever scenarios were possible, and whatever Eliot's and Merriam's reactions might have been to any proposals for a greatly different NRPB, in the unwillingness of each to yield wholly to the other, a significantly different NRPB never had a chance of being born, much less of surviving.

22

Does the United States Need a Reconstituted NRPB Today?

Would the well-being and prosperity of the United States be enhanced for the 1980s and beyond by the establishment and operation of a reconstituted national planning board? The National Resources Planning Board and its predecessors existed from 1933 to 1943, performed certain functions then, and filled a particular role then. Times have changed. If the NRPB had continued, it doubtless would have changed, at least to some degree, over the years. Should a new national planning agency be created to perform some of the functions of the old NRPB, plus perhaps others, minus perhaps still others?

Beckman, writing twenty years ago, decided in the negative:

> It is evident that history has passed by NRPB's government-wide approach to federal planning organization. There is no significant popular, political, or administrative support for the NRPB objective of promoting comprehensive central planning at all levels of government— especially at the national level. There was little sustained support even during the Board's existence. While some specific gaps on substantive federal activities still remain, we now seem to be committed to the principle that long-range as well as immediate federal planning should be undertaken by that department or agency of the executive branch which has a continuing operating responsibility in the fields most directly associated with the planning. New functions are assigned to existing agencies or, where appropriate, a new agency is established to meet emerging needs or set new national goals. It is not merely a question of who is performing the old NRPB functions. The nation is

264

facing different problems and has different approaches as well as new organizations for meeting its planning needs. Executive office planning facilities have been, and in the future should be, established only where the multiagency scope of the planning activity, the special needs of the President, or the uniqueness of the problem require provision for such a facility.[1]

Some of the remaining alumni of the NRPB with whom I consulted in the preparation of this book have argued that Beckman's analysis, presented in more detail in chapter 20, deals only with the specific functions performed by the NRPB, not with its overall or comprehensive planning function. In their view, this latter function was not being performed by any federal agency in 1960, when Beckman wrote, nor is it being performed today. To these persons, the need for a comprehensive overall official national planning agency is as great today as it was during the 1930s and 1940s.

Sundquist, writing in 1978, has put very well the case for greatly strengthened national planning. He argues strongly for a national growth policy—a policy of fostering and promoting jobs in areas of the country where people live who do not have jobs, or not enough jobs. He traces the evolution of the idea that the government should set goals for employment and production, from the Employment Act of 1946 down through the Nixon and Ford administrations in particular, and into the Carter administration. He argues that there is substantial popular and political support for a positive national growth policy. He concludes:

> If the United States is to have a national growth policy, the government must be organized to develop one. What is needed is a center of strategic thinking and analysis, of policy development, and of overseeing and evaluating the execution of policy. . . . the coordinating mechanism would need to be located in the Executive Office of the President, on a par with the Council of Economic Advisers and the Office of Management and Budget. Whatever it might be called and wherever located, the new growth policy unit would take charge of preparing the President's biennial national urban report, just as the Council of Economic Advisers prepares the President's annual economic report. Once the policy objectives were established, the unit would monitor the consistency of federal programs, including tax programs, with those objectives. It would design and recommend new programs. Ideally, it would

---

[1] Norman Beckman, "Federal Long-Range Planning—The Heritage of the National Resources Planning Board," *Journal of the American Institute of Planners,* vol. XXVI, no. 2 (May 1960) p. 97.

also be involved in federal efforts to encourage the development of state and local growth policies and regional development plans that would both help to carry out the national policies and make their own contribution to national growth planning. If the organization is formed, policy will follow. If the policy is developed, the organization will have to follow. Perhaps it is not important which comes first. But the time has come to execute the laws of 1970. The geographical distribution of jobs and people is too important to be left any longer to chance.[2]

As one reads Sundquist, one can almost hear Charles Eliot speaking. Sundquist is talking about "national growth policy" in the context of the 1978 national problems, as he sees them; Eliot talked about comprehensive national planning in the context of the problems of the 1930s and 1940s, as he saw them.[3] But there is a strong thread of support for a comprehensive national planning organization common to both. It may be significant, or it may be simply because Sundquist began his consideration with the Employment Act of 1946, but he does not anywhere in his article mention the NRPB and its predecessors.

Major National Problems That Might Seem to Argue for a New NRPB

It is easy to compile a dreary list of major national problems on which a consistent and competent national policy is urgently needed in the United States today; no prize is offered for the longest and most horrendous such list. Many of the problems on such a list would be old and persistent ones but some would be new, at least in their magnitude and precise form. I briefly consider major national problems in four areas: economic problems, environmental problems, political problems, and problems of governmental coordination.

Of the major economic problems confronting the United States in 1980, none is more serious than continuing inflation. The evils of massive and continued inflation have been described by many economists and others. Inflation is worldwide and its persistence is a major facet of the problem. Certainly the United States has not learned to control it; our modest efforts to live with it, by such measures as indexing

---

[2] James L. Sundquist, "Needed: A National Growth Policy," *The Brookings Bulletin,* vol. 14, no. 4 (Winter–Spring 1978) p. 5.

[3] Charles W. Eliot, 2nd, *Final Report—Status of Work, National Resources Planning Board,* December 31, 1943 (see pp. 23–26 particularly).

welfare payments and wages to the cost of living, reduce the adverse impacts upon people while at the same time virtually guaranteeing continued inflation.

Another and closely related problem is the persistent tendency of the economic machine to operate at less than full capacity, producing periodic or recurrent economic depressions and continued unemployment, particularly for some classes of the population. Is some form of economic planning, to overcome these deficiencies, necessary? Warken has traced the numerous proposals for some form of economic syndicalism, to marry private business and public agency participation into a guaranteed full output economy, which arose during the 1920s and the 1930s before the New Deal.[4] Numerous private organizations, including the U.S. Chamber of Commerce, made proposals to this end. They all came to nothing, measured in terms of actual implementation. While they were set aside by the New Deal, the idea persisted. It runs strongly through the essays in Galloway's book.[5] As we have noted, one of the most articulate and closely reasoned proposals was that advanced by Mordecai Ezekiel.[6] Advocates of such economic planning and of a government–business partnership stressed the efficacy of their proposals and the preservation of democracy and of individual freedoms. Surely the problem of full economic output is much with the United States today and is not unrelated to the inflation problem.

While there are many environmental and natural resource issues, I limit this discussion to two: the need to control adverse externalities in the environment and energy. Many economic activities produce adverse environmental externalities—they may also produce favorable externalities, but I do not pursue these here. A factory providing employment and producing needed goods also produces smoke which afflicts people living nearby. This is the classic externality. While this particular form may be slightly outdated by new technologies, the factory which produces chemicals with unknown but possible serious adverse effects upon people is very much with us, as is the power plant which produces needed electricity but also adverse environmental consequences. I need not try here to produce a complete catalogue of such problems or

---

[4] Philip M. Warken, "A History of the National Resources Planning Board" (doctoral dissertation, Ohio State University, 1969).

[5] George B. Galloway and Associates, *Planning for America* (New York, Henry Holt and Company, 1941).

[6] Mordecai Ezekiel, *Jobs for All* (New York, Knopf, 1939); and *$2500 a Year* (New York, Harcourt, Brace, 1936).

to rank them according to their seriousness. We can simply say, these problems are persistent and not yet fully solved in the United States.

The problem of sources of energy, its general availability and especially the availability of gasoline when demanded, and its cost are obvious national economic (as well as technical and political) problems in the United States today. Although there has been much talk about national energy policy, none is evident. As I heard one senator say about national energy policy: the Administration has a dozen, the Congress has 535, and the country has none.

While there are a host of political problems, a few seem the most important. One is the general public distrust of governmental integrity, the general disbelief in almost anything that is said by almost any political leader, and the general cynicism toward motivation and integrity of governmental figures. There has been a notable rise in the number and influence of special interest groups on the national or federal scene —groups which have no regard for a consistent national policy. There has been a serious decline in the power and efficacy of the political parties; a kind of political nihilism has seemed to replace structured decision making, with the result that the formulation and implementation of national policy on any issue is difficult. A feeling of a lack of national consensus and of national purpose pervades much of U.S. life.

Coordination of federal agencies is a perennial problem, grown more difficult as the number of agencies and the variety of federal programs has expanded. This problem permeates every field of government activity. There is increasing concern that the federal establishment has outgrown the ability of any political party, or of the president, or of the Congress to control it. The increasing number and variety of national programs which invade nearly every area of national economic activity adds to the seriousness of this problem.

Suppose that each of the foregoing problems reached an acute stage simultaneously, presenting the people and the government of the United States with a truly national emergency—something vastly more serious than exists in 1980.

In times of past national emergencies, notably the two World Wars and the Great Depression of the 1930s, the United States turned strongly toward some form of national planning. In "normal" times, the private economy operates within a framework of laws and institutions, such as laws relating to contracts, systems of weights and measures, organized commodity and securities exchanges, and the like. In the emergencies, these normal restraints and aids have been supplemented and to a degree replaced by more direct government action. When a war is on, the government undertakes the allocation of scarce raw materials, for instance; or when depression does not yield readily to private actions, public works, public welfare and unemployment relief, and other governmental measures are undertaken. Each major emergency in the past has had both distinctive features and also features in common with other emergencies.

How serious would an emergency have to be before a significant majority of the American people would actively support measures to deal with it and be willing to bear their costs? The willingness of the Congress to give President Roosevelt broad emergency powers in 1933 is in sharp contrast with the reluctance of the Congress to act decisively and promptly on President Carter's rather specific energy proposals in the late 1970s, to use but one example. Might there come into office a new president with a strong national consensus behind him and strong convictions on his part as to what he wanted to do, more or less like Roosevelt? No such political leader can be readily identified in either party today. If there were a national consensus that an acute emergency existed and that something innovative and aggressive should be done, would this more or less inexorably lead to the establishment of some form of national planning organization?

Overall National Planning Since 1943

The abolishment of the NRPB in 1943 did not end the problems which it had been created to consider. The Second World War was on, and much planning of that war effort was under way. Such planning was strong, in the sense that it greatly affected the war effort as well as the civilian economy. The United States geared up for war far more effectively and far more quickly than did its enemies, all of whom had had war planning efforts of much longer duration. The war planning in the United States has been criticized as being less than perfect and no doubt it was by its own objectives, but it did help "win the war."

Graham has traced the development of overall national planning in the United States over the period from 1929 to 1976.[7] The following discussion is based on his book.

---

[7] Otis L. Graham, Jr., *Toward a Planned Society from Roosevelt to Nixon* (New York, Oxford University Press, 1976). Graham consistently capitalizes Planning to mean comprehensive national planning.

An effort to get a Full Employment Act was undertaken by liberals in the Congress in 1945; the act that passed called for an annual report from the president and ". . . committed the government, in effect, to spend until full employment was achieved." The idea of national planning as such was played down, although plans were to be prepared. The president was given a Council of Economic Advisers and Congress established the Joint Committee on the Economic Report (pp. 86–90).

"When the Employment Act finally cleared Congress and was signed by Harry Truman, the prospects for Planning were not merely bleak, but nonexistent." During Truman's Administration, even the liberals muted their endorsement of planning. The Hoover Commission was created and operated during Truman's Administration, to deal with government organization, not planning, but its proposals would have affected the problem of program coordination within government (p. 91).

"Eisenhower would not have been surprised to find historians concluding that his presidency did not move the country noticeably toward Planning, or away from it. . . . Planning was not an issue, not a word that either party used. It was something the Russians did" (p. 120). Eisenhower did have a National Security Council, primarily to deal with international problems. It will be recalled that this was the time when Beckman wrote that there was no effective support for national planning.

The Kennedy and Johnson administrations were more concerned with gaining control over the apparatus of the federal government than they were with planning. But it was during their administrations that federal support to local planning and requirements for local planning as requisites for federal grants-in-aid were embodied in legislation for housing, highways, water and sewers, public works of other kinds, and the like. Although there was considerable discussion during these administrations, it was left to the Nixon Administration to obtain legislation for a national growth policy. Graham argues that there was little real planning during the Kennedy-Johnson years. Johnson did indeed try to impose a Planning-Programming-Budgeting-System (PPBS) upon a (wisely) reluctant bureaucracy, with little or no lasting effect.

Nixon, according to Graham, took many steps toward planning and equally many steps away from it. It was under him, in 1969, that Daniel Patrick Moynihan organized a National Goals Research Staff, which was supposed to analyze alternatives and stimulate debate but not to engage in planning; it issued exactly one annual report and then quietly died. Nixon also authorized a Domestic Council, which was not notably more effective. The Economic Stabilization Act, Graham says, "thrust upon a reluctant executive the authority to impose wage and price controls" (p. 215). Nixon did use this authority in 1971 to impose wage and price controls, without notable success in arresting the inflation then under way. The Housing and Urban Development Act of 1970 called for a biennial report on urban growth. The first two reports prepared under this act were widely criticized as being inadequate and unsatisfactory. Graham summarizes the Nixon years: "The era of Planning was still over the horizon when Nixon returned to San Clemente, but the discussion of Planning—what kind, directed toward which social ends—could now begin in the United States" (p. 263).

Graham goes on to point out how unreceptive President Ford was toward the idea of planning, and indeed toward governmental activism generally.

Graham, in what seems to me a curious interpretation of the evidence he so well organizes and presents, believes there has been a consistent trend toward planning during the whole 1929–1976 period. He says, "So Planning irresistibly presses forward, here at the end of America's second century" (p. 303). He has indeed shown that the problems of performance of the economy, coordination of federal programs, and capacity and willingness to meet new economic and social challenges are matters of continuing concern at the national level. Every president, regardless of his philosophical or ideological position, has been forced to cope with these matters. There has indeed been continued support for planning throughout this period; but there has been continued opposition also. A statistician would have a hard time calculating a trend line if a planning-over-time chart could be developed. It is difficult to see that planning under President Ford was much advanced compared with planning under President Hoover, or that planning under President Carter is as advanced as was planning under President Franklin D. Roosevelt. The problems remain; planning existed in some form throughout, but has not notably advanced in effectiveness or acceptance.

The latest major step in the development of national economic planning is the Humphrey–Hawkins Full Employment and Balanced Growth Act.[8] First introduced in the spring of 1976, largely as a Democratic

---

[8] In compiling the very brief account in this paragraph, I read news articles about the Humphrey–Hawkins Bill in the following periodicals: *Business Week,* May 31, 1976; June 14, 1976; and November 28, 1977; *Fortune,* November 20, 1978; and January 29, 1979; *Harper's,* October 1976; *National Review,* May 14,

political manuever intended to embarrass President Ford in his effort at election, it included an unequivocal commitment for federal employment programs to offset any lack of full employment in the private economy. The bill was to a substantial extent sponsored by the same groups which had pushed for the Employment Act of 1946 and was intended to go substantially farther than the earlier act. The bill was greatly watered down during its consideration in the Congress, including provision for more flexibility in reaching its employment goals, the addition of a provision to reduce and ultimately to eliminate inflation, and the deletion of any specific mechanisms for attaining the goals it contains. Even liberal economists had been disturbed by the original act's likelihood of substantially increased inflation. The act passed in the fall of 1978 and was signed by President Carter. While it was far more an employment and a fiscal objectives act than a planning act, yet its implementation would require extensive planning within the federal government. The act requires a report by the president, as part of his annual economic report, as to the extent to which the objectives of the act have been met and as to his specific plans for meeting them in the ensuing five years.

The 1980 *Economic Report of the President* discusses the provisions of the Humphrey–Hawkins Act at some length, describes the situation at the end of 1979, when unemployment was still well above the target goals and inflation was still both high and rising, and puts forth the president's plans for the next five years, as required by the act.[9] "... the goals of a 4 percent unemployment rate and 3 percent inflation by 1983 are no longer practicable" (p. 93). "The Administration believes that simultaneous progress toward the unemployment rate and inflation goals cannot be made by relying solely on aggregate demand policies" (p. 95). Experience to date with the Act has largely confirmed the criticisms of its opponents, who argued that its goals were unrealistic and unattainable, and that the Act was little more than a pious hope that could not possibly be realized in practice.

As I consider the 1943–80 period, my interpretation of events, as far as national economic planning is concerned, differs considerably from that of Graham. I would briefly summarize this period as follows:

1976; February 4, 1977; and April 28, 1978; *New Leader,* February 27, 1978; *New Republic,* March 27, 1976; June 12, 1976; November 12, 1977; and December 17, 1977; *Newsweek,* May 31, 1976; August 2, 1976; August 16, 1976; and March 5, 1979; *U.S. News and World Report,* February 16, 1976; and November 28, 1977.

[9] *Economic Report of the President,* transmitted to the Congress January 1980 (Washington, GPO, 1980).

1. There has been a continuing substantial, but much less than majority, support for the idea of national planning *as such*. There has also
been a continuing, perhaps greater, opposition to the general idea of
planning, though less emotionally so than at the time of the NRPB's
death.

2. There has been greater support, quite possibly amounting to a
majority of the electorate, for the idea of doing something about persistent unemployment and persistent inflation; but there is far from agreement as to what should be done, or how, and far from a willingness to
pay the costs. There has also been a continuing skepticism and opposition to any substantial effort to modify the workings of the economy.

3. The problems of coordination of the programs and agencies of the
federal government and of control of the governmental establishment by
the elected political leaders has continued to plague every president,
regardless of party or of ideological convictions. These problems have
not been critical but they have been serious and they remain unsolved.

4. On the basic issue of the role of national planning in the economy
of the country, there has been no clear decision; the arguments and the
issues today are closely similar to those of the late 1920s and early 1930s.

The State of Planning in the United States Today

Public planning at all levels of government has proliferated greatly in the
United States in recent years. There is a large volume of activity which
is called, or which might be called planning; its characteristics, even its
quality, may be called into question but there is little doubt that the
quantity is large.

At the federal level there is a great deal of activity which may not
be called planning but which clearly fits within the framework of planning as I have outlined it. The Housing and Urban Development Act of
1970 calls for a biennial report, similar to that required by the
Humphrey–Hawkins Act, described above. These and other laws require
periodic reports from the president, or he makes such reports under
more general powers and obligations, and these can all be considered a
form of national planning. Many departments and agencies prepare plans
for future activities in their respective fields. Some of these plans may be
labelled "comprehensive" but few or none of them would be so considered by national planners. Under the stimulus of various private

interest groups and of the federal bureaucracy, the Congress has passed
laws calling for renewable resources planning (the Renewable Resources
Planning Act of 1974 and the National Forest Management Act of
1976), for water planning, and others.

The federal government conducts or finances much research of the
kind I described earlier as the idea stimulation role of the NRPB. The
National Institutes of Health conduct much research aimed at improvement of the physical and mental health of the people. The National
Science Foundation finances much research by universities and other
nonfederal organizations. The National Academy of Sciences/National
Research Council makes extensive use of committees, in a manner highly
reminiscent of the NRPB, to study important scientific and policy matters
referred to it by various parts of the executive branch; and, like NRPB
committees, these committees typically make recommendations with
important policy objectives or implications. The Office of Technology
Assessment also makes somewhat similar studies, usually at the suggestion of some member of the Congress, and directed primarily to the
Congress. Congress has established its own Budget Office, to provide
perspective on the president's budget, with all the policy implications
inherent in budget review. The General Accounting Office in recent
years has not only postaudited many federal programs for compliance
with the law and for achievement but has also developed suggestions for
new approaches to many problems.

Federal agency coordination is one concern, at least at some levels,
of the Office of Management and Budget. The White House staff has
responsibilities in this direction also, given to it by the president. It is
very difficult for an outsider to know the inner workings of these groups;
he must rely on media accounts for descriptions of workings and for
accounts of results. The latter are not impressively good.

It is arguable—some of the alumni of the NRPB have argued in
statements to me—that there is today in the whole federal establishment
a serious lack of any truly comprehensive federal planning of the kind
which the NRPB aspired to—but did not fully attain. But no one, I
think, can deny that there is a great deal of activity, either called planning or that might be so called, in the federal government today.

Planning by state and local governments has also proliferated greatly
in recent years, driven by two major considerations: (1) the necessity
of developing plans in order to get federal grants-in-aid; and (2) a growing unwillingness on the part of large sectors of the total public to let

a totally uncontrolled private market determine where, when, and how physical development, including housing, may take place. The result is that planning is both pervasive and overlapping. The frequent rhetoric against planning which was common in the NRPB days has become muted, although rumblings are sometimes still heard, but the fact is that planning is exceedingly common at all governmental levels today. This is not, of course, to assert that it is highly competent at all levels.

The extent of federal grants-in-aid to state and local governments is greater than many persons realize, having increased in dollar amounts from $11 billion in 1965 to $80 billion in 1978, and in number of planning assistance programs from four in 1962 to nineteen in 1977.[10] The largest sums in 1978 were in the following categories: education, employment, training, and social services, $21 billion; income security, $14 billion; health, $13 billion; and others ranged on downward. One of the oldest forms of grant-in-aid, agriculture, got a mere $400 million in 1978—one of the smallest of all. Changing times have brought great changes in the role of the federal government. State grants-in-aid to local government (not counting federal funds merely passed through) in 1976 were nearly $14 billion.

Each grant-in-aid program naturally asks the recipient: What are you going to do with the money? and this invariably means some kind of a plan must be prepared. But the correlation between one set of plans and another is often poor or wholly lacking. For instance, in the field of economic and community development the Department of Housing

---

[10] In the preparation of this section I have been greatly aided by the opportunity to read an unpublished paper by Pat Choate, of the Academy for Contemporary Problems. He in turn utilizes the following materials, among others, which I have also drawn upon: (1) Advisory Commission on Intergovernmental Relations, *Categorical Grants: Their Role and Design* (Washington, 1978); (2) Advisory Commission on Intergovernmental Relations, *The Intergovernmental Grant System as Seen by Local, State, and Federal Officials* (Washington, 1977); (3) A background paper, "Nonmetropolitan Growth and Economic Development" (Washington, 1978); (4) Office of Management and Budget, *Report to the Congress, Implementation of the Joint Funding Simplification Act of 1974 (Public Law 93-150)* (Washington, February 1979); (5) Office of Management and Budget, *Reorganization Study of Local Development Assistance Programs* (Washington, December 1978); (6) The Council of State Planning Agencies, *State Planning for Economic Development* (Washington, 1976); (7) Bureau of the Census, *Regional Organizations* (Washington, 1978); and (8) The General Accounting Office, *Federally Assisted Areawide Planning: Need to Simplify Policies and Practices* (Washington, 1977). None of these is responsible for my interpretations which follow in this section.

and Urban Development, the Department of Agriculture, and the Department of Commerce each operate programs and provide funds to states
and local governments. Although these three programs offer basically
the same services to recipient governments, there are substantial differences in the operations of the individual programs. Each has slightly
different criteria and each has a separate delivery system. Local governments seeking grants for these purposes must not only prepare separate
applications to each agency, but often essentially separate plans as well.
To use another example, there are no less than seven federal water and
sewage treatment grant programs, each with its own particular terms,
each requiring not only separate applications but also to a large extent
separate planning by recipient governments.

But the proliferation of planning in the United States today is not
solely due to the grants-in-aid programs. In chapter 12 we noted the
great increase in local planning organizations since NRPB days. Each
of these local planning organizations prepares one or more plans, and
these plans typically lead to some degree of restriction on individual
actions in development, particularly housing, trade, and manufacture in
urban and suburban areas. There is fairly general agreement that these
controls have added to costs of development and a persuasive case can
be made that they have added more to such costs than they are worth.[11]
A major item in the cost is the need by the developer to get permission
from each of several local agencies, and the attendant delays and costs
associated therewith.

By 1980 there is an almost complete commitment in the United States
to the idea that grants-in-aid require planning and to the idea that local
development must to some degree be planned or "coordinated" by public
bodies. There is a lot of brave talk at all levels of government about the
desirability of "comprehensive," "integrated," and otherwise coordinated
functional plans, but there is precious little accomplishment to match the
talk. The conditions under which grants are made dominate plans far
more than do the resource, economic, social, or technological conditions
of the area or the development planned for. The planners make their

---

[11] Fred E. Case, "The Impact of Land Use and Environmental Controls on
Housing Costs," in *The Cost of Housing,* Proceedings of the Third Annual Conference, Federal Home Loan Bank of San Francisco (December 1977). Case cites
a number of reports, of which Fred Bosselman, Duane A. Feurer, and Charles L.
Siemon, *The Permit Explosion: Coordination of the Proliferation* (Washington,
Urban Land Institute, 1976) is one of those more directly pertinent to the discussion here.

plans more with an eye to what will get their application for a grant approved than they do to the conditions they are planning for. Duplication of planning and fragmentation of planning dominate the whole U.S. planning scene today. There have been some efforts at the national level and at some local levels to reduce or eliminate the duplication, overlapping, and even conflict among plans, but such efforts have been limited or half-hearted, and generally ineffective.

At the same time, the link between planning and action has often been weak or missing. That is, the grant-in-aid is made under certain conditions, or the permission to develop is made under certain conditions, but the follow-up is often weak or missing, so that the ultimate result sometimes bears little resemblance to the plan.

This state of planning in the United States might seem to argue for a reconstituted National Resources Planning Board with some authority. Before one jumps to that conclusion, other factors must be considered.

What Are the Lessons from the Past?

If a reconstituted NRPB or any other national overall planning organization were to be established, there are a number of attributes which it should have.

Clear definition of role. Whether the new national planning organization has a broad or a narrow definition of its role or roles, that definition should be clear. The clarity should extend to the agency itself, to the president and the rest of the executive branch, to the Congress, and to the nation as a whole. Whether one supported or opposed the role or roles of the planning agency, one should know clearly what it sought to do, and why one supported or opposed it. Clarity of basic role is perhaps more important today than ever, because of the real likelihood of a legal or court challenge to the agency from some dissatisfied group.

Firm legislative base. It might be difficult for a new national planning agency to get a firm legislative base, but it is essential that it do so. Such a legislative base would avoid some of the continual controversy that was so debilitating to the NRPB and which in the end played such a considerable role in its demise. A clear legislative base is necessary for the functioning of the planning agency as well as for its survival in the face of inevitable criticism. The process of obtaining a legislative base would go a long way toward clarifying the role or roles of the agency. While congressional hearings and debates are often time-consuming, on the whole the process produces a compromise or a result which more nearly reflects a national consensus than any other process we have been able to devise. If a president cannot get a firm legislative base for his national planning agency, then the probabilities are high that it cannot function effectively.

Administrative structure compatible with its role. If the new national planning agency were to have any operating, or coordinating, or decision-making role, then a part-time administrative board is *not* an acceptable administrative structure. A full-time, fully responsible administrator is highly desirable. He might have an advisory board or council or outside advisers, if he chose. If he did not so choose, then providing one in legislation is ineffectual. A small (three, perhaps) full-time board may be able to function like a single administrator. There must be a single final decision point within the agency. If the planning agency is primarily oriented to research, an administrative board may be satisfactory, but even then there should be a single administrator with some power. The general rule is that the administrative structure should be fully compatible with the agency's role—anything else is a needless hostage to fortune, as the NRPB experience clearly demonstrates.

Roles and methods of operation must be fully compatible. Whatever roles the agency is given by its enabling legislation, its own internal methods of operation must be fully compatible with those roles. There are powerful arguments for limited as well as clearly defined roles for an overall national planning agency. Too many roles, even if clearly defined, are likely to be competitive and conflicting. In particular, I am strongly convinced that the same planning agency cannot be a coordinator of federal agencies and advisory to the president, on the one hand, and at the same time seek publicity for its results and seek to play a national educational role, on the other. The agency's posture vis-à-vis other federal agencies, its use of staff, and other aspects of its operations should be carefully considered and evaluated in terms of their compatibility with the assigned roles.

Methods of operation and time span of activities. A new overall national planning agency should determine its internal methods of operation in light of the time span of its interests and activities, as defined in its basic legislation. If the new agency has the task of advising the president and his administration on current issues, then it must have direct access to the president, must meet his needs to the limit of its ability, must avoid embarrassing the administration by publicity or by careful leaks, and generally must seek to be part of an administration team. Under these circumstances, the agency must gear itself to produce answers quickly—day before yesterday—to questions posed to it by the president or other major administration figure. On the other hand, if the agency has its major responsibility in the formulation of long-range plans and alternatives—and by "long-range" I mean something of the order of ten to twenty years ahead—then it must seek to produce results which will be useful not only to the present administration but for the next one-to-three administrations, irrespective of their party. For this role it must avoid undue embarrassment to the current administration, but it need not be so concerned with immediate issues as with more basic and persistent ones, and immediate access to the president is less important. For this role its communication with the Congress and the public may be crucial.

An Idea Stimulator/Financer?

As I have noted in earlier chapters, the NRPB and its predecessor agencies had as one of its broad roles or responsibilities the generation of new ideas, either by its own research or by research it stimulated. Moreover, it had considerable success in this role, although many of the ideas were controversial and were one factor in its ultimate demise.

The need for new ideas is always great, whether it be the nation, or a state, or a private business firm, or an educational or research institution which is considered. There are never enough new ideas and those which do come forward are never good enough. What are the alternative solutions to evident problems? What are the probable benefits and what are the probable costs and constraints on any alternative? While this is a universal problem, it exists for the national government and for the national problems mentioned earlier. One possible role for a reconstituted NRPB would be the production, stimulation, and financing of research or other new ideas for dealing with evident or imminent problems.

But, as a researcher itself, what could a reconstituted NRPB do that the National Academy of Sciences/National Research Council, or the various departments with their research and planning units, or the Office of Technology Assessment, or the General Accounting Office, or the Library of Congress cannot do among the federal agencies? Or that the Brookings Institution, the American Enterprise Institute for Public Policy Research, the Potomac Institute, the National Planning Association, the National Bureau of Economic Research, the Institute for Policy Studies, the Urban Institute, or Resources for the Future (or some other organization which I have inadvertently omitted) could not do, among the private organizations? Ideas come from people, especially trained and specialized thinkers (whatever their professional backgrounds). Could a reconstituted NRPB attract better thinkers than can the present agencies and organizations? Could it do so only by robbing existent organizations, or could it be a factor in the development of more persons and/or the greater development of the individuals who would in any case be drawn into this kind of work? Would the same men and women be more effective if drawn into a reconstituted NRPB than if they were connected with one of the existing public agencies or private organizations?

A somewhat similar range of questions should be raised about the establishment of a reconstituted NRPB which was given the role of financing research by public agencies or by private or semiprivate organizations. What could the reconstituted NRPB do better than the National Science Foundation, the various government departments and agencies, and private foundations? What is the likelihood that the administration and the Congress would give a reconstituted NRPB significant funds for the financing of research, and, if such funds were made available, how far would they be *net*—that is, would funds to this new agency largely come out of funds that otherwise would be provided to existent agencies? Could a reconstituted NRPB really make wiser choices in its allocation of available funds than do present government agencies and private foundations? If the nation is prepared to put more money into research on important national policy problems, is it better to put such additional money into a reconstituted NRPB than into an existing organization?

In considering the questions I have raised in this section, one should be as realistic as possible about both existing and proposed new organizations. The deficiencies of existing organizations can easily be argued by their critics. But would a new organization do any better?

If a reconstituted NRPB were to be an idea stimulator/financer, its ideas would have to be communicated to the public as well as to the president. This would require report publication, as the NRPB did; but it might also well involve communication by new methods, such as television, which were not existent when the NRPB was alive. It would be particularly important, I think, that such a reconstituted NRPB communicate directly and on a personal level with the Congress as well as with the rest of the executive branch. The kind of aloofness from the Congress which the NRPB maintained would be fatal to an idea stimulator/financer and the argument that it advised the president would have even less validity than it had during the NRPB's life. If a reconstituted NRPB of the idea stimulator/financer type were to survive over a period of years or indefinitely, through changes in administrations and Congresses, then it would need a broad base of understanding and support.

As a Coordinator of Federal Programs?

It will be recalled from earlier chapters that one role the NRPB and its predecessors played was the coordination of various federal programs, especially some of the public works programs. If a new NRPB were created, one possible role would be to serve as a coordinator of various and diverse federal programs. Probably most observers and all critics of every recent national administration would agree on the desirability of better coordination among the many and diverse federal programs touching nearly every aspect of modern life. Each of the most recent six or seven presidents has been seriously concerned with this problem. In this chapter we have briefly described some of the incoherence in present-day federal planning. Today one has only to read any daily newspaper to have some fresh examples of the lack of coordination. Could a new NRPB help bring some order out of this?

In theory, the responsibility for federal program coordination rests with the by now very extensive White House staff, and upon such presidential agencies as the Office of Management and Budget. One of the marked developments with respect to the American presidency in the past generation has been the enormous increase in staff directly serving the president. One of its tasks is to assure at least an adequate degree of coordination among agencies and programs. If the present performance is less than ideal, or even less than satisfactory, what reason is there to think that a new NRPB could do any better?

The problem is always with the president, not with the White House staff. If he is unable to get his administration to operate in a cooperative and consistent fashion to deal with the difficult national problems of today, the deficiency lies not in numbers or capabilities of staff, but rather in the president himself and in his use of staff.

It might well be argued that a formal national planning agency is not needed and might even be counterproductive to federal agency coordination from the White House. That is, as part of his Executive Office, any president might have a small group of senior persons with somewhat diverse backgrounds, personally known and trusted by him, freed of direct operating responsibilities, to seek in various ways to promote and secure better coordination among the federal agencies. There is little gain from Congress thrusting either planning or reporting responsibility on a reluctant president. If he took a direct and personal interest in such a group within his office, it could be highly effective—and not prominent in the public eye.

It should be recalled again that my position is that program coordination and idea stimulation are mutually incompatible roles for an overall national planning agency. If the current or any future administration decides to establish a national planning agency to assist in federal program coordination, such an agency should not also be given the responsibility for idea stimulation and financing. Or, if some reconstituted NRPB is given the idea stimulation and financing role, it should not be asked also to assume the agency and program coordination role.

Any direct coordinating role for a national planning agency or staff unit in the president's office must be an "inside" operation; that is, it must have access not only to the president but also to most documents except perhaps the most top secret ones. But there might be a role for a private planning organization or group of private planning organizations, in postauditing federal programs. That is, the National Planning Association or some other private group might undertake periodic, possibly annual, postaudits of federal programs, using such information as was publicly available or as it could find, and expressing its judgment as to how well the agencies had carried out their missions. If done with great competence and skill, such postauditing could make every federal agency more alert to its responsibilities. Such postaudits would, of course, be published and their wide distribution would be a major factor in their influence. Fulfillment of this private planning role would take a great deal of ability, substantial funds, and an appropriate organization within the private group.

As Part of a Major Federal Economic Operating Agency?

The New Deal was possible only because the situation which preceded it had become intolerable to so many people. The demand was for action, even when the nature of the best action was most unclear. If such a crisis situation came about again, the demands for national action would rise greatly. One way those demands might find expression would be some form of direct federal economic action. Something like this has already been proposed for some aspects of the energy problem. However such action might be organized, the agency or agencies would almost certainly require some kind of a planning unit. The latter would not be the direct "operator" but a staff unit to the operating agency.

There are, of course, precedents for a vastly enlarged federal role in the economy of the nation. The Reconstruction Finance Corporation was established in the Hoover administration although it was so starved for funds that it became effective only during the New Deal and the war years. It loaned money to many private organizations and actually took over many operating functions, either of companies that had gone bankrupt or of new enterprises created for special tasks. There was the National Recovery Administration, established under special act at the beginning of the New Deal which actually sought the kind of economic syndicalism described earlier. That act was declared unconstitutional— thereby rescuing President Roosevelt from one of his most serious errors on the economic front, for NRA was neither helping the economy very much nor achieving an acceptable degree of economic democracy in the process. During World War II there was the War Production Board and the whole war mobilization effort, under which supplies of raw materials and production goods were allocated and rationed to industries to help directly in the war effort. One could find other less known illustrations. All of these efforts were begun in times of extreme national difficulty— severe depression or war—and served only because of those emergencies. Merely listing the times and conditions in which these exercises in national economic planning and operation functioned is enough to suggest that probably nothing like this would ever again be established in anything but extreme emergency.

How severe would the national emergency have to be, for the country as a whole and its elected representatives to endorse—not merely accept—a major direct federal involvement in economic planning and operation? One can only speculate that the emergency would have to be very serious. I can conceive of even a highly conservative president reluctantly accepting direct federal involvement in the economy of the country under some circumstances. If he did, he would be directly in the tradition of every president, beginning at least with Franklin Roosevelt.

A consideration which perhaps should be the most sobering of all is: if a general economic operating agency were established at the federal level to cope with an emergency, could the country ever again get rid of it when or if the emergency ended? I do not mean that free elections and choice by elected representatives would thereby cease, but rather that, once such an agency had become operative, it could not be dispensed with—even if only modestly successful. Not only would there be an entrenched and possibly highly durable bureaucracy, but all manner of private economic interests would develop an interest in seeing it continue, just as many industries acquire vested interests in tariffs or many parts of the country acquire vested interests in continued subsidized federal water development programs.

If any such federal economic operating program and agency were established, it surely would require an economic planning unit, or a new unit would have to be established in the Office of the President, or both. The demands upon such a unit would be very great and it could hardly expect to avoid serious scrutiny and criticism. Since the existence of a direct federal economic program is unlikely, and its nature, if one should be undertaken, is so uncertain, there is little reason to speculate further on the best form and best methods of operation of its planning organization. However, if something like this organization should come into existence, the lessons from the NRPB experience as I have tried to develop them would be valuable.

A Reconstituted NRPB—Yes or No?

Now, assuming anyone gets this far and is willing to read the last few paragraphs, I do *not* intend to come up with a ringing plea for the reestablishment of the NRPB, nor do I intend to come up with an all-out rejection of the idea. The answer about a reconstituted NRPB depends entirely, in my judgment, on the role that one envisages for it, and on consistent concomitants to that role.

I think there is some room for an idea stimulator/financer type of NRPB, especially for dealing with national problems of a longer-range type. One may doubt that it would be wholly successful and surely it would not, and should not, wholly displace the National Science Foundation and the many other public and private organizations functioning in this field. But it might make a significant net contribution to national thought and thereby to national welfare. Much would depend upon the persons attracted to it.

I can see some role for a national coordinating agency, although I think this task should be taken over more competently by the White House staff which is now supposed to fill this function. Possibly some of that staff could be reorganized into a national planning agency, generally comparable to the Council of Economic Advisers.

My most positive conviction and position is: *not both of these roles in one agency*. Create either, or neither, or both; but not one agency for these diverse and incompatible roles. One agency trying to do both would almost surely fail at one or both roles—fail internally and with the Congress and the public.

Lastly, and most basic of all: a final answer depends on the president, whoever he may be. A president who would use a planning organization effectively, including listening to it, might get a great deal out of it; a president who either gave it nothing to do, or gave it impossible tasks, or paid no attention to it, would gain nothing from it, and he might well be embarrassed by its actions or even by its existence. This book—and now that I am at the end of its writing, I would argue, any book—cannot give a positive answer to the matter of a new or reconstituted NRPB. What it can do, and what I hope it will do, is to point out how the nation could best establish an overall national planning board, if it chose to do so, and what should be avoided if the prospects for a useful agency are to be the best.

APPENDIXES

Appendix A

Documentary History of Official Actions Relating to the National Resources Planning Board

This appendix is a simple account of the official documents relating to the National Resources Planning Board, including establishment of agencies or units, enumeration of functions and powers, and abolishment. Some documents are reproduced in their entirety; others, especially if long, are reproduced only in those parts which relate to the NRPB. There is nothing in this appendix on the events leading up to each action, nothing on the rationale for the action taken, and nothing on the performance under the action. These matters are discussed in the body of this report. This appendix does not include internal documents of NRPB, relating to its internal organization and functioning. The official documents which follow are in chronological order and include the following:

1. The Employment Stabilization Act of 1931, which created a Federal Employment Stabilization Board and, among other things, established the principles of advance planning for public works.

2. Executive Order 6166, of June 10, 1933, which, among many other things, abolished the Federal Employment Stabilization Board and transferred its records (and presumably its duties) to the Federal Emergency Administration of Public Works.

3. National Industrial Recovery Act of 1933, which, among its many provisions, created a Federal Emergency Administration of Public Works with very extensive powers and duties, and empowered the president to establish agencies to carry out the act.

4. Order of the Administrator of Public Works, July 20, 1933, which established the National Planning Board of three members and spelled out their functions.

289

5. Executive Order 6221, July 26, 1933, which postponed the effective date of Executive Order 6166 until sixty days after the convening of the second session of the 73rd Congress.

6. Executive Order 6623, March 1, 1934, again abolishes Federal Employment Stabilization Board, and transfers its functions and records to a new office in the Department of Commerce.

7. Executive Order 6777, June 30, 1934, abolishes the National Planning Board of the Federal Emergency Administration of Public Works, and creates the National Resources Board consisting of five secretaries of departments, the administrator of the Federal Emergency Relief Administration, and the same three citizens who had constituted the National Planning Board; and set forth its functions.

8. Executive Order 7065, June 7, 1935, abolishes the National Resources Board, establishes a National Resources Committee of the same membership and similar functions, but with an advisory committee of the three citizen members.

9. Reorganization Act of 1939 in its entirety; it was under this authority that the following action was taken.

10. Reorganization Plan No. 1, April 3, 1939, abolished the National Resources Committee, established the National Resources Planning Board, of very similar organization and functions; and set forth in much detail other reorganization matters not directly affecting NRPB.

11. Executive Order 8248, September 8, 1939, established divisions in the office of the president and spelled out their functions, including the role of NRPB.

12. Executive Order 8455, June 26, 1940, outlined in some detail the six year advance planning of public works by the federal government, and the role of NRPB in this activity.

13. Independent Offices Appropriation Act of 1944, which, among other matters, terminated NRPB.

1. Employment Stabilization Act of 1931 (2/10/31; 46 Stat. 1084) (Created Federal Employment Stabilization Board, a direct ancestor of National Resources Planning Board; establishes advance planning for Public works.)

CHAP. 117.—An Act To provide for the advance planning and regulated construction of public works, for the stabilization of industry, and for aiding in the prevention of unemployment during periods of business depression.

Be it enacted by the Senate and House of Representatives of the United States of America in Congress assembled, That this Act may be cited as the "Employment Stabilization Act of 1931."

DEFINITIONS

Sec. 2. When used in this Act—

(a) The term "board" means the Federal Employment Stabilization Board established by section 3 of this Act;

(b) The term "United States," when used in a geographical sense, includes the several States and Territories and the District of Columbia;

(c) The term "public works emergency appropriation" means an appropriation made in pursuance of supplemental estimates transmitted to the Congress under the provisions of this Act.

(d) The term "construction agencies" shall mean the following departments, bureaus, and independent agencies and such others as the President may designate from time to time:

Of the Department of Agriculture, the Bureau of Public Roads, the Bureau of Plant Industry, the Forest Service, the Bureau of Dairy Industry, and the Bureau of Animal Industry;

Of the Department of Commerce, the Aeronautics Branch, the Coast and Geodetic Survey, the Bureau of Fisheries, and the Bureau of Lighthouses;

Of the Department of Interior, the Bureau of Indian Affairs, the Bureau of Reclamation, and the National Park Service;

Of the Department of the Treasury, the Coast Guard, the Public Health Service, and the Office of the Supervising Architect;

Of the Department of War, the office of the Quartermaster General, and the office of the Chief of Engineers;

Of the Department of Justice, the Bureau of Prisons;

Of the Department of the Navy, the Bureau of Yards and Docks;

The Department of Labor;

The Post Office Department;

Of the independent agencies, the Veterans' Administration, the office of Public Buildings and Public Parks of the National Capital, the District of Columbia, the Architect of the Capitol, and the Panama Canal.

(e) The term "construction" shall include also repairs and alterations, and the purchase of such materials, supplies, and equipment as may be necessary as a part of, or incident to, such construction, repairs, or alterations.

(f) The term "authorized construction" shall include those projects which have been specifically authorized by Congress, and those projects which do not require specific legislative authorization, such as repairs and alterations.

FEDERAL EMPLOYMENT STABILIZATION BOARD

Sec. 3. (a) There is hereby established a board to be known as the Federal Employment Stabilization Board, and to be composed of the Secretary of the Treasury, the Secretary of Commerce, the Secretary of Agriculture, and the Secretary of Labor. It shall be the duty of the board to advise the President from time to time of the trend of employment and business activity and of the existence or approach of periods of business depression and unemployment in the United States or in any substantial portion thereof; to cooperate with the construction agencies in formulating methods of advance planning; to make progress reports; and to perform the other functions assigned to it by this Act.

(b) The board is authorized to appoint, in accordance with the civil-service laws, a director and such experts, and clerical and other assistants, and to make such expenditures (including expenditures for personal services and rent at the seat of Government and elsewhere, for law books, books of reference, and periodicals) as may be necessary for the administration of this Act, and as may be provided for by the Congress from time to time. The compensation of the director and such experts and clerical and other assistants shall be fixed in accordance with the classification Act of 1923, as amended. The director and his staff may be domiciled in and attached to one of the executive departments. There is hereby authorized to be appropriated annually such sum as may be necessary for the expenses of the board.

BASIS OF ACTION OF BOARD

SEC. 4. (a) In advising the President the board shall take into consideration the volume, based upon value, of contracts awarded for construction work in the United States, or in any substantial portion thereof, during any three-month period in comparison with the corresponding three-month period of three previous calendar years.

(b) The board may also take into consideration the index of employment prepared by the Department of Labor, and any other information concerning employment furnished the Department of Labor or by any other public or private agency, and any other facts which it may consider pertinent.

PUBLIC WORKS EMERGENCY APPROPRIATION

SEC. 5. Whenever, upon recommendation of the board, the President finds that there exists, or that within the six months next following there is likely to exist, in the United States or any substantial portion thereof, a period of business depression and unemployment, he is requested to transmit to the Congress by special message, at such time and from time to time thereafter, such supplemental estimates as he deems advisable for emergency appropriations, to be expended during such period upon authorized construction in order to aid in preventing unemployment and permit the Government to avail itself of the opportunity for speedy, efficient, and economical construction during any such period. Except as provided in this Act, such supplemental estimates shall conform to the provisions of the Budget and Accounting Act, 1921.

WORKS ON WHICH APPROPRIATION USED

SEC. 6. Such emergency appropriations are authorized and shall be expended only—

(a) For carrying out the provisions of the Federal Highway Act, as now or hereafter amended and supplemented;

(b) For the preservation and maintenance of existing river and harbor works, and for the prosecution of such projects heretofore and hereafter authorized as may be most desirable in the interest of commerce and navigation;

(c) For prosecuting flood-control projects heretofore or hereafter authorized; and

(d) For carrying into effect the provisions of the Public Buildings Act, approved May 25, 1926, as now or hereafter amended and supplemented, in respect to public buildings within and without the District of Columbia.

(e) For prosecuting such other construction as may now or hereafter be authorized by the Congress, and which is or may be included in the six-year advance plans, as hereinafter provided.

ACCELERATION OF EMERGENCY CONSTRUCTION

SEC. 7. For the purpose of aiding in the prevention of unemployment during periods of business depression and of permitting the Government to avail itself of opportunity for speedy, efficient, and economical construction during such periods the President may direct the construction agencies to accelerate during such periods, to such extent as is deemed practicable, the prosecution of all authorized construction within their control.

ADVANCE PLANNING

SEC. 8. (a) It is hereby declared to be the policy of Congress to arrange the construction of public works so far as practicable in such manner as will assist in the stabilization of industry and employment through the proper timing of such construction, and that to further this object there shall be advance planning, including preparation of detailed construction plans, of public works by the construction agencies and the board.

(b) Each head of a department or independent establishment having jurisdiction over one or more construction agencies shall direct each such construction agency to prepare a six-year advance plan with estimates showing projects allotted to each year. Such estimates shall show separately the estimated cost of land, the estimated cost of new construction, and the estimated annual cost of operation and of repairs and alterations.

(c) Each construction agency shall also prepare a program for prompt commencement and carrying out of an expanded program at any time. This program shall include organization plans. It shall also include the plans for the acquisition of sites and the preparation of advance detailed construction plans for not less than one year in advance, except where in the judgment of the board this would not be practicable.

(d) Such programs, plans, and estimates for the six-year period shall be submitted to the board and to the Director of the Bureau of the Budget.

The Director of the Bureau of the Budget shall report to the President from time to time consolidated plans and estimates.

(e) Each construction agency shall keep its six-year plan up-to-date by an annual revision of the plans and estimates for the unexpired years and by annually extending the plan and estimates for an additional year.

(f) The President is requested each year, before recommending the amount of construction appropriations for the next fiscal year to take into consideration the volume of construction in the United States, the state of employment, and the activity of general business.

(g) The board shall collect information concerning advance construction plans and estimates by States, municipalities, and other public and private agencies which may indicate the probable volume of construction within the United States or which may aid the construction agencies in formulating their advance plans.

Approved, February 10, 1931.

2. Executive Order 6166, June 10, 1933, Organization of Executive Agencies

(Abolished Federal Employment Stabilization Board, transferred its functions to the Federal Emergency Administration of Public Works.)

WHEREAS section 16 of the act of March 3, 1933 (Public, No. 428, 47 Stat. 1517), provides for reorganizations within the executive branch of the Government; requires the President to investigate and determine what reorganizations are necessary to effectuate the purposes of the statute; and authorizes the President to make such reorganizations by Executive order; and

WHEREAS I have investigated the organization of all executive and administrative agencies of the Government and have determined that certain regroupings, consolidations, transfers, and abolitions of executive agencies and functions thereof are necessary to accomplish the purposes of section 16;

NOW, THEREFORE, by virtue of the aforesaid authority, I do hereby order that:

SECTION 1—*Procurement*

(Only that part of Section 1 which is pertinent to National Resources Planning Board is reproduced here.)

The Federal Employment Stabilization Board is abolished, and its records are transferred to the Federal Emergency Administration of Public Works if and when said administration is authorized and established.

SECTION 22—*Effective Date*

In accordance with law, this order shall become effective 61 days from its date; *Provided,* That in case it shall appear to the President that the interests of economy require that any transfer, consolidation, or elimination be delayed beyond the date this order becomes effective, he may, in his discretion, fix a later date therefor, and he may for like cause further defer such date from time to time.

THE WHITE HOUSE,
    June 10, 1933.

Franklin D. Roosevelt

3. National Industrial Recovery Act, June 16, 1933 (48 Stat. 195) (Created a Federal Emergency Administration of Public Works, outlined its powers and duties; empowered the President to establish agencies to carry out the Act. Only those parts of the Act relating to NRPB are included here.)

AN ACT

To encourage national industrial recovery, to foster fair competition, and to provide for the construction of certain useful public works, and for other purposes.

Be it enacted by the Senate and House of Representatives of the United States of America in Congress assembled,

TITLE I—*Industrial Recovery*

DECLARATION OF POLICY

SECTION 1. A national emergency productive of widespread unemployment and disorganization of industry, which burdens interstate and foreign commerce, affects the public welfare, and undermines the standards of living of the American people, is hereby declared to exist. It is hereby declared to be the policy of Congress to remove obstructions to the free flow of interstate and foreign commerce which tend to diminish the amount thereof; and to provide for the general welfare by promoting the organization of industry for the purpose of cooperative action among trade groups, to induce and maintain united action of labor and management under adequate governmental sanctions and supervision, to eliminate unfair competitive practices, to promote the fullest possible utilization of the present productive capacity of industries, to avoid undue restriction of production (except as may be temporarily required), to increase the consumption of industrial and agricultural products by increasing purchasing power, to reduce and relieve unemployment, to improve standards of labor, and otherwise to rehabilitate industry and to conserve natural resources.

ADMINISTRATIVE AGENCIES

SEC. 2. (a) To effectuate the policy of this title, the President is hereby authorized to establish such agencies, to accept and utilize such voluntary and uncompensated services, to appoint, without regard to the provisions of the civil service laws, such officers and employees, and to utilize such Federal officers and employees, and, with the consent of the State, such State and local officers and employees, as he may find necessary, to prescribe their authorities, duties, responsibilities, and tenure, and, without regard to the Classification Act of 1923, as amended, to fix the compensation of any officers and employees so appointed.

(b) The President may delegate any of his functions and powers under this title to such officers, agents, and employees as he may designate or appoint, and may establish an industrial planning and research agency to aid in carrying out his functions under this title.

(c) This title shall cease to be in effect and any agencies established hereunder shall cease to exist at the expiration of two years after the date of enactment of this Act, or sooner if the President shall by proclamation or the Congress shall by joint resolution declare that the emergency recognized by section 1 has ended.

TITLE II—*Public Works and Construction Projects*

FEDERAL EMERGENCY ADMINISTRATION OF PUBLIC WORKS

SECTION 201. (a) To effectuate the purposes of this title, the President is hereby authorized to create a Federal Emergency Administration of Public Works, all the powers of which shall be exercised by a Federal Emergency Administrator of Public Works (hereafter referred to as the "Administrator"), and to establish such agencies, to accept and utilize such voluntary and uncompensated services, to appoint, without regard to the civil service laws, such officers and employees, and to utilize such Federal officers and employees, and, with the consent of the State, such State and local officers and employees as he may find necessary, to prescribe their authorities, duties, responsibilities, and tenure, and, without regard to the Classification Act of 1923, as amended, to fix the compensation of any officers and employees so appointed. The President may delegate any of his functions and powers under this title to such officers, agents, and employees as he may designate or appoint.

(b) The Administrator may, without regard to the civil service laws or the Classification Act of 1923, as amended, appoint and fix the compensation of such experts and such other officers and employees as are necessary to carry out the provisions of this title; and may make such expenditures (including expenditures for personal services and rent at the seat of government and elsewhere, for law books and books of reference, and for paper, printing and binding) as are necessary to carry out the provisions of this title.

(c) All such compensation, expenses, and allowances shall be paid out of funds made available by this Act.

(d) After the expiration of two years after the date of the enactment of of this Act, or sooner if the President shall by proclamation or the Congress shall by joint resolution declare that the emergency recognized by section 1 has ended, the President shall not make any further loans or grants or enter upon any new construction under this title, and any agencies established hereunder shall cease to exist and any of their remaining functions shall be transferred to such departments of the Government as the President shall designate: *Provided*, That he may issue funds to a borrower under this title prior to January 23, 1939, under the terms of any agreement, or any commitment to bid upon or purchase bonds, entered into with such borrower prior to the date of termination, under this section, of the power of the President to make loans.

SEC. 202. The Administrator, under the direction of the President, shall prepare a comprehensive program of public works, which shall include among other things the following: (a) Construction, repair, and improvement of public highways and park ways, public buildings, and any publicly owned instrumentalities and facilities; (b) conservation and development of natural resources, including control, utilization, and purification of waters, prevention of soil or coastal erosion, development of water power, transmission of electrical energy, and construction of river and harbor improvements and flood control and also the construction of any river or drainage improvement required to perform or satisfy any obligation incurred by the United States through a treaty with a foreign Government heretofore ratified and to restore or develop for the use of any State or its citizens water taken from or denied to them by performance on the part of the United States of treaty obligations heretofore assumed: *Provided*, That no river or harbor improvements shall be carried out unless they shall have heretofore or hereafter been adopted by the Congress or are recommended by the Chief of Engineers of the United States Army; (c) any projects of the character heretofore constructed or carried on either directly by public authority or with public aid to serve the interests of the general public; (d) construction, reconstruction, alteration, or repair under public regulation or control of low-cost housing and slum-clearance projects; (e) any project (other than those included in the foregoing classes) of any character heretofore eligible for loans under subsection (a) of section 201 of the Emergency Relief and Construction Act of 1932, as amended, and paragraph (3) of such subsection (a) shall for such purposes be held to include loans for the construction or completion of hospitals the operation of which is partly financed from public funds, and of reservoirs and pumping plants and for the construction of dry docks; and if in the opinion of the President it seems desirable, the construction of naval vessels within the terms and/or limits established by the London Naval Treaty of 1930 and of aircraft required therefor and construction of heavier-than-air aircraft and technical construction for the Army Air Corps and such Army housing projects as the President may approve, and provision of original equipment for the mechanization or motorization of such Army tactical units as he may designate: *Provided, however,* That in the event of an international agreement for the further limitation of armament, to which the United States is signatory, the President is hereby authorized and empowered to suspend, in whole or in part, any such naval or military construction or mechanization and motorization of Army units: *Provided further,* That this title shall not be applicable to public works under the jurisdiction or control of the Architect of the Capitol or of any commission or committee for which such Architect is the contracting and/or executive officer.

SEC. 203. (a) With a view to increasing employment quickly (while reasonably securing any loans made by the United States) the President is authorized and empowered, through the Administrator or through such other agencies as he may designate or create, (1) to construct, finance, or aid in the construction or financing of any public-works project included in the program prepared pursuant to section 202; (2) upon such terms as the President shall prescribe, to make grants to States, municipalities, or other public bodies for the construction, repair, or improvement of any such project, but no such grant shall be in excess of 30 per centum of the cost of the labor and materials employed upon such project; (3) to acquire by purchase, or by exercise of the power of eminent domain, any real or personal property in connection with the construction of any such project, and to sell any security acquired or any property so constructed or acquired or to lease any such property with or without the privilege of purchase: *Provided,* That all moneys received from any such sale or lease or the repayment of any loan shall be used to retire obligations issued pursuant to section 209 of this Act, in addition to any other moneys required to be used for such purpose; (4) to aid in the financing of such railroad maintenance and equipment as may be approved by the Interstate Commerce Commission as desirable for the improvement of transportation facilities; and (5) to advance, upon request of the Commission having jurisdiction of the project, the unappropriated balance of the sum authorized for carrying out the provisions of the Act entitled "An Act to provide for the construction and equipment of an annex to the Library of Congress", approved June 13, 1930 (46 Stat. 583); such advance to be expended under the direction of such Commission and in accordance with such Act: *Provided,* That in deciding to extend any aid or grant hereunder to any State, county, or municipality the President may consider whether action is in process or in good faith assured therein reasonably designed to bring the ordinary current expenditures thereof within the prudently estimated revenues thereof. The provisions of this section and section 202 shall extend to public works in the several States, Hawaii, Alaska, the District of Columbia, Puerto Rico, the Canal Zone, and the Virgin Islands.

(b) All expenditures for authorized travel by officers and employees, including subsistence, required on account of any Federal public-works projects, shall be charged to the amounts allocated to such projects, notwithstanding any other provisions of law; and there is authorized to be employed such personal services in the District of Columbia and elsewhere as may be required to be engaged upon such work and to be in addition to employees otherwise provided for, the compensation of such additional personal services to be a charge against the funds made available for such construction work.

(c) In the acquisition of any land or site for the purposes of Federal public buildings and in the construction of such buildings provided for in this title, the provisions contained in sections 305 and 306 of the Emergency Relief and Construction Act of 1932, as amended, shall apply.

(d) The President, in his discretion, and under such terms as he may prescribe, may extend any of the benefits of this title to any State, county, or municipality notwithstanding any constitutional or legal restriction or limitation on the right or power of such State, county, or municipality to borrow money or incur indebtedness.

SEC. 204. (a) For the purpose of providing for emergency construction of public highways and related projects, the President is authorized to make grants to the highway departments of the several States in an amount not less than $400,000,000, to be expended by such departments in accordance with the provisions of the Federal Highway Act, approved November 9, 1921, as amended and supplemented, except as provided in this title, as follows:

(1) For expenditure in emergency construction on the Federal aid highway system and extensions thereof into and through municipalities. The amount apportioned to any State under this paragraph may be used to pay all or any part of the cost of surveys, plans, and of highway and bridge construction including the elimination of hazards to highway traffic, such as the separation of grades at crossing, the reconstruction of existing railroad grade crossing structures, the relocation of highways to eliminate railroad crossings, the widening of narrow bridges and roadways, the building of footpaths, the replacement of unsafe bridges, the construction of routes to avoid congested areas, the construction of facilities to improve accessibility and the free flow of traffic, and the cost of any other construction that will provide safer traffic facilities or definitely eliminate existing hazards to pedestrian or vehicular traffic. No funds made available by this title shall be used for the acquisition of any land, right of way, or easement in connection with any railroad grade elimination project.

(2) For expenditure in emergency construction on secondary or feeder roads to be agreed upon by the State highway departments and the Secretary of Agriculture: *Provided*, That the State or responsible political subdivision shall provide for the proper maintenance of said roads. Such grants shall be available for payment of the full cost of surveys, plans, improvement, and construction of secondary or feeder roads, on which projects shall be submitted by the State highway department and approved by the Secretary of Agriculture.

(b) Any amounts allocated by the President for grants under subsection (a) of this section shall be apportioned among the several States seven-eighths in accordance with the provisions of section 21 of the Federal Highway Act, approved November 9, 1921, as amended and supplemented (which Act is hereby further amended for the purposes of this title to include the District of Columbia), and one-eighth in the ratio which the population of each State bears to the total population of the United States, according to the latest decennial census and shall be available on July 1, 1933, and shall remain available until expended; but no part of the funds apportioned to any State need be matched by the State, and such funds may also be used in lieu of State funds to match unobligated balances of previous apportionments of regular Federal-aid appropriations.

(c) All contracts involving the expenditure of such grants shall contain provisions establishing minimum rates of wages, to be predetermined by the State highway department, which contractors shall pay to skilled and unskilled labor, and such minimum rates shall be stated in the invitation for bids and shall be included in proposals for bids for the work.

(d) In the expenditure of such amounts, the limitations in the Federal Highway Act, approved November 9, 1921, as amended and supplemented, upon highway construction, reconstruction, and bridges within municipalities and upon payments per mile which may be made from Federal funds, shall not apply.

(e) As used in this section the term "State" includes the Territory of Hawaii and the District of Columbia. The term "highway" as defined in the Federal Highway Act approved November 9, 1921, as amended and supplemented, for the purposes of this section, shall be deemed to include such main parkways as may be designated by the State and approved by the Secretary of Agriculture as part of the Federal-aid highway system.

(f) Whenever, in connection with the construction of any highway project under this section or section 202 of this Act, it is necessary to acquire rights of way over or through any property or tracts of land owned and controlled by the Government of the United States, it shall be the duty of the proper official of the Government of the United States having control of such property or tracts of land with the approval of the President and the Attorney General of the United States, and without any expense whatsoever to the United States, to perform any acts and to execute any agreements necessary to grant the rights of way so required, but if at any time the land or the property the subject of the agreement shall cease to be used for the purposes of the highway, the title in and the jurisdiction over the land or property shall automatically revert to the Government of the United States and the agreement shall so provide.

(g) Hereafter in the administration of the Federal Highway Act, and Acts amendatory thereof or supplementary thereto, the first paragraph of section 9 of said Act shall not apply to publicly owned toll bridges or approaches thereto, operated by the highway department of any State, subject, however, to the condition that all tolls received from the operation of any such bridge, less the actual cost of operation and maintenance, shall be applied to the repayment of the cost of its construction or acquisition, and when the cost of its construction or acquisition shall have been repaid in full, such bridge thereafter shall be maintained and operated as a free bridge.

SEC. 205. (a) Not less than $50,000,000 of the amount made available by this Act shall be allotted for (A) national forest highways, (B) national forest roads, trails, bridges, and related projects, (C) national park roads and trails in national parks owned or authorized, (D) roads on Indian reservations, and (E) roads through public lands, to be expended in the same manner as provided in paragraph (2) of section 301 of the Emergency Relief and Construction Act of 1932, in the case of appropriations allocated for such purposes, respectively, in such section 301, to remain available until expended.

(b) The President may also allot funds made available by this Act for the construction, repair, and improvement of public highways in Alaska, the Canal Zone, Puerto Rico, and the Virgin Islands.

SEC. 206. All contracts let for construction projects and all loans and grants pursuant to this title shall contain such provisions as are necessary to insure (1) that no convict labor shall be employed on any such project; (2) that (except in executive, administrative, and supervisory positions), so far as practicable and feasible, no individual directly employed on any such project shall be permitted to work more than thirty hours in any one week; (3) that all employees shall be paid just and reasonable wages which shall be compensation sufficient to provide, for the hours of labor as limited, a standard of living in decency and comfort; (4) that in the employment of labor in connection with any such project, preference shall be given, where they are qualified, to ex-service men with dependents, and then in the following order: (A) To citizens of the United States and aliens who have declared their intention of becoming citizens, who are bona fide residents of the political subdivision and/or county in which the work is to be performed, and (B) to citizens of the United States and aliens who have declared their intention of becoming citizens, who are bona fide residents of the State, Territory, or district in which the work is to be performed: *Provided,* That these preferences shall apply only where such labor is available and qualified to perform the work to which the employment relates; and (5) that the maximum of human labor shall be used in lieu of machinery wherever practicable and consistent with sound economy and public advantage.

SEC. 207. (a) For the purpose of expediting the actual construction of public works contemplated by this title and to provide a means of financial assistance to persons under contract with the United States to perform such construction, the President is authorized and empowered, through the Administrator or through such other agencies as he may designate or create, to approve any assignment executed by any such contractor, with the written consent of the surety or sureties upon the penal bond executed in connection with his contract, to any national or State bank, or his claim against the United States, or any part of such claim, under such contract; and any assignment so approved shall be valid for all purposes, notwithstanding the provisions of sections 3737 and 3477 of the Revised Statutes, as amended.

(b) The funds received by a contractor under any advances made in consideration of any such assignment are hereby declared to be trust funds in the hands of such contractor to be first applied to the payment of claims of subcontractors, architects, engineers, surveyors, laborers, and material men in connection with the project, to the payment of premiums on the penal bond or bonds, and premiums accruing during the construction of such project on insurance policies taken in connection therewith. Any contractor and any officer, director, or agent of any such contractor, who applies, or consents to the application of, such funds for any other purpose and fails to pay any claim or premium hereinbefore mentioned, shall be deemed guilty of a misdemeanor and shall be punished by a fine of not more than $1,000 or by imprisonment for not more than one year, or by both such fine and imprisonment.

(c) Nothing in this section shall be considered as imposing upon the assignee any obligation to see to the proper application of the funds advanced by the assignee in consideration of such assignment.

SHORT TITLE

SEC. 304. This Act may be cited as the "National Industrial Recovery Act." Approved, June 16, 1933, 11:55 a.m.

4. Order of the Administrator of Public Works, July 20, 1933 (Appoints a National Planning Board of three members, outlines its functions.)

SEC. 2. *The central organization.* (a) The Planning Board. Its functions are: (1) To advise and assist the Administrator in the preparation of the "Comprehensive program of public works" required by the Recovery Act, through—

1. *The preparation, development, and maintenance* of comprehensive and coordinated plans for regional areas in cooperation with national, regional, State, and local agencies; based upon

2. *Surveys and research concerning* (a) The distribution and trends of population, land uses, industry, housing and natural resources; and (b) the social and economic habits, trends, and values involved in development projects and plans; and through

3. The analysis of projects for coordination in location and sequence in order to prevent duplication or wasteful overlaps and to obtain the maximum amount of cooperation and correlation of effort among the departments, bureaus, and agencies of the Federal, State, and local governments.

5. Executive Order 6221, July 26, 1933
(Postpones effective date of Executive Order 6166)

Under the provisions of Section 22, of Executive Order No. 6166, dated June 10, 1933, issued pursuant to Section 16 of the Act of March 3, 1933 (Public No. 428, 47 Stat. 1517), the effective date of Section 18, of said Executive Order No. 6166, relating to co-operative vocational education and rehabilitation, payments for agricultural experiment stations, co-operative agricultural extension work, and endowment and maintenance of colleges for the benefit of agriculture and the mechanic arts, and the effective date for the abolishment of the Federal Employment Stabilization Board and the transfer of its records to the Federal Emergency Administration of Public Works, as provided in the last paragraph of Section 1 of said Executive Order, are hereby deferred until sixty days after the convening of the second session of the 73rd Congress.

Franklin D. Roosevelt

THE WHITE HOUSE
July 26, 1933

6. Executive Order 6623, March 1, 1934
(Abolishes Federal Employment Stabilization Board, establishes Office in Department of Commerce.)

WHEREAS section 16 of the act of March 3, 1933 (ch. 212, 47 Stat. 1517), provides for reorganizations within the executive branch of the government, requires the President to investigate and determine what reorganizations are necessary to effectuate the purposes of the act, and authorizes the President to make such reorganizations by Executive Order; and

WHEREAS section 1 of Executive Order No. 6166 of June 10, 1933, provides in part as follows:

"The Federal Employment Stabilization Board is abolished, and its records are transferred to the Federal Emergency Administration of Public Works if and when said administration is authorized and established." and

WHEREAS the effective date of the above-quoted provision of section 1 of Executive Order No. 6166 has been further deferred by Executive Order of this date until such time as the functions of said Board may be transferred as hereinafter provided; and

WHEREAS after further investigation I find and declare that the establishment in the Department of Commerce of an office to be known as the Federal Employment Stabilization Office, and the transfer thereto of the functions of said Board, would be in the public interest and would affectuate the purposes of said section 16;

NOW, THEREFORE, by virtue of the authority vested in me by the aforesaid section 16 of the act of March 3, 1933, it is ordered that the above-quoted provision of section 1 of Executive Order No. 6166 of June 10, 1933, be, and it is hereby, revoked.

It is further ordered that the said Federal Employment Stabilization Board be, and it is hereby, abolished.

There is hereby established in the Department of Commerce an office to be known as the Federal Employment Stabilization Office, and there are hereby transferred to such Office the functions of the Federal Employment Stabilization Board, together with its Director and other personnel, and records, supplies, equipment, and property of every kind.

The unexpended balances of appropriations and/or allotments of appropriations of the Federal Employment Stabilization Board are hereby transferred to the Federal Employment Stabilization Office, Department of Commerce.

This order will become effective in accordance with the provisions of section 1 of Title III of the act of March 20, 1933 (ch. 3, 48 Stat. 8, 16).

Franklin D. Roosevelt

DONE IN TRIPLICATE.
THE WHITE HOUSE,
    March 1, 1934.

7. Executive Order 6777, June 30, 1934
(Abolishes National Planning Board, establishes National Resources Board.)

By virtue of the authority vested in me by the National Industrial Recovery Act (Public, No. 67, 73d Congress), I hereby establish the National Resources Board, consisting of the Secretary of the Interior (Chairman), the Secretary of War, the Secretary of Agriculture, the Secretary of Commerce, the Secretary of Labor, the Federal Emergency Relief Administrator, Frederic A. Delano, Charles E. Merriam, and Wesley C. Mitchell.

An Advisory Committee, consisting of Frederic A. Delano (Chairman), Charles E. Merriam, and Wesley C. Mitchell, is hereby constituted, to which additional members may be added from time to time by order of the President.

There is also established a Technical Committee with no fixed membership or tenure of office to be selected by the Board.

The functions of the Board shall be to prepare and present to the President a program and plan of procedure dealing with the physical, social, governmental and economic aspects of public policies for the development and use of land, water and other national resources, and such related subjects as may from time to time be referred to it by the President.

The Board shall submit a report on land and water use on or before December 1, 1934. The program and plan shall include the coordination of projects of Federal, State and local governments and the proper division of responsibility and the fair division of cost among the several governmental authorities.

The Board may appoint such officers and employees without regard to the Classification Act or Executive Orders fixing salary schedules, and establish such field offices, as in its opinion may be required; and defray, where necessary, the cost of such investigations and reports as may be made at the request of the Board by other departments and agencies of the Federal Government.

The National Planning Board of the Federal Emergency Administration of Public Works is hereby abolished, and all of its powers, duties, records, personnel, equipment, and funds are hereby transferred to the National Resources Board.

The Committee on National Land Problems, created by Executive Order No. 6693, of April 28, 1934, is hereby abolished.

The Federal Emergency Administration of Public Works is hereby directed to allot to the National Resources Board the sum of One Hundred Thousand Dollars ($100,000), and such additional sums as may be approved from time to time by the President, to carry out its functions.

THE WHITE HOUSE,
    June 30, 1934.

Franklin D. Roosevelt

8. Executive Order 7065, June 7, 1935
(Abolishes National Resources Board, establishes National Resources Committee.)

By virtue of and pursuant to the authority vested in me under the Emergency Relief Appropriation Act of 1935, approved April 8, 1935, 49 Stat. 115, and to provide a means of obtaining information essential to a wise employment of the emergency appropriation made by said Act, I hereby establish an agency within the Government to be known as the National Resources Committee, consisting of the Secretary of the Interior (Chairman), the Secretary of War, the Secretary of Agriculture, the Secretary of Commerce, the Secretary of Labor, the Federal Emergency Relief Administrator, Frederic A. Delano, Charles E. Merriam, and Wesley C. Mitchell, who shall serve as members without compensation.

A committee advisory thereto, consisting of Frederic A. Delano (Chairman), Charles E. Merriam, and Wesley C. Mitchell, is hereby constituted, to which advisory committee members may be added from time to time by the President. The compensation of the members of the advisory committee shall be fixed by the President.

I hereby prescribe the functions and duties of the National Resources Committee as follows:

(a) To collect, prepare and make available to the President, with recommendations, such plans, data and information as may be helpful to a planned development and use of land, water, and other national resources, and such related subjects as may be referred to it by the President.

(b) To consult and cooperate with agencies of the Federal Government, with the States and municipalities or agencies thereof, and with any public or private planning or research agencies or institutions, in carrying out any of its duties and functions.

(c) To receive and record all proposed Federal projects involving the acquisition of land (including transfer of land jurisdiction) and land research projects, and in an advisory capacity to provide the agencies concerned with such information or data as may be pertinent to the projects. All executive agencies shall notify the National Resources Committee of such projects as they develop, before major field activities are undertaken.

In the performance of such duties and functions and within such amounts as may be allocated by the President, expenditures are hereby authorized for necessary supplies and equipment; law books and books of reference, directories, periodicals, newspapers and press clippings; travel expenses, including the expense of attendance at meetings when specifically authorized by said committee; rental at the seat of Government and elsewhere; printing and binding; and incidental expenses; and I hereby authorize the said committee to accept and utilize such voluntary and uncompensated services and, with the consent of the State, such State and local officers and employees, and appoint without regard to the provisions of the civil service laws, such officers and employees, as may be necessary, prescribe their duties and responsibilities and, without regard to the Classification Act of 1923, as amended, fix their compensation: *Provided*, That in so far as practicable, the persons employed under the authority of this Executive Order shall be selected from those receiving relief.

The National Resources Board and the advisory committee established by Executive Order No. 6777, dated June 30, 1934, are hereby abolished, and all personnel, property, records, rights, etc., of said Board are hereby transferred to said National Resources Committee.

There is hereby transferred to the National Resources Committee the unexpended balance of all moneys heretofore made available for expenditure by the National Resources Board, which moneys shall be available for discharge of obligations lawfully incurred by said Board; and for the expenses of the National Resources Committee hereunder funds will be hereafter allocated to said Committee from the appropriation made by the Emergency Relief Appropriation Act of 1935.

This Executive Order shall take effect at the close of business on June 15, 1935.

Franklin D. Roosevelt

THE WHITE HOUSE,
    June 7, 1935.

9. Reorganization Act of 1939

AN ACT

To provide for reorganizing agencies of the Government, and for other purposes.

Be it enacted by the Senate and House of Representatives of the United States of America in Congress assembled, That this Act may be cited as the "Reorganization Act of 1939".

TITLE I—*Reorganization*

PART I

SECTION 1. (a) The Congress hereby declares that by reason of continued national deficits beginning in 1931 it is desirable to reduce substantially Government expenditures and that such reduction may be accomplished in some measure by proceeding immediately under the provisions of this Act. The President shall investigate the organization of all agencies of the Government and shall determine what changes therein are necessary to accomplish the following purposes:

(1) To reduce expenditures to the fullest extent consistent with the efficient operation of the Government;

(2) To increase the efficiency of the operations of the Government to the fullest extent practicable within the revenues:

(3) To group, coordinate, and consolidate agencies of the Government, as nearly as may be, according to major purposes;

(4) To reduce the number of agencies by consolidating those having similar functions under a single head, and to abolish such agencies as may not be necessary for the efficient conduct of the Government; and

(5) To eliminate overlapping and duplication of effort.

(b) The Congress declares that the public interest demands the carrying out of the purposes specified in subsection (a) and that such purposes may be accomplished in great measure by proceeding immediately under the provisions of this title, and can be accomplished more speedily thereby than by the enactment of specific legislation.

SEC. 2. When used in this title, the term "agency," means any executive department, commission, independent establishment, corporation owned or controlled by the United States, board, bureau, division, service, office, authority, or administration, in the executive branch of the Government.

SEC. 3. No reorganization plan under section 4 shall provide—

(a) For the abolition or transfer of an executive department or all the functions thereof or for the establishment of any new executive department;

(b) In the case of the following agencies, for the transfer, consolidation, or abolition of the whole or any part of such agency or of its head, or of all or any of the functions of such agency or of its head: Civil Service Commission, Coast Guard, Engineer Corps of the United States Army, Mississippi River Commission, Federal Communications Commission, Federal Power

Commission, Federal Trade Commission, General Accounting Office, Interstate Commerce Commission, National Labor Relations Board, Securities and Exchange Commission, Board of Tax Appeals, United States Employees' Compensation Commission, United States Maritime Commission, United States Tariff Commission, Veterans' Administration, National Mediation Board, National Railroad Adjustment Board, Railroad Retirement Board, the Federal Deposit Insurance Corporation, or the Board of Governors of the Federal Reserve System; or

(c) For changing the name of any executive department or the title of its head, or for designating any agency as "Department" or its head as "Secretary"; or

(d) For the continuation of any agency beyond the period authorized by law for the existence of such agency; or

(e) For the continuation of any function of any agency beyond the period authorized by law for the exercise of such function; or

(f) For authorizing any agency to exercise any function which is not expressly authorized by law.

Sec. 4. Whenever the President, after investigation, finds that—

(a) the transfer of the whole or any part of any agency or the functions thereof to the jurisdiction and control of any other agency; or

(b) the consolidation of the functions vested in any agency; or

(c) the abolition of the whole or any part of any agency which agency or part (by reason of transfers under this Act or otherwise, or by reason of termination of its functions in any manner) does not have, or upon the taking effect of the reorganizations specified in the reorganization plan will not have, any functions, is necessary to accomplish one or more of the purposes of section 1 (a), he shall—

(d) prepare a reorganization plan for the making of the transfers, consolidations, and abolitions, as to which he has made findings and which he includes in the plan. Such plan shall also—

(1) designate, in such cases as he deems necessary, the name of any agency affected by a reorganization and the title of its head;

(2) make provision for the transfer or other disposition of the records, property (including office equipment), and personnel affected by such transfer, consolidation, or abolition;

(3) make provision for the transfer of such unexpended balances of appropriations available for use in connection with the function or agency transferred or consolidated, as he deems necessary by reason of the transfer or consolidation for use in connection with the transferred or consolidated functions, or for the use of the agency to which the transfer is made, but such unexpended balances so transferred shall be used only for the purposes for which such appropriation is originally made;

(4) make provision for winding up the affairs of the agency abolished; and

(e) transmit such plan (bearing an identifying number) to the

Congress, together with a declaration that, with respect to each transfer, consolidation, or abolition referred to in paragraph (a), (b), or (c) of this section and specified in the plan, he has found that such transfer, consolidation, or abolition is necessary to accomplish one or more of the purposes of section 1 (a). The delivery to both Houses shall be on the same day and shall be made to each House while it is in session.

The President, in his message transmitting a reorganization plan, shall state the reduction of expenditures which it is probable will be brought about by the taking effect of the reorganizations specified in the plan.

SEC. 5. The reorganizations specified in the plan shall take effect in accordance with the plan:

(a) Upon the expiration of sixty calendar days after the date on which the plan is transmitted to the Congress, but only if during such sixty-day period there has not been passed by the two Houses a concurrent resolution stating in substance that the Congress does not favor the reorganization plan.

(b) If the Congress adjourns sine die before the expiration of the sixty-day period, a new sixty-day period shall begin on the opening day of the next succeeding regular or special session. A similar rule shall be applicable in the case of subsequent adjournments sine die before the expiration of sixty days.

SEC. 6. No reorganization under this title shall have the effect—

(a) of continuing any agency or function beyond the time when it would have terminated if the reorganization had not been made; or

(b) of continuing any function beyond the time when the agency in which it was vested before the reorganization would have terminated if the reorganization had not been made; or

(c) of authorizing any agency to exercise any function which is not expressly authorized by law.

SEC. 7. For the purposes of this title any transfer, consolidation, abolition, designation, disposition, or winding up of affairs, referred to in section 4 (d), shall be deemed a "reorganization".

SEC. 8. (al) All orders, rules, regulations, permits, or other privileges made, issued, or granted by or in respect of any agency or function transferred to, or consolidated with, any other agency or function under the provisions of this title, and in effect at the time of the transfer or consolidation, shall continue in effect to the same extent as if such transfer or consolidation had not occurred, until modified, superseded, or repealed.

(b) No suit, action, or other proceeding lawfully commenced by or against the head of any agency or other officer of the United States, in his official capacity or in relation to the discharge of his official duties, shall abate by reason of any transfer of authority, power, and duties from one officer or agency of the Government to another under the provisions of this title, but the court, on motion or supplemental petition filed at any time within twelve months after such transfer takes effect, showing a necessity for a survival of such suit, action, or other proceeding to obtain a settlement of the questions involved, may allow the same to be maintained by or against the head of the agency or other officer of the United States to whom the authority, powers, and duties are transferred.

(c) All laws relating to any agency or function transferred to, or consolidated with, any other agency or function under the provisions of this title, shall, insofar as such laws are not inapplicable, remain in full force and effect.

SEC. 9. The appropriations or portions of appropriations unexpended by reason of the operation of this title shall not be used for any purpose, but shall be impounded and returned to the Treasury.

SEC. 10. (a) Whenever the employment of any person is terminated by a reduction of personnel as a result of a reorganization effected under this title, such person shall thereafter be given preference, when qualified, whenever an appointment is made in the executive branch of the Government, but such preference shall not be effective for a period longer than twelve months from the date the employment of such person is so terminated.

(b) Any transfer of personnel under this title shall be without change in classification or compensation, except that this requirement shall not operate after the end of the fiscal year during which the transfer is made to prevent the adjustment of classification or compensation to conform to the duties to which such transferred personnel may be assigned.

SEC. 11. If the reorganizations specified in a reorganization plan take effect, the reorganization plan shall be printed in the Statutes at Large in the same volume as the public laws, and shall be printed in the Federal Register.

SEC. 12. No reorganization specified in a reorganization plan shall take effect unless the plan is transmitted to the Congress before January 21, 1941.

PART 2

SEC. 21. The following sections of this part are enacted by the Congress:

(a) As an exercise of the rule-making power of the Senate and the House of Representatives, respectively, and as such they shall be considered as part of the rules of each House, respectively, but applicable only with respect to the procedure to be followed in such House in the case of resolutions (as defined in section 22); and such rules shall supersede other rules only to the extent that they are inconsistent therewith; and

(b) With full recognition of the constitutional right of either House to change such rules (so far as relating to the procedure in such House) at any time, in the same manner and to the same extent as in the case of any other rule of such House.

SEC. 22. As used in this part, the term "resolution" means only a concurrent resolution of the two Houses of Congress, the matter after the resolving clause of which is as follows: "That the Congress does not favor the reorganization plan numbered ———— transmitted to Congress by the President on ———— ————, 19—.", the blank spaces therein being appropriately filled; and does not include a concurrent resolution which specifies more than one reorganization plan.

SEC. 23. A resolution with respect to a reorganization plan shall be referred to a committee (and all resolutions with respect to the same plan shall be referred to the same committee) by the President of the Senate or the Speaker of the House of Representatives, as the case may be.

SEC. 24. (a) If the committee to which has been referred a resolution with respect to a reorganization plan has not reported it before the expiration of ten calendar days after its introduction (or, in the case of a resolution received from the other House, ten calendar days after its receipt), it shall then (but not before) be in order to move either to discharge the committee from further consideration of such resolution, or to discharge the committee from further consideration of any other resolution with respect to such reorganization plan which has been referred to the committee.

(b) Such motion may be made only by a person favoring the resolution, shall be highly privileged (except that it may not be made after the committee has reported a resolution with respect to the same reorganization plan), and debate thereon shall be limited to not to exceed one hour, to be equally divided between those favoring and those opposing the resolution. No amendment to such motion shall be in order, and it shall not be in order to move to reconsider the vote by which such motion is agreed to or disagreed to.

(c) If the motion to discharge is agreed to or disagreed to, such motion may not be renewed, nor may another motion to discharge the committees be made with respect to any other resolution with respect to the same reorganization plan.

SEC. 25. (a) When the committee has reported, or has been discharged from further consideration of, a resolution with respect to a reorganization plan, it shall at any time thereafter be in order (even though a previous motion to the same effect has been disagreed to) to move to proceed to the consideration of such resolution. Such motion shall be highly privileged and shall not be debatable. No amendment to such motion shall be in order and it shall not be in order to move to reconsider the vote by which such motion is agreed to or disagreed to.

(b) Debate on the resolution shall be limited to not to exceed ten hours, which shall be equally divided between those favoring and those opposing the resolution. A motion further to limit debate shall not be debatable. No amendment to, or motion to recommit, the resolution shall be in order, and it shall not be in order to move to reconsider the vote by which the resolution is agreed to or disagreed to.

SEC. 26. (a) All motions to postpone, made with respect to the discharge from committee, or the consideration of, a resolution with respect to a reorganization plan, and all motions to proceed to the consideration of other business, shall be decided without debate.

(b) All appeals from the decisions of the Chair relating to the application of the rules of the Senate or the House of Representatives, as the case may be, to the procedure relating to a resolution with respect to a reorganization plan shall be decided without debate.

SEC. 27. If, prior to the passage by one House of a resolution of that House with respect to a reorganization plan, such House receives from the other House a resolution with respect to the same plan, then—

(a) If no resolution of the first House with respect to such plan has been referred to committee, no other resolution with respect to the same plan may be reported or (despite the provisions of section 24 (a)) be made the subject of a motion to discharge.

(b) If a resolution of the first House with respect to such plan has been referred to committee—

(1) the procedure with respect to that or other resolutions of such House with respect to such plan which have been referred to committee shall be the same as if no resolution from the other House with respect to such plan had been received; but

(2) on any vote on final passage of a resolution of the first House with respect to such plan the resolution from the other House with respect to such plan shall be automatically substituted for the resolution of the first House.

TITLE II—*Budgetary Control*

Sec. 201. Section 2 of the Budget and Accounting Act, 1921 (U. S. C., 1934 edition, title 31, sec. 2), is amended by inserting after the word "including" the words "any independent regulatory commission or board and".

TITLE III—*Administrative Assistants*

Sec. 301. The President is authorized to appoint not to exceed six administrative assistants and to fix the compensation of each at the rate of not more than $10,000 per annum. Each such administrative assistant shall perform such duties as the President may prescribe.

Approved, April 3, 1939.

10. Presidential Reorganization Plan No. 1, April 3, 1939
(53 Stat 1423)
(Abolishes National Resources Committee, establishes National Resources Planning Board, abolishes Federal Employment Stabilization Office.)

REORGANIZATION PLAN NO. I

Prepared by the President and transmitted to the Senate and the House of Representatives in Congress assembled, April 25, 1939, pursuant to the provisions of the Reorganization Act of 1939, approved April 3, 1939

PART 1.—EXECUTIVE OFFICE OF THE PRESIDENT

Section 1. *Bureau of the Budget.*—The Bureau of the Budget and all of its functions and personnel (including the Director and Assistant Director) are hereby transferred from the Treasury Department to the Executive Office of the President; and the functions of the Bureau of the Budget shall be administered by the Director thereof under the direction and supervision of the President.

Section 2. *Central Statistical Board.*—The Central Statistical Board and all of its functions and personnel (including the Chairman and the members of the Board) are hereby transferred to the Bureau of the Budget in the Executive Office of the President. The Chairman of the Board shall perform such administrative duties as the Director of the Bureau of the Budget shall direct.

Section 3. *Central Statistical Committee Abolished and Functions Transferred.*—The Central Statistical Committee is hereby abolished, and its functions are transferred to the Director of the Bureau of the Budget to be administered by him under the direction and supervision of the President. The Director of the Bureau of the Budget shall promptly wind up any outstanding affairs of the Central Statistical Committee.

Section 4. *National Resources Planning Board.*—(*a*) The functions of the National Resources Committee, established by Executive Order No. 7065 of June 7, 1935, and its personnel (except the members of the Committee) and all of the functions of the Federal Employment Stabilization Office in the Department of Commerce and its personnel are hereby transferred to the Executive Office of the President. The functions transferred by this section are hereby consolidated, and they shall be administered under the direction and supervision of the President by the National Resources Planning Board (hereafter referred to as the Board), which shall be composed of five members to be appointed by the President. The President shall designate one of the members of the Board as Chairman and another as Vice Chairman. The Vice Chairman shall act as Chairman in the absence of the Chairman or in the event of a vacancy in that office. The members of the Board shall be compensated at the rate of $50 per day for time spent in attending and traveling to and from meetings, or in otherwise exercising the functions and duties of the Board, plus the actual cost of transportation: *Provided,* That in no case shall a member be entitled to receive compensation for more than thirty days' service in two consecutive months.

(*b*) The Board shall determine the rules of its own proceedings, and a majority of its members in office shall constitute a quorum for the transaction of business, but the Board may function notwithstanding vacancies.

(*c*) The Board may appoint necessary officers and employees and may delegate to such officers authority to perform such duties and make such expenditures as may be necessary.

Section 5. *National Resources Committee Abolished.*—The National Resources Committee is hereby abolished, and its outstanding affairs shall be wound up by the National Resources Planning Board.

Section 6. *Federal Employment Stabilization Office Abolished.*—The Federal Employment Stabilization Office is hereby abolished, and the Secretary of Commerce shall promptly wind up its affairs.

Section 7. *Transfer of Records and Property.*—All records and property (including office equipment) of the several agencies transferred, or the functions of which are transferred, by this Part are hereby transferred to the Executive Office of the President for use in the administration of the agencies and functions transferred by this Part.

Section 8. *Transfer of Funds.*—So much of the unexpended balances of appropriations, allocations, or other funds available (including those available for the fiscal year ending June 30, 1940) for the use of any agency in the exercise of any functions transferred by this Part, or for the use of the head of any department or agency in the exercise of any functions so transferred, as the Director of the Bureau of the Budget shall determine, shall be transferred to the Executive Office of the President for use in connection with the exercise of functions transferred by this Part. In determining the amount to be transferred the Director of the Bureau of the Budget may include an amount to provide for the liquidation of obligations incurred against such appropriations, allocations, or other funds prior to the transfer: *Provided,* That the use of the unexpended balances of appropriations, allocations, or other funds transferred by this section shall be subject to the provisions of section 4 (d)(3) and section 9 of the Reorganization Act of 1939.

Section 9. *Personnel.*—Any personnel transferred by this Part found to be in excess of the personnel necessary for the efficient administration of the functions transferred by this Part shall be re-transferred under existing law to other positions in the Government service, or separated from the service subject to the provisions of section 10(a) of the Reorganization Act of 1939.

11. Executive Order 8248, September 8, 1939
(Organizes the Office of the President, including defining the role of the National Resources Planning Board in that Office.)

EXECUTIVE ORDER 3243—ESTABLISHING THE DIVISIONS OF THE EXECUTIVE OFFICE OF THE PRESIDENT AND DEFINING THEIR FUNCTIONS AND DUTIES

By virtue of the authority vested in me by the Constitution and Statutes, and in order to effectuate the purposes of the Reorganization Act of 1939, Public No. 19, Seventy-sixth Congress, approved April 3, 1939, and of Reorganization Plans Nos. I and II submitted to the Congress by the President and made effective as of July 1, 1939 by Public Resolution No. 2, Seventy-sixth Congress, approved June 7, 1939, by organizing the Executive Office of the President with functions and duties so prescribed and responsibilities so fixed that the President will have adequate machinery for the administrative management of the Executive branch of the Government, it is hereby ordered as follows:

I

There shall be within the Executive Office of the President the following principal divisions, namely: (1) The White House Office, (2) the Bureau of the Budget, (3) the National Resources Planning Board, (4) the Liaison Office for Personnel Management, (5) the Office of Government Reports, and (6) in the event of a national emergency, or threat of a national emergency, such office for emergency management as the President shall determine.

II

The functions and duties of the divisions of the Executive Office of the President are hereby defined as follows:

1. *The White House Office.*—In general, to serve the President in an intimate capacity in the performance of the many detailed activities incident to his immediate office. To that end, The White House Office shall be composed of the following principal subdivisions, with particular functions and duties as indicated:

(a) *The Secretaries to the President.*—To facilitate and maintain quick and easy communication with the Congress, the individual members of the Congress, the heads of executive departments and agencies, the press, the radio, and the general public.

(b) *The Executive Clerk.*—To provide for the orderly handling of documents and correspondence within The White House Office, and to organize and supervise all clerical services and procedure relating thereto.

(c) *The Administrative Assistants to the President.*—To assist the President in such matters as he may direct, and at the specific request of the President, to get information and to condense and summarize it for his use. These Administrative Assistants shall be personal aides to the President and shall have no authority over anyone in any department or agency, including the Executive Office of the President, other than the personnel assigned to their immediate offices. In no event shall the Administrative Assistants be interposed between the President and the head of any department or agency, or between the President and any one of the divisions in the Executive Office of the President.

2. *The Bureau of the Budget.*—(a) To assist the President in the preparation of the Budget and the formulation of the fiscal program of the Government.

(b) To supervise and control the administration of the Budget.

(c) To conduct research in the development of improved plans of administrative management, and to advise the executive departments and agencies of the Government with respect to improved administrative organization and practice.

(d) To aid the President to bring about more efficient and economical conduct of Government service.

(e) To assist the President by clearing and coordinating departmental advice on proposed legislation and by making recommendations as to Presidential action on legislative enactments, in accordance with past practice.

(f) To assist in the consideration and clearance and, where necessary, in the preparation of proposed Executive orders and proclamations, in accordance with the provisions of Executive Order No. 7298 of February 18,1936.

(g) To plan and promote the improvement, development, and coordination of Federal and other statistical services.

(h) To keep the President informed of the progress of activities by agencies of the Government with respect to work proposed, work actually initiated, and work completed, together with the relative timing of work between the several agencies of the Government; all to the end that the work programs of the several agencies of the Executive branch of the Government may be coordinated and that the monies appropriated by the Congress may be expended in the most economical manner possible with the least possible overlapping and duplication of effort.

3. *The National Resources Planning Board.*—(a) To survey, collect data on, and analyze problems pertaining to national resources, both natural and human, and to recommend to the President and the Congress long-time plans and programs for the wise use and fullest development of such resources.

(b) To consult with Federal, regional, state, local, and private agencies in developing orderly programs of public works and to list for the President and the Congress all proposed public works in the order of their relative importance with respect to (1) the greatest good to the greatest number of people, (2) the emergency necessities of the Nation, and (3) the social, economic, and cultural advancement of the people of the United States.

(c) To inform the President of the general trend of economic conditions and to recommend measures leading to their improvement or stabilization.

(d) To act as a clearing house and means of coordination for planning activities, linking together various levels and fields of planning.

4. *The Liaison Office for Personnel Management.*—In accordance with the statement of purpose made in the Message to Congress of April 25, 1939, accompanying Reorganization Plan No. I, one of the Administrative Assistants to the President, authorized in the Reorganization Act of 1939, shall be designated by the President as Liaison Officer for Personnel Management and shall be in charge of the Liaison Office for Personnel Management. The functions of this office shall be:

(a) To assist the President in the better execution of the duties imposed upon him by the Provisions of the Constitution and the laws with respect to personnel management, especially the Civil Service Act of 1883, as amended, and the rules promulgated by the President under authority of that Act.

(b) To assist the President in maintaining closer contact with all agencies dealing with personnel matters insofar as they affect or tend to determine the personnel management policies of the Executive branch of the Government.

5. *The Office of Government Reports.*—(a) To provide a central clearing house through which individual citizens, organizations of citizens, state or local governmental bodies, and, where appropriate, agencies of the Federal Government, may transmit inquiries and complaints and receive advice and information.

(b) To assist the President in dealing with special problems requiring the clearance of information between the Federal Government and state and local governments and private institutions.

(c) To collect and distribute information concerning the purposes and activities of executive departments and agencies for the use of the Congress, administrative officials, and the public.

(d) To keep the President currently informed of the opinions, desires, and complaints of citizens and groups of citizens and of state and local governments with respect to the work of Federal agencies.

(e) To report to the President on the basis of the information it has obtained possible ways and means for reducing the cost of the operation of the Government.

III

The Bureau of the Budget, the National Resources Planning Board, and the Liaison Office for Personnel Management shall constitute the three principal management arms of the Government for the (1) preparation and administration of the Budget and improvement of administrative management and organization, (2) planning for conservation and utilization of the resources of the Nation, and (3) coordination of the administration of personnel, none of which belongs in any department but which are necessary for the over-all management of the Executive branch of the Government, so that the President will be enabled the better to carry out his Constitutional duties of informing the Congress with respect to the state of the Union, of recommending appropriate and expedient measures, and of seeing that the laws are faithfully executed.

IV

To facilitate the orderly transaction of business within each of the five divisions herein defined and to clarify the relations of these divisions with each other and with the President, I direct that the Bureau of the Budget, the National Resources Planning Board, the Liaison Office for Personnel Management, and the Office of Government Reports shall respectively prepare regulations for the governance of their internal organizations and procedures. Such regulations shall be in effect when approved by the President and shall remain in force until changed by new regulations approved by him. The President will prescribe regulations governing the conduct of the business of the division of The White House Office.

V

The Director of the Bureau of the Budget shall prepare a consolidated budget for the Executive Office of the President for submission by the President to the Congress. Annually, pursuant to the regular request issued by the Bureau of the Budget, each division of the Executive Office of the President shall prepare and submit to the Bureau estimates of proposed appropriations for the succeeding fiscal year. The form of the estimates and the manner of their consideration for incorporation in the Budget shall be the same as prescribed for other Executive departments and agencies.

The Bureau of the Budget shall likewise perform with respect to the several divisions of the Executive Office of the President such functions and duties relating to supplemental estimates, apportionments, and budget administration as are exercised by it for other agencies of the Federal Government.

VI

Space already has been assigned in the State, War and Navy Building, adjacent to The White House, sufficient to accommodate the Bureau of the Budget with its various divisions (including the Central Statistical Board), the central office of the National Resources Planning Board, the Liaison Office for Personnel Management, and the Administrative Assistants to the President, and although for the time being, a considerable portion of the work of the National Resources Planning Board and all of that of the Office of Government Reports will have to be conducted in other quarters, if and when the Congress makes provision for the housing of the Department of State in a building appropriate to its function and dignity and provision is made for the other agencies now accommodated in the State, War and Navy Building, it then will be possible to bring into this building, close to The White House, all of the personnel of the Executive Office of the President except The White House Office.

This Order shall take effect on September 11th 1939.

Franklin D. Roosevelt

THE WHITE HOUSE
    September 8, 1939.

12. Executive Order 8455, June 26, 1940
(Establishes a planning procedure for federal public works and defines the role of the National Resources Planning Board therein.)

EXECUTIVE ORDER 8455—DESIGNATING ADDITIONAL CONSTRUCTION AGENCIES AND PROVIDING FOR THE PLANNING AND PROGRAMMING OF CONSTRUCTION UNDERTAKEN OR AIDED BY THE FEDERAL GOVERNMENT

By virtue of the authority vested in me by the Constitution and by the laws of the United States, including the Employment Stabilization Act of

1931 (46 Stat. 1084), the Budget and Accounting Act, 1921 (42 Stat. 20), and Reorganization Plan No. I, made effective July 1, 1939, by Public Resolution No. 20, 76th Congress, approved June 7, 1939, it is ordered as follows:

1. I hereby designate as "construction agencies", in addition to those agencies listed in section 2(d) of the said Employment Stabilization Act of 1931, all departments, independent offices and establishments, bureaus, agencies, and divisions of the Federal Government, including Government-owned corporations, which now or may hereafter:

(a) Plan, initiate, undertake, or engage in construction financed in whole or in part by the Federal Government, by contract, force account, Government plant and hired labor, or other similar procedures (all such agencies being hereinafter referred to as "construction agencies (Class I)"), or

(b) Aid construction activity through grants-in-aid, loans, or other forms of financial assistance or through guaranties from the Federal Government (all such agencies being hereinafter referred to as "construction agencies (Class II)").

2. In order to facilitate and assist in the advance planning of construction undertaken by the Federal Government, all construction agencies (Class I) shall prepare and keep up-to-date, in accordance with section 8 of the Employment Stabilization Act of 1931, six-year advance plans and programs of their public-works construction, to be financed in whole or in part by the Federal Government, and shall submit reports on such plans and programs and on any such construction in the manner herein provided.

3. Beginning with the submission to the Bureau of the Budget in September 1940 of the estimates for the Budget for the fiscal year 1942, each construction agency (Class I) shall submit annually with its budget estimates, for the joint use of the Bureau of the Budget and the National Resources Planning Board, its six-year advance plan and program of public-works construction with a schedule of priorities for the projects assigned for construction to each of the six years.

4. Each construction agency (Class I) shall submit a report to the National Resources Planning Board, for the joint use of the Board and the Bureau of the Budget, when the agency undertakes any examination, survey, investigation, or research directed toward the preparation of any reports, plans, programs, or estimates of construction costs for any project proposed to be constructed and financed in whole or in part by the Federal Government.

5. Each construction agency (Class I) shall submit a report to the National Resources Planning Board, for the joint use of the Board and the Bureau of the Budget, when the agency completes any examination, survey, investigation, or research directed toward the preparation of any reports, plans, programs, or estimates of construction costs for any project to be constructed and financed in whole or in part by the Federal Government. Any subsequent revision by a construction agency (Class I) of an

original report on any such examination, survey, investigation, or research shall be reported to the Board in the manner prescribed herein.

6. Each construction agency (Class I), in submitting any report to the Congress or to any committee or member thereof on the results of any examination, survey, investigation, or research directed toward the preparation of any reports, plans, programs, or estimates of construction costs for any project to be constructed and financed in whole or in part by the Federal Government, shall include therein a statement as to the relationship of such report to the program of the President. Such reports shall be submitted to the Bureau of the Budget before the agency submits them to the Congress or to any committee or member thereof, and the Bureau of the Budget shall advise the agency as to the relationship of such report to the program of the President.

7. Each construction agency (Class I) shall make such reports to the National Resources Planning Board, for the joint use of the Board and the Bureau of the Budget, as may be requested by the Board or required by the rules and regulations issued hereunder, on the status of any project being constructed and financed in whole or in part by the Federal Government.

8. Each construction agency (Class II) shall submit to the National Resources Planning Board, for the joint use of the Board and the Bureau of the Budget, such reports as the Board may request on any of its plans, programs, or estimates (including any examination, survey, investigation, or research directed toward the preparation of any reports, plans, programs, or estimates) of the cost of any construction for which financial aid, assistance, or guaranty is to be provided by such agency, or on the status of any construction activity receiving any financial aid, assistance, or guaranty from such agency.

9. The Director of the Bureau of the Budget and the Chairman of the National Resources Planning Board shall jointly make such detailed rules and regulations as may be necessary to provide for the effective operation of this Executive order, and whenever necessary shall jointly determine whether a particular agency is to be regarded as a construction agency (Class I) or as a construction agency (Class II).

10. If the Director of the Bureau of the Budget and the Chairman of the National Resources Planning Board shall jointly find that the immediate or future application of any or all of the provisions of this Executive order or of any rules and regulations issued hereunder is impracticable, they may, upon their own initiative or upon request from the chief of any construction agency, temporarily exempt any such agency or any project from such provisions.

Franklin D. Roosevelt

THE WHITE HOUSE
    June 26, 1940.

13. Independent Offices Appropriation Act 1944 (57 Stat 170)
(Abolishes National Resources Planning Board effective August 31,
1943 and directs that its functions shall not be transferred to any other
agency.)

NATIONAL RESOURCES PLANNING BOARD

Salaries and expenses: For all expenses incident to the discontinuance
of the work of the Board, including personal services in the District of
Columbia and elsewhere, printing and binding, traveling expenses, and the
payment of accumulated and accrued annual leave of employees of the
Board due them after June 30, 1943, $30,000: *Provided,* That the National
Resources Planning Board is abolished effective August 31, 1943, and the
functions exercised by such Board shall not be transferred to any other
agency and shall not be performed after such date except as hereafter provided by law or as authorized in the ensuing proviso of this paragraph with
respect to winding up the Board's affairs: *Provided further,* That the Director
of the Board is authorized after August 31, 1943, and until January 1, 1944,
to perform such duties and to exercise such administrative authority as may
be incident to the effectuation of the discontinuance of the Board: *Provided
further,* That the records and files of the Board shall be transferred to the
National Archives.

The appropriation herein made for the National Resources Planning
Board shall constitute the total amount to be available for obligation by such
agency during the fiscal year 1944 and shall not be supplemented by funds
from any source.

Appendix B

Chronological List of Major Reports

The National Archives in March 1946 prepared a *Preliminary List of Published and Unpublished Reports of the National Resources Planning Board 1933–1943* (SR 3 (46-3) Record Group No. 187) which includes about 1600 items. This report is extremely valuable as a guide to the National Resources Planning Board materials in Archives. ". . . it is both the most complete list, with respect to number of titles, of that agency's printed and processed reports that has been attempted in a single compilation and the only listing anywhere of a considerable quantity of reports that exist only in manuscript form. . . . Regional office reports are included in the appendix of this list, and in considerable number, but only insofar as they are found in the Washington office . . . or as their presence in the regional office files has been disclosed by reference service in response to particular requests." (p. vii) At the same time, Archives warns that its list ". . . does not, therefore, purport to be a complete list of the reports of the Board . . .", because it is limited to materials physically within the Archives and may omit some reports not available there. For the purposes of this study, the Archives' list is sufficiently near complete to be fully adequate.

The Archives *List* is not a publication, in the sense that it has been generally available to the public. "It has been compiled primarily for internal use in the National Archives. . . . A few copies have been reproduced in multilithed form in order that extra copies may be available for the convenience of members of the staff of the National Archives and for limited distribution to Government officials and others having specific need for it." (p. ii) The *List* is organized in three parts: Part I consists of reports relating to particular subjects, within each section of which the reports are listed by title alphabetically; Part II consists of general recommendations and administrative reports and organization materials, arranged chronologically;

and Part III consists of circular letters, circulars, and bulletins, also chronologically. Part I takes 89 pages in the *List,* while Part II includes only 8
pages and Part III 5 pages. To these Parts is added an appendix of regional
reports, arranged by region, thereunder by subject, and finally alphabetically
by title, and it includes 36 pages of the *List.*

The Archives *List* is extremely valuable for its purpose but its very detail
makes the grasping of the range and meaning of NRPB's reporting difficult.
Many of the documents listed were of limited or transitory value—the big
trees are obscured by the undergrowth of bushes. For my purposes, a
selection of "major reports," while difficult, is essential and also for my
purposes a different arrangement of the list of reports is necessary. These
are discussed below.

The National Resources Planning Board had published, in one place or
another, "Publications of the National Resources Planning Board 1934–
1943." The purpose of that publication was to advise the general public
how it could obtain reports of the Board. That publication mostly, but not
invariably, omitted mimeographed or other processed reports and it did
not include the internal documents, preliminary drafts, and other materials
included in the Archives *List.* It did include reports about regions if these
reports had been issued by the Board in Washington, but it excluded
regional offices of the NRPB. The arrangement of this list is by subject
matter and, within each subject matter group, chronologically. The listing
is somewhat confusing since some titles are included under the subject matter
heading and again under a grouping of pamphlets. The NRPB list was
undoubtedly highly useful for its purpose, that of informing the general
public. The list also includes some "related works" or government publications closely related to NRPB work and interest but not strictly by the NRPB
itself. The arrangement of materials in the NRPB list is not well suited
to my purposes.

The focus of this appendix is chronological, for several reasons. Time
flows only in one direction and a chronological listing is incontrovertible in
its arrangement, whereas a subject matter listing may be open to varying
interpretations either by the compiler of the list or by its user. My list, as
will be seen, does include a subject matter designation of each report.
Admittedly, the reader who wants a complete account of the "land" or
"water" reports has to sort through the chronological list to get it. There are
problems in a few cases of knowing what the date of publication actually
was. But my major reason for compiling a chronological list was that I am
interested to trace the development and the operations of NRPB and a
chronological account of the relationships among the numerous activities and
interests of NRPB is extremely useful for my purpose.

In the table at the end of this appendix, the NRPB publications are
arranged chronologically by date, using both month and year of publication
if available. When only a year is given, the report is listed between the
June and the July reports of that year. The governing date is the one listed
on the cover page of the report, if one is given there and if there is no good

reason to challenge it. In some cases, the date is that of the transmittal letter of the report, if there is one. For a few, resort had to be to the Government Printing Office identification date for the report. And a few reports are simply undated by any measure; these have been included at the end of the table. It is obvious that this chronological listing of reports is not an annotated bibliography, much less an evaluation of the significance or the consequences of the publication. These latter functions are, to a degree, exercised in the main body of this study.

A brief account of the procedure I followed in compiling this chronological list of NRPB reports may be helpful in understanding its nature. I worked primarily from the Archives *Preliminary List;* it included, I think, every report that the NRPB list included. In the analysis which follows, I have included every printed report of the NRPB and all "major" mimeographed reports, whether the report was by the Board (or its predecessors) or by one of its committees or by an individual employed by the Board or serving as a consultant or advisor to it, and whether the report was issued by the Washington office or by one of its eleven regional offices. Knowing something of the procedures that had to be followed in order to get a government report printed in those days, I reasoned that such approval was sufficient evidence of the inherent value or the public demand for the report. The difficult question was: What should be considered a "major" mimeographed or processed report?

In some ways, it is more revealing of what I included in my list to describe what I excluded. I excluded from my list all the items in the Archives *List* which fell into one of the following categories:

1. all typed manuscripts. It will be recalled that all of the reports of the Board were pre-Xerox, hence the few carbons that could be made by typing could have had only a limited circulation. It took mimeographing to attain what might today be achieved by Xeroxing.

2. all mimeographed statements or reports of 10 pages or less, as well as a good many longer ones, on the general theory that such short statements would have been less important and/or had lesser circulation than longer ones.

3. mostly but not entirely, all preliminary drafts of reports. When a preliminary draft was shortly replaced by a revised or final mimeographed or printed draft, I have excluded it. But some reports labeled as "preliminary" were never followed by a final draft and have beeen included. So have some preliminary reports that I judged had considerable dissemination and circulation as such. Here is clearly a field where differences of judgment may enter.

4. all circular letters, circulars, and bulletins which were for internal circulation within NRPB and its staff. While they may be highly valuable as a source of information about the internal operations of the NRPB, they were not publications in the sense that most of the other reports are here.

5. all speeches by NRPB staff, including those by its director and those by board members, and all internal memos which there was reason to believe

circulated only within NRPB staff. While these too may be useful as information on NRPB operations, I felt they did not qualify as major reports in the sense I used the term.

6. most of the many regional war and defense impact and area reports. I count 80 such reports in the Archives *List,* some of which were quite short; I have included only 7 of the longer ones, as a sample, generally choosing the longest such report from each region making such reports.

Appendix table B-1 lists some 370 "major" reports of the NRPB and its predecessor agencies. For later convenience in reference, I have given each report a number; this number does not appear on the NRPB or Archives *List,* but is strictly my own invention. Each report is listed by its title. In a very few cases, there is doubt if the report is really a separate one or is another name for another included report. Since a number of reports were issued with closely similar titles, it is not a simple matter to determine whether a report is the same or different from another one.

Each report has been given a subject matter classification. This was one of the more difficult parts of compiling this table. How does one classify a report which deals with the planning of water development in the postwar period: as planning, as "war" including postwar, as water, or as public works? In general, I followed the Archives subject matter classification but with considerable grouping of its detailed classes. The basic difficulty is that the Archives classification is not clearly and easily mutually exclusive; nor, for that matter, is any other classification likely to be unequivocally mutually exclusive. Perhaps no other part of this appendix table is more subject to challenge than this subject matter classification.

The appendix table also lists information as to whether a report was issued in Washington or in some regional office. It will be noted that in a considerable number of cases, a mimeographed report on a subject was issued in the originating region, followed later by a printed report from Washington. The mimeographed version may have had a significant circulation. Information is also given on the method of reproduction and on the length of the reports. Since the latter is in terms of pages of different size, its information should be used with care.

Finally, my tabulation of the NRPB reports in table B-1 was carefully checked by Dr. Harold R. Pinkett of the National Archives staff. Using the definitions and standards just described in this chapter, he checked my list of reports for possible errors, omissions, and duplicates or items not meeting the standards set in this chapter. He found enough items not in conformity with my standards that the result is significantly more accurate than if he had not made such a check. The final decisions about table B-1 were mine and I absolve him of responsibility for any remaining errors while at the same time acknowledging the great help he gave me.

Table B-1. Chronological List of Major Reports of National Resources Planning Board,[a] 1934–1943

My Number[b]	Title[c]	Subject Matter[d]	Where Published[e]	Method Repro.[f]	Length (pages)[g]
	1934: National Planning Board				
1	Criteria and Planning for Public Works, by Russell V. Black	Works	Wash	Mim	182
2	Final Report—1933–34, National Planning Board	Gen	Wash	Pr	119
	1934: National Resources Board				
3	Preliminary Program of Work, National Resources Board	Gen	Wash	Mim	32
4	Development of the Rivers of the United States (H. Doc. No. 395,73d,2d)	Water	Wash	Pr	423
5	A Report on National Planning and Public Works in Relation to Natural Resources and Including Land Use and Water and Mineral Resources, with Findings and Recommendations	Gen[h]	Wash	Pr	455
	1935: National Resources Board				
6	Division of Costs of Public Works, Conference Papers, nos. 1–13, 15	Works	Wash	Mim	132
7	Second Report of the Board, with Findings and Recommendations, June 15, 1935	Gen	Wash	Mim	83
8	Basic Data for a Tentative and Preliminary Plan for New England	Plan	I	Mim	37
9	Second Report of the Board with Findings and Recommendations	Gen	Wash	Mim	83
10	Inventory of the Water Resources of the North Atlantic Drainage Area, by H. K. Barrows	Water	Wash	Mult	62
11	Inventory of the Water Resources of the South Atlantic and Eastern Gulf Drainage Area	Water	Wash	Mult	53

No.	Title			
12	Inventory of the Water Resources of the Great Lakes, St. Lawrence River, and Red River of the North Drainage Area	Water	Wash	Mult	48
13	Inventory of the Water Resources of the Mississippi River Drainage Area	Water	Wash	Mult	64
14	Inventory of the Water Resources of the South Pacific and Great Basin Drainage Areas	Water	Wash	Mult	50
15	Inventory of the Water Resources of the Southwest and Western Gulf Drainage Area	Water	Wash	Mult	29
16	Inventory of the Water Resources of the North Pacific Drainage Area	Water	Wash	Mult	117
17	Inventory of the Water Resources of the Colorado River Drainage Area, by H. T. Cory	Water	Wash	Pr	27
18	State Planning—Review of Activities and Progress	Plan	Wash	Pr	310
19	Economics of Planning of Public Works, by J. Maurice Clark	Works	Wash	Pr	194
20	Supplementary Reports of the Land Planning Committee to the National Resources Board (in two volumes, eleven parts, each part paged separately, each published as separate also), 1935–38	Land	Wash	Pr	1,073

1935: National Resources Committee

21	Report on Water Pollution	Water	Wash	Mim	82
22	Human Resources, by W. Rex Crawford	Pop	Wash	Mim	63
23	The Loan of Expert Personnel Among Federal Agencies, by James W. Fesler	Gen	Wash	Mim	53
24	Columbia Basin Study, Report of the Pacific Northwest Regional Planning Commission (part of a longer report)	Plan	IX	Mim	41
25	Regional Factors in National Planning	Plan	Wash	Pr	223
26	Standards and Specifications for Hydrologic Data, Report of the Special Advisory Committee to the Water Resources Committee	Water	Wash	Mult	45

(Table continues on next page)

327

Table B-1 (continued)

My Number[b]	Title[c]	Subject Matter[d]	Where Published[e]	Method Repro.[f]	Length (pages)[g]
	1936: National Resources Committee				
27	Federal Agencies Concerned with Water Use and Control	Water	Wash	Mim	37
28	The Effects upon Operating Efficiency of the British Experiment in Production Control in the Coal Industry, by George W. Strasser	Energy	Wash	Mim	88
29	Classified Guide to Material in the Library of Congress Covering Urban Community Development	Plan	Wash	Mim	102
30	Regional Planning Report, Part I—Pacific Northwest	Plan	Wash	Pr	192
31	Regional Planning Report, Part II—St. Louis Region	Plan	Wash	Pr	68
32	Progress Report with Statements of Coordinating Committees	Gen	Wash	Pr	61
33	Urban Population Changes in the United States, by Warren S. Thompson	Pop	Wash	Mim	64
34	A Method for Determining Certain Conversion Characteristics of the Underground Bituminous Coal Mining Industry Which Will Constitute a Part of a Technique to Be Used in Forecasting, by Harry P. Sweeny	Energy	Wash	Mim	24
35	Regional Planning Report, Part III—New England	Plan	Wash	Pr	101
36	Interim Report to the National Resources Committee by the Research Committee on Urbanism	Plan	Wash	Mim	189
37	Connecticut River Valley Water Resources Data	Water	I	Mim	44
38	Connecticut River Valley Water Resources Bibliography	Water	I	Mim	134
39	Deficiencies in Basic Hydrologic Data	Water	Wash	Pr	66
40	Consolidation and Coordination of Transport Terminals and Their Probable Effects on the Urban Community, by Ernest P. Goodrich	Trans	Wash	Mim	164
41	Drainage Basin Problems and Programs	Water	Wash	Pr	540

42	Public Works Planning	Plan	Wash	Pr	221
43	State Planning, Programs and Accomplishments	Plan	Wash	Pr	123
44	Trends in Urban Government, by Albert Lepawsky	Plan	Wash	Mim	157

1937: National Resources Committee

45	The Role of the Urban Community in the National Economy	Plan	Wash	Mim	246
46	Columbia Gorge Conservation and Development	Plan	IX	Mim	71
47	Preliminary Report on Baltimore-Washington-Annapolis Area	Plan	Wash	Mim	77
48	Rural Zoning—a Monograph	Plan	I	Mim	76
49	Suggested Symbols for Plans, Maps, and Charts	Plan	Wash	Mim	38
50	Our Cities, Their Role in the National Economy	Plan	Wash	Pr	88
51	Progress Reports and Report Digests	Gen	Wash	Mim	311
52	Technological Trends and National Policy Including the Social Implications of New Inventions, Report of the Subcommittee on Technology	Indust	Wash	Pr	338
53	Second Report of the Special Advisory Committee on Water Pollution and Summary of State Legislation Affecting Water Pollution	Water	Wash	Pr	54
54	Technology and Planning (pamphlet)	Indust	Wash	Pr	31
55	Regional Planning Report, Part V—Red River of the North	Water	Wash	Pr	80
56	Our Cities (pamphlet)	Plan	Wash	Pr	35
57	Population Statistics, 1. National Data	Pop	Wash	Pr	107
58	Population Statistics, 2. State Data [1]	Pop	Wash	Pr	(60)
59	Population Statistics, 3. Urban Data	Pop	Wash	Pr	52
60	Members of Joint State-Federal Basin Committees	Water	Wash	Mim	81
61	Progress Report, Statement of the Advisory Committee	Gen	Wash	Pr	20
62	Some Factors in the Development of Housing Policies in the United States	Hous	Wash	Mim	561

(*Table continues on next page*)

Table B-1 (continued)

My Number [b]	Title [c]	Subject Matter [d]	Where Published [e]	Method Repro. [f]	Length (pages) [g]
63	Regional Planning Report, Part IV, Baltimore-Washington-Annapolis Area	Plan	Wash	Pr	65
64	Alaska: Its Resources and Development, Preliminary Draft of Item 65, 2 vols.	Plan	X	Mim	393
65	Regional Planning Report, Part VII, Alaska—Its Resources and Development	Plan	Wash	Pr	213
66	Drainage Basin Committee reports—some 22 drainage basins, each separately paged, published separately as well as in one volume	Water	Wash	Pr	837
67	Suggestions Concerning Government and Administration in the Territory of Alaska, by Charles McKinley, James C. Rettie, and Oscar Gass	Plan	Wash	Mim	85
68	Water Resources of New England	Water	I	Mim	483
	1938: National Resources Committee				
69	Information on Flood Control in the Mississippi River Basin	Water	Wash	Mim	121
70	Status and Future of State and Regional Planning, New England	Plan	I	Mim	87
71	Status and Future of State and Regional Planning, Middle Atlantic	Plan	II	Mim	105
72	Status and Future of State and Regional Planning, Southeastern	Plan	III	Mim	83
73	Status and Future of State and Regional Planning, Ohio-Great Lakes	Plan	IV	Mim	90
74	Status and Future of State and Regional Planning, Region II	Plan	V	Mim	41
75	Status and Future of State and Regional Planning, Missouri Valley	Plan	VI	Mim	43
76	Status and Future of State and Regional Planning, Southwest	Plan	VIII	Mim	52
77	Status and Future of State and Regional Planning, Pacific Northwest	Plan	IX	Mim	85
78	Drainage Basin Problems and Programs, 1937 revision	Water	Wash	Pr	154
79	Proceedings of the National Zoning Conference, Chicago, Illinois, December 1937	Plan	Wash	Mim	168
80	Regional Planning Report, Part IV, Upper Rio Grande vol. 1, text; vol. 2, maps	Plan	Wash	Pr	566
81	Water Planning (pamphlet)	Water	Wash	Pr	40

Table B-1 (continued)

My Number[b]	Title[c]	Subject Matter[d]	Where Published[e]	Method Repro.[f]	Length (pages)[g]
	1939: National Resources Committee				
104	Energy Resources and National Policy	Energy	Wash	Pr	435
105	Federal Relations to Research (pamphlet)	Resear	Wash	Pr	30
106	Progress Report, Report on the Period 1935–39	Gen	Wash	Mim	143
107	Consumer Expenditures in the United States (2 vols.)	Econ	Wash	Mim	400
108	From the Ground Up	Plan	I	Pr	54
109	A New Definition of Local Planning, by Russell Van Nest Black	Plan	Wash	Mim	64
110	Regional Planning Report, Part VIII, Northern Lake States	Plan	Wash	Pr	63
111	The Accomplishments of the Maryland State Planning Commission and Recommendations on Future Activities, by V. O. Key	Plan	Wash	Mim	40
112	Consumer Expenditures in the United States	Econ	Wash	Pr	195
113	The Consumer Spends His Income (pamphlet)	Econ	Wash	Pr	47
114	County and Municipal Planning: A Statement of Improved Practices and Procedures, by Russell Van Nest Black	Plan	Wash	Mim	77
115	Introductions and Outlines for a Manual on the Planning of Small Water Storage Projects	Water	Wash	Mim	68
116	The Northern Lake States Region (pamphlet)	Plan	Wash	Pr	35
117	Our Energy Resources (pamphlet)	Energy	Wash	Pr	41
118	Progress Report, Statement of the Advisory Committee	Gen	Wash	Pr	173
119	Regulation of the Bituminous Coal Industry in the United States, by Roger N. Quirk	Energy	Wash	Mim	395
120	The Structure of the American Economy: I. Basic Characteristics	Econ	Wash	Pr	396

No.	Title				
82	Forest Resources of the Pacific Northwest	Land	Wash	Pr	86
83	The Future of State Planning	Plan	Wash	Pr	117
84	The Future of State Planning Boards as Shown by Their Recent Reports, by Harold F. Gosnell	Plan	Wash	Mim	116
85	Planning Our Resources (pamphlet)	Plan	Wash	Pr	35
86	Deficiencies in Hydrologic Research	Water	Wash	Mim	181
87	The Distribution of Consumer Income in 1935–36, by Hildegarde Kneeland, 2 vols.	Econ	Wash	Mim	277
88	Problems of a Changing Population	Pop	Wash	Pr	306
89	Research of the Federal Government in Natural Sciences and Technology, by Charles M. Wiltse	Resear	Wash	Mim	67
90	Federal Expenditures for Research, 1937 and 1938, by E. R. Gray	Resear	Wash	Mim	104
91	Recreation in New England	Land	I	Mim	26
92	Regional Planning (pamphlet)	Plan	Wash	Pr	28
93	Suggested Symbols for Plans, Maps, and Charts	Plan	Wash	Pr	32
94	Low Dams: A Manual of Design for Small Water Storage Projects	Water	Wash	Pr	431
95	Patterns of Resource Use	Gen	Wash	Pr	149
96	Population Problems (pamphlet)	Pop	Wash	Pr	28
97	The States and Planning (pamphlet)	Plan	Wash	Pr	30
98	Suggested Procedure for Population Studies by State Planning Boards	Pop	Wash	Mim	87
99	Consumer Incomes in the United States—Their Distribution in 1935–36	Econ	Wash	Pr	104
100	A Plan for New England Airports	Trans	I	Mim	–
101	Planning Technicians' Conference, Sept. 19–Oct. 1, 1938, in several				
102	Progress R				

No.	Title	Category	Location	Type	Page
121	Housing Monograph Series, No. 1, Residential Building	Hous	Wash	Pr	19
122	Housing Monograph Series, No. 2, Legal Problems in the Housing Field	Hous	Wash	Pr	75
123	Housing Monograph Series, No. 3, Land, Materials, and Labor Costs	Hous	Wash	Pr	104
124	Planning Facts (pamphlet)	Plan	Wash	Pr	11
125	State Conservation of Resources, by Clifford J. Hynning	Plan	Wash	Pr	115
126	Supplementary Report of the Urbanism Committee, II, Urban Planning and Land Policies	Plan	Wash	Pr	366
127	Supplementary Report of the Urbanism Committee, I, Urban Government	Plan	Wash	Pr	303
128	Water Pollution in the United States	Water	Wash	Pr	165

1939: National Resources Planning Board

No.	Title	Category	Location	Type	Page
129	The Planning Function in Local Government, by Robert A. Walker	Plan	Wash	Mim	209
130	Migration and the Development of Economic Opportunity in the Pacific Northwest	Econ	IX	Mim	240
131	Planning for the Rehabilitation of North Dakota, by Charles McKinley	Plan	Wash	Mim	50
132	Study of Advisory Committees in the Federal Government, by Norman N. Gill	Gen	Wash	Mim	134
133	Who's Who in the National Resources Planning Board, 1939	Gen	Wash	Mim	62
134	Preliminary Draft of a Directory of Federal Construction Agencies, by Robert E. Simpson	Gen	Wash	Mim	233
135	Regional Planning Report, Part IX, The Northern Great Plains	Plan	Wash	Pr	14
136	A Confidential Report on Regional and State Planning in Region IX	Plan	IX	Mim	88
137	Housing Progress and Problems	Hous	Wash	Mim	65

1940: National Resources Planning Board

No.	Title	Category	Location	Type	Page
138	Price Flexibility and Full Employment of Resources, by Alvin E. Hansen	Econ	Wash	Mim	25
139	Hydrologic, Hydraulic, and Sanitary Engineering Nomenclature	Water	Wash	Mim	384

(Table continues on next page)

Table B-1 (continued)

My Number[b]	Title[c]	Subject Matter[d]	Where Published[e]	Method Repro.[f]	Length (pages)[g]
140	The Southern Forests	Land	Wash	Mim	39
141	Deficiencies in Hydrologic Research, 1940	Water	Wash	Pr	93
142	Interim Report, Upper Mississippi Basin Committee	Plan	IV	Mult	164
143	Northern Great Plains (pamphlet)	Plan	Wash	Pr	44
144	Proceedings, North Central Aviation Planning Conference	Plan	VI	Mim	106
145	Symposium on State Water Law of the Pacific Northwest	Water	Wash	Mim	101
146	Capital Requirements: A Study in Methods as Applied to the Iron and Steel Industry, by Louis J. Paradiso under the direction of Gardiner C. Means	Econ	Wash	Pr	54
147	Capital Requirements, A Study in Methods as Applied to the Iron and Steel Industry	Econ	Wash	Pr	51
148	Federal Aids to Local Planning	Plan	Wash	Pr	151
149	Housing—The Continuing Problem (pamphlet)	Hous	Wash	Pr	60
150	Public Land Acquisition, Part I: Rural Lands	Land	Wash	Pr	25
151	Summary of Statutes Affecting Water in the 31 Eastern States, by Sheldon D. Klein	Water	Wash	Mim	117
152	Our National Resources: Facts and Problems (pamphlet)	Plan	Wash	Pr	45
153	Subject Index of Reports by the National Planning Board, National Resources Board, National Resources Committee	Gen	Wash	Pr	76
154	Index of Reports, 1934-1939 (pamphlet)[i]	Gen	Wash	Pr	(201)
155	The Structure of the American Economy: II. Toward Full Use of Resources	Econ	Wash	Pr	48
156	Supplement to the Patterns of Resource Use	Econ	Wash	Pr	44
157	Production and Utilization of Techniques—Coal, by A. C. Fieldner and W. E. Rice	Energy	Wash	Mim	86
158	Upper Gila River Basin Report	Water	Wash	Mim	236

159	Analytical Study of Railroad Car Equipment, by R. N. Janeway	Trans	Wash	Mim	97
160	A Comprehensive Regional Development Plan for New England	Plan	I	Mim	37
161	National Planning in Latin America, by Lewis L. Lorwin	Plan	Wash	Mim	124
162	A Plan for Development and Conservation of the Resources of the Inter-mountain Region	Plan	VII	Mim	64
163	Planned Regional Development in the Middle Atlantic States	Plan	II	Mim	61
164	Proposed Regional Development Plan, South Central Region	Plan	V	Mim	75
165	Regional Development Plan for the Territory of Alaska, by H. A. Bauer	Plan	X	Mim	92
166	The Long-Range Planning of the Location of New Productive Capacity, by P. Sargant Florence	Econ	Wash	Mim	72
167	A National Policy for Development of Water Resources	Water	Wash	Mim	96
168	Principles for the Evaluation of Public Works as These Affect the Land, by Carl L. Alsberg	Land	Wash	Mim	43
169	Standard Budgets for Determination of Levels of Living of Varying Degrees of Adequacy, by L. Epstein	Econ	Wash	Mim	62
170	The Economic Effects of the Federal Public Works Expenditures 1933–1938, by J. K. Galbraith, assisted by G. G. Johnson	Econ	Wash	Pr	131
171	Public Works and Employment Planning in Germany, 1933–1939, by Lewis L. Lorwin	Plan	Wash	Mim	108
172	Rationale of Air Transportation, by J. Parker Van Zandt	Trans	Wash	Mim	77
173	Stabilization of Planning in Sweden, 1929–1939, by Lewis L. Lorwin	Plan	Wash	Mim	73
174	Development of Resources and Stabilization of Employment in the United States, Part II, Six-Year Programs of Public Works of Federal Agencies, confidential	Econ	Wash	Mult	139
175	Housing: The Continuing Problem	Hous	Wash	Pr	220
176	National Income, Consumer Welfare, and Full Employment	Econ	Wash	Mim	54

(Table continues on next page)

Table B-1 (continued)

My Number[b]	Title[c]	Subject Matter[d]	Where Published[e]	Method Repro.[f]	Length (pages)[g]
177	Problems of Transportation Policy—Review of Basic Issues and Alternative Solutions	Trans	Wash	Mim	53
178	Public Works and Land Use Adjustment	Land	Wash	Mim	52
179	Research—A National Resource, II. Industrial Research	Resear	Wash	Pr	370
	1941: National Resources Planning Board				
180	Development of Resources and Stabilization of Employment in the United States	Econ	Wash	Pr	409
181	Development of Resources and Stabilization of Employment in the United States, Part I. The Federal Program for National Development	Econ	Wash	Pr	101
182	Development of Resources and Stabilization of Employment in the United States, Part II. Regional Development Plans	Econ	Wash	Pr	244
183	Development of Resources and Stabilization of Employment in the United States, Part III. Functional Development Plans	Econ	Wash	Pr	63
184	Industrial Location in Relation to Size of Plant, Concern, and Production Center, by Edgar M. Hoover	Econ	Wash	Mim	54
185	Public Land Acquisition in a National Land Use Program, Part I—Rural Lands, Part II—Urban Lands	Land	Wash	Pr	63
186	The Role of Public Action in Transportation Abroad, by Ludwig M. Homberger	Trans	Wash	Mim	68
187	War-Time Planning in Germany, 1939–1940, by Lewis L. Lorwin	Plan	Wash	Mim	116
188	Industrialization of Rural Areas in the Southern Piedmont, by Rupert B. Vance, assisted by Ruth Criwell Leafer	Econ	Wash	Mim	50
189	Land Classification in the United States	Land	Wash	Pr	151
190	Rates and Rate Structure (Railroads), by D. Philip Locklin	Trans	Wash	Mim	136

191	Report on Economic Phases of Our Foreign and Domestic Water Transportation	Trans	Wash	Mim	148
192	Diversification as a Locational Policy, by Edgar M. Hoover	Econ	Wash	Mim	45
193	Functions, Organization, Authority, Activities, Publications	Gen	Wash	Pr	11
194	Price Policies and Industrial Location, by H. Gardner Ackley	Econ	Wash	Mim	46
195	Transport Coordination, by Ralph L. Dewey	Trans	Wash	Mim	65
196	Area Analysis: Upper Snake Basin, by J. D. Wood and William E. Folz	Gen	Wash	Mim	85
197	Family Expenditures in the United States, Statistical Tables and Appendixes	Econ	Wash	Pr	209
198	Industrial Studies, Preliminary Edition for Technical Criticism, Middle Atlantic	Indust	II	Mim	193
199	Locational Experiences of the Cotton Industry, by Seth Hammond	Econ	Wash	Mim	48
200	Long-Range Programming of Municipal Public Works	Works	Wash	Pr	72
201	Our Public Works Experience (pamphlet)	Works	Wash	Pr	36
202	Research—A National Resource: III. Business Research	Resear	Wash	Pr	70
203	Development of Resources and of Economic Opportunity in the Pacific Northwest	Plan	IX	Mim	180
204	Interest Rates, An Analysis of Supply and Demand Factors, by Murray Shields	Econ	Wash	Mult	120
205	Progress Report, 1940–1941	Gen	Wash	Pr	81
206	Preliminary Discussion on the Conservation of Cultural Resources in Civilian Defense	War	Wash	Mim	61
207	Progress Report, 1939–41[1]	Gen	Wash	Pr	(25)
208	Geographic Distribution of Resources, by Wilbert G. Fritz and John K. Rose	Gen	Wash	Mim	82
209	Government Ownership and Operation of Railroads, by Ralph L. Dewey	Trans	Wash	Mim	77
210	Housing and Related Problems Today	Hous	Wash	Mim	20
211	The Influence of Transportation on the Location of Economic Activities, by Edward S. Lynch	Trans	Wash	Mim	81
212	National Defense Transportation Policy, by Andrew Stevenson	Trans	Wash	Mim	54
213	The Position of Labor, by Edwin M. Fitch and Joseph M. Gillman	Trans	Wash	Mim	96

(Table continues on next page)

337

Table B-1 (continued)

My Number[b]	Title[c]	Subject Matter[d]	Where Published[e]	Method Repro.[f]	Length (pages)[g]
214	Railroad Financing, 1890–1940, by W. H. S. Stevens	Trans	Wash	Mim	136
215	Transportation and Public Promotional Policy, by Wilfred Owen	Trans	Wash	Mim	91
216	After Defense—What? (pamphlet)	War	Wash	Pr	18
217	Public Works and National Planning in Selected Countries	Plan	Wash	Mult	173
218	Consumer Demand at Full Production	Econ	Wash	Mim	59
219	Effects of Changes in Location of Industries on Labor, by Elinor Pancoast	Indus	Wash	Mim	66
220	Gains in Oil and Gas Production, Refining and Utilization Technology, by H. C. Miller and B. G. Shea	Energy	Wash	Pr	39
221	Integration of Processes in Plants, Concerns, and Production Centers, by Edgar M. Hoover	Econ	Wash	Mim	33
222	A Preliminary Regional Development Program, Region VI, 1941 Revision	Plan	VI	Mim	70
223	Regional Development Plan, Mountain States Region	Plan	VII	Mim	106
224	Regional Development Plan—Pacific Southwest	Plan	VIII	Mim	121
225	Taxation of Industrial Corporation in Washington and Oregon, by James C. Rettie	Econ	IX	Mim	80
226	American Transportation Policy: Summary Report	Trans	Wash	Mim	64
227	Conference Group on Post-Defense Planning for Children and Youth: Proceedings	Plan	Wash	Hect	171
228	New Concepts in Transport Regulation, by James C. Nelson	Trans	Wash	Mim	136
229	Planning for Post-Defense Land-Use Adjustment, New England	Plan	I	Mim	34
230	Post-Defense Economic Development in Alaska	War	X	Mim	54
231	Quantitative Relations of Saving, Consumption and Investment to National Income, by Mordecai Ezekiel	Econ	Wash	Mim	94

No.	Title	Category	Region	Type	Pages
232	Regional Development Plan, Lakes States and Ohio Valley, 1941	Plan	IV	Mim	117
233	Research and Progress in the Production and Use of Coal, by A. C. Fieldner and W. E. Rice	Energy	Wash	Pr	49
234	The Transportation System Today, by G. Lloyd Wilson and Joseph L. White	Trans	Wash	Mim	63
235	Water Regimen Data: Pacific Northwest Drainage Basins	Water	IX	Mim	148
236	Area Analysis: Willamette Valley, by H. A. Bauer	Gen	Wash	Mim	24
237	Regional Development Plan: New England	Plan	I	Mim	35
238	Regional Development Program: Lake States and Ohio Valley, Summary	Plan	IV	Mim	35
239	Regional Development Program: Missouri Valley Region, Summary	Plan	VI	Mim	34
240	Regional Development Plan: Mountain States Region, Summary	Plan	VII	Mim	40
241	The St. Louis Defense Area, Missouri	War	VI	Mim	115
242	Post-Defense Planning for Children and Youth, by Paul T. David, Paul R. Hanna, D. L. Harley, and Floyd W. Reeves	War	Wash	Mim	56

1942: National Resources Planning Board

No.	Title	Category	Region	Type	Pages
243	After the War—Full Employment (pamphlet)	War	Wash	Pr	19
244	Area Analysis: Delmarva Area, by George T. Renner	Gen	Wash	Mim	81
245	Area Analysis: Pennsylvania Anthracite Region, by Raymond E. Murphy	Gen	Wash	Mim	55
246	Bibliography of Reports of State, Territorial, and Regional Planning Agencies	Plan	Wash	Mim	28
247	The Location of the Aircraft Industry, by W. Glenn Cunningham	Indus	Wash	Mim	55
248	A National Program of Public Works for Range Conservation	Works	Wash	Mim	138
249	A National Program of Public Works for Recreational Land	Works	Wash	Mim	44
250	National Resources Development, Report for 1942	Gen	Wash	Pr	227
251	Post-War Planning: A Bibliography, by Letha F. McCance	War	Wash	Mim	41
252	Security, Work, and Relief Policies	Econ	Wash	Pr	640
253	Area Analysis: Northern Sierra Nevada, by David Weeks	Gen	Wash	Mim	80

(*Table continues on next page*)

My Number[b]	Title[c]	Subject Matter[d]	Where Published[e]	Method Repro.[f]	Length (pages)[g]
254	Area Analysis: Republican River Basin, by Byron C. Denny	Gen	Wash	Mim	55
255	Area Analysis: San Luis Valley, by Morris E. Garnsey	Gen	Wash	Mim	28
256	Area Analysis: Southwestern Rhode Island, by Edward A. Ackerman	Gen	Wash	Mim	57
257	Hampton Roads Regional Water Supply Study, by Abel Wolman, John Geyer, and W. F. Day	Water	Wash	Mult	210
258	A National Program of Public Works for Forest Conservation	Works	Wash	Mim	214
259	Northern California Redwood Area Analysis, by P. M. Barr	Gen	Wash	Mim	39
260	Post-War Planning in Great Britain, by Luther Gulick and E. N. Thompson	War	Wash	Mim	80
261	Regional Resource Development, Report for 1942	Plan	Wash	Mim	up (230)
262	Education for Planners	Plan	I	Mim	80
263	Report on Mobile Defense Area, Alabama	War	Wash	Mim	71
264	Small Manufacturing Firms and Locational Policy, by Edna Sugihara	Indus	Wash	Mim	51
265	After Victory—A Housebuilding Industry	Hous	Wash	Mim	26
266	Area Analysis: Glaciated Sand Region, Wisconsin, by Loyal S. Durand, Jr.	Gen	Wash	Mim	96
267	Composite Report on Albany-Corvallis Defense Area	War	IX	Mim	51
268	Area Analysis of a Gum Naval Stores County, Clinch County, Georgia, by John W. Lehman	Gen	Wash	Mim	80
269	Baltimore Area—War and Post-War	War	II	Mult	58
270	Better Cities—Building America (pamphlet) by Charles S. Ascher	Plan	Wash	Pr	22
271	Composite Report on San Bernardino County	War	VIII	Mim	43
272	International Public Works and Economic Development, by Lewis L. Lorwin	Works	Wash	Mim	312
273	Transportation and National Policy	Trans	Wash	Pr	513

No.	Title				
274	Area Analysis: Salt River Valley, Arizona, by Sheldon K. Baker	Gen	Wash	Mim	73
275	The Effect of Agriculture on the Location of Industry, by Raymond P. Christensen	Econ	Wash	Mim	117
276	The External Trade of the Pacific Northwest	Econ	IX	Mim	88
277	Interstate Water Compacts, 1785 to 1941	Water	Wash	Mim	159
278	Pecos River Joint Investigation, Reports and Atlas (2 vols.) Summarized in Regional Planning Report, Part X (1941)	Plan	Wash	Pr	406
279	Regional Planning Report, Part XI, The Southeast	Plan	Wash	Pr	250
280	Report on Hartford Defense Area, State of Connecticut	War	I	Mim	65
281	National Roster of Scientific and Specialized Personnel	Gen	Wash	Pr	47
282	Water and Power in Puerto Rico, by Donald P. Griffin	Water	XI	Mim	44
283	Bibliography and Abstracts on the Subject of Agriculture in Alaska, 1867–1942, by George Sundborg	Land	X	Mim	139
284	Composite Report on New Orleans, La., Military and War Production Area	War	V	Mim	154
285	Post-War Climate of Opinion	Gen	Wash	Mim	92
286	State Planning, June 1942	Plan	Wash	Pr	134
287	Area Analysis—A Method of Public Works Planning	Gen	Wash	Mim	56
288	Industrial Development Studies: Middle Atlantic Region	Plan	Wash	Pr	50
289	The Integration of Federal and Non-Federal Research as a War Problem, by Richard H. Heindel	Resear	Wash	Mim	122
290	Memorandum on Public Works Planning for the Post-War Period, by Frank W. Herring and Robert W. Hartley	Works	Wash	Mim	40
291	The Role of the Housebuilding Industry, Building America (pamphlet)	Hous	Wash	Pr	29
292	Urban Financing, by Edwin H. Spengler, assisted by Celia Sperling and Isabelle Pass	Plan	Wash	Mim	73
293	The Wastage of Human Resources, by Lawrence K. Frank	Pop	Wash	Mim	111

(Table continues on next page)

Table B-1 (continued)

My Number[b]	Title[c]	Subject Matter[d]	Where Published[e]	Method Repro.[t]	Length (pages)[g]
294	City of Anchorage—Anchorage Public Improvement Program, 1942–1947	Plan	X	Mim	67
295	City of Sitka—Sitka Public Improvement Program, 1942–1947	Plan	X	Mim	42
296	A Preliminary View of Industrial Possibilities in South Central Region: Arkansas, Louisiana, Oklahoma, Texas	Indus	V	Mim	43
297	Regional Planning: A Long-Range Regional Development Program for the Southeast in Wartime	Plan	III	Mim	829
298	After the War—Toward Security (pamphlet)	War	Wash	Pr	61
299	The Future of Transportation (pamphlet)	Trans	Wash	Pr	43
300	Post-War Planning—Full Employment, Security, Building America (pamphlet)	War	Wash	Pr	32
301	Public Works and Rural Land Use	Land	Wash	Pr	167
302	Supplementary Analysis of the External Trade of the Pacific Northwest, by James E. Maxwell	Econ	IX	Mim	24
303	Tax Delinquency and Rural Land-Use Development	Land	Wash	Pr	190
304	Arkansas Valley: Regional Planning Part XII	Plan	V	Mim	225
305	Development of Resources and of Economic Opportunity in the Pacific Northwest	Econ	Wash	Pr	178
306	International Economic Development—Public Works and Other Problems, by Lewis L. Lorwin	Plan	Wash	Pr	111
307	Final Draft of the Puerto Rico Planning Bill, by Alfred Bettman	Plan	XI	Mim	55
308	The Framework of an Economy of Plenty, by R. J. Watkins	Econ	Wash	Mim	58
309	Highway Transportation: A Program to Meet the Impacts of War, by Wilfred Owen	Trans	Wash	Mim	52
310	After the War—Full Employment (pamphlet)	War	Wash	Pr	19

No.	Title				
311	Forestry in New England, by Henry I. Baldwin	Land	I	Mim	57
312	Industrial Development Studies: Mountain States Region	Indus	Wash	Pr	62
313	Industrial Development Studies: Pacific Northwest Region	Indus	Wash	Pr	39
314	Industrial Development Studies: Pacific Southwest Region	Indus	Wash	Pr	66
315	Industrial Location and Natural Resources	Indus	Wash	Pr	360
316	Preliminary Memorandum on Wartime Programing of Facilities and Construction, by Robert W. Hartley	Plan	Wash	Mim	42

1943: National Resources Planning Board

No.	Title				
317	National Resources Development Report for 1943, Part I: Post-War Plan and Program	Gen	Wash	Pr	81
318	National Resources Development Report for 1943, Part II: Wartime Planning for War and Post War	War	Wash	Pr	116
319	Some Major Problems in the Operation of the Law of Water Rights in the West	Water	Wash	Pr	323
320	Summary of Federal Post-War Planning Programs	War	Wash	Mim	51
321	Analysis of Taxation in New York City, by Edwin H. Spengler, assisted by Celia Sperling and Isabelle Pass	Plan	Wash	Mim	44
322	Area Analysis, Including Suggested Immediate and Post-War Adjustments, Kootenai County, Idaho, with Reference to Adjoining Counties, by Norman Nybroten	Gen	IX	Mim	121
323	Post-War Plan and Program	War	Wash	Pr	12
324	Urban Taxation, by Edwin H. Spengler, assisted by Celia Sperling and Isabelle Pass	Plan	Wash	Mim	65
325	After the War—Land Use for Better Food, by Hollis W. Peter	War	Wash	Mim	37
326	Development Study of the Alabama-Coosa Basin Area Prospectus	Gen	III	Mim	64
327	Human Conservation—The Story of Our Wasted Resources, by Lawrence K. Frank with the assistance of Louise K. Kiser	Pop	Wash	Pr	126

(Table continues on next page)

343

Table B-1 (continued)

My Number[b]	Title[c]	Subject Matter[d]	Where Published[e]	Method Repro.[f]	Length (pages)[g]
328	Summary Justification of Estimates of Appropriations (House)	Gen	Wash	Mim	67
329	Area Analysis—A Method of Public Works Planning	Gen	Wash	Pr	40
330	A Development Plan for Puerto Rico	Plan	XI	Mim	63
331	A Development Plan for the Virgin Islands of the United States	Plan	XI	Mim	84
332	Editorial Reaction to National Resources Planning Board Reports	Gen	Wash	Mim	13
333	Post-War Problems of the Aircraft Industry, by Melvin A. Brenner	War	Wash	Mim	47
334	International Fisheries Cooperation Between Canada and the United States in the North Pacific	Water	IX	Mim	70
335	Plan for Development and Control of Water Resources (several parts)	Water	Wash	Mim	237
336	Preliminary Draft of the Northern Lakes States Regional Report	Plan	IV	Mim	124
337	Puget Sound Region: War and Post-War Development	War	IX	Mim	231
338	Better Rural Life, by Ayers Brinser	Gen	I	Mim	42
339	The North Pacific Planning Project, Report of Progress	Plan	Wash	Pr	39
340	Principal Federal Sources of Hydrologic Data	Water	Wash	Pr	76
341	Puget Sound Region, War and Post-War Developments	War	Wash	Pr	160
342	Rural Population Distribution with Reference to Public Works Projects and Programs	Works	Wash	Mim	90
343	Summary Justification of Estimates of Appropriations (Senate)	Gen	Wash	Mim	46
344	After the War, 1918–1920, Military and Economic Demobilization of the United States, Effect Upon Employment and Income, by Paul A. Samuelson and Everett E. Hagen	War	Wash	Pr	45
345	A Decade of Regional Planning in New England	Plan	I	Mim	31
346	Demobilization and Readjustment (report of a conference)	War	Wash	Pr	106

No.	Title	Category	Location	Type	Pages
347	Highway Transportation: Wartime Problems and Future Development, by Wilfred Owen	Trans	Wash	Mim	49
348	Location of War Plants in Britain and Post-War Problems of Reconversion, by P. Sargant Florence	War	Wash	Mim	47
349	Magnesium After the War, by James W. Alfriend, Jr.	War	Wash	Mim	33
350	Post-War Problems of the Shipbuilding Industry, by Lawrence A. Oosterhous	War	Wash	Mim	46
351	Post-War Problems of the Steel Industry, by Marion W. Worthing	War	Wash	Mim	39
352	Post-War Problems of the Synthetic Rubber Industry, by Melvin A. Brenner	War	Wash	Mim	42
353	Post-War Transportation Studies	War	Wash	Mim	40
354	Regional Planning Report, Part XI, Southeastern Region	Plan	Wash	Pr	250
355	Regional Planning Report, Part XII, Arkansas Valley	Plan	Wash	Pr	109
356	State Water Law in the Development of the West	Water	Wash	Pr	138
357	External Trade of Alaska, 1931–1940: An Analysis of the Inbound and Outbound Shipments of a Frontier Region, with Emphasis on the Possibilities for Expanding Its Trade and Strengthening Its Internal Economy, by Joseph L. Fisher	Econ	X	Mult	25
358	Estimates of Future Population, 1940–2000, by Warren S. Thompson and P. K. Whelpton	Pop	Wash	Pr	137
359	Final Report—Status of Work, by Charles W. Eliot	Gen	Wash	Mim	30
360	Guide to the Files of the National Resources Planning Board and Predecessor Agencies: Ten Years of National Planning, 1933–1943, by Charles W. Eliot, assisted by Harold A. Merrill	Gen	Wash	Mim	188

Undated Reports

No.	Title	Category	Location	Type	Pages
361	Area Analysis: Northern Lake States	Gen	Wash	Mim	111
362	Developments in the American Petroleum Industry, 1914-19, by H. C. Fowler	Energy	Wash	Mim	84

(Table continues on next page)

345

Table B-1 (continued)

My Number[b]	Title[c]	Subject Matter[a]	Where Published[e]	Method Repro.[f]	Length (pages)[g]
363	Estimates of the National Income, Industrial Production, and Employment for the Fiscal Years 1940–41 and 1941–42	Econ	Wash	Mim	60
364	Fuel Supply and Requirements for the War Economy (August 1943)	Energy	Wash	Mim	191
365	Human Resources, by Goodwin Watson	Pop	Wash	Mim	165
366	Locality Report, Colorado Springs Defense Area, Colorado	War	VII	Mim	56
367	Major Elements for Consideration in a Denver Metropolitan Area Project (August 1942)	Plan	Wash	Mim	13
368	Population Problems (pamphlet)	Pop	Wash	Pr	12
369	Forest Resource Conservation: National Significance and Objectives	Land	Wash	Mim	75
370	Columbia Basin Report (in several parts)	Plan	Wash	Mim	489

Notes to Table B-1

a And predecessor organizations: National Planning Board, July 20, 1933 to June 30, 1934; National Resources Board, July 1, 1934 to June 7, 1935; National Resources Committee, June 8, 1935 to June 30, 1939; and National Resources Planning Board, July 1, 1939 to December 31, 1943.

b My number is purely for reference in this study; it does not appear in any NRPB or Archives list.

c This is an attempt to list every major report of the National Resources Planning Board and its predecessor agencies. The list is as closely chronological as possible; some reports bear month as well as year dates on the cover, and these dates have been taken as controlling even when letters of transmittal or other documents suggest the actual publication date may have been different. Other reports bear only year of publication on the cover; these have been listed at approximately mid-year unless some evidence suggests a different date. Reports of the same month have been listed alphabetically by title. Where reports indicate individual authorship, author(s) are listed; otherwise, reports are by staff or committees of organization.

ᵈ Subject matter designation follows closely that used by the Archives in its list of publications, but with some grouping. General groups include the following: economics, including consumer income and expenditures, finance and prices, national income, and security, work, and relief; energy, including coal, petroleum and other forms of energy; general, including area analyses, progress reports and programs of the NRPB, general reports, and personnel; housing; industry, including location, aircraft, iron and steel, magnesium and aluminum, rubber, ship building, technology and general industry; land, including forestry, land classification, public land, public works and land, recreation, taxation, and general land matters; planning, including local, national, regional and regions, state, urban, and other countries; population, including human resources, population changes and growth; public works, including general public works, distribution of costs and benefits of public works, municipal public works; research; transport, including air, water, railroad, and general; war, including defense, war, and postwar planning; and water including compacts, drainage basins, valley plans, flood control, hydrology, pollution, silt and salinity, small water developments, water law and rights, and water generally.

ᵉ Washington office or region. Numbers apply to regions as follows: I, New England; II, Middle Atlantic; III, Southeastern; IV, Ohio-Great Lakes; V, South Central; VI, Missouri Valley; VII, Intermountain-Great Plains; VIII, Southwest; IX, Pacific Northwest; X, Alaska; and XI, Caribbean.

ᶠ Method of reproduction: Pr = printed; Mim = mimeographed; and Mult = multilithed.

ᵍ Length is number of arabic-numbered pages; to this number would often be added a few roman-numbered pages at the beginning for letter of transmittal, acknowledgements, contents, and the like. Printed publications were typically 9⅛″ x 11⅜″, "census size," which Eliot and Merrill in Guide to Files (p. 58) explain was chosen as "a size which would take maps, plans, and other illustrations without too great reduction on the single page or with a single folding''; pamphlets were mostly 6″ x 9″ size; and mimeographed reports generally government typewriter paper size, 8″ x 10½″.

ʰ Although listed here as "general," this report included a very long part on land, including agriculture, another long part on water, and a great deal of general economic, including demographic, analysis.

ⁱ This report is listed in some NRPB documents but no copy exists in the files at the National Archives. Length estimated.

Index

Advisory Commission on Intergovernmental Relations, 249, 250
Agricultural Adjustment Act, 26, 28, 34
Agricultural Adjustment Administration, 3, 191
Agricultural planning, 3, 22, 23, 26, 31, 34, 191
  NRPB reports on, 108–111
Agriculture, U.S. Department of, 88, 108, 109, 119, 120, 149, 276
Air transportation, NRPB report on, 160
American Assembly of Columbia University, 15, 251
American Council on Education, 126
American Enterprise Institute for Public Policy Research, 280
Area (regional) analysis, NRPB report on, 170
Ascher, Charles S., 61
Automobile transportation, NRPB report on, 158–162

Baker, Jacob, 108
Bankhead, John H., 2nd, 230
Barrows, Harlan H., 71, 78, 115, 116n
Baugh, Virgil E., 41n, 43n, 76n, 78n, 81n, 86n
Beckman, Norman, 199, 202, 203n, 211, 212n, 214, 237, 238n, 244, 257, 258n, 264, 265, 270
Beveridge, Sir William Henry, 137
Beveridge Report, 142
Bigger, Frederick, 133n
Birth rates, NRPB reports on, 109, 125–131
Bishop, Jim, 238n

Black, Russell Van Nest, 146, 172n
Blaisdell, Thomas C., Jr., 50, 70, 132, 149, 153, 178
Blouke, Pierre, 133n
Board of Surveys and Maps, 114
Bonem, Gilbert W., 119n
Bosselman, Fred, 276n
Branch, Melville C., Jr., 193
Brookings Institution, 15, 95, 251, 252, 280
  "Capacity" studies, 33–34, 109, 148
Brownlow, Louis, 42, 47, 61, 63n, 203, 217
Budd, Ralph, 178
Budget and Accounting Act of 1921, 202
Bureau of Labor Statistics, 149, 152
Bureau of Mines, 88, 201
Bureau of Reclamation, 112
Bureau of the Budget, 10, 148, 202, 203, 228, 260
  See also Office of Management and Budget
Burns, Eveline M., 137, 139, 141, 231
Burton, Harold H., 231
Business statistics, NRPB reports on, 136
Byrd, Harry F., 220, 232

Cannon, Clarence, 229n, 238, 240
Capper, Arthur, 231
Carter, Jimmy, 205, 269, 271, 272
Carter Administration, 265, 272
Case, Fred E., 276n
Census Bureau, 131, 134
Census data, 125–131
Central Statistical Board, 149

Chamber of Commerce, 267
Chapin, F. Stuart, Jr., 173*n*
Chavez, Dennis, 231
Chawner, Lowell J., 133*n*
Chicago Plan, 173
Choate, Pat, 275*n*
City planning, 34–35, 166
  for wartime, 180–181
  NRPB reports on, 162–164, 172–174
Civilian Conservation Corps, 26
Civilian demobilization, 185
Clark Amendment, 218–220
Classification Act, 42
Clawson, Marion, 110*n*
Colby, Charles C., 170
Columbia river basin planning, 167
Colwell, H. R., 41
Commerce, U.S. Department of, 276
  Committee on Business Research, 136
Commission on Rural Poverty, 244
Committee for Economic Development,
  15, 251
Committee on National Land Problems,
  108
Committee on Recent Social Trends,
  83, 89, 109, 148
  See also President's Research Com-
    mittee on Social Trends
Committee on the Basis of a Sound
  Land Policy, 58
Commodity trade flows, NRPB report
  on, 157
Congress. See U.S. Congress.
Construction industry, NRPB reports
  on, 131–133
Consumer incomes and expenditures,
  NRPB reports on, 148–152
Cooke, Morris L., 44, 112, 115
Coolidge, Calvin, 24
Corps of Engineers, 10, 12, 98, 112,
  116, 124, 148, 157, 203, 212, 259
Country Life Commission, 162
Crane, Jacob, 133*n*
Crop yields, NRPB reports on, 108–111
Cultural resources, preservation of, 180
Currie, Lauchlin, 149
Cutting, Bronson, 56

Danaher, John A., 231
Davis, James J., 231
Davis, Joseph S., 21*n*, 22*n*, 35*n*, 129
Defense planning (World War II),
  NRPB reports on, 177–181
Delano, Frederic A., 6, 10, 33, 35, 43–
  46, 49, 50, 52, 58–60, 64, 66–69,
  72–75, 82, 83, 97, 99, 116, 132,
  138, 143, 146, 149, 158, 159, 161,
  173, 179, 195, 209, 211, 221, 226,
  229*n*, 236, 239, 240, 261
  See especially 58–60, 221
Demobilization planning, 181–186
Demographic issues, NRPB reports on,
  109, 125–131
Dennison, Henry S., 49, 50, 69, 73, 74
Depression, economic (1929), 2–3, 16,
  21, 23–29, 32, 34, 35, 87, 109, 173
Dern, George H., 56, 69, 72
Dirksen, Everett, 229
Douglas, Lewis W., 26
Drainage basin planning, NRPB reports
  on, 111–119, 165, 167
Draper, Earle S., 166*n*
Droughts, NRPB reports on, 111–119
Dykstra, C. A., 71

Eccles, Marriner, 149
Economic planning, 27–29, 266–269
  NRPB reports on, 144–157
Economic potential, Brookings "Capacity" studies on, 33–34, 109, 148
Economic Stabilization Act, 271
Education, NRPB reports on, 128
Eisenhower, Dwight D., 270
Eisenhower, Milton, 71
Eisenhower Administration, 263
Eliot, Charles W., 2nd, 3, 6, 10, 15, 35,
  39*n*, 42, 43, 45, 46, 47*n*, 50, 52, 59,
  64–65, 71, 73–77, 80*n*, 81–83, 86*n*,
  93–97, 99, 102, 108, 111, 115,
  119*n*, 120, 121*n*, 143, 146, 149,
  162, 173, 179, 192–195, 199–201,
  205, 206, 210, 211, 213, 214, 215*n*,
  216, 217, 221, 229, 233–236, 239,
  240, 242, 251, 255, 263, 266
  See especially 64–65, 221, 233–235
Eliot–Merriam differences, 7, 10, 63,
  65–68, 70, 75, 212, 221, 233, 235,
  239
Emergency Banking Act, 3, 26, 28
Emergency Relief Appropriation Acts,
  5, 46, 218
Employment, New Deal programs, 3,
  26, 57
  NRPB reports on, 141, 145–148, 156–
    157, 182, 183, 185
  See also Full employment, and spe-
    cific New Deal agencies, e.g.,
    Works Progress Administration
Employment Act of 1946, 186, 252–253,
  265, 266
Employment Stabilization Act of 1931,
  41, 49, 157, 218, 220, 290–294
Energy resources, NRPB reports on,
  121–123

Environmental planning, 266–269
See also Natural resources
Euclid zoning decision, 173
Evans, Mercer G., 133*n*
Executive branch planning agency, proposed, 265–266, 281–283
See also Federal planning agency
Executive branch reorganization, 41, 47–50, 61, 63, 95–96, 202, 204, 218, 244, 261, 270
Ezekiel, Mordecai, 28*n*, 149, 267

Family expenditures, NRPB reports on, 148–152
Farm income, NRPB reports on, 148–152
Farmland use, NRPB reports on, 108–111
FDR. *See* Roosevelt, Franklin Delano (FDR)
Federal Employment Stabilization Board, 36, 41, 218, 219, 289
Federal Farm Board, 34
Federal planning, 30–32, 35–36, 89–99, 266–269
for the 1980s, 273–285
NRPB reports on, 165–175
opposition to, 94–96
regional offices for, 189–191
since 1943, 269–273
Federal planning agency, proposed, 3, 15–18, 266–269, 277–285
in executive branch, 265–266, 281–283
Federal research activities, NRPB reports on, 133–136
Feurer, Duane A., 276*n*
Fieldner, A. C., 88
Fiscal policy, NRPB report on, 145
Fisher, Joseph L., 13, 70
Flood control, NRPB reports on, 111–119
Ford, Gerald, 271, 272
Ford Administration, 265
Ford Foundation, 251
Forest land use, NRPB reports on, 108–111
Forest Service, 110, 119, 191, 201
Frank, Lawrence K., 130
Friedman, Milton, 13, 70, 152
Fritz, Wilbert G., 70, 177*n*, 178
Fuel resources, NRPB report on, 121–123
Full employment, Hansen report on, 12, 129, 182, 227, 231, 232
Full Employment Act, proposed, 270–273

Galbraith, J. K., 13, 70, 87*n*, 146
Galloway, George B., 21*n*, 28*n*, 166*n*, 174*n*, 200*n*, 219, 256*n*, 267
Gannett, Frank, 95, 96
General Accounting Office, 274, 280
George, Walter F., 231
Gill, Corrington, 41
Glass, Carter, 35, 230, 238
Gordon, Lincoln, 13, 70, 178
Government planning. *See* Federal planning
Graham, Otis L., Jr., 269–272
Gray, L. C., 108, 119, 120
Great Depression, 2–3, 16, 21, 23–29, 32, 34, 35, 87, 109, 173
Green, William, 137
Gulick, Luther, 47, 63*n*
Gutheim, Frederick, 35*n*

Haber, William, 137
Hansen, Alvin H., 12, 129, 182, 227, 231, 232
Harding, Warren G., 22
Hartley, Robert W., 240*n*, 243
Hayden, Carl, 217, 262
Hayden Bill, 218, 262
Health care, NRPB reports on, 128, 141
Henderson, Leon, 149
Herring, Frank W., 50, 70
Highway transportation, NRPB reports on, 158–162
Hill, Lister, 232
Historic preservation, 180
Holmes, Beatrice Hort, 118*n*
Hoover, Herbert, 2, 23–25, 30–32, 41, 173, 271
Hoover Administration, 22–25, 30–32, 35–36, 283
Hoover Commissions, 244, 270
Hopkins, Harry L., 46, 57, 69, 73, 149, 200
House of Representatives, U.S. *See* U.S. Congress
Housing, New Deal loan program, 3, 26
NRPB reports on, 131–133
Housing Administration, 57
Housing and Urban Development, U.S. Department of, 164, 276
Housing and Urban Development Act of 1970, 271, 273
Hufschmidt, Maynard M., 147, 148*n*
Human resources, NRPB reports on, 127–128, 136–143
Humphrey-Hawkins Full Employment and Balanced Growth Act, 271–273

Ickes, Harold L., 3, 5, 6, 42–47, 49–53, 55–57, 61, 64, 68, 69, 72, 111, 113,

119, 121, 146, 148, 149, 176n, 200,
    201, 211, 256
See especially, 55–57
Incomes and expenditures, consumer,
    NRPB reports on, 148–152
Independent Offices Appropriations Act
    of 1941, 219
    Clark Amendment to, 218–220
Independent Offices Appropriations Act
    of 1944, 321
Industrial development, NRPB reports
    on, 134–135, 152–154
Institute for Policy Studies, 280
Interest rates, NRPB report on, 157
Interior, U.S. Department of the, 88,
    108, 120
Iron and steel industry, NRPB report
    on, 152–153
Irrigation, NRPB reports on, 111–119

Jackson, Dorothy, 43
Janeway, Robert, 178
Johnson, G. G., Jr., 87n, 146
Johnson Administration, 270
Joint Committee on the Economic Re-
    port, 270
Judd, Charles H., 71, 134

Kahn, Herman, 209n
Kaiser, Edward J., 173n
Karl, Barry D., 30n, 32n, 45n, 46n, 50,
    51, 56n, 60–62, 136, 210n, 213,
    228, 237, 239, 240n, 256, 257
Kennedy Administration, 270
Keynes, John Maynard, 182, 232
Keyserling, Leon H., 133n
Kiser, Louise K., 130
Kneeland, Hildegarde, 150
Knutson, Harold, 220
Kreps, Theodore H., 133n

Land Grant College Association, 108
Land use planning, NRPB reports on,
    108–111, 119–121
Leith, C. K., 113
Leontief, Wassily, 13, 70
Lepawsky, Albert, 42n, 62, 83n, 144–
    146, 248n, 256, 257n,
Library of Congress, 134, 280
Local planning, 34–35, 166
    for wartime, 180–181
    NRPB reports on, 162–164, 172–174
Lodge, Henry Cabot, Jr., 231
Lubin, Isador, 149

Magnuson, Warren G., 229
Maloney, Francis, 231

Manpower, NRPB roster, 179–180
Manvel, Allen D., 174n
McKellar, Kenneth, 230–232
McLaughlin, Glenn E., 70, 154, 178,
    221n
McMillan Commission, 35
McNary, Charles L., 231
Mead-Lynch Bill, 240
Means, Gardiner, C., 149, 153, 155
Merriam, Charles E., 6, 10, 32, 33, 42–
    47, 49–52, 56, 60–64, 69, 73, 83,
    85, 89, 93, 97, 99, 143, 148, 149,
    173, 179, 195, 200, 203, 210–212,
    214, 217, 221, 222, 235–237, 239,
    255–257, 261, 263
    See especially 60–63, 221
Merriam–Eliot differences, 7, 10, 63, 65–
    68, 70, 75, 212, 221, 233, 235, 239
Merriam, John C., 33
Merrill, Harold A., 43, 64, 73–77, 80n,
    81, 82, 83n, 86n, 99, 102, 108n,
    111n, 115, 120, 121n, 193n, 194,
    199–201, 205, 206, 211, 213, 214,
    215n, 216, 217, 233, 242
Miami Conservancy District, 112
Mid-Century Conference, 251
Military bases, effects on communities,
    180–181
Military demobilization, 185
Miller, John, 181n, 194, 195
Millett, John D., 179, 212, 228, 256
Mineral resources, NRPB reports on,
    113–114, 121–123
Mississippi Valley Committee, 44, 112,
    115
Missouri river basin planning, 167
Mitchell, Wesley Clair, 32, 43–46, 49,
    69, 73, 211
Monetary policy, NRPB report on, 145
Morgenthau, Henry, 145, 149
Mott, James W., 220
Moulton, Harold G., 33n
Moynihan, Daniel Patrick, 270
Myers, William I., 71, 119, 120

National Academy of Sciences/National
    Research Council, 16, 79, 121, 126,
    135, 274, 280
National Advisory and Legislative Com-
    mittee on Land Use, 34
National Advisory Commission on Food
    and Fiber, 244
National Bureau of Economic Research,
    280
National Capital Park and Planning
    Commission, 3, 6, 34–35, 42, 59,
    64, 173

National Commission on Urban Problems, 244

National Committee to Uphold Constitutional Government, 95–96

National defense planning, NRPB reports on, 177–181

National Forest Management Act of 1976, 274

National Goals Research Staff, 270

National income data, NRPB reports on, 148–152

National Industrial Recovery Act of 1933, 3, 5, 26, 28, 46, 295–302

National Industrial Recovery Administration, 16

National Institutes of Health, 274

National Land Use Committee, 34, 108

National planning. *See* Federal planning

National Planning Association, 15, 251, 252, 280, 282

National Planning Board (predecessor of NRPB), 3–6, 30, 33, 36, 42–44, 53, 60, 72, 73, 76, 80, 82, 86–87, 92, 98, 108, 145, 146, 171, 173, 201, 210, 257, 260
  final report, 44, 45, 92–93
  Land Planning Committee, 108, 109
  number of meetings, 74
  relations with U.S. Congress, 215–218

National Power Policy Committee, 121

National Recovery Administration, 283

National Resources Board (predecessor of NRPB), 5, 6, 8, 44–46, 57, 72, 73, 76, 82, 83, 92, 99, 108, 185, 199, 210–212, 257
  Exploratory Committee on Competing Fuels, 121
  land use planning, 46, 108–111, 119–121
  Mineral Policy Committee, 121–123
  national planning report (1934), 78
  number of meetings, 74
  relations with U.S. Congress, 215–218
  water use planning, 44, 46, 78, 111–115

National Resources Committee (predecessor of NRPB), 5, 6, 8, 13, 46, 47, 49, 51, 57, 69, 72, 73, 76, 102, 171, 185, 199, 212, 213, 257
  Industrial Committee, 149, 153, 155
  Land Planning Committee, 119–121
  number of meetings, 74
  relations with U.S. Congress, 215–218
  Research Committee on Urbanism, 162

  Technical Committee on Regional Planning, 167–169
  Water Committee, 165, 200, 201

National Resources Planning Board (NRPB), agencies responsible for NRPB functions, 243–248, 250–253
  table, 245–247
  appropriations for, 5, 11–13, 36, 214–220, 228–232
  evaluation of, 15–18, 255–263
  formal divisions, 50
  historical background, 21–29
  influence of Delano, 58–60
  influence of Eliot, 64–68
  influence of Ickes, 55–57
  influence of Merriam, 60–63, 65–68
  influence of Roosevelt, 52–55, 208–213, 237–241
  influence on attitudes toward planning, 249–250, 253–254
  legacy, 13–15, 242–254
  legal authority, 5, 41–42, 46, 49, 95, 218, 289–321
  liquidation, 11–13, 64, 233–236, 260–261
  number of meetings, 74
  organization, 4–7, 47–51, 72–85
    table, 40
  predecessor agencies, 30–36, 39–46, 215–218
    See also National Planning Board; National Resources Board; National Resources Committee
  relations with other federal agencies, 9–11, 199–207
  relations with regional, state, and local planning agencies, 81–83, 189–198, 248–249
  relations with U.S. Congress, 5, 6, 10–13, 36, 62, 66, 85, 124, 201, 214–222, 225–226, 228–232, 236, 238, 257, 258
  Statement on Freedom and Rights, 184
  view of federal planning, 92–94, 97–99

NRPB activities, 3–4
  assistance to planning agencies, 11, 81–83, 99, 192–194, 248–249
  federal agency coordination, 98–99
  idea development and stimulation, 87–89
  planning, 88–99
  policy formulation, 98–99
  social research, 99

NRPB committees, 69–75, 77–79, 206–207

Energy Resources Committee, 121–123

Fiscal and Monetary Advisory Board, 144, 145

Industrial Committee, 131, 132, 155

Land Committee, 119–121, 170

Long-Range Work and Relief Policies Committee, 136

Minerals Policy Committee, 114

Population Problems Committee, 126–131

Public Works Committee, 146

Science Committee, 126, 133–136

Transportation Committee, 205–206

Urbanism Committee, 131

Water Resources Committee, 98, 115–121, 123, 147, 203, 205, 206

NRPB personnel, 69–73, 76

alumni, 13, 70, 250

Cabinet officers, 69, 72–73

central office staff, 70–71, 75–77, 206–207, 233

consultants, 79–80

field (regional) offices, 11, 80–81, 84, 189–191, 194–196, 222

See also NRPB committees

NRPB reports, 7–8, 88, 99–104, 226–227, 234, 242–243

characteristics of, tables, 77, 100–101, 103

chronological list of, 322–347

table, 326–347

final report, 234

national planning report of 1934, 107–115

on city planning, 172–174

on defense and war planning, 177–181

on economics, 144–157

on full employment, 12, 129, 182, 227, 231, 232

on housing, 131–133

on natural resources, 107–124, 227

on population, 125–131

on postwar planning, 181–186

on regional planning, 166–170

on scientific, industrial, and business research, 133–136

on state planning, 171–172

on transportation, 158–162, 226, 253

on urban structure, 162–164

on welfare and security, 136–143, 227, 253

National Roster of Scientific and Specialized Personnel, 179–180

National Science Foundation, 14, 16, 260, 274, 280, 285

National Security Council, 270

National Transportation Agency, proposed, 159–160

Natural resources, NRPB reports on, 107–124

New Deal (FDR) Administration, 2–3, 7, 12, 21, 24–29, 36, 42, 49, 64, 87, 142, 144, 145, 167, 173, 191, 204, 216, 219, 226, 267, 283

planning activities, 256–258

New England Regional Planning Commission, 168–170

New York Regional Plan, 173

Nixon, Edgar B., 209n, 213n

Nixon, Richard M., 271

Nixon Administration, 265, 270, 271

Nourse, Edwin G., 33n

Office of Defense Health and Welfare Services, 180–181

Office of Education, 57

Office of Emergency Management, 177

Office of Management and Budget, 265, 274, 281

See also Bureau of the Budget

Office of Production Management, 201

Office of Technology Assessment, 274, 280

Ogburn, William F., 61, 71

Outdoor Recreation Resources Review Commission, 244

Pacific Northwest Regional Commission, 168, 170

Paley Commission, 244

Paradiso, Louis J., 153

Perkins, Frances, 46, 52n, 53, 69, 72, 149, 256

Perloff, Harvey S., 174n

Person, Harlow S., 115

Personal income, NRPB reports on, 148–152

Planning. See City planning; Federal planning; Regional planning; State planning

Planning Committee for Mineral Policy, 121

Polenberg, Richard, 48n, 95n, 202n

Political parties, decline of, 268

Population, NRPB reports on, 109, 125–131

Postwar planning, NRPB reports on, 181–186

Potomac Institute, 15, 251, 280

President's Commission on National Goals, 244

President's Committee on Administrative Management, 47–48, 61, 63, 95, 202, 218, 261

See also Executive branch reorganization
President's Council of Economic Advisers, 14, 144, 186, 265, 270, 285
President's Domestic Council, 270
President's Materials Policy Commission, 244
President's Research Committee on Social Trends, 30–32
See also Committee on Recent Social Trends
Presidential Reorganization Plans, 41, 49, 50, 204, 218, 312–314
See also Executive branch reorganization
Prohibition Amendment, 27
Public Administration Clearing House, 42, 47
Public assistance, NRPB reports on, 127–128, 136–143
Public housing, NRPB reports on, 131–133
Public Land Law Review Commission, 244
Public welfare, NRPB reports on, 127–128, 136–143
Public Works Administration, 3, 6, 42, 43, 57, 145
Public works programs, 3, 26, 34–36, 43, 44
NRPB reports on, 145–148, 156–157, 165, 183, 185

Rail transportation, NRPB reports on, 158–162
Rand Corporation, 15, 251
Randall, Robert W., 194
Reconstruction Finance Corporation, 24, 26, 283
Recreational land use, NRPB reports on, 111
Recreational water use, NRPB reports on, 112
Reed, Clyle M., 230
Regional planning, 189–198, 248–249
NRPB reports on, 166–170
population issues in, 125–131
Renewable Resources Planning Act of 1974, 274
Reorganization Act of 1939, 50, 307–312
See also Executive branch reorganization
Research and development, NRPB reports on, 133–136
Reservoir planning, NRPB reports on, 111–119

Resources for the Future, 15, 251–252, 280
Ricc, W. E., 88
River basin planning, NRPB reports on, 111–119, 165, 167
Rivers and Harbors Congress, 4, 10, 12, 203–204
Roadway construction, NRPB reports on, 158–162
Rockwell, Landon G., 216, 233, 234, 258
Roosevelt, Franklin Delano (FDR), 2, 12, 16, 25–27, 36, 48, 49, 56–61, 63, 68, 95, 97, 108, 121, 141, 142, 145, 176, 177, 202, 217, 225–228, 256, 269, 271, 283
and the NRPB, 5–6, 9, 13, 44, 45, 47, 50, 52–55, 67, 87, 137–138, 148–149, 156, 181, 208–213, 218, 220, 228, 237–241, 261, 262
See especially 52–55, 208–213, 237–241
views on conservation, table, 209
Roosevelt, Theodore, 56, 163
Roosevelt (New Deal) Administration, 2–3, 7, 12, 21, 24–29, 36, 42, 49, 64, 87, 142, 144, 145, 167, 173, 191, 204, 216, 219, 226, 267, 283
Roper, Daniel C., 69, 72
Rosenman, Samuel I., 52n, 256
Ruml, Beardsley, 49, 50, 68, 69, 73, 74, 148, 149
Rural Electrification Administration, 115
Russell, Horace, 133n

Samuelson, Paul A., 13, 70
Saville, Thorndike, 71, 78, 115
Sawyer, D. H., 41
Schlesinger, Arthur M., Jr., 21n, 22n, 27, 44, 45, 52n, 55, 58, 66
Schnepfe, Fred E., 41
Scientific research, NRPB reports on, 133–136
Scientists, NRPB roster, 179–180
Scott, Mel, 172n
Securities Act, 28
Securities and Exchange Commission, 3, 23
Segoe, Ladislas, 174n
Senate, U.S. See U.S. Congress
Siemon, Charles L., 276n
Smith, Harold D., 69, 202n, 203, 231
Smith, Lester W., 180
Social Science Research Council, 7, 47, 50, 60, 83, 89, 126, 136, 140, 260
Social welfare, NRPB reports on, 127–128, 136–143

Soil Conservation Service, 191, 204
Soil Erosion Service, 191
Somers, Herman Miles, 177n, 185n
Spending habits, consumer, NRPB reports on, 148–152
State planning, 189–198, 248, 249
  NRPB reports on, 171–172
Steel industry, NRPB reports on, 152–153
Stevens, Raymond, 135
Stock market crash, 23–25
Stock market regulation, 3, 23, 28
Sundquist, James L., 265, 266
Sweezy, Paul M., 155

Taft, Robert A., 162, 183, 231, 232
Taxation, NRPB report on, 157
Temporary National Economic Committee, 155–156, 182
Tennessee Valley Authority, 3, 26, 112, 167, 168, 204–205
Thompson, Dorothy, 138
Thompson, George N., 133n
Thompson, Warren S., 71
Timber land use, NRPB reports on, 108–111
Toll, Seymour, 173n
Toon, Malcolm, 13, 70
Town planning, 34–35, 166
  for wartime, 180–181
  NRPB reports on, 162–164, 172–174
Transportation, NRPB reports on, 158–162, 205–206
Truman, Harry S, 263, 270
Truman Administration, 270
Truman Committee, 138, 142
Tugwell, Rexford G., 2n, 21n, 25n, 52n, 56, 57n
Twentieth Century Fund, 15
Tydings, Millard E., 232

U.S. Congress, appropriations for NRPB, 5, 11–13, 36, 214–220, 228–232
  budget office, 274
  relations with NRPB, 5–6, 10, 13, 36, 62, 66, 85, 124, 201, 214–222, 225–226, 228–232, 236, 238, 257, 258
  Senate committee on water policy, 244
U.S. Supreme Court, Euclid zoning decision, 173
  NIRA decision, 5, 28, 46
  Roosevelt reorganization "packing" plan, 49, 95, 202, 218, 261
Unemployment. See Employment

Urban Institute, 280
Urban planning, 34–35, 166
  for wartime, 180–181
  NRPB reports on, 162–164, 172–174

Van Nuys, Frederick, 231
Vandenberg, Arthur H., 231
Vickery, William S., 155

Wagner, Robert, 36
Wallace, Henry A., 46, 69, 72, 119, 120, 149, 200, 201
War Manpower Commission, 180
War planning (World War II), NRPB reports on, 177–181
War Production Board, 16, 153, 154, 178, 201, 283
Warken, Philip W., 28n, 58n, 116n, 136n, 137n, 141, 142, 177n, 178n, 181, 201, 203, 217, 219, 227n, 228, 258, 267
Warren, Lindsay Carter, 219
Water resources, NRPB reports on, 4, 107, 111–121, 165, 167, 205
Watkins, Ralph J., 50, 70, 122, 159, 161n, 178, 206, 221n
Watson, Gen. Edwin M. "Pa," 239, 240
Welfare, public, NRPB reports on, 127–128, 136–143
White, Gilbert F., 14, 70, 115, 255, 256n
White, Harry D., 149
White, Philip L., 66–68, 116n, 141, 201, 213, 215–219, 220n, 226n, 228–230, 231n, 236, 237, 239n, 240n, 258
Wigglesworth, Richard B., 219
Wilbur, Ray Lyman, 42
Wildavsky, Aaron, 89n, 91
Wildlife refuges, NRPB reports on, 108–111
Wiley, Alexander, 231
Wilson, Edwin B., 71, 135
Wilson, M. L., 108, 119, 120, 162
Wilson Administration, 54
Wollman, Nathaniel, 119n
Wolman, Abel, 71, 78, 115, 116n, 206
Woodring, Harry H., 69, 201
Works Progress Administration, 57, 73, 82, 149
World War II planning, 16, 177–181
  effect on NRPB, 225–226

Yantis, George F., 49, 68, 69, 74, 179, 195, 221n, 239
Young, Owen D., 71, 159, 161, 206

Zoning issues, 173, 248–249

About the Author

Marion Clawson has had a long and distinguished career in the U.S. government serving many years in the Department of Agriculture and at the Department of Interior where he was director of the Bureau of Land Management. Well-known for his many books on land economics, natural resources, the economics of outdoor recreation, agricultural policy, and forest policy—he has also been an advisor to the Department of Housing and Urban Development, and has served on many government and professional committees and boards.

In 1955, he joined Resources for the Future to direct studies on land and water use and later to serve as acting president and then vice president. He is a fellow of the American Agricultural Economics Association and of the American Academy of Arts and Sciences. In 1976, he received the American Motors Conservation award, and in 1980 received the Theodore C. Blegen award of the Forest History Society for the best article on forest history published in 1979. He is presently a fellow emeritus and consultant in residence at RFF.